Human Populations

Frontispiece: the two photographs show three Tamang children, who are all the same age (born in September 1980) but who have achieved very different heights and weights. The upper photograph was taken in July 1983. The lower photograph, taken in 1990, shows that these growth differentials are maintained, but also — and more importantly — that all three children have survived.

Human Populations

Diversity and Adaptation

Edited by

A. J. BOYCE

*Institute of Biological
Anthropology, University of Oxford*

and

V. REYNOLDS

*Institute of Biological
Anthropology, University of Oxford*

Oxford   New York   Tokyo

OXFORD UNIVERSITY PRESS

1995

Oxford University Press, Walton Street, Oxford OX2 6DP

Oxford   New York
Athens   Auckland   Bangkok   Bombay
Calcutta   Cape Town   Dar es Salaam   Delhi
Florence   Hong Kong   Istanbul   Karachi
Kuala Lumpur   Madras   Madrid   Melbourne
Mexico City   Nairobi   Paris   Singapore
Taipei   Tokyo   Toronto
and associated companies in
Berlin   Ibadan

Oxford is a trade mark of Oxford University Press

Published in the United States
by Oxford University Press Inc., New York

A catalogue record for this book is available from the British Library

Library of Congress Cataloging in Publication Data
Human populations : diversity and adaptation/edited by A. J. Boyce
and V. Reynolds.
Includes bibliographical references.
1. Physical anthropology.   2. Nature and nurture.   3. Social
evolution.   I. Boyce, A. J. (Anthony J.)   II. Reynolds, V.
GN50.8.H86   1995   304.2–dc20   94–34343
ISBN 0 19 852294 0

Typeset by EXPO Holdings, Malaysia

Printed in Great Britain by
Bookcraft (Bath) Ltd
Midsomer Norton, Avon

To past and present
students in biological
anthropology

Preface

Human populations can be defined as collectivities of people living together and sharing a number of biological and social characteristics. Such populations differ from one another in many respects. There are genetic differences, which may be the result of natural selection or random genetic drift (chapter by Boyce, Harding and Martinson). There are morphological differences which may be the result of genetic factors but are also influenced by nutrition, and other environment features (Brush, Schmitt). There are cultural differences which to a greater or lesser extent control human fertility (Bittles, Coleman, Reynolds).

A further kind of diversity in human populations is their disease associations. Because of the different climatic zones of the world, different disease vectors and agents alter the disease environment of human beings. All cultures attempt to control disease, but in much of the world these attempts are far from successful, leading to differential patterns of morbidity and mortality in different populations (Almedom, Attenborough and Alpers, Panter-Brick, Parker).

All of these processes distinguished above interact with each other to produce the diversity of populations we encounter across the world. Such diversity has led to a variety of explanations. In the nineteenth century, populations were placed on a scale from 'primitive' to 'advanced'. With the impact of Darwinism proper, processes of natural selection were sought that might be capable of explaining inter-population differences in skin colour, eye colour, body size and shape. Subsequently the study of population genetics has led to the discovery of the selective advantages of particular genes, together with an understanding that not all genetic differences are the product of natural selection, but that neutral processes operate as well.

Human history is to some extent the history of population migrations, and as a result the world's populations are not discrete entities but grade into each other at the genetic, morphological and cultural levels. These gradations are not uniform, however, and populations are structured as a result of patterns of mate choice (Clegg, Macbeth, Mascie-Taylor, White).

The present volume, presented as a Festschrift to Professor Geoffrey Ainsworth Harrison on the occasion of his retirement explores all these aspects of human diversity and the various ways in which they constitute adaptations to the diverse environments in which human populations live.

Oxford   A. J. B.
March 1995   V. R.

Contents

Contributors

A. M. Almedom, Tropical Health Epidemiology Unit, London School of Hygiene and Tropical Medicine, London

M. P. Alpers, Institute of Medical Research, Goroka, Papua New Guinea

R. D. Attenborough, Department of Prehistory and Anthropology, Australian National University, Canberra, ACT, Australia

A. H. Bittles, School of Applied Science, Edith Cowan University, Perth, Western Australia

A. J. Boyce, Institute of Biological Anthropology, Oxford University, Oxford

G. Brush, Institute of Biological Anthropology, Oxford University, Oxford

E. J. Clegg, Department of Biomedical Sciences, University of Aberdeen, Aberdeen

D. A. Coleman, Department of Applied Social Studies and Social Research, Oxford University, Oxford

R. M. Harding, MRC Molecular Haematology Unit, Institute of Molecular Medicine, John Radcliffe Hospital, Headington, Oxford

H. M. Macbeth, Department of Social Studies, Oxford Brookes University, Oxford

J. J. Martinson, MRC Molecular Haematology Unit, Institute of Molecular Medicine, John Radcliffe Hospital, Headington, Oxford

C. G. N. Mascie-Taylor, Department of Biological Anthropology, Cambridge University, Cambridge

C. Panter-Brick, Department of Anthropology, Durham University, Durham

M. Parker, Department of Public Health, St Mary's Hospital Medical School, London

V. Reynolds, Institute of Biological Anthropology, Oxford University, Oxford

L. H. Schmitt, Department of Anatomy and Human Biology, University of Western Australia, Nedlands, Perth, Western Australia

N. G. White, School of Genetics and Human Variation, La Trobe University, Bundoora, Victoria, Australia

1

Patterns of marriage in the Isle of Harris

E. J. CLEGG

Introduction

It is well recognized that mate selection in marriage does not occur at random
(see van den Berghe 1979). Many factors may influence it, for example: the
degree of relatedness (O'Brien *et al.* 1979); the high correlation between
spouses' ages (Hajnal 1963; Leslie 1983*a,b*); the decline in mating frequency
with increasing separation between spouse's residences (Boyce *et al.* 1967;
Boyce 1984; Swedlund 1988); and the existence of assortative mating for
various overt biological or cultural characteristics (Rao *et al.* 1979). In addition
there may be a secular factor in a given population, resulting from changes in
residence and social class distribution, improvements in communications, etc.
(Küchemann *et al.* 1967).

The question of who marries whom is obviously important in the determination of the genetic structure of a population. Departures from random mating or
out-mating lead to subdivision of a larger effective population into smaller-sized
subunits, with the risk of inbreeding — whether through assortative mating for
genetically determined phenotypic characteristics or through consanguinity —
and hence decreased heterozygosity with a putative loss of Darwinian fitness
(Cavalli-Sforza and Bodmer 1971).

In terms of their possible effects on its breeding structure, a population's marriages may be classified on an ordinal scale of endogamy/exogamy, the former
being between spouses from the same population unit, the latter between
spouses from distant units. Intermediate degrees will depend on the degree of
separation between units. Although, conventionally, units are defined in spatial
terms, spouse's ages, social class, or occupation may be treated also as discrim-
inating variables.

The present work examines the effects of some geographic and socio-cultural
variables on the pattern of marriage in Harris, an Outer Hebridean island off the
north-west coast of Scotland (Fig. 1.1). It is, however, not a true island, being
conjoined to Lewis to the north by an inhospitable tract of mountain and moor-
land. Since 1855, when vital registration began in Scotland, its population has
varied between 3000 and 5000 (Geddes 1955; Thompson 1968), all resident on
or near the coast and engaged predominantly in occupations related to crofting,
an economy which includes small-scale agriculture, fishing, and tweed-weaving

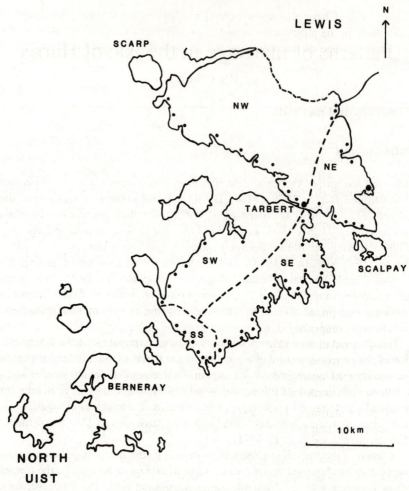

Fig. 1.1 Map of the Isle of Harris, showing settlements and subdivision into regions.

(Hunter 1976, 1991). Over this period, apart from Lord Leverhulme's short-lived venture in the 1920s (Nicolson 1960) there has been no significant indus-trialization and while there has been some degree of socio-economic and occupational change (for example an increase in paid employment, both skilled and unskilled, and a decrease in the number of individuals giving their occupa-tion as 'crofter'), compared with many other parts of the UK, Harris, together with most Outer Hebridean islands has in this respect remained fairly stable. What has changed has been population size and age structure, with a rapid increase up to the First World War and an equally rapid decline thereafter

(Clegg 1975). Changes in age structure have involved decreased proportions of individuals in the reproductive age groups and marked secular variation in the sex ratio, the age of marriage, and the proportions remaining celibate (Clegg 1975).

Materials and methods

The data used in this study were obtained from copies of certificates of first marriage held at the General Register Office, Edinburgh. They ranged in date from 1855 to 1984. All registers covering the various islands of the Outer Hebrides were examined; all marriages in which at least one spouse was resident in Harris were included in the analysis.

Relevant information on the certificates included dates of marriages, ages and residences of the spouses, and their fathers' occupations. For the purpose of analysis, the raw data were modified. Regarding residences of spouses two variables were created:

1. Residence of couple, based on groom's place of residence. Three categories were recognized (Fig. 1.1): (a) North Harris; (b) South Harris; and (c) islands, comprising Berneray, Scalpay, and Scarp (other islands had very small populations and/or were abandoned during the period of the study). As well as forming parts of a single residence category, each island was allocated to its nearest mainland region — Berneray to south south Harris, Scalpay to north-east Harris, and Scarp to north-west Harris (Fig. 1.1).

2. Type of marriage, whether: (a) local — each spouse residing in the same population unit (village or island); (b) regional — spouses resident in the same region of Harris (Fig. 1.1), although not in the same population unit; (c) Harris — spouses resident in different regions of Harris; (d) Outer Hebrides — one spouse resident in Harris, the other elsewhere in the Outer Hebrides.

It was not possible to create a fifth category in which one spouse was resident outwith the Outer Hebrides, as the custom of matrilocal marriage would have truncated this category by missing those unions in which the bride was resident elsewhere. While it is possible to estimate the total number of such marriages (Clegg 1975) this estimate cannot be subdivided by place of residence within Harris or by groom's occupation.

An additional complexity was that the custom became increasingly common over time, of solemnizing marriage in places outwith the Outer Hebrides (e.g. Glasgow or Inverness), irrespective of the residences of the spouses. Thus not all relevant unions could be ascertained. It was assumed that there was no systematic association between the type of marriage or place of residence or groom's occupation, and probability of such external solemnization. Regarding groom's occupation the following categories were recognized:

(1) fishermen;

(2) crofters;

(3) seamen;

(4) low status land occupations — labourers, cottars, servants, shepherds, weavers; and

(5) high status land occupations — skilled, managerial and professional occupations.

A total of 1914 marriages between bachelors and spinsters were ascertained. The data, transformed as above, were analysed using the Statistical Package for the Social Sciences (SPSS). Being categorical in nature the methods used included chi-square goodness-of-fit and log-linear methods, including model fitting using hierarchical and logit techniques (Gilbert 1981; Norušis 1991; Halli and Rao 1992). Hierarchical methods were used to ascertain the overall significance of particular associations and interactions between variables. Logit methods were used to test the significance, within significant interactions, of particular associations between categories of variables; marriage type was the dependent variable.

Results

Figures 1.2 and 1.3 show changes in the numbers (Fig. 1.2) and percentages (Fig. 1.3) of marriages, classified as to marital type, groom's residence, and groom's occupation.

There was a considerable decline in marriages between 1855 and 1984. It was most marked for local and regional marriages and least marked for Harris-wide unions. Marriages with partner from elsewhere in the Outer Hebrides, after an initial decline, increased significantly after 1915–24 and by 1975–84 formed the greatest proportion of all marriages.

The decline in marriages was not dependent on the groom's place of residence within Harris, but grooms from elsewhere in the Outer Hebrides became more common. Where groom's occupation was concerned the main decline was in numbers and proportions of fishermen. Other occupations showed relatively small changes except upper status occupations, which rose both proportionately and absolutely so that by the 1930s they formed the greatest proportion of all marriages.

Table 1.1 is a contingency table showing numbers of marriages of different types by groom's place of residence and occupation. There were wide divergences between observed cell numbers and those expected if the variables were independent of one another.

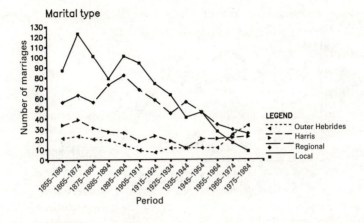

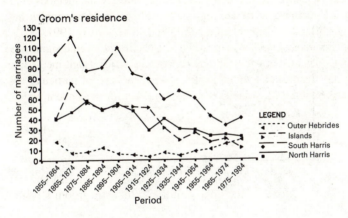

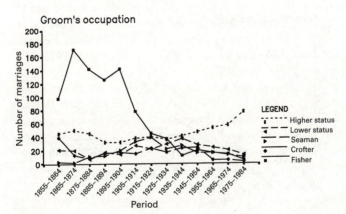

Fig. 1.2 Numbers of marriages over successive 10-year periods, by marital type, groom's residence, and groom's occupation.

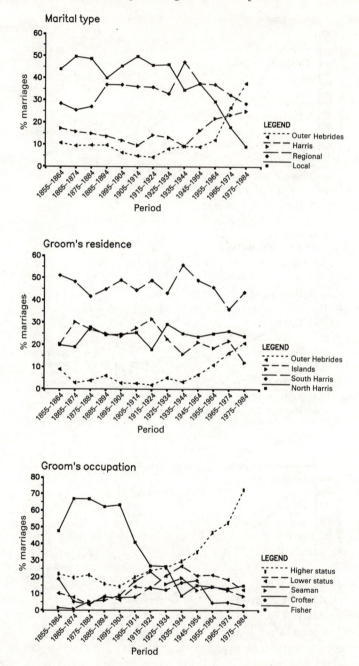

Fig. 1.3 Proportions of marriages over successive 10-year periods, by marital type, groom's residence, and groom's occupation.

Table 1.1. Distribution of types of marriage by groom's residence and occupation, 1855–1984

Type of Marriage	Groom's residence	Groom's occupation				
		Fisher	Crofter	Seaman	Lower	Upper
Local	North Harris (obs.)	72	16	9	23	37
	(exp.)	98.51	21.41	23.12	26.65	48.29
	South Harris (obs.)	161	34	38	44	55
	(exp.)	191.62	41.65	44.97	51.84	93.93
	Islands (obs.)	224	24	53	13	45
	(exp.)	93.11	20.24	21.85	25.19	45.64
Regional	North Harris (obs.)	55	14	13	43	64
	(exp.)	79.23	17.22	18.59	21.43	38.84
	South Harris (obs.)	204	69	50	60	101
	(exp.)	154.11	33.49	36.17	41.69	75.54
	Islands (obs.)	7	0	1	0	1
	(exp.)	74.88	16.27	17.57	20.26	36.70
Harris	North Harris (obs.)	32	6	8	18	46
	(exp.)	33.92	7.37	7.96	9.18	16.63
	South Harris (obs.)	47	11	10	20	36
	(exp.)	65.98	14.34	15.48	17.85	32.34
	Islands (obs.)	25	7	12	2	12
	(exp.)	32.06	6.97	7.52	8.67	15.72
Outer Hebrides	North Harris (obs.)	9	1	4	7	15
	(exp.)	10.69	2.32	2.51	2.89	5.24
	South Harris (obs.)	7	0	0	2	8
	(exp.)	20.79	4.52	4.88	5.62	10.19
	Islands (obs.)	22	6	5	2	4
	(exp.)	10.10	2.20	2.37	2.73	4.95

Chi-square = 702.826; d.f. = 50; $P < 0.0001$.

Hierarchical log-linear analysis revealed that the most economical model included the associations between marital type and groom's residence ($\chi^2 = 466.104$, d.f. = 6, $P < 0.001$), and marital type $\times$ groom's occupation ($\chi^2 = 32.933$, d.f. = 12, $P = 0.001$). The three-way interaction term was not significant ($\chi^2 = 33.353$, d.f. = 24, $P = 0.1864$).

For further analysis the logit method was used, the model comprising marital type both as a main effect and the dependent variable, with groom's residence and occupation as separate independent variables. A linear-by-linear component (Norušis 1991) was introduced by using the product of marital type (coded Local = 1; Regional = 2; Harris = 3; Outer Hebrides = 4) $\times$ date of marriage (expressed as a decimal year) as a covariate. In order to examine the possible effects of population increase and decline, the period of the study was divided into two, 1855–1914, during which population rose, and 1915–84 when it fell.

Table 1.2 shows chi-square values for goodness-of-fit to the model for the two periods, and overall. The fit was reasonably good over each period. Table 1.3 is the contingency table for 1855–1984, showing the reasonably good fit of expected to observed cell numbers.

Table 1.4 shows deviation parameter estimates for the main effect of marital type. During 1855–1914 there were non-significant excesses of local and regional marriages and deficits of Harris-wide and Outer Hebrides marriages. During 1915–84 the deficit in the latter became almost statistically significant. Over the whole period there were significant excesses of local and deficits of Outer Hebridean marriages.

Table 1.5 shows deviation parameter estimates for the association between marital type and groom's place of residence. Both North and South Harris generally showed strong tendencies away from local marriages and toward regional marriages, the negative local trend being more marked in North Harris and the positive regional trend being greater in South Harris. Both parts of mainland Harris showed few trends where more distant unions were concerned, except that South Harris showed a distinct trend away from Outer Hebridean unions.

The islands, taken together, showed patterns generally opposite in sign to mainland Harris. There were strong trends to local and away from regional unions and a strong positive trend to marriages elsewhere in the Outer Hebrides. However, there appeared to be considerable heterogeneity between the three islands (Table 1.6), in which the regional and Harris categories of marriage type have been aggregated. Scalpay showed a positive but non-significant trend to local marriage, a significant trend to regional/Harris marriage and a significant trend away from Outer Hebridean marriages. Berneray showed a significant trend to local marriage and a significant trend away from regional/Harris marriages, while Scarp showed only a significant trend away from local marriages; for both these islands trends to more distant unions were positive but not statistically significant.

Table 1.7 shows deviation parameter estimates for the association between marital type and groom's occupation. Significant associations were confined to fishermen and upper status grooms. The former showed significant or almost significant trends to local marriages, particularly during the 1915–84 period, and

Table 1.2. Goodness-of-fit of observed data to expectation based on model

Period	Number of cases	Chi-square	d.f.	P
1855–1914	1179	21.576	23	0.546
1915–84	735	18.647	23	0.722
1855–1984	1914	23.823	23	0.414

Table 1.3. Distribution of types of marriage by groom's residence and occupation, 1855–1984. Expected numbers derived from model

Type of marriage	Groom's residence	Groom's occupation				
		Fisher	Crofter	Seaman	Lower	Upper
Local	North Harris (obs.)	72	16	9	23	37
	(exp.)	65.57	10.98	11.60	27.27	41.57
	South Harris (obs.)	161	34	38	44	55
	(exp.)	167.03	35.21	34.92	39.71	55.13
	Islands (obs.)	224	24	53	13	45
	(exp.)	224.40	27.81	53.47	13.02	40.30
Regional	North Harris (obs.)	55	14	13	43	64
	(exp.)	62.25	16.76	12.77	36.31	60.92
	South Harris (obs.)	204	69	50	60	101
	(exp.)	198.13	66.08	49.69	66.63	103.48
	Islands (obs.)	7	0	1	0	1
	(exp.)	5.62	0.16	1.55	0.07	1.60
Harris	North Harris (obs.)	32	6	8	18	46
	(exp.)	29.42	6.58	6.95	20.95	46.11
	South Harris (obs.)	47	11	10	20	36
	(exp.)	45.49	12.64	13.35	16.70	35.82
	Islands (obs.)	25	7	12	2	12
	(exp.)	29.10	4.77	9.71	2.35	12.07
Outer Hebrides	North Harris (obs.)	9	1	4	7	15
	(exp.)	10.76	2.68	2.69	6.48	13.40
	South Harris (obs.)	7	0	0	2	8
	(exp.)	8.36	0.06	0.04	2.97	5.57
	Islands (obs.)	22	6	5	2	4
	(exp.)	18.88	4.26	6.27	1.56	8.03

Chi-square = 23.823; d.f = 23; P = 0.414.

Table 1.4 Deviation parameters for the main effect of marital type

Type of marriage	Coefficient ± SE		
	1855–1914	1915–84	1855–1984
Local	3.773 ± 2.125	2.984 ± 1.646	2.439 ± 0.878 ****
Regional	0.946 ± 0.726	0.862 ± 0.588	0.561 ± 0.314
Harris	−0.946 ± 0.714	−0.799 ± 0.555	−0.480 ± 0.300
Outer Hebrides	−3.773 ± 2.138	−3.047 ± 1.677 *	−2.520 ± 0.889 ****

* 0.02 <P< 0.05; **** P< 0.001.

Table 1.5. Deviation parameters for the association between type of marriage and groom's residence

Type of marriage	Groom's residence	Coefficient ± SE		
		1855–1914	1915–84	1855–1984
Local	North Harris	−0.500 ± 0.091 ****	−0.670 ± 0.123 ****	−0.593 ± 0.071 ****
	South Harris	−0.141 ± 0.094	−0.260 ± 0.112 ****	−0.207 ± 0.069 ****
	Islands	0.641 ± 0.109 ****	0.930 ± 0.144 ****	0.750 ± 0.082 ****
Regional	North Harris	0.492 ± 0.143 ****	0.527 ± 0.162 ****	0.543 ± 0.104 ****
	South Harris	1.145 ± 0.140 ****	1.049 ± 0.157 ****	1.157 ± 0.103 ****
	Islands	−1.637 ± 0.239 ****	−1.577 ± 0.273 ****	−1.700 ± 0.177 ****
Harris	North Harris	0.033 ± 0.114	0.077 ± 0.131	0.008 ± 0.082
	South Harris	−0.072 ± 0.114	−0.243 ± 0.128 *	−0.142 ± 0.083
	Islands	0.039 ± 0.138	0.165 ± 0.177	0.134 ± 0.103
Outer Hebrides	North Harris	−0.026 ± 0.171	0.065 ± 0.191	0.044 ± 0.122
	South Harris	−0.932 ± 0.206 ****	−0.547 ± 0.215 ****	0.808 ± 0.143 ****
	Islands	0.958 ± 0.186 ****	0.482 ± 0.242 *	0.767 ± 0.134 ****

* 0.02 <P< 0.05; *** 0.001 <P< 0.01; **** P< 0.001.

Table 1.6. Deviation parameters for the association between type of marriage and groom's island of residence

Island	Type of marriage	Coefficient ± SE
Scalpay	Local	0.186 ± 0.123
	Regional/Harris	0.303 ± 0.155 *
	Outer Hebrides	−0.489 ± 0.190 ***
Berneray	Local	0.346 ± 0.140 **
	Regional/Harris	−0.543 ± 0.193 ***
	Outer Hebrides	0.188 ± 0.227
Scarp	Local	−0.533 ± 0.151 ****
	Regional/Harris	0.231 ± 0.192
	Outer Hebrides	0.302 ± 0.231

* 0.02 <*P*< 0.05; ** 0.01 <*P*< 0.02; *** 0.001 <*P*< 0.01; **** *P*< 0.001.

Table 1.7. Deviation parameters for the association between type of marriage and groom's occupation

Type of marriage	Groom's occupation	Coefficient ± SE		
		1855–1914	1915–84	1855–1984
Local	Fisher	0.168 ± 0.097	0.281 ± 0.147*	0.222 ± 0.075***
	Crofter	−0.148 ± 0.182	−0.126 ± 0.179	−0.081 ± 0.125
	Seaman	0.270 ± 0.202	0.041 ± 0.145	0.091 ± 0.114
	Lower	−0.029 ± 0.168	0.102 ± 0.165	−0.019 ± 0.111
	Upper	−0.261 ± 0.138*	−0.298 ± 0.133**	−0.213 ± 0.089***
Regional	Fisher	0.037 ± 0.111	0.128 ± 0.177	−0.035 ± 0.079
	Crofter	0.078 ± 0.193	0.036 ± 0.209	0.109 ± 0.133
	Seaman	0.081 ± 0.245	−0.187 ± 0.167	−0.034 ± 0.131
	Lower	−0.118 ± 0.190	0.088 ± 0.152	0.019 ± 0.109
	Upper	−0.077 ± 0.144	−0.065 ± 0.129	−0.058 ± 0.090
Harris	Fisher	−0.041 ± 0.126	−0.240 ± 0.208	−0.107 ± 0.094
	Crofter	0.008 ± 0.223	−0.395 ± 0.244	−0.146 ± 0.158
	Seaman	0.261 ± 0.251	−0.067 ± 0.190	0.007 ± 0.145
	Lower	−0.207 ± 0.239	0.280 ± 0.184	0.023 ± 0.133
	Upper	−0.021 ± 0.164	0.421 ± 0.142***	0.223 ± 0.099**
Outer Hebrides	Fisher	−0.164 ± 0.209	−0.168 ± 0.266	−0.080 ± 0.145
	Crofter	0.062 ± 0.398	0.484 ± 0.395	0.119 ± 0.260
	Seaman	−0.611 ± 0.462	0.212 ± 0.286	−0.064 ± 0.235
	Lower	0.354 ± 0.337	−0.470 ± 0.325	−0.023 ± 0.214
	Upper	0.359 ± 0.280	−0.058 ± 0.241	0.048 ± 0.162

* 0.02 <*P*< 0.05; ** 0.01 <*P*< 0.02; *** 0.001 <*P*< 0.01.

Table 1.8. Deviation parameters for the linear-by-linear covariant, marriage type by date of marriage

	Coefficient ± SE	
1855–1914	1915–84	1855–1984
0.0020 ± 0.0016	0.0016 ± 0.0012	0.0011 ± 0.0006

overall. The latter showed avoidance of local marriage during all periods and a significant trend towards Harris-wide marriages latterly (but not a trend towards more distant, Outer Hebridean, unions).

Table 1.8 shows that in all periods the linear-by-linear association between marital type and the date of marriage failed to reach the level of statistical significance.

Discussion

The results of this study show that over the period 1855–1984 both place of residence and occupation of grooms affected the degree of endogamy/exogamy of marriages. Overall, there appears to have been no change in the distributions of the different types of marriage, which was largely independent of population increase during 1855–1914 or decrease during 1915–84 (Table 1.4).

As far as the effects of grooms' place of residence on marital type are concerned, there is a clear distinction between mainland Harris and the islands, the former showing strong trends away from local and towards regional marriages, the latter showing equally strong trends in the opposite directions and an additional positive trend to marriages with partners from elsewhere in the Outer Hebrides. The major difference between North and South Harris is that the latter shows a strong trend away from marriages elsewhere in the Outer Hebrides.

The trend to regional marriage in South Harris is considerably greater than in North Harris and the trend away from the local marriage less. Perhaps this is due to the denser settlement pattern in South Harris (Fig. 1.1), which would make easier movement to find a mate outside the village, but within the neighbourhood. The difference between North and South Harris in respect of Outer Hebridean marriages is again explicable on a geographical basis (Fig. 1.1). South Harris is not close to any other part of the Outer Hebrides, but North Harris not only forms the boundary with Lewis, but also is traversed by the main road connecting Tarbert, the principal commercial centre of Harris, and Stornoway in Lewis. Thus both position and ease of communication can explain the difference between North and South Harris in this respect.

The islands show a quite different pattern of relationships, with strong tendencies to local and Outer Hebridean marriages and away from regional unions, but as Table 1.6 indicates, they are not homogeneous within the group. Scalpay shows a significant trend to more distant marriages in Harris and away from Outer Hebridean unions, Berneray a significant trend to local and away from regional and Harris marriages, and Scarp only a significant trend away from local unions.

Again, the geographical situation of these three islands may explain the differences. Scalpay is close to north-east Harris, but distant from other regions and from other Outer Hebridean areas. Berneray is much closer to North Uist than to Harris, and it is somewhat surprising that there seems to be no significant trend to Outer Hebridean unions (although the sign is positive). Scarp is close to both north-west Harris and Uig in Lewis, which may account for the large negative local coefficient. Thus there are two almost equally possible non-local marital types, neither reaching a value of their coefficient which is statistically significant.

Thus it appears that in these small populations, both of mainland Harris and its principal islands, patterns of marriage are much affected by local geographical features, particularly the presence or absence of sea passages between neighbouring parts. The avoidance of local (endogamous) marriage in mainland Harris is surprising and is not readily explicable on the basis of most conventional models of marital movement (see Jorde 1980 for a comprehensive review), which as a rule identify a negative relationship between marriage frequency and degree of spatial separation between spouses' residences.

Groom's occupation (Table 1.7) does not seem to be as important a determinant of variation in marriage type as does place of residence, but its effects are fairly clear-cut and are limited to two groups only, fishermen and higher status occupations. Over the whole period fishermen exhibit a significant tendency towards local and, less clearly, away from Harris-wide and Outer Hebridean unions, while upper status individuals show reverse trends, which become more clear-cut during 1915–84. An explanation for this might be that this group, which includes the most affluent individuals, would have been less affected by the economic adversity which affected the Highlands and Islands during the early/middle twentieth century, and more able to take advantage of the improvements in communications during the same period (Nicolson 1960), enabling them to travel further in search of mates.

For fisherman grooms the explanation is perhaps more complex. Unpublished work (Clegg in preparation) suggests that they were on average younger than other grooms; therefore they may be expected to have been less affluent and thus more constrained in their choice of mates. In addition, evidence from other fishing/agricultural communities (Baillie 1984; Sherren 1988; Smith and Sherren 1989) suggests that fishers as a group are more endogamous. This probably results from the necessity of interfamily cooperation in running a fishing enterprise (Gray 1978) and the value, in intergenerational terms, of keeping a boat and its crew within the extended family.

Thus within the variables considered in this study the two main factors affecting patterns of marriage within Harris appear to be where the groom lives and his occupation. Change in population size does not seem to have any major effect and when other variables are taken into account time itself appears to have little influence.

The two parts of mainland Harris, North and South appear to form a reasonably coherent entity in which marriages tend to occur within regions rather than in local communities, but not to any great extent further afield. Thus, major subdivision of the effective population by endogamy is probably avoided, given the arbitrary nature of the regional boundaries. The islands present a different and much more heterogeneous picture with (Scarp excepted) a greater tendency of their relatively small populations to marry endogamously. While Scalpay and Scarp show tendencies towards more distant marriages (or avoidance of local marriages) Berneray shows strong propensities to local unions and away from regional unions and little trend to more distant marriages. While in Scalpay and Scarp there appear to be factors reducing any tendency to endogamy, they appear to be absent in Berneray.

Acknowledgements

I am indebted to the Economic and Social Research Council and the Carnegie and Leverhulme Trusts for financial support and to the Registrar-General for Scotland for permission to extract vital data and to his staff for their continued cheerful cooperation in this task.

References

Baillie, S. R. (1984). *The structure of population in fishing communities in North-East Scotland*. PhD thesis, University of Aberdeen.

Berghe, P. L. van den (1979). *Human family systems: an evolutionary view*. Elsevier, New York.

Boyce, A. J., Küchemann, C. F., and Harrison, G. A. (1967). Neighbourhood knowledge and the distribution of marriage distances. *Annuals of Human Genetics, 30*, 335–8.

Boyce, A. J. (ed.) (1984). *Migration and mobility: biosocial aspects of human movement*. Taylor and Francis, London.

Cavalli-Sforza, L. L. and Bodmer, W. F. (1971). *The genetics of human populations*. Freeman, San Francisco.

Clegg, E. J. (1975). Marriages in Lewis and Harris, 1861–1966. In *Biosocial interactions in population adaptation* (ed. E. S. Watts, F. E. Johnston and G. W. Lasker), pp. 147–63. Mouton, The Hague.

Geddes, A. (1955). *The isle of Lewis and Harris.* Edinburgh University Press.

Gilbert, G. N. (1981). *Modelling society.* Allen & Unwin, London.

Gray, M. (1978). *The fishing industries of Scotland, 1790–1914. A study in regional adaptation.* Oxford University Press.

Hajnal, J. (1963). Concepts of random mating and the frequency of consanguineous marriages. *Proceedings of the Royal Society of London B,* **159**, 125–77.

Halli, S. S. and Rao, K. V. (1992). *Advanced techniques of population analysis,* pp. 119–39. Plenum, New York.

Hunter, J. (1976). *The making of the crofting community.* Donald, Edinburgh.

Hunter, J. (1991). *The claim of crofting: the Scottish Highlands and Islands, 1930–1990.* Mainstream, Edinburgh.

Jorde, L. B. (1980). The genetic structure of subdivided human populations: a review. In *Current developments in anthropological genetics,* Vol. 1 (ed. J. H. Mielke and M. H. Crawford), pp. 135–208. Plenum, New York.

Küchemann, C. F., Boyce, A. J., and Harrison, G. A. (1967). A demographic and genetic study of a group of Oxfordshire villages. *Human Biology,* **39**, 251–76.

Leslie, P. W. (1983*a*). Cohorts, overlapping generations and consanguinity estimates. *Annals of Human Biology,* **10**, 257–65.

Leslie, P. W. (1983*b*). Age correlation between mates and average consanguinity in age-structured human populations. *American Journal of Human Genetics,* **35**, 962–77.

Nicolson, N. (1960). *Lord of the Isles. Lord Leverhulme in the Outer Hebrides.* Weidenfeld & Nicolson, London.

Norušis, M. J. (1990). *SPSS advanced statistics user's guide,* pp. 150–207. SPSS, Chicago.

O'Brien, E., Jorde, L. B., Rönnlof, B., Fellman, J. O., and Eriksson, A. W. (1979). Consanguinity avoidance and mate choice in Sottunga, Finland. *American Journal of Physical Anthropology,* **79**, 235–46.

Rao, D. C., Morton, N. E., and Cloninger, C. R. (1979). Path analysis under generalized assortative mating.1. Theory. *Genetical Research,* **33**, 175–88.

Sherren, S. J. (1988). *Migration and genetic structure among North Yorkshire coastal populations.* Ph.D. thesis. University of Durham.

Smith, M. T. and Sherren, S. J. (1989). The one-dimensional stepping stone model of migration: an application to British coastal populations. *Collegium Antropologicum,* **13**, 97–104.

Swedlund, A. C. (1988). Mating distance and historical population structure: a review. In *Human mating patterns* (ed. C. G. N. Mascie-Taylor and A. J. Boyce), pp. 15–29. Cambridge University Press.

Thompson, F. (1968) *Harris and Lewis, Outer Hebrides.* David & Charles, Newton Abbott.

2

Fertility in Britain: variation and its significance

D. A. COLEMAN

The significance of human fertility differentials

Differences in human fertility can have biological, social, and political consequences. Biological consequences arise if genotypically distinct individuals or genetically definable groups have different average rates of fertility or reproduction. Genetic differences may have social significance, especially if linked to 'visible minorities'. Alternatively, they may be hidden polymorphisms of medical or evolutionary interest. Quite independently of any biological connection, if members of socially defined groups have distinctive characteristics which can be transmitted culturally from one generation to the next, and also have non-average fertility, then the characteristics of that society will change. That in turn may have political consequences, if the groups concerned are ethnic or religious rivals, or even recognizable in cultural or phenotypic ways. Quite apart from any group categorization, if individuals with particular characteristics which are socially or biologically heritable, have more children than others then those characteristics are likely to spread in the population; whether they are those of Galton's 'hereditary genius' (Eysenck 1993) or the characteristics of 'problem families', or of an 'underclass'.

In human biology, variance of heritable population characteristics is the raw material of evolutionary change. Systematic differential replacement of different heritable forms in the population from one generation to another is the outward sign that such evolutionary change is occurring. In even the most promising of human populations, however, the potential for observing evolutionary change is very low, as Hiorns and Harrison (1970) have pointed out. Human generation length of about 27 years, and the (by animal standards) relatively modest rates of mortality and fertility inevitably make evolution a long-term process requiring sample sizes which pre-industrial man is seldom able to provide even if post-industrial research grants could pay for them. No surprise, therefore, that studying evolutionary processes among modern human beings seems even less promising.

The lower limits of human survival, an expectation of life at birth of about 20 years, are determined by the maximum sustainable average level of human fertility. In theory, this is often estimated to be about 16 children ever born ('natural fecundity'). In practice, the most favourable and unusual combination of circumstances for maximizing fertility were those observed among the North American rural religious isolate populations known as the Hutterites in the first half of this century. Thanks to relatively favourable health circumstances, relatively early marriage, short periods of breast feeding and a religious prohibition on family planning, the Hutterites averaged about 10 children ever born. Before the modern period, it is not believed that most human populations deliberately attempted to limit the number of births occurring in marriage to any 'target', although various practices affected the commencement of fertility and the spacing of births. Such fertility in the absence of parity-specific birth control is known as 'natural' fertility and it differs considerably between populations (Leridon and Menken 1982; Diggory *et al.* 1988).

In more 'normal' combinations of circumstances, those of pre-industrial cultivators in the early phases of economic development (which tends to increase fertility for a time), the maximum observed average family size is about eight children per woman (for example Kenya and North Yemen in the 1970s). Over larger populations over longer period of time, the maximum average is probably nearer seven. Many pre-industrial European populations, especially in Western Europe, had an average of about five births per woman, thanks to a unique combination of late, and frequently avoided marriage. A few nomadic hunting and gathering populations, notably the !Kung bushmen, have achieved even lower levels of average fertility without recourse to parity specific birth control or high levels of abortion (Howell 1986). Such limits to fertility put a low upper limit upon the population growth of human populations before the modern period. Pre-modern population growth rates can seldom have exceeded 1 per cent per year in the absence of migration. On average, over the greater part of human history, average annual growth rates have been hardly distinguishable from zero.

In post-transitional human populations, low mortality rates have taken expectation of life at birth to about 75 years, such that over 97 per cent of female babies born in Europe in the 1980s are likely to survive to age 50. Mean family size among industrial populations has declined to less than two (total fertility rate around 1990 was about 1.7), with, it would appear, considerably reduced opportunities for variance in reproduction. This chapter will concentrate upon differences in fertility. In the modern world, especially since the contraceptive revolution, fertility differentials have tended to be much more significant agents of demographic change than have differences in mortality, continuing a pattern noted by Malthus.

In looking at human reproductive differentials in modern society, attention will be focused upon reproductive differences between individuals and populations and their cultural correlates. In fact most biological (genetic) change in modern human populations now proceeds through a reverse effect, whereby relatively physiologically unimportant, visible or invisible genetic differences experience changes in the degree to which they are represented in the population by correlation with socio-economic characteristics which affect fertility or mortality through social mechanisms: ethnicity, religion, social class, and so on. These are the more direct (although possibly transient) determining factors of reproductive differences. This is a kind of 'passenger' evolution. Examples include the pace at which the human species is on average becoming more brown and black, with corresponding changes in the relative frequency of particular polymorphic alleles and biometrical characteristics, simply because of the much larger pace of population growth (for non-biological reasons) of Asian and African populations with those characteristics. In the latter half of the twentieth century, these population growth rates have ranged between 2 and 3 per cent per year, even reaching 4 per cent for a short time in some countries. These growth rates are without historical precedent; European 'rapid' population growth in the nineteenth century seldom exceeded 1.5 per cent, and Europe is now set for population decline. When the demographic transition, and thereby zero population growth, is achieved in African and Asian countries, as is expected some time in the next century, a radically new distribution of human genetical differences will then have been established; which, if the demographic transition is then complete across the world, will be likely to change only very slowly henceforth.

Because timing of the onset of fertility decline has varied across the world, disequilibrium in growth rates is radically changing the numerical balance of human populations of different racial and geographical origins. China and most countries in South-East Asia have had low or at least falling fertility rates for between 10 and 30 years. Most of Latin America is following. There are slow changes in India, hardly any in most of the Muslim nations of South Asia, the Middle East, and Africa (Egypt, Tunisia, Indonesia, Malaysia, and Turkey are exceptions). Only very few African countries have shown any reduction in fertility (Kenya, Zimbabwe, Botswana) and those only since the middle 1980s; none is in West, Muslim, or Francophone Africa. India is nearly certain to overtake China within a couple of decades as the world's most populous country. Muslim countries and Africa are projected to be the centre of demographic attention in future decades. This is not only changing the distribution of human population stocks on a world-wide basis, it also affects Europe itself through the demographic behaviour of immigrant populations of Third World origin.

This chapter will examine differences in fertility, with particular reference to Britain. At the national as well as at the world level, demographic change occasioned by cultural differences in fertility may change the balance of ancestry in the population with respect to social class, geographical and ethnic origin, educational level, and so on. At various times in the past, such variance has aroused interest in case it affects the distribution of biological characteristics, capacity or performance, for example in stature or intellect, and in the increase or decline of the relative numbers of persons who may, whether through biological or social processes, bring particular benefits to or impose costs upon the society. Changes in population representation may become visible, if biologically trivial but socially important characteristics such as skin colour and physiognomy happen to be associated with particular ethnic groups, as they are among groups of recent Third World immigrant origin in western Europe. Demography provides convenient ways of measuring ancestry irrespective of its evolutionary (in)significance.

Variance of family size

The variability of demographic behaviour and its analysis

Demography and population genetics have many terms and formulae in common, especially a shared interest in relative rates of population growth and reproduction, whose key parameter of intrinsic growth Fisher (1930) termed the 'Malthusian parameter'. But there are substantial differences in the way that statistics are employed. Much genetic modelling and analysis in biometrical genetics, for example, is based upon partitioning the variance observed in continuously distributed characteristics between its genetic and other components.

In demography, more attention has conventionally been given to summary statistical indicators between subpopulations, such as the total fertility rate or the expectation of life. Demographic analysis seldom concerns itself with the dispersal or variability of demographic phenomena around these averages or medians, which are infrequently accompanied by any statistics on dispersal. Statistics of dispersal such as the variance are little quoted, and analyses seldom based upon them; although distributional aspects of fertility analysis, in a slightly different sense, have attracted recent attention (Lutz 1989) especially in the context of distribution of family sizes and of births by birth order and by the parity of women. This relative neglect arises partly because of the 'whole population' nature of much demographic data. In whole populations, all differences are real. Much demographic analysis is concerned with relative or absolute levels of population growth, the mathematics of which require overall rates of fertility or growth, not measures of dispersal. The exponential nature of population growth means that quite small levels of growth or differences in growth levels rapidly generate substantial demographic consequences or divergences in population size. Demographic study of complex societies depends to a considerable extent upon the tabulations and statistics generated by official data collection bodies. The raw data relating to millions of individuals or events are seldom available and might not be welcomed in view of the immense labour of computing the statistics on which to base such calculations. The rise of public use samples of individual anonymized records from the census, available since the 1970 US Census and for the first time in the UK from the 1991 Census (SAR — Sample of Anonymized Records) may awaken new interest in the dispersion of charac-teristics previously described as means. However, analysis of such surveys as the General Household Survey (e.g. Murphy 1987), that includes information on family size, has recently provided us with some of the first estimates of the pro-portion of overall variability in the tempo and quantum of family size, which can be accounted for by membership of various social groups (Ni Bhrolchain 1993).

In modern societies, of which England and Wales is a typical example, family size and birth order are strongly concentrated around a mean of about two chil-dren. Of births to married women in 1990, for example, 40 per cent were first births, 37 per cent were second births and 16 per cent were third births. Only 7 per cent of births were of order four and over. This is a distribution strongly clustered around a two-child family. But in statistical terms it represents rather a high degree of variance. Children only come in integer values, not in fractions. A second child represents 100 per cent more than a first, a third child 50 per cent more than a second, a fourth child is double the mean of two, and so on. This means that in conventional statistical, as opposed to demographic terms, the variance, standard deviation, and related statistics of family size are extremely high, much more so than those of biological variables such as stature or weight. In respect of height, no individuals are even 30 per cent greater than the mean and few are double the mean with respect to weight.

Evidently there is much potential for evolution to work on, even if that poten-tial is not realized. How does this compare with the condition in populations with natural fertility or only partly controlled fertility? Table 2.1 compares the completed fertility of women aged 45–49 years in England and Wales, measured in 1971, with that of women in Great Britain who married between 1900 and 1909, measured in 1946, and that of women aged 45–49 years in Thailand in 1960. The Thai data refer to women who had not begun to use contraception on any important scale. They therefore represent an example of 'natural' fertility. The British marriage cohorts of 1900–09 were in the middle of the fertility tran-sition. The mean completed family size for England and Wales in 1971 (2.13 for all married women, 2.43 for fertile women only) is typical of the controlled fer-tility of a mid-twentieth century industrial society. These data are only available for married women, but in the two decades before 1971 illegitimacy was only about 5 per cent. They are in fact the latest available full data on completed family size in England and Wales, thanks to the failure of the British census since 1971 to ask retrospective questions on fertility. The British transitional data yield a mean family size of 3.95 (4.35 if only fertile women are included; i.e. those who have had at least one child). The Thai completed fertility in 1960 was equivalent to an average of 6.3 children per woman (6.5 for fertile women only; almost everyone marries in Thailand).

In the data from Thailand, representing a 'natural fertility' population, the largest recorded family size is only two and a half times the mean and the smallest

Table 2.1. Children ever-born

(a) Thailand 1960

Children ever-born	Women aged 45–49 years	Distribution (%)	Cumulated distribution (%)	Children	Distribution (%)	Cumulative distribution (%)	Deviation of each sibship size from mean	Total squared deviation	Replacement ratio (% children/ % women)
0	14 352	3.2	3.2	0	0	0	-6.3	564 219	0.0
1	26 548	5.8	9.0	26 548	0.9	0.9	-5.3	737 315	15.9
2	29 268	6.4	15.4	58 536	2.0	3.0	-4.3	533 641	31.8
3	33 271	7.3	22.8	99 813	3.5	6.5	-3.3	355 763	47.7
4	39 448	8.7	31.5	157 792	5.5	12.0	-2.3	203 272	63.6
5	44 928	9.9	41.3	224 640	7.9	19.9	-1.3	72 464	79.5
6	48 252	10.6	52.0	289 512	10.1	30.0	-0.3	3 518	95.4
7	49 401	10.9	62.8	345 807	12.1	42.1	0.7	26 326	111.4
8	46 789	10.3	73.1	374 312	13.1	55.2	1.7	140 035	127.3
9	41 112	9.0	82.2	370 008	13.0	68.2	2.7	306 404	143.2
10	32 439	7.1	89.3	324 390	11.4	79.5	3.7	451 321	159.1
11	20 500	4.5	93.8	225 500	7.9	87.4	4.7	458 644	175.0
12	15 278	3.4	97.2	183 336	6.4	93.8	5.7	501 621	190.0
13	6 804	1.5	98.7	88 452	3.1	96.9	6.7	308 173	206.8
14	3 196	0.7	99.4	44 744	1.6	98.5	7.7	190 970	222.7
15	1 635	0.4	99.8	24 525	0.9	99.4	8.7	124 608	238.6
16	669	0.1	99.9	10 704	0.4	99.7	9.7	63 336	254.5
17	434	0.1	100.0	7 378	0.3	100.0	10.7	49 968	270.4
All women	454 324	100.0		2 855 997	100.0			5 091 597	

all children children/woman 6.3
fertile only 6.5

mean sibship 8.1
mean sibs 7.1

sum sq 5 091 597
variance 11.2
SD 3.3
CVar 53.3

Note: sum sq = sum of squares, SD = standard deviation, CVar = coefficient of variation. Replacement ratios are equal to the ratio of each birth order (1, 2, 3, etc.) to the mean birth order of this distribution which is 6.27.
Source of data: Shryock and Siegel 1976 table 17–4.

(b) Great Britain 1946

Children ever-born	Women married 1900–09	Distribution (%)	Cumulated distribution (%)	Children	Distribution (%)	Cumulative distribution (%)	Deviation of each birth order from mean	Total squared deviation	Replacement ratio (% children/ % women)
0	7 279	9.0	9.0	0	0.0	0.0	−4.0	113 571	0.0
1	9 762	12.1	21.2	9 762	3.1	3.1	−3.0	84 954	25.3
2	12 641	15.7	36.8	25 282	7.9	11.0	−2.0	48 067	50.6
3	11 631	14.4	51.3	34 893	11.0	22.0	−1.0	10 497	75.9
4	9 982	12.4	63.7	39 928	12.5	34.5	0.1	25	101.2
5	7 822	9.7	73.4	39 110	12.3	46.8	1.1	8 624	126.5
6	6 306	7.8	81.2	37 836	11.9	58.6	2.1	26 501	151.8
7	4 791	5.9	87.1	33 537	10.5	69.2	3.1	44 568	177.1
8	3 591	4.5	91.6	28 728	9.0	78.2	4.1	58 901	202.3
9	2 623	3.3	94.9	23 607	7.4	85.6	5.1	66 893	227.6
10	1 896	2.4	97.2	18 960	6.0	91.6	6.1	69 398	252.9
11	1 023	1.3	98.5	11 253	3.5	95.1	7.1	50 846	278.2
12	627	0.8	99.3	7 524	2.4	97.5	8.1	40 631	303.5
13	320	0.4	99.7	4 160	1.3	98.8	9.1	26 209	328.8
14	148	0.2	99.8	2 072	0.7	99.4	10.1	14 948	354.1
15	125	0.2	100.0	1 875	0.6	100.0	11.1	15 263	379.4

All women 80 567 | 100.0 | 100.0 | all children 318 527 | 100.0

children/woman 4.0   fertile only 4.3

mean sibship 6.1   mean sibs 5.1

sum sq 679 896.3
variance 8.4
SD 2.9
CVar 73.5

Note: sum sq = sum of squares, SD = standard deviation, CVar = coefficient of variation. Replacement ratios are equal to the ratio of each birth order (1, 2, 3, etc.) to the mean birth order which is 3.95.
Source of data: Glass and Grebenik 1954 Part 2 table F.1.
N.B. Sample data from 1946 Fertility Census.

(c) England and Wales 1971

Children ever-born	Women aged 45–49 years	Distribution (%)	Cumulated distribution (%)	Children	Distribution (%)	Cumulative distribution (%)	Deviation of each sibship size from mean	Total squared deviation	Replacement ratio (% children/ % women)
0	158 760	12.4	12.4	0	0.0	0.0	-2.1	720 278	0.0
1	303 175	23.7	36.1	303 175	11.1	11.1	-1.1	387 124	47.0
2	410 630	32.1	68.2	821 260	30.2	41.3	-0.1	6 940	94.0
3	214 810	16.8	85.0	644 430	23.7	64.9	0.9	162 590	140.9
4	101 055	7.9	92.9	404 220	14.8	79.8	1.9	353 379	187.9
5	45 105	3.5	96.4	225 525	8.3	88.1	2.9	371 525	234.9
6	22 315	1.7	98.1	133 890	4.9	93.0	3.9	334 210	281.9
7	11 210	0.9	99.0	78 470	2.9	95.9	4.9	265 866	328.8
8	5 905	0.5	99.5	47 240	1.7	97.6	5.9	203 468	375.8
9	3 125	0.2	99.7	28 125	1.0	98.6	6.9	147 490	422.8
10	1 780	0.1	99.9	17 800	0.7	99.3	7.9	110 248	469.8
11	820	0.1	99.9	9 020	0.3	99.6	8.9	64 515	516.7
12	485	0.0	100.0	5 820	0.2	99.8	9.9	47 247	563.7
13	175	0.0	100.0	2 275	0.1	99.9	10.9	20 677	610.7
14	105	0.0	100.0	1 470	0.1	99.9	11.9	14 794	657.7
15	40	0.0	100.0	600	0.0	100.0	12.9	6 625	704.7
16	20	0.0	100.0	320	0.0	100.0	13.9	3 848	751.6
17	5	0.0	100.0	85	0.0	100.0	14.9	1 106	798.6
18			100.0			100.0	15.9		
19			100.0			100.0	16.9		
20	10	0.0	100.0	200	0.0	100.0	17.9	3 193	939.5
All women	1 279 530	100.0		2 723 925	100.0			3 225 124	

all children 2 723 925   children/woman 2.1   fertile only 2.4

mean sibship 3.3   mean sibs 2.3

sum sq 3 225 124   variance 2.5   SD 1.6   CVar 74.6

Note: sum sq = sum of squares, SD = standard deviation, CVar = coefficient of variation. Replacement ratios are equal to the ratio of each birth order (1, 2, 3, etc.) to the mean birth order of this distribution which is 2.13.
Source data: Census 1971, England and Wales Fertility Tables, Vol. 1, table 1, HMSO (1979).

is only 16 per cent of the mean. Thirty-two per cent of all births are within one more or less of the mean in these Thai data compared with 37 per cent of the births to the British women married in 1900–09 and 68 per cent of births in the England and Wales cohorts measured in 1971. The variances and standard deviations of the completed fertilities in the three populations naturally are highest in the Thai data (11.2, 3.3 respectively), intermediate in the British transitional data (8.4, 2.9) and lowest in the 1971 census data (2.5, 1.6), as might be apparent from the distributions shown in Fig. 2.1. However, the coefficient of variation,

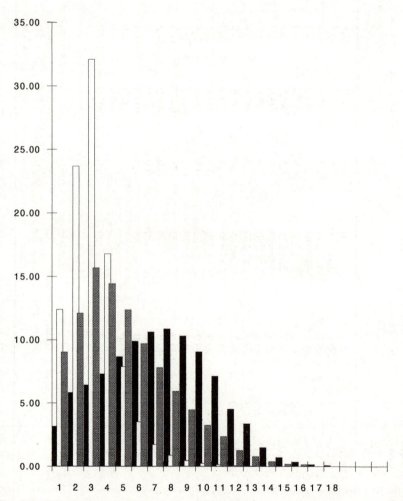

Fig. 2.1 Distribution per cent of the number of children ever-born to women aged 45–49 years, selected countries. ■, Thailand 1960; □, England and Wales 1971, ▨, GB 1946.

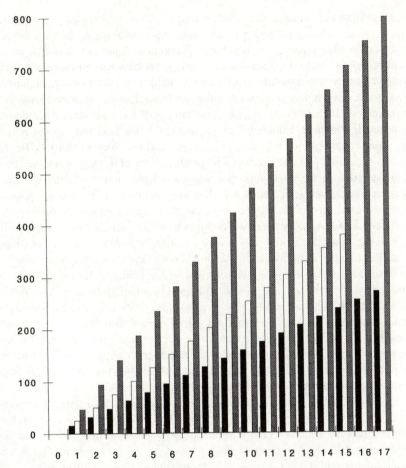

Fig. 2.2 Replacement ratios of mothers at given completed family sizes, at fertility levels of three selected populations (100 = replacement in next generation, ignoring mortality). ■, Thailand 1960; □, Great Britain 1946; ▩, England and Wales 1971. Source: data from Table 2.1.

which corrects estimates of dispersion for differences in mean, tells a somewhat different story. It is substantially higher in the two British populations (74.6 in 1971, 73.5 in 1946) than in the 1960 Thai population (53.3). This reflects the fact that one or two children more or less than the average contributes much more to variability in populations where average family size is low. All these coefficients of variation are relatively high. 'Biological' variables typically have coefficients of variation under 15, 'social' variables over 30 (Snedecor and Cochrane 1967).

A comparison between the relative frequency of mothers of given family sizes, and the relative frequency of children, shows how higher fertility women can increase their representation in future generations (ignoring mortality, which is not likely to make a significant difference). Women who produce about the average family size naturally approximately hold their own in the next genera- tion. Such women may or may not have any biological or social characteristics in common. If they do not, such variability will have no detectable conse- quences. In Thailand, women producing one child only have only 16 per cent of the representation in the next generation compared with their own. In the British marriage cohorts of 1900, women who produced one child only would see their representation in the next generation drop to 25 per cent, while in 1971 such women would manage to limit the decline to 47 per cent. In low fertility popula- tions the effects of extra children over the population average are correspond- ingly enhanced. An additional two children over the average category of family size in the Thai case would only secure an increase in representation of 43 per cent. But two extra children in Britain in 1900 would increase the representation in the next generation by 52 per cent and in England and Wales in 1971, by about 88 per cent (Fig. 2.1). Also in low fertility populations very large family size, although rare, can secure very large proportionate increases in population representation. Thus a 10-child family in England and Wales 1971 would increases its mother's representation in the next generation by about 4.7 times, compared with 2.5 times in the British marriage cohorts at the turn of the century, and just 59 per cent in the Thai example. This is one of several reasons for the interest in high-fertility families in modern societies.

It might be noted in passing that these tables also show the difference between family sizes from the child's and from the mother's point of view (Langford 1982). Thus while the average size of family of fertile women in England and Wales was 2.43, the mean size of sibship was 3.31 and the mean number of sibs of the average child was therefore 2.31 (assuming all children survived).

The two-child family and its variability

Trends in fertility in Western societies practising birth control have concentrated family size on an average of two children. But despite the rise of the two-child family norm this century, most women married since 1930 have not produced this exact norm. Three-quarters of women had at least one child more or less than the average. This was particularly true earlier in the century when one-child as well as larger families were more common (Glass and Grebenik 1954). Even in 1971, when one-child and larger families had become more rare, only 44 per cent of families of women married in 1961–65 were two-child families, and that proportion is likely to have decreased as some women went on to higher parity births (Table 2.2). It is only since the late 1980s that even half of all completed families have been two-child families. By the time they had reached age

Table 2.2. Distribution of family size by year of marriage, England and Wales, 1911–65 at the 1971 census

Year of marriage	Number of children								Total
	0	1	2	3	4	5	6	7 or more	
1911–15	139	193	224	159	102	64	42	77	1000
1921–25	178	252	245	139	76	43	26	41	1000
1931–35	175	270	266	143	70	35	18	23	1000
1941–45	97	258	331	167	77	34	18	18	1000
1951–55	112	179	334	197	100	42	20	16	1000
1961–65	113	205	444	175	48	11	3	1	1000

Note: Family size of some women married 1961–65 would not be completed by 1971. OPCS (1983) Fertility Report from the 1971 Census, t. 4.7 (p. 36). HMSO, London.

36 years, with their fertility almost complete, 52 per cent of the mothers in the 1946 cohort of births had two children, 16 per cent just one and 32 per cent three or more (Kiernan 1987).

Failure to reproduce

Childlessness is an important component of the distributional aspect of fertility. Minimum levels of childlessness in human populations appear to be about 2 per cent, an apparently irreducible biological minimum. Such low figures are normally only found for whole populations in non-industrial societies where marriage is nearly universal and usually early, but they can also be found in appropriate subdivisions of modern societies. For example, in England and Wales the proportion of women married below age 20 who were still childless after 20 years was about 2 per cent among women married in 1951, 3 per cent among women married in 1956.

Involuntary childlessness is a peculiarly human phenomenon, with no obvious parallel in the animal world. Its prevalence is difficult to estimate. Demographic statistics on childlessness include both the voluntarily and involuntarily childless. The former are very rare in non-European societies, where marriage has traditionally been nearly universal and child-bearing one of its necessary aims. It will be noted that the level of childlessness is low in the Thai data above and highest in the data for England and Wales 1971. It is usually thought that within marriage in modern societies the proportions of voluntary and involuntary childlessness are approximately equal, but that fluctuations in overall childlessness between cohorts are due to changes in choice about childlessness, not changes in fecundity.

In England and Wales the average proportion of each marriage cohort still without children after 20 years of marriage (all ages at marriage together) has varied between 10 and 15 per cent (e.g. 1951 13 per cent, 1956 10 per cent). The lowest proportion of any cohort of married women to remain childless by age 50 is about 7 per cent. Eight per cent of all women aged 40–44 years, whether married or not, had no liveborn children at the time of the 1987 General Household Survey. Infecundity rises with age for a variety of biological reasons.

In the 27 countries studied in the World Fertility Survey in the 1970s, the proportion of married women still childless by age 40–49 years varied from 1.5 to 6.7 per cent (mostly near the lower figure) and historical data suggest that 3 per cent of couples are already sterile at the beginning of reproductive life (Bongaarts and Potter 1983, Vaessen 1984). The trend towards later marriage and child-bearing especially among career women has sharpened interest in how far children can be deferred before running into substantial increasing risks of sterility. Historical data from non-contracepting European populations reinforces a view from contemporary data that the risk rises gradually from youth until about age 40 years. At age 25 years, 6 per cent of women were sterile, 24 per cent at age 40 years, and the proportion then rises more steeply (Menken 1985; Trussell and Wilson 1985).

Voluntary childlessness

Perhaps 5 per cent of married couples choose to be childless in modern Britain, and an unknown but probably growing number of those who do not marry, either living alone or (more usually) cohabiting. It is widely supposed that this proportion will grow substantially in Britain as in other Western societies. The trend in successive cohorts certainly suggests that this is the case. The proportion of all women still childless by age 25–29 years doubled from 20 per cent in 1961 to 40 per cent in 1981 and by 1984 had reached 47 per cent; levels not seen since early this century. Most of these women may still start families in their late 20s or 30s, but time is running out. Only 10 per cent of the 1940–44 birth cohort of women remained childless. A higher proportion of this cohort married than any this century. With the decline in marriage and the postponement, and possibly in some cases the cancellation of child-bearing, this figure has been forecast to rise to at least 15 per cent and possibly 20 per cent among the women born in 1960–64 (Werner 1986; OPCS 1988).

Such high future levels of childlessness, however, do not fit the consistent response to questions in the annual General Household Survey that only about 5–7 per cent of women intend to remain childless; although it is true that up to 20 per cent of women fail to reply to this question. This uncertainty makes it particularly interesting to know whether intentionally childless women are different in social status, personality, or attitudes from those who wish to have children, and whether theirs are attitudes which could readily become more wide-spread. According to surveys of childless couples, the motives for remaining childless are mixed: hedonistic, ideological, and medical (Baum and Cope 1980; Campbell 1985; Kiernan 1989). No particular personality type seemed to pre-dominate. The intentionally childless married woman is more likely than average to be well-educated, employed, and married to a husband in a profes-sional or managerial job. While most of those who were delaying children cited economic reasons first (70 per cent), only 41 per cent of those who intended to remain childless mentioned the costs. The most important consideration was freedom of action; an understandable response, as child-bearing may be regarded as equivalent to a 15-year sentence of partial house arrest, without remission for good behaviour.

Group differences in fertility: social class

In Britain, it is natural to think of fertility differentials first in the form of social class. This is despite the fact that social class is a rather fragile and labile cat-egory. In its precise categories it is a classification or scale imposed on popula-tions by academics and bureaucrats rather than one which is claimed by them. Most people might identify themselves as 'working class' or 'middle class' but would be unlikely to specify 'Registrar-General's Social Class IV' or 'SEG 12'. By contrast religious or national or regional identities are often self-ascribed, in a detailed way, by their proud adherents. Furthermore, movement between social classes 'officially' defined, across generations and through mar-riage, is common, and in these respects Britain is no less mobile than its indus-trial neighbours, contrary to popular mythology (Erikson and Goldthorpe 1993). Many individuals in the course of changing their jobs or developing their careers throughout their life would be classified according to different social classes. None the less, social class continues to attract interest, whether in the form of the 'official' Registrar-General's scale or through various empiri-cally based replacements offered for it, as a dimension which accounts statisti-cally for some population variability in a wide range of demographic and other variables.

At the beginning of the fertility transition, from 1870 to 1910, in Britain as in most Western countries, the professional and middle classes adopted family planning earlier than most manual workers (Teitelbaum 1984; Coale and Watkins 1986). The consequence was the creation of the well-known roughly inverse linear relation between social class and family size which became appar-ent in the latter half of the nineteenth century (Fig. 2.3). Over this period family size in social class I fell by 33 per cent, that in social class VII by 10 per cent. The social classification used then was not the same as that used today and was not arranged in so hierarchical a fashion. It included elements of industrial

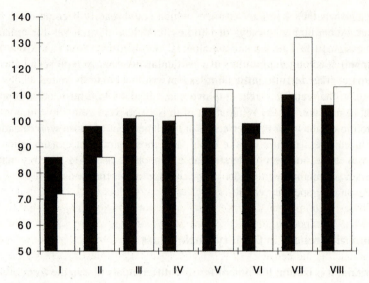

Fig. 2.3 Completed family size by social class, marriages 1851–61 (■) and 1881–86 (□), England and Wales 1911. Mean for each cohort = 100. Source: Royal Commission on Population (1949), Report, table XX.

sector classification which are nowadays treated separately. The classes in Fig. 2.3 are:

I   Professional and higher administrative
II   Employers in industry and retail
III   Skilled workers
IV   Intermediate between III and V
V   Unskilled labourers
VI   Textile workers
VII   Miners
VIII   Agricultural labourers

Up to the marriages of the early twentieth century the social differentials remained constant, although overall fertility fell in all groups to a national average of little over two children. Thus, with the average in each year set at 100, non-manual wage earners had 81 per cent of average fertility in the marriages of 1890–99 and 81 per cent in the marriages of 1920–24, and manual wage earners had 112 per cent of average fertility in each of those marriage cohorts (Glass and Grebenik 1954). This linear relationship had at one time been assumed to be permanent. In fact it has changed considerably since then.

Since at least the marriages of the 1930s the lowest average fertility has been found, not at the top of the social scale, but among families where the husband is in social class IIIN (clerical workers, clerks, salesmen). In the census of 1951 average family size where the husband was in social class I was 1.57 children compared with to 1.48 for social class II. Fertility then rose to considerably higher levels among the families of unskilled manual workers in social class V. By 1961 average fertility in social class II was almost as high as that in class III, while that of IV and V — semi-skilled and unskilled workers — had fallen by one-tenth or more. By the 1971 census this J-shaped curve was long established (Table 2.3), with fertility lowest in social class IIIN and still highest in social class V.

However, the analysis by Werner (1985) of births in the late 1970s and early 1980s suggested that, while social class differentials were considerably less than in the past, age-specific fertility rates, and therefore the total fertility rate, were then lowest in non-manual workers and particularly in social class I and II. This somewhat unexpected finding, which refers only to current period fertility within marriage, and not to completed family size, cannot be confirmed by census data, as the censuses of 1981 and 1991 failed to ask questions on completed fertility. During the period of declining fertility of the 1970s, fertility in social class I and V moved even closer together, as births (within marriage) in the latter social class have fallen faster (Werner 1985). However, this is due in part to the rise of illegitimate births, which more frequently occur to women of manual backgrounds but where the occupation of the father is often not registered. However, in the aggregate, social class differences in fertility appear to be diminishing, as well as possibly changing their form. The old inverse linear relationship, however, is starkly apparent with respect to births to teenage mothers (Babb 1993) and to births outside marriage (most teenage births are illegitimate).

Table 2.3. Social class differences in average fertility, 1971

Period of marriage	Husband's social class						
	I	II	IIIN	IIIM	IV	V	All
1941–45	2.04	1.99	1.86	2.20	2.24	2.47	2.14
1946–50	2.11	2.02	1.90	2.24	2.29	2.57	2.19
1951–55	2.25	2.17	2.00	2.34	2.36	2.66	2.29
1956–60	2.23	2.12	2.00	2.29	2.31	2.58	2.25
1961–65	1.80	1.76	1.66	1.89	1.93	2.14	1.85
1966–70	0.60	0.66	0.62	0.85	0.92	1.05	0.79
All periods	1.75	1.81	1.62	1.95	2.03	2.26	1.91
All periods, by woman's class	1.45	1.61	1.35	1.65	1.95	2.39	1.70

Note: Fertility of recent marriage cohorts, especially 1966–70, is incomplete at 1971. 'Inadequately described' and 'others' omitted from table.
Sources: OPCS (1983) Fertility Report from the 1971 Census OPCS Series DS no. 5,t.5.7, t. 5.30. HMSO, London. OPCS (1979) Census 1971 Fertility Tables, vol. ii, t. 24. HMSO, London.

Britain's exceptionally high frequency of teenage births should be noted; they were higher than any country in Western Europe in 1990 and two or three times higher than most.

Fewer births can be classified according to the mother's own occupation (50 per cent in 1990) than according to men's, and there are other problems of comparability (Cooper and Botting 1992; Botting and Cooper 1993). Information on the mother's own occupation has only been collected at the registration of birth since 1986. For earlier periods analysis depends on the Census (which last asked questions about fertility in 1971), the Longitudinal Study and surveys. As might be expected in view of the more direct impact of the opportunity costs of child-bearing upon women, fertility is related to social class based on women's own occupation in a more linear fashion than to men's. Average family size at age 36 among the 1946 birth cohort of women was 2.0 among women in social class I increasing to 2.7 among women in social class V.

Despite lower average fertility and a later start, fewer women in social class I and II ended up childless in 1971 than did women in class IV and V, and one-child families are least common in these two highest classes (Fig. 2.4). Higher fertility in class I and II than in IIIN is partly due to the relative rarity of families with just one child or none. Family size in class I and II is concentrated on two- and three-child families more than in any other class. The two-child 'norm' is a

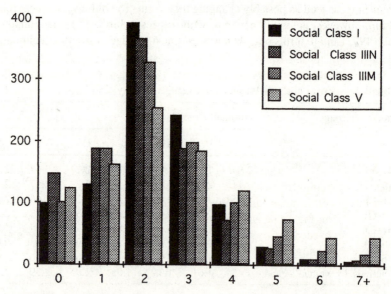

Fig. 2.4 1971 Proportionate distribution of numbers of children ever-born to married women (married once only under age 45 years, enumerated with husband) by husband's social class, year of marriage 1951–55.

middle-class norm. Families above three children are more frequent in the manual social classes, especially class V. Manual workers have higher average fertility because they are more likely to have big families, not because they avoid having really small ones. Forty-one per cent of wives of manual workers married in 1955–60 had at least four children in 1971 compared with 29 per cent in the non-manual group.

Patterns of starting and spacing children differ more by social class than does the simple average. In the 1946 birth cohort, the class effects on family size were mediated mostly through differences in timing of first birth (Kiernan 1987). In the 1970s and 1980s, middle class couples married 2–3 years later than working class couples and start their families 2 years later after marriage. As a consequence wives in social class I and II in 1986 produced their first child when they were more than 4 years older than wives in social class IV and V. In 1975, women with husbands in social class V gave birth for the first time a mere 9 months after marriage, as at most times in the past. By 1990 this interval increased by a half (49 per cent) to 13 months. If premarital conceptions are eliminated from the calculation, the social class gradient in the duration of time from marriage to first birth is only half as steep as before, from 45 months in social class I to 24 months in class V.

Despite all these interesting differences according to social class, the proportion of variability accounted for by social class membership and other social group variables is relatively small. The maximum average difference between social classes was equivalent to half a child, whereas differences in average according to age at commencing child-bearing were equivalent to about one child. This timing of the beginning of child-bearing is the single most important explanatory factor in a recent multivariate analysis. Net of that and other factors, social class could account for between 6 and 8 per cent of the observed variance, in both the tempo and quantum components of fertility — about the same as other variables such as educational level and housing tenure (Ni Bhrolchain 1993).

Births outside marriage

Since the beginning of the 1980s, generalizations based on statistics gathered about births within marriage have become less representative of all births. In the 1950s, as in the 1930s and in most previous centuries, births outside marriage seldom exceeded 5 per cent of the total in England and Wales and most other Western countries. Since the 1960s, the proportion of births occurring outside marriage has risen dramatically (Cooper 1991) to over 30 per cent in 1992. Less is known about the characteristics of these births. When births are registered by the mother alone, no data can be collected about the occupational status of the father. This can only be done when the birth is jointly registered by both parents. In 1992 in England and Wales, 76 per cent of births outside marriage were jointly registered and 72 per cent of these parents (55 per cent of the parents of all births outside marriage) gave the same address. Where the same address is given, it is believed that the couple is usually cohabiting, and it is also believed that the majority of births to cohabiting couples are jointly registered (Haskey and Coleman 1986). Relatively high proportions of couples in several social classes cohabit before marriage and generally outside marriage, and there is no simple relationship between the propensity to cohabit and social class. However, child-bearing while cohabiting is much more prevalent among manual workers, especially in social class V, as also is 'conventional' illegitimacy. Five per cent of all births in 1983 in class I + II, and 16 per cent to class IV + V occurred outside marriage but within formal unions (as inferred from the joint registration of the births; Werner (1985)). The distribution of births by mother's and by father's social class, for all cases where the information is available irrespective of marital or cohabiting status, for the years 1986–90 was 37 per cent of births to non-manual occupations according to the husband's occupation, and 31 per cent according to the mother's.

The shifts in legitimate fertility by social class match shifts in family intentions. In the 1940s and 1950s working class women expected to have more babies than middle class women. These preferences and expectations were reversed by the 1970s, and seem to offer further evidence in support of Becker's (1981) view that the better-off will eventually have more children than others. Women born in 1955–59, with non-manual fathers expected rather more children (2.24–2.12) than women from manual backgrounds, and the new difference is maintained in the most recent cohorts.

Space forbids detailed exploration of other factors. Educational level is associated with social class but some analyses suggest that at least up to the 1971 census, graduates (a small proportion of all women) may be more fertile than others, with women who stopped at 'A' levels having the lowest fertility (Grebenik 1983). Demographic differences in respect of housing tenure have been shown to be substantial and partly independent of social class, with the tenants of social housing beginning union formation and child-bearing considerably earlier than households in other tenures, including private renting. In council tenure, more than in private renting or ownership, family size is larger, teenage births and births outside marriage and single parent families more prevalent, and marriages more likely to end in divorce (Babb 1993), even when social class is taken into account (Murphy and Sullivan 1985). Some previous work is reviewed in Coleman (1990) and Ni Bhrolchain's (1993) substantial multivariate analysis deals with all these and other factors.

The underlying relationship between reproduction and status

In the past it is quite possible that better-off classes had higher fertility than the poor. They enjoyed better health and were able (in the West European system) to marry earlier. This is known in pre-war Poland and France and has also been noted in some unmodernized post-war Third World populations. Becker's model of fertility and its determinants (Becker 1981) suggests that in the long run we will return to a similar pattern, once the spread of education has minimized contraceptive ignorance and unwanted fertility. Under conditions of complete fertility control, births are expected to be delayed and numbered to permit the satisfaction of material aspirations. Thus the better off, able as in the past to satisfy these aspirations more readily, may end up with a larger average family size even though the direct and opportunity costs of their children are higher than average. Some evidence from reproductive intentions and from reproductive behaviour in Britain and elsewhere suggests that this may be occurring. It is not surprising that higher male income might be associated with larger family size, where most couples plan their families. The earning ability of men is not compromised by the number of children they have. But the movement of married women into the work-force is supposed to have been one of the main reasons for the decline in fertility since the 1960s, because of the opportunity cost for women, in terms of income forgone, involved in child care. However, work-force participation by women appears nowadays to be a less effective impediment to having a third- or higher-order child that used to be the case in Norway, Sweden, and Britain (Kravdal 1992). While women with a higher wage at the start of marriage have smaller families according to the British 1980 Women and Employment Survey, the depressing effect upon fertility weakens as women's income increases further (Ermisch 1988).

The social origins of future generations

In the event, there has been a shift in the relative contribution which each social class has made to each birth cohort and therefore to each future generation (Table 2.4). In 1970 only 22 per cent of births occurred in social class I or II families. By 1982, the proportion had reached 32 per cent, the same as in 1986. This trend has been driven both by shifts in fertility and in the distribution of occupations. There has been a long-term move away from manual and less skilled occupations towards skilled, service, and professional jobs (Boston 1984; Werner 1985). During the fall in fertility in the 1970s, all legitimate births fell by 24 per cent between 1970 and 1975, and a further 3.4 per cent by 1985. Births in manual workers' families, particularly to women in class 4 and 5, fell by a third. Births to routine non-manual workers families (IIIN) fell by roughly the national average. But women with husbands in class I and II did not share this decline at all.

The social class origin of each generation has often been thought to be significant with respect to the kinds of attitudes, abilities, and values inherited by each new generation. The statistical distribution of such origins is influenced by changes in the distribution of occupations through social and economic change,

Table 2.4.   Social class distribution of live births England and Wales 1971–90

Year	I&II	IIIN	IIIM	IV&V	Other	All
Legitimate births only						
(numbers in thousands)						
1971	154.7	75.3	297.7	160.1	29.5	717.3
1976	140.8	55.5	204.6	110.2	19.4	530.5
1981	163.3	60.4	198.2	111.4	20.1	553.4
1986	160.1	55.2	179.5	101.1	23.8	519.7
1990	177.4	53.2	168.8	85.3	21.4	506.1
Jointly registered births outside marriage (numbers in thousands)						
1981	6.2	3.0	20.6	15.6	1.7	47.1
1986	13.3	5.8	38.3	31.8	4.3	93.5
1990	23.1	9.5	62.7	44.6	5.6	145.5

	I&II	IIIN	IIIM	IV&V	All
Legitimate births only (per cent of total excluding 'other')					
1971	22.5	10.9	43.3	23.3	100
1976	27.5	10.9	40.0	21.6	100
1981	30.6	11.3	37.2	20.9	100
1986	32.3	11.1	36.2	20.4	100
1990	36.6	11.0	34.8	17.6	100
Jointly registered births outside marriage (per cent of total excluding 'other')					
1981	13.7	6.6	45.4	34.4	100
1986	14.9	6.5	42.9	35.7	100
1990	16.5	6.8	44.8	31.9	100

	I&II	IIIN	IIIM	IV&V	All	% all births
All births of known social origin, inside and outside marriage (per cent of total excluding 'other')						
1981	169.5	63.4	218.8	127.0	578.7	91.2
1986	173.4	61.0	217.8	132.9	585.1	88.5
1990	200.5	62.7	231.5	129.9	624.6	88.5
All births of known social origin, inside and outside marriage (per cent of total excluding 'other')						
1981	29.3	11.0	37.8	21.9	100.0	91.2
1986	29.6	10.4	37.2	22.7	100.0	88.5
1990	32.1	10.0	37.1	20.8	100.0	88.5

Source: OPCS Birth Statistics (1977) Series FM1 No. 4 (1988); Series FM1 No. 15 (1990); Series FM1 No. 19, tables 11.1, 11.5. All HMSO, London.

through social mobility, and through differential fertility. All of these factors may have fairly transient effects. The apparent shift in the distribution of births between classes had already made an important difference in the balance of class origins of future generations. In 1971, for example, there were about 224 000 births to fathers in non-manual groups, compared with 469 000 to 'manual' fathers — a ratio of 1: 2.1. But by 1980, 'non-manual births' remained almost the same — 226 000; 'manual' births had fallen to 333 000 — a ratio of 1:1.5. In 1986 the respective numbers were 215 000 and 281 000–a ratio of 1:1.3, with 37 per cent of legitimate births in 1990 occurring to families with fathers in social class I and II (OPCS 1992). But these statistics refer only to legitimate births. In 1986 21 per cent of births were illegitimate, by 1990 30 per cent. A high proportion of these where the occupation of father or mother's chief economic supporter is known are in manual occupations, particularly in social class IV and V (34 per cent in 1981). In these births in 1990 only 17 per cent were of social class I and II origin, 45 per cent social class IIIM and 32 per cent IV and V a slight change to favour class I and II since 1981. In 1990 births within marriage comprised 506 141 or 72 per cent of the total of 706 140 births, those jointly registered were a further 145 500 or 21 per cent. Most but not all of these can be assigned to social class origins I–V. We can therefore say that of those 624 600 (88.5 per cent) of births whose social origins were known in 1990, that 32 per cent were from class I and II origins (slightly increased from 1981), 29.3 and 20.8 per cent were of social class IV and V origins (slightly lower than in 1981). The social origins of the remaining 11 per cent of births of unknown social origins are likely to be at least as biased towards the unskilled and semi-skilled origins as were those jointly registered. If that were so, then the proportion of all births from class I + II would be not more than 31 per cent and that from class V + IV not less than 22 per cent.

Contemporary controversies

Victorian eugenists and biometricians such as Francis Galton and Karl Pearson expressed concern about higher working class fertility during what we now know to be the earlier phases of the demographic transition, and its supposed consequences for social welfare and national average ability. The Royal Commission on Population (1949) while uncertain that the trend of 'national intelligence' really was downwards, felt that 'it is clearly undesirable for the welfare and cultural standards of the nation that our social arrangements should be such as to induce those in the higher income groups and the better educated and more intelligent within each income group to keep their families not only below replacement level but below the level of others'. This general kind of concern goes back at least to the time of Malthus, who argued that welfare arrangements to supplement low wages through the poor laws promoted early and imprudent marriage and thereby increased the level of poverty through the larger family size which would, in the days before contraception, usually follow earlier marriage.

In fact post-war research showed that there was no empirical evidence to sustain these fears, as average intelligence showed a slight increase from the 1930s (Thompson 1946). The view that population variation in ability and other aspects of behaviour have a strong genetic component is well supported (Mascie-Taylor 1990), although it does not follow from this that average differences between subpopulations such as social classes are a result of differences in the distribution of genes. Arguments on the measurement and the inheritance of ability and its social distribution remained hot issues in the 1950s and 1960s (Thoday and Parkes 1968).

Since the early twentieth century there has been considerable interest in what were then called 'problem families' and what has now become known as the 'underclass' (Murray 1984). Problem families were distinguished by numerous progeny raised in debased material and social circumstances, requiring attention from more than one of the welfare services, and were held to be responsible for more than their fair share of delinquency and dependency in the present and future generations (Blacker 1937; Wolfinden 1950). Our interest depends upon whether: (a) such characteristics are handed on to the future generations to any significant extent, through whatever mechanisms of inheritance, so as to maximize the chances of the progeny of such families replicating the same circumstances for their own offspring and (b) whether those persons in such categories in the present generation have higher than average fertility, thus maintaining or increasing the prevalence of such conditions in society.

The transmission of such dependence over generations — the so-called Cycle of Disadvantage — has been a major sociological controversy since the 1960s (Rutter and Madge 1976; Heath 1981). Some elements of this complex of problems have been shown to be transmitted over generations, at least to some degree. For example, the Medical Research Council cohort studies show that parents of teenage mothers had usually married young themselves, and that both generations were from large families, had low levels of education and were concentrated in manual occupations (Kiernan 1980). Mothers of illegitimate babies, and teenage mothers, have been shown to have lower than averaged measured intelligence (Kiernan and Diamond 1982). However, studies of the transmission of poverty revealed only a partial transmission of income levels across generations. Fathers and sons were most similar in income level at the very lowest level and at the highest (Shorrocks 1988). About half the cases of deprivation in any generation had arisen anew in that generation (Madge 1988).

Specifically hereditarian views on these matters, always controversial, were discredited by the exposure of the fabrications of Sir Cyril Burt, although Sir Cyril now appears to have been at least partly rehabilitated (Fletcher 1991). While a substantial body of evidence suggests that inherited characteristics account, in general, for a good deal of the observed variation in human ability in modern societies, such views make little explicit contribution to the modern debate on the underclass and are avoided by most of the present protagonists. This is dangerous territory. It has been suggested that Sir Keith Joseph's political career was permanently blighted by his blunt suggestions that there would be advantages to society, as well to the individuals concerned, if the teenage mothers of problem children would curb or delay their child-bearing more effectively (Joseph 1972).

The term 'underclass' is an American import intended to describe an American phenomenon (in the USA, especially a black urban phenomenon). It is associated with the Chicago school of libertarian economists and social and political scientists, such as Charles Murray (Murray 1990), to describe a group of poor people distinguished from other poor people not just by low income but also by specific delinquent behaviour, unemployability, disproportionate dependency on welfare and social housing, and among whom reproduction primarily takes place outside marriage. The notion of a behaviourally distinct group of poor people, long familiar as the 'undeserving poor' is accepted by some British commentators (Field 1989) and rejected by others (Walker 1990; Halsey 1993). The debate on the existence of such an underclass is potentially of demographic interest. Their problems are allegedly transmitted across generations; a high proportion of births outside marriage is claimed to be both an important characteristic and a causal element in the process (Dennis and Erdos 1992). In earlier studies higher fertility groups among poor people have been attributed to poor education and of weak ability to control life events (Askham 1975), or at least the belief that such events are not within conscious control. Recently, a parallel controversy has arisen as to whether single women with few prospects use early child-bearing as a quick route to subsidized adult status and independent household through the provisions of the welfare and housing allocation system; or at least that these systems weaken inhibitions against such behaviour (Garfinkel and McLanahan 1986; Duncan and Hoffman 1991; Ermisch 1991).

Group differences in fertility: ethnic minorities

Ethnicity and social class are to some extent rivals in the explanation of social phenomena. Some sociologists (Barry 1970) are inclined to discount any independent effect of 'culture' or 'values' upon behaviour, demographically measured or otherwise, regarding cultural constructs as transient and unstructured epiphenomena of fundamentally economic pressures which can survive only in the gaps of socio-economic explanations. At the time of writing the tide of opinion in demography flows firmly in favour of the independent importance of socially inherited culture and religious values which independently structure attitudes and behaviour affecting work, marriage and fertility (Reynolds 1988), political responses and national and international politics (Moynihan 1993).

Some social scientists, especially from non-numerate disciplines whose wider influence had hitherto been marginalized by modern economics, like the societies they study, have become almost triumphalist (Gellner 1993) in re-asserting the importance of cultural, 'ideational', ethnic, and religious factors. Within demography, disillusion with the failure of economic and development indicators to provide more than partial explanations for demographic transition, together with improvements in the development of proxy and direct instruments for measuring attitudes, have promoted models of demographic change and differentials based on 'values' and 'ideational' change (Simons 1986; Lesthaeghe and Meekers 1986; Cleland and Wilson 1987).

Few of these ideas have been applied to the demographic study of ethnic minority differentials, which have attracted great interest in Western countries (OECD 1991) because of the high rates of population growth of such immigrant minorities. Since the Second World War most Western European countries have acquired substantial non-European immigrant communities. Initially, all had higher fertility than their European host populations, not surprisingly in view of the pre-transitional societies from which most had emigrated. That, together with continued immigration, gives them growth rates of over 4 per cent per year, higher than any population in the world. This transplantation of populations to social, intellectual, and material circumstances very different from those in which their high-fertility demographic regimes had developed makes for a remarkable large-scale demographic 'experiment'; which has been far from adequately explored from the viewpoint of demographic theory.

In particular this 'experiment' may highlight the effects of religion upon fertility. Most of the world's religions assume more or less strongly that their followers will affirm both their faith and its institutions through reproduction. But some at least are compatible, in 'modernized' form, with the adoption of low fertility norms (Reynolds and Tanner 1973). Hinduism and Islam are perhaps the chief defining principle of the culture of some ethnic groups, the more so as they recognize no clear separation between the secular and the religious. Faith and observance are high among most immigrant populations, most of whom originate from poor rural backgrounds. It is generally supposed, following demographic transition theory, that immigrant populations will experience accelerated social change and that the raised costs of children in developed societies, the wider opportunities for women, and changes in literacy, education, and attitude will lead these vital rates to converge on the low fertility of the host population.

In the UK there is considerable diversity among immigrant fertility patterns (Table 2.5). Among West Indian immigrants, fertility has fallen to about the same level as the population average, although about 40 per cent of households are headed by women, and illegitimacy has remained about 50 per cent of births. The birth rate to Asian immigrant women born in India and in East Africa has also fallen to about the same level as the national average. Fertility among the

Table 2.5. Total fertility rate of women born in the New Commonwealth, for England and Wales, 1971–91

Birthplace	1971*	1981	1983	1985	1987	1988	1989	1990	1991
Total	2.4	1.8	1.8	1.8	1.8	1.8	1.8	1.9	1.9
UK	2.3	1.7	1.7	1.7	1.8	1.8	1.8	1.9	1.8
Total outside UK	–	2.5	2.4	2.5	2.4	2.4	2.3	2.3	2.4
New Commonwealth	4.0	2.9	2.8	2.9	2.8	2.8	2.7	2.6	2.5
India	4.3	3.1	2.8	2.9	2.7	2.8	2.4	2.2	2.1
Pakistan and Bangladesh	9.3	6.5	6.1	5.6	5.2	4.9	4.7	4.7	4.6
East Africa (Asian)	2.7	2.1	2.0	2.1	2.0	2.0	1.9	1.8	1.8
Rest of Africa (African)	4.2	3.4	3.1	3.0	3.2	3.6	4.2	4.1	4.2
West Indies	3.4	2.0	1.8	1.8	1.9	1.8	1.6	1.6	1.5
Malta, Gibraltar, Cyprus		2.1	2.1	2.2	2.0	2.0	1.9	1.7	1.3
Hong Kong, Malaysia, Singapore, Brunei	2.7	1.7	1.9	2.0	1.8	1.9	1.7	1.7	1.7
Rest of New Commonwealth		2.3	2.4	2.3	2.5	2.7	2.4	2.2	2.4
Rest of world	NA	2.0	1.9	2.0	1.9	2.0	1.9	2.0	2.2

* OPCS Monitor, Series FM1 84/9.
Sources: OPCS Birth Statistics 1985, Series FM1 No. 12 table 9.5. OPCS Birth Statistics 1987 Series FM1 No. 16 table 9.5. 1992 Series FM1 No. 19 table 9.5. 1993 Series FM1 No. 20 table 9.5. All HMSO, London.

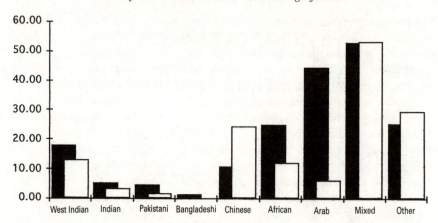

Fig. 2.5 Percentage of men and women of specified ethnic groups currently married to whites, Great Britain 1985–88, all birthplaces of partners. Women, □; men, ■.
Sources: data from Labour Force Surveys 1985–88. Note: includes informal unions.

Muslim Pakistanis and Bangladeshis, although falling, remains very high by European standards (Coleman 1994).

New Commonwealth Muslim immigrant communities in Britain (Pakistanis and Bangladeshis) have the lowest rate of out-marriage of any ethnic minorities (Fig. 2.5). In particular hardly any women from these immigrant communities are married to whites (almost all whites can be assumed to be non-Muslim). However, a high proportion of Arab men in Britain, most of whom are also Muslim, are married to whites. This underlines the importance of being cautious about making generalizations about 'universal' religious behaviour which may also be influenced in particular groups by ethnic, regional, or income factors. There is no religious prohibition in Islam against men marrying non-Muslim women, for it is assumed that the wife will convert. Arabs in Britain do not come from poor North African or Commonwealth countries but predominantly from Arabia and the Gulf. Most are educated and well off. By contrast, West Indian society, at least nominally Christian, is relatively free of such strictures and has traditionally been relaxed about the choice of partner, a pattern associated with the informality and relative impermanence of sexual unions. African and Arab men, at least in immigrant communities in the West, likewise have few inhibitions against unions with persons outside their ethnic origin, at least with whites.

These attitudes and behaviours are rapidly changing. Fertility is declining among immigrant women themselves. Furthermore, it appears that there is a substantial difference between the fertility and marriage patterns of New Commonwealth (NC) immigrants and those of their children born in the UK, who have been exposed to a different economic, educational, and moral environment. The relatively small sample size of the only data source on the ethnic origin of the partners in current unions, the Labour Force Survey, makes detailed analysis difficult. But in general, although little is known about differences in fertility, persons of NC immigrant origin born in the UK appear to be much more prone to form unions with whites than were their parents. Much more precise comments on this subject will be possible once the results of the 1991 Census (which asked a question on ethnic origin) are analysed (see Berrington, in preparation).

So numerous have such unions become that a mixed population of over 300 000 persons has arisen in Britain, over 70 per cent of them born in the UK and about half of mixed West Indian/White ancestry. By the late 1980s they comprised 20 per cent of the 0–4 age group of the whole ethnic minority population in the UK. The majority of those already in unions (70 per cent) have formed unions with whites. This group is important and interesting for a variety of reasons. Marriages across religious and ethnic boundaries have created a new population of individuals of diverse origins, which belongs to no well-established existing 'group' (traditional 'Anglo-Indians' of mixed origin form only a small minority in this new population). Many, it seems, have been happy to describe themselves as being of 'mixed' origin (often adding supplementary detail) in response to questions on ethnic group in the annual Labour Force Survey from 1981, which included the category 'mixed'.

This category has been abolished in the revised ethnic grouping adopted for the 1991 census, and has now been dropped from subsequent rounds of the Labour Force Survey. This deprives us of information on a most important and growing group of people, whose behaviour might offer many insights into the process of integration in Britain (Nanton 1992). This step, which appears to have been taken in response to political pressures, may itself have effects upon how people in Britain view themselves. The introduction of census questions on language with restricted choice of answers is alleged to have polarized self-identity in the Austro-Hungarian domains in the late nineteenth century, for example (Hobsbawm 1990).

Group differences in fertility: the religious dimension

How important is the religious dimension in the preservation of these fertility differences? A priori, religious attitudes seem highly likely to be able to account for differences in values affecting reproduction, as many religions have much to say about the social, or rather spiritual control of reproduction and the relations between the sexes. Sexual restraint outside marriage was an essential element of the Western European marriage pattern and the regime which depended on it. In Islam, family honour depends upon the safeguarding of the purity of unmarried girls, and the penalty for adultery is death. The roles and relative standing of the sexes are defined in considerable detail in the Koran. Buddhist attitudes emphasize restraint and encourage enlightenment through learning (not just religious learning). These are believed to facilitate early achievement of low fertility and an early passage through the demographic transition (e.g. Thailand; Knodel *et al.* 1987).

The effects of religious adherence on fertility are not easy to establish empirically or to explain theoretically. A number of questions are involved. Do members of one denomination in a population in fact have different vital rates from others or from non-believers? Do countries where that denomination is numerically preponderant have higher birth rates than others? Do any such differences depend on whether the religious community concerned is in a minority in the whole population (the 'minority status' hypothesis)? Do adherents of particular religions behave differently with respect to the proximate determinants of fertility: marriage, sex, contraception, abortion, breast feeding? Can any differences which are observed be attributed to non-religious socio-economic factors such as differences in income, occupation, or educational level, which are known to have a predictable effect on fertility (the 'characteristics' theory)? Do religious adherents have higher preferences concerning family size, and do these differences vary with the degree of religious observance or fervour? Does the religion concerned place emphasis on specific injunctions about reproduction, the status of women and polygamy, or on recourse to contraception or abortion?

Empirical testing of such notions is difficult. Many countries do not record religious denomination in censuses or on the registration of vital events. A few, such as Germany and Switzerland, note the denomination on the registration of marriages but not at birth and death. No such records are kept in the UK except for a voluntary question on religious denomination in the Northern Ireland census. Such records in any case are of dubious value when religious faith is weak or non-existent, as in many residents of industrial society. While many non-believers may retain a nominal affiliation, such questions really need to be qualified by supplementary enquiries on frequency of observance, intensity of religious belief, or its importance to the individual, as they usually are in surveys. Even empirical data depend too much on surveys, or on proxy variables such as ethnicity or birthplace, or geographical residence, which are vulnerable to the 'ecological fallacy' in statistical inference.

Roman Catholicism and its demography

For example, it is widely assumed that Roman Catholics have higher fertility than non-Catholics. This is only partly true. There are of course many empirical examples which appear to support such a case. In the early modern period, many (Catholic) South German villages showed high birth rates (up to total fertility rate = 8) and high infant mortality (Knodel and van de Walle 1967). This appears to be due to religious attitudes which enhanced fertility and infant mortality indirectly, as a by-product of moralizing views on breast feeding and sex.

The Roman church adopted the view (which does not seem at all inherent in general Catholic doctrine) that sexual intercourse damaged breast milk (an erroneous opinion also held by other cultures, for example in tropical Africa). Accordingly, as neither adultery or polygamy (the African solution, (Lesthaeghe 1986)) were permitted, and sexual continence was not to be expected for a full year, breast feeding was minimized or abandoned (Fildes 1988) with much emphasis on wet nursing and early weaning, with highly deleterious consequences for birth spacing and infant mortality. Protestant regions did not follow this practice to anything like the same degree, and the result is apparent in higher birth rates and infant mortality in many Catholic countries and provinces in the early modern period (Flinn 1981).

In Britain, Roman Catholics were late in adopting family planning in the nineteenth century, and those few areas with relatively high proportions of Roman Catholics had correspondingly higher average fertility (Teitelbaum 1984). Within Western countries today, Catholic populations tend to be indistinguishable demographically from their Protestant counterparts unless they are also ethnically distinct and/or recent immigrants from higher fertility countries, such as the Irish-born in Britain or Hispanics in America (except Cubans, who have lower than average fertility; Coleman 1992). In Britain and the USA, non-ethnic Roman Catholic populations have not had significantly higher fertility than non-Catholics since the 1970s at the latest (Westoff and Jones 1979); although there is some evidence this pattern may be reviving in the USA.

Looking at countries as a whole, it is true that many Latin American countries have preserved higher fertility for longer than similarly poor or poorer countries in the Far East. Although almost all are showing declining fertility, there are few low-fertility achievers in Latin America. Likewise, Spain and Portugal preserved higher than average fertility until about 1980, as did Catholic Quebec until the 1970s. In both cases the collapse of the birth rate has occurred at the same time as a flight from religion and traditional values. Ireland and Poland remain bastions of Catholic observance and preserve higher fertility than the European average, although both religion and fertility appear to be in decline. But the general notion that Catholic countries are late to adopt family planning cannot be sustained when it was (Catholic) pre-revolutionary France that was the first national population in the world to show clear signs of the general adoption of birth control within marriage; starting in the 1770s in some (but not all) urban and rural areas about a century before any other country did do. Catholic Hungary showed, in some rural areas, the same precocious fertility decline. Non-revolutionary countries with almost entirely Catholic populations such as Belgium and Austria showed perfectly ordinary fertility declines. Catholic French-speaking (Walloon) Belgians showed much earlier fertility declines than their Dutch speaking (Fleming) Belgian neighbours (Lesthaeghe 1978).

In the industrial world of the 1980s, Catholic countries now have lower average fertility (Fig. 2.6). Mean total fertility rate of 14 predominantly Roman

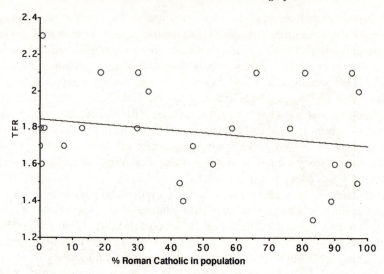

Fig. 2.6 Relation between the percentage of Roman Catholics in the population and the total fertility rate, in 26 Western countries in the 1980s. $y = -0.001x + 1.847$, $r^2 = 0.04$. $n = 26$, $P = 0.3$.

Catholic industrial countries around 1990 was 1.72; that of 12 predominantly Protestant ones was 1.80. The lowest national fertility in Europe, and in the world, is that of Italy (1.3) with Catholic Spain, Portugal, and Quebec in Canada not far behind. The highest, probably now overtaking Ireland and Poland, are Lutheran Sweden (2.1) and Protestant USA and New Zealand (2.1); the latter have 25 per cent Roman Catholic minorities. Fig. 2.7 shows recent trends in two selected groups of predominantly Protestant, and Roman Catholic countries.

However, there remains a strong inverse relationship between the proportion of Roman Catholics and the proportion of live births born outside marriage ($n = 26$, $r^2 = 0.51$, $P = 0.0001$). The proportion declines from about 40 per cent in countries almost entirely non-Catholic to about 15 per cent or less in highly Catholic countries. 'Catholic' fertility appears to have been replaced with 'Protestant' illegitimacy.

How are we to interpret these apparently confusing data? A number of possible *post-hoc* explanations offer themselves. Most of them underline the importance of eliminating confounding variables but usually involve handing on the responsibility for explaining the root causes of change to other subjects. Ireland, Spain, and Portugal were relatively poor rural societies until relatively recently, where higher fertility would be expected on socio-economic grounds alone. A rapid retreat from faith and observance was noted in many Western countries in the 1960s (Britain, the Netherlands; Simons 1986) and especially in the southern

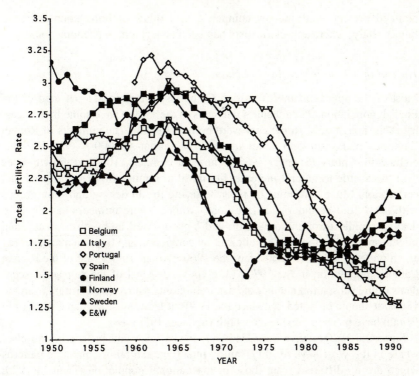

Fig. 2.7 Trends in total fertility rate, selected European countries 1950–91. Predominantly Protestant countries have black chart symbols, predominantly Roman Catholic countries have white. □ Belgium; △ Italy; ◇ Portugal; ▽ Spain; ● Finland; ■ Norway; ▲ Sweden; ◆ England and Wales. Sources: data from Council of Europe, 1993.

European countries in the 1970s, where referenda on abortion and divorce were held (successfully) for the first time. If that caused the decline in fertility which followed then the view that religious attitudes influence fertility levels is supported, even by the example of the decline of those religious values.

The culture of Catholicism, like that of other universal religions, is not uniform but adapts to local conditions and to social change. In the early twentieth century, Day (1968) has shown that Catholic fertility was usually only higher than that of their neighbours when Catholics were in a minority, especially when the community was 'pillarized' on religious lines as in the Netherlands. In this respect, the majority Catholic population in Poland and Ireland may be regarded as 'honorary minorities' as far as the status of the church is concerned. Both had to survive under the domination of the homeland by neighbouring countries of alien religion where the sole remaining substantial institution to protect national identity was the Catholic church, which thereby retained prestige and support compared with other Catholic countries (e.g. France, Italy) where anti-clericalism had become a common phenomenon.

The end of 'Catholic' fertility in Britain

Most of the approximately 5 million Catholics in Britain (11 per cent of the English population, 25 per cent of the Scots in the 1970s) have some Irish ancestry even though only 16 per cent were born in Ireland. The numbers of Roman Catholics had shrunk to small numbers — about 40 000 — by the mid-eighteenth century (Spencer 1982). The approximately 100-fold growth since then owes little to natural increase, but more to immigration from Ireland and conversion. Much care must be taken in trying to 'do demography' on groups with such fluid boundaries as religious groups, where numbers can grow or decline rapidly through conversion and lapse as well as by birth, death, and migration. Conversions to Catholicism, by conviction and through marriage, ran at a high level from the 1860s until the 1960s. About 10 per cent of the Roman Catholic population in the 1970s were converts. Most of the rest are descendants of the substantial number of Irish immigrants who entered Britain from the 1840s. It should be noted that since the 1970s at least, most Roman Catholics in Britain have married outside their faith (Spencer 1975).

Since the 1970s native born Catholics in the USA and in Britain and elsewhere in the West have fertility, family intention, and family planning patterns which are no different from those of the national population (Dunnell 1979; Westoff and Jones 1979; Cartwright 1987). In Britain only a relatively small difference exists between the fertility of Irish immigrants and others. There is a slight tendency for the (Vatican approved) rhythm method to be used more often by Catholics than by others, both in Britain and in Catholic countries such as Italy. By the mid-1970s, about 4 per cent of British Catholic couples used this approved method, compared with 2 per cent of non-Catholics. Patterns of contraceptive usage even among Irish born women in Britain have not been significantly different from the general population since the 1970s (Cartwright 1987). The use of the pill, rhythm method, and female sterilization were more common among the Irish women, and the sheath and IUD less so.

By that time the occupational and geographical distribution of Roman Catholics was only slightly different from that of the general population, and differences have narrowed since (Hornsby-Smith 1987). This is less true of the Irish born; a higher proportion of whom are manual workers living in urban areas. In England it has never made any sense to talk of a Roman Catholic 'ethnic group' population as to an increasing extent religion, or religious tradition, is all that distinguishes them from their fellow citizens. Among the indigenous people of most Western countries, religious faith and practice is now important for only a minority and even the demography of the devout appears to be little different from that of others, even though people with religious commitments have more conservative attitudes and behaviour than do others, especially in respect of living arrangements (Lesthaeghe and Moors 1993). For many years, family planning has for most people been regarded as a necessary morally neutral or positive act of restraint, emancipated from religious inhibitions. For these reasons, specifically religious affiliation among indigenous European populations attracts little interest among analysts of fertility. This may seem surprising, as demographic interest in values and attitudes as factors affecting living arrangements and family formation has never been higher. But organized religion is far from being the only vehicle for moral values and preferences.

Islamic attitudes to reproduction

By contrast, there is considerable interest in the demographic behaviour of immigrant ethnic and religious minorities, especially that of Islam, which are linked to wider cultural differences. Since the 1950s western Europe has acquired a Muslim population of over 5 million (up to 900 000 of them in Britain; Peach 1990). While this population has varied origins (Nielsen 1992) they have preserved, despite substantial social change, distinctive demographic patterns — notably higher fertility and low levels of intermarriage compared not only with the indigenous population and other immigrants of Third World origin. The isolation of specifically religious effects in such immigrant minorities is complicated not only by the socio-economic correlates and minority effects mentioned above, but also by the more over-arching role of Islam and some other non-European religions in offering at least ideally, a complete framework for law and governance of society as well as for individual morality.

The injunctions of Islam appear a priori to have great potential for maximizing its membership. Conversion is simple, departure difficult, indeed punishable by death as apostasy. Intermarriage with other faiths is forbidden for woman and permitted to men on the presumption that children will be raised by the mother and must be raised as Muslims. (In the past the Roman church only permitted its adherents — of either sex — to marry a non-Catholic with religious rites if promises were made to raise the children as Catholics.) Marriage and child-bearing are held to be morally superior to celibacy and childlessness. Monasticism, powerful in Buddhism and Christianity, is forbidden in Islam, although mystical but not celibate sufi brotherhoods are popular. Fertility at least of men is favoured by polygyny and unlimited concubinage with slaves where slavery is permitted; particularly appropriate for a religion of conquest, which regards itself as the natural and inevitable replacement of earlier, incomplete revelations.

Authoritative statements as early as the 1930s deny that the Koran prohibits contraception, but many of the rural faithful none the less assume that contraception is contrary to religion. It is characteristic of simple societies to assume that the conservative retention of traditional ways has the support of religion.

Recent Islamic fundamentalist regimes demolished 'Western' family planning programmes, although the Iranian regime has re-established its own. A preference for sons, spurred by the Islamic law giving twice the inheritance to sons, and patrilineal society, encourages couples to continue until a sufficient number of boys are born. Islam provides the most specific injunctions on the roles of women. Their seclusion and restriction to the domestic sphere, regarded as the ideal if not practised, inhibits female education, effectively prevents their participation in the work-force in Islamic societies and inhibits it among immigrant communities. In Britain, the female work-force participation rates of Muslim immigrant minorities (Pakistanis and Bangladeshis) is the lowest of any immigrant group (Department of Employment 1993).

Islamic countries as a group have the highest fertility (Weeks 1988). While fertility decline has occurred in Muslim states of the Middle East, the Maghreb, and especially in Turkey and Indonesia, no Muslim country has yet reached replacement fertility. Islamic ethnic minorities tend to have the highest fertility of any ethnic minority group: for example Muslims in India (Breton 1988) and in Israel (Friedlander and Goldscheider 1984) as well as in Europe. However, the isolation of the specific influences of Islam on fertility is compounded, as in the discussion about Roman Catholicism, by parallel effects of poverty, minority status, and other factors. Islamic countries include some of the poorest in the world (e.g. Bangladesh, Afghanistan, most of north-west Africa) and their high fertility has been attributed to these socio-economic attributes rather than to Islam (Weeks 1988).

Conclusions

Despite beginning with rather idealistic comments on the desirability of considering variation in fertility in Britain and elsewhere using population statistics on variability rather than group averages, the constraints of available data and published work have in fact obliged most of the comments in this chapter to revert to the familiar territory of group averages and other simple statistics. This will not change as much as might have been hoped through the availability of individual anonymized records through the 1991 census, because the 1991 census, like other British censuses after 1971, has failed to ask questions on fertility, and the vital registration system only records the most limited information: age, occupation, and birthplace. However, analysis on the basis of co-resident children ('own children') will be possible, and the recent more extensive use of the General Household Survey for multivariate analysis, mentioned above, has shown how illuminating an analysis of all fertility variability can be.

It has long been possible to analyse the fertility of different social and ethnic categories of the British population separately in terms of group averages. While it is possible to state which sections of the population, defined by one characteristic, are contributing most to the next generation and which are contributing least, it is not so easy to do so with respect to more than one characteristic. Moreover, when the overall variability of fertility in the British population is investigated using individual-level data (necessarily with a limited set of variables), it is instructive to see how relatively little of the total variability can be attributed statistically to such conventional social, geographical, and other factors. Much of the variability of fertility and of the representation of individuals in the next generation is simply unaccounted for and must be set down to individual choice or chance at our present level of knowledge. We are, perhaps only just beginning to appreciate how little we know about the factors which influence the chances of individuals or families being represented in future generations.

Social class differences in fertility persist but are considerably weaker than they were and are less clear in form. While professional women in their own right still have lower fertility than average, some evidence points to the emergence of a positive association with fertility at the top of the educational and social scale; a development of considerable theoretical and practical importance. Among persons of unskilled backgrounds, with the lowest level of education, fertility remains relatively high.

Whether an 'underclass' can be satisfactorily defined remains to be demonstrated, but some patterns of early union formation and child-bearing are prone to be repeated over generations. Births outside marriage, both to single women and to cohabiting couples, are particularly frequent among this group. If births outside marriage can be regarded as a category, they comprise the fastest growing group in the population, increasing by 5 per cent from 1988 to 1989 and by 8 per cent from 1989 to 1990.

Even if the overall fertility of women who produce births outside marriage is no higher than average, the rapid growth of this group underlines the importance of establishing definitively whether the handicaps attributed to upbringing in a single-parent or even a cohabiting couple justify current anxieties. In these respects the mediating effects of subsidies and allocation systems in social housing needs to be clarified.

Despite declining birth rates, births to immigrant minorities are still increasing, partly as a result of higher fertility rates than average especially among Pakistanis, Bangladeshis, and Africans, and also as a consequence of youthful age structures. Together with reinforcement from continuing immigration, populations of immigrant origin in Britain, as in many Western countries are increasing on average by about 4 per cent per year, ranging from 2 per cent among West Indians to over 5 per cent among Bangladeshis (Haskey 1992). The effect of the higher birth rate of immigrant minorities is disclosed by concomitant racial differences and thereby has visibly impressive demographic consequences. Even assuming that their fertility transition will be complete within a decade, and that immigration will cease, the population of visible immigrant origin is likely to stabilize at approximately double their present number, and proportion, in the British population (Berrington in preparation). That reflects on a small-scale the shift in the balance of population origins throughout the world.

References

Askham, J. (1975) *Fertility and deprivation: a study of differential fertility among working-class families in Aberdeen*. Cambridge University Press.

Babb, P. (1993). Teenage conceptions and fertility in England and Wales 1971–91. *Population Trends* **74**, 12–17.

Barrett, D. (ed.) (1982). *World Christian encyclopaedia: a comparative study of churches and religions in the modern world 1900–2000*. Oxford University Press, Nairobi.

Barry, B. (1970). *Sociologists, Economists and Democracy*. Collier Macmillan, London.

Baum, F. and Cope, D. R. (1980). Some characteristics of intentionally childless wives in Britain. *Journal of Biosocial Science*, **12**, 287–99.

Becker, G. (1981). *A treatise on the family*. Harvard University Press, Cambridge, MA.

Berrington, A. (in preparation). Marital status and the inter-ethnic union. In Coleman D. A. and Salt J. (ed.) *Demographic characteristics of the ethnic minority populations* . HMSO, London.

Blacker, C. P. (ed.) (1937). *A social problem group*? Oxford University Press, London.

Bongaarts, J. and Potter, R. G. (1983) *Fertility, biology and behavior: an analysis of the proximate determinants*. Academic Press, New York.

Boston, G. F. P. (1984). *Occupation, industry, social class and socio-economic groups 1911–1981*. An unpublished working paper available from OPCS, Titchfield, Hants.

Botting, B. and Cooper, J. (1993). Analysing fertility and infant mortality by mother's social class as defined by occupation — Part II. *Population Trends*, **74**, 27–33.

Breton, R. (1988). Réligion et évolution démographique en Inde. *Population*, **43**, 1089–122.

Campbell, E. (1985). *The childless marriage*. Tavistock Publications, London.

Cartwright, A. (1987). Family intentions and the use of contraception among recent mothers 1967–84. *Population Trends*, **49**, 31–4.

Cleland, J. and Wilson, C. (1987). Demand theories of the fertility transition, an iconoclastic view. *Population Studies*, **41**, 5–30.

Coale, A. J. and Watkins, S. C. (1986). *The decline of fertility in Europe*. Princeton University Press.

Coleman, D. A. (1990). The demography of social class. In *Biosocial aspects of social class* (ed. C. G. N. Mascie-Taylor), pp. 59–116. Oxford University Press.

Coleman, D. A. (1992). The demography of Hispanic America. In *Handbooks to the modern world: the United States* (ed. G. Hodgson), pp. 752–94. Facts on File Inc., New York.

Coleman D. A. (1994). Trends in fertility and intermarriage among immigrant populations in Western Europe as measures of integration. *Journal of Biosocial Science*, **26**, 107–36.

Cooper, J. (1991). Births outside marriage: recent trends and associated demographic and social changes. *Population Trends*, **63**, 8–18.

Cooper, J. and Botting, B. (1992). Analysing fertility and infant mortality by mother's social class as defined by occupation. *Population Trends*, **70**, 15–21.

Council of Europe (1991). *Recent demographic developments in the Member States of the Council of Europe and Yugoslavia*. Council of Europe, Strasburg.

Council of Europe (1993). *Recent demographic developments in Europe and North America 1992*. Council of Europe Press, Strasburg.

Day, L. H. (1968). Nationality and ethno-centrism: some relationships suggested by an analysis of Catholic–Protestant differentials. *Population Studies*, **22**, 25.

Dennis, N. and Erdos, G. (1992). *Families without fatherhood*. Institute of Economic Affairs Health and Welfare Unit, London.

Diggory, P., Potts, M., and Teper, S. (ed.) (1988). *Natural human fertility: social and biological determinants*. Macmillan, London.

Duncan, G. J. and Hoffman, S. D. (1991). Teenage underclass behaviour and subsequent poverty: have the rules changed? In *The urban underclass* (ed. C. Jencks and E. Peterson). The Brookings Institution, Washington DC.

Dunnell, K. (1979). *Family formation 1976*. HMSO, London.

Employment, Department of (1993). Ethnic minorities in the workforce. *Employment Gazette*, **101**, 2, 25–43.

Erikson, R. and Goldthorpe, J. H. (1993). *The constant flux: a study of class mobility in industrial societies*. Clarendon Press, Oxford.

Ermisch, J. F. (1988). *Purchased child care, optimal family size and mothers' employment: theory and econometrical analysis*. Centre for Economic Policy Research, London.

Ermisch, J. F. (1991). *Lone parenthood: an economic analysis*. Cambridge University Press.

Eurostat (1991). *Demographic statistics 1990*. Office for official publications of the European Communities, Luxemburg.

Eysenck, H. J. (1993). Intelligence and hereditary genius. In *Sir Francis Galton FRS: the legacy of his ideas. 28th Annual Symposium of the Galton Institute* (ed. R. Chester), pp. 62–74. Macmillan, London.

Field, F. (1989). *Losing out: the emergence of Britain's underclass*. Blackwell, London.

Fildes, V. (1988). *Wet nursing: a history from antiquity to the present*. Basil Blackwell, Oxford.

Fisher, R. A. (1930). *The genetical theory of natural selection*. Clarendon Press, Oxford.

Fletcher, R. (1991). *Science, ideology and the media: the Cyril Burt scandal*. Transactions, New Brunswick.

Flinn, M. W. (1981). *The European demographic system 1500–1820*. Johns Hopkins University Press, Baltimore.

Friedlander, D. and Goldscheider, C. (1984). Israel's population: the challenge of pluralism. *Population Bulletin*, **39**.

Garfinkel, I. and McLanahan, S. S. (1986). *Single mothers and their children: a new American dilemma*. Urban Institute Press, Washington DC.

Gellner, E. (1993). What do we need now? Social anthropology and its new global context. *Times Literary Supplement*, July 16 1993, **4711**, 3–4.

Glass, D. V. and Grebenik, E. (1954). *The trend and pattern of fertility in Great Britain. A Report on the family census of 1946. Papers of the Royal Commission on Population*. HMSO, London.

Grebenik, E. (1983) *Fertility report from the 1971 census*. HMSO, London.

Halsey, A. H. (1993). Changes in the family. *Childhood and Society.*

Haskey, J. and Coleman, D. A. (1986). Cohabitation before marriage. A comparison of information from parish registers and the General Household Survey. *Population Trends*, **43**, 15–17.

Heath, A. R. (1981). *Social Mobility*, (Chapter 5). Fontana, Glasgow.

Hiorns, R. W. and Harrison, G. A. (1970). Sampling for the detection of natural selection by age-group genetic differences. *Human Biology*, **42**, 53–64.

HMSO (1979). Census 1971, England and Wales Fertility Tables. Vol. 1, table 1. HMSO, London.

Hobsbawm, E. J. (1990). *Nations and nationalism since 1780*. Cambridge University Press.

Hornsby-Smith, M. P. (1987). *Roman Catholics in England: studies in social structure since the Second World War*. Cambridge University Press.

Howell, N. (1986). Feedbacks and buffers in relation to scarcity and abundance. Studies of hunter-gatherer populations. In *The state of population theory: forward from Malthus* (ed. D. A. Coleman and R. S. Schofield), pp. 156–87. Basil Blackwell, Oxford.

Joseph, S. K. (1972). The cycle of deprivation: speech to the Conference of Preschool Playgroups Association, 29 June 1972.

Kiernan, K. (1980). Teenage motherhood: associated factors and consequences. The experiences of a British birth cohort. *Journal of Biosocial Science*, **12**, 393–405.

Kiernan, K. (1987). *Demographic experiences of early adulthood: a longitudinal study*. Ph.D. thesis, London University.

Kiernan, K. E. (1989). Who remains childless? *Journal of Biosocial Science*, **21**, 387–498.

Kiernan, K. and Diamond, I. (1982). Family origin and educational influences on age at first birth. The experiences of a British birth cohort. In *CPS Working Paper No. 82–1*. Centre for Population Studies, London School of Hygiene and Tropical Medicine.

Knodel, J. and van de Walle, E. (1967) Breast feeding, fertility and infant mortality: an analysis of some early German data. *Population Studies*, **31**, 109–32.

Knodel, J., Chamratrithirong, A., and Debavalya, N. (1987). *Thailand's reproductive revolution: rapid fertility decline in a third-world setting*. University of Wisconsin Press, Madison.

Kravdal, Ø. (1992). The weak impact of female labour force participation on Norwegian third-birth rates. *European Journal of Population*, **8**, 247–63.

Langford, C. M. (1982). Family size from the child's point of view. *Journal of Biosocial Science*, **14**, 319–27.

Leridon, H. and Menken, J. (1982). *Natural fertility: patterns and determinants*. Editions Ordina, Liège.

Lesthaeghe, R. J. (1978). *The decline of Belgian fertility 1800–1970*. Princeton University Press.

Lesthaeghe, R. (1986). On the adaptation of sub-Saharan systems of reproduction. In *The state of population theory: forward from Malthus* (ed. D. A. Coleman & R. S. Schofield), pp. 212–38. Basil Blackwell, Oxford.

Lesthaeghe, R. and Meekers, D. (1986). Value changes and the dimensions of familism in the European Community. *European Journal of Population*, **2**, 225–68.

Lesthaeghe, R. and Moors, G. (1993). *Living arrangements, socio-economic position and values among young adults: a pattern description for France, Germany, Belgium, and the Netherlands 1990*. Centrum Sociologie, Free University of Brussels.

Lutz, W. (1989). *Distributional aspects of fertility*. Academic Press, London.

Madge, N. (1988). Inheritance, chance and choice in the transmission of poverty. In *The political economy of health and welfare* (ed. M. Keynes, D. A. Coleman, and N. Dimsdale), pp. 26–35. Macmillan, London.

Mascie-Taylor, C. G. N. (1990). The biology of social class. In *Biosocial aspects of social class* (ed. C. G. N. Mascie-Taylor), pp. 117–42. Oxford University Press.

Menken, J. (1985). Age at fertility: how late can you wait? *Demography*, **22**.

Moynihan, D. P. (1993). *Pandaemonium; ethnicity in international politics*. Oxford University Press.

Murphy, M. (1987). Differential family formation in Great Britain. *Journal of Biosocial Science*, **19**, 463–85.

Murphy, M. and Sullivan, O. (1985). Housing tenure and family formation in contemporary Britain. *European Sociological Review*, **1**, 230–43.

Murray, C. (1984). *Losing ground: American social policy 1950–1980*. Basic Books, New York.

Murray, C. (1990). *The emerging British underclass*. Institute of Economic Affairs Health and Welfare Unit, London.

Nanton, P. (1992). Official statistics and problems of inappropriate ethnic categorization. *Policy and Politics*, **20**, 277.

Ni Bhrolchain, M. (1993). Recent fertility differentials in Britain. In *New perspectives on fertility in Britain. Studies on medical and population subjects*, No. 55. (ed. M. Ni Bhrolchain), pp. 93–108. HMSO, London.

OECD (1991). *Migration: The demographic aspects*. OECD, Paris.

OPCS (1979). *Census 1971. Fertility tables, vol. ii*. OPCS, London.

OPCS (1983). Fertility report from the 1971 census. OPCS series DS no. 5. OPCS, London.

OPCS (1989). Population projections, mid 1987 based. Monitor PP2 89/1, OPCS, London.

OPCS Birth Statistics (1977). Series FM1 No. 40. OPCS, London.

OPCS Birth Statistics (1985). Series FM1 No. 12. OPCS, London.

OPCS Birth Statistics (1987). Series FM1 No. 16. OPCS, London.

OPCS Birth Statistics (1988). Series FM1 No. 15. OPCS, London.

OPCS Birth Statistics (1990). Series FM1 No. 19. OPCS, London.

OPCS Birth Statistics (1992). Series FM1 No. 19. OPCS, London.

Peach, G. C. K. (1990). The Muslim population of Great Britain. *Ethnic and Racial Studies*, **13**, 414–19.

Reynolds, V. (1988). Religious rules, mating patterns and fertility. In *Human mating patterns* (ed. C. G. N. Mascie-Taylor and A. J. Boyce). Cambridge University Press.

Reynolds, V. and Tanner, R. E. S. (1973). *The biology of religion*. Longman, London.

Royal Commission on Population (1949) *Report*. Cmd 7695. HMSO, London.

Rutter, M. and Madge, N. (1976). *Cycles of disadvantages*. Heinemann, London.

Shorrocks, A. F. (1988). Inequality of economic opportunity. In *The political economy of health and welfare* (ed. M. Keynes, D. A. Coleman, and N. H. Dimsdale), pp. 47–71. Macmillan, London.

Shryock, H. S. and Siegel J. S. (1976). *The methods and materials of demography (condensed edition)* (ed. E. G. Stockwell). Academic Press, London.

Simons, J. (1986). Culture, economy and reproduction in contemporary Europe. In *The state of population theory: forward from Malthus* (ed. D. A. Coleman and R. S. Schofield), pp. 256–78. Basil Blackwell, Oxford.

Snedecor, G. W. and Cochrane, W. G. (1967). *Statistical methods*. Iowa State University Press, Ames.

Spencer, A. E. C. W. (1975). The demography of Catholicism. *The Month*, **236**, 100–5.

Spencer, A. E. C. W. (1982). Catholics in Britain and Ireland — regional contrasts. In *The demography of immigrant and minority groups in the United Kingdom*. (ed. D. A. Coleman), pp. 213–43. Academic Press, London.

Teitelbaum, M. (1984). *The British fertility decline*. Princeton University Press.

Thoday, J. M. and Parkes, A. S. (ed.) (1968). *Genetical and environmental influences on behaviour*. Oliver and Boyd, Edinburgh.

Thompson, S. G. H. (1946). *The trend of national intelligence: the Galton Lecture 1946*. Eugenics Society (now Galton Institute), London.

Trussell, J. and Wilson, C. (1985). Sterility in a population with natural fertility. *Population Studies*, **39**, 269–86.

Vaessen, M. (1984). *Childlessness and infecundity: world fertility survey comparative studies*, No. 31. International Statistical Institute, Voorburg, Netherlands.

Walker, A. (1990). Blaming the victims. In IEA (Eds.), *The emerging British underclass* pp. 49–58. IEA, London.

Weeks, J. R. (1988). The demography of Islamic nations. *Population Bulletin*, **43**.

Werner, B. (1985). Fertility trends in different social classes 1970–1983. *Population Trends*, **41**, 5–12.

Werner, B. (1986). Trends in first, second, third and later births. *Population Trends*, **45**, 26–33.

Westoff, C. and Jones, C. F. (1979). The end of 'Catholic' fertility. *Demography*, **16**, 209.

Wolfinden, R. C. (1950). *Problem Families in Bristol*. The Eugenics Society and Cassell and Co., London.

3

Interaction between religions and reproduction in human populations

V. REYNOLDS

Introduction

Studies of the ways in which religious affiliation affects people's attitudes to, and realization of, their reproductive potential have tended in the main to focus on a number of issues, in particular how strongly pronatalist sects may promote high fertility rates (Eaton and Mayer 1953; Hostetler and Huntington 1967, 1971; Reynolds and Tanner 1983; Reynolds 1988; Coleman, Chapter 2), or conversely how reduced fertility can come about in religious groups (Lesthaeghe 1977, 1980; Coale and Watkins 1986; Lesthaeghe and Wilson 1986; Landers 1990; Stevenson and Everson 1990). Most of the latter studies have concerned Christian sects, with the notable exception of Chamie (1981) who investigated fertility decline among educated Muslims in the Lebanon.

Such studies raise a number of wider issues that are less often addressed, probably because they are further removed from the empirical data and reach into some contentious areas of argument in sociology and economic history. For example, there is the question 'To what extent are people's reproductive decisions determined by their religious affiliation and to what extent by secular, economic considerations?' This question is not overly contentious in itself. For example, Westoff and Ryder (1977) demonstrated that from 1916 to 1950 there was a progressive increase in the use of artificial methods of birth control and it became more popular among younger Catholics in various countries (see Table 3.1); this they interpreted in terms of secular factors such as the cost of education, the provision by the state of welfare benefits for the aged, and so on.

Here we already see a widely held hypothesis at work, namely that the secular forces of modernization, technological sophistication, and state provision for the needy, can to a greater or lesser extent overrule people's religious beliefs and convictions. The last Papal encyclical on contraception, *Humanae Vitae*, published by Pope Paul VI in 1968, firmly continued traditional proscription of artificial birth control. There has been no wavering by the central authority, yet Catholics in developed countries have changed their practices so that today

Table 3.1.   Percentage of US white Catholic women not conforming to Church teaching on birth control (from Westoff and Ryder 1977)

	Age of women				
Year of birth	20–24	25–29	30–34	35–39	40–44
1916–20				28	45
1921–25			30	46	43
1926–30		37	40	52	50
1931–35	30	40	50	50	
1936–40	43	54	68		
1941–45	51	74			
1946–50	78				

Catholics in some Western countries have achieved lower fertility rates than Protestants. Does this conclusively demonstrate that secular forces override religious ones and that religions must eventually adapt or lose the battle for people's minds?

This idea presents difficulties. There are signs of a religious revival in the USA at the present time, and just because secular forces have been stronger than religious ones in the twentieth century does not guarantee that they will be stronger in the twenty-first. Nor were they stronger for a sizeable minority of the population during the twentieth century. For example, a study of voluntary childlessness among Catholic and non-Catholic women in the USA (Poston 1990) showed that despite declining differences in fertility and contraception between Catholics and non-Catholics, voluntary childlessness was still considerably rarer among Catholics. In other words, though they might reduce their family size they were less likely than non-Catholics to decide not to have any children at all. Here we can perhaps see the pronatalist ethic of Catholicism still at work.

Religion and reproduction in the modern context

The question of religious inputs into reproductive decisions remains an important one. Let us take the case of Lebanon already referred to. Chamie studied fertility in the context of pre-civil war Lebanon, when slow westernization was taking place in the Muslim community. He found that the more educated sector was starting to limit family size. But after Chamie's study there was a civil war and westernization became associated with America and Christianity; there have been no follow-up studies but it is likely that there (as in other countries where Islamic vs. Christian civil war has flared up and devastated whole cities and countries) this change of attitude to family size was reversed during social disintegration, collapse of educational structures, and a reversion to fundamentalism. ·

Islam is not doctrinally opposed to contraception, but it is very pronatalist. Women have low status relative to men, marriage is universal, divorce and remarriage are easy, and the role of women is traditionally, and still in many countries today, in the home, being a wife and mother. Reynolds (1988) showed that total fertility rates (TFR) for 29 Muslim countries in 1980 were higher than the world average (3.8) or the average for the less developed countries (4.4). In 16 countries surveyed by Nagi (1983) the TFR was 6.5 or higher in 1980. Some Muslim countries do show declining fertility, notably Malaysia, Indonesia, Turkey, Tunisia, and Egypt. But most do not.

We thus come to an interesting fact about religions and religious attitudes, namely that they are not necessarily doomed to disappear as the world converges on a bright and technologically sophisticated future (following the so-called 'convergence hypothesis'). Instead, for all we know, the world may be heading towards a series of calamities in which traditional religious views will grow stronger. We should not take it for granted that either convergence or smaller family size are inevitable in the long run. We cannot assume that the 'demographic transition' will occur in one place after another until the whole world is on a low birth-rate, low death-rate schedule. Nagi (1983) in a study of 29 Muslim countries during the period 1960–80 showed that Muslim fertility remained high during this period, that there was no discernible fertility decline in relation to modernization, and that the only causal factor related to fertility decline was the existence of family planning programmes in certain areas.

Table 3.2 is derived from data presented by Nagi (1983). Nagi presented TFRs for 29 Muslim countries, and allocated each country a score ranging from 0 to 100 based on a composite index of socio-economic development (Maudlin and Berelson 1978). As Table 3.2 shows, there is no correlation between TFR for these Islamic countries and their socio-economic status ($r = -0.179$, $P = 0.352$, NS).

There may be countries, as there are at present, where modernization meets insuperable obstacles. Much of Africa remains unmodernized and shows no real signs of modernizing. Much of the Islamic world shows signs of a cyclical return to fundamentalism that prevents modernization from taking place. Islam is a fast growing religion, and we can never be sure what this single fact implies for humanity as a whole. ·

Table 3.2. Total fertility rate (TFR) and socio-economic status (SES) in 29 Islamic countries (after Nagi 1983)

Country	TFR	SES
Algeria	6.9	54
Egypt	4.9	58
Libya	7.0	73
Morocco	6.5	53
Sudan	6.7	28
Tunisia	5.4	62
Guinea	6.2	17
Mali	6.7	9
Mauritania	5.9	19
Niger	7.1	13
Nigeria	6.9	31
Senegal	6.5	32
Somalia	6.1	12
Chad	5.9	18
Iraq	6.6	70
Jordan	6.9	75
Kuwait	6.1	90
Lebanon	4.1	85
Saudi Arabia	6.9	43
Syria	7.0	68
Turkey	4.4	64
North Yemen	6.5	18
South Yemen	6.7	32
Afghanistan	6.6	15
Bangladesh	6.0	24
Iran	5.8	62
Pakistan	6.1	43
Indonesia	4.5	43
Malaysia	4.2	71

Adaptation

A widely used concept in anthropology is that of 'adaptability' or 'adaptation' (Harrison 1966; Blurton Jones and Reynolds 1978). This concept can be used for cultural as well as physical features. The central argument made by Reynolds and Tanner (1983) was that differences in the degree of pronatalism and antinatalism found in the world's religions were not just coincident with economic and demographic differences but were adaptive to them. A little more precisely, the doctrines and dogmas and rules of the Islamic, Christian, Hindu, Judaic, and Buddhist faiths contained messages about age at marriage, use of contraceptives,

Table 3.3. Comparison between Muslim–Hindu and Protestant countries

	t	P
Crude birth rate	16.96	< 0.0001
Total fertility rate	15.86	< 0.0001
Expectation of life at birth	−12.66	< 0.0001
Infant mortality rate	11.92	< 0.0001
Per capita GNP (US$)	−6.89	< 0.0001

expected family size, abortion, remarriage, and so on that were 'sensible' in a purely secular way for people living in those particular economic and environmental circumstances. As a result we find religions such as Islam and Hinduism expressing pronatalist attitudes in countries with high levels of infant mortality, low expectation of life at birth, and low income levels, whereas Protestant Christianity which promotes antinatalist attitudes is found mainly in affluent countries with low levels of infant mortality and high expectation of life at birth. Comparison between Muslim–Hindu countries on the one hand and Protestant ones on the other yields highly significant results (see Table 3.3).

Reynolds and Tanner did not go into detail about how such supposed adaptedness might have come about, except to indicate that the transmission process would have been cultural, that is an oral or written tradition handed down from generation to generation by parents and, in the wider society, by the guardians of morality who exist in every society, including professional and semi-professional agents of established churches, temples, etc. The question is: how do parents, or guardians of morality, know what level of pronatalism to teach the next generation? In a static environment there is no problem; you teach the next generation to do as you did yourself. If you had many children, or if your generation had many children, then you teach the next generation to have many children, and vice versa. However, static environments have not been a feature of the twentieth century and may be the exception rather than the rule. In a changing environment, how do parents and other authorities know what to advise? It is a problem we are only too familiar with in the West, where rapid change has been the context in which the present generation (and the previous one) have lived their lives, and the whole issue of parental 'advice' has become problematic.

What is needed is a theory that links up secular, technological, social, commercial, and industrial change with moral belief systems in such a way that neither is a simple dependent variable on the other. For example, if we refer back to Table 3.1 (Westoff and Ryder 1977) we can note the increasing percentage of women not conforming to Catholic teaching on birth control during the period concerned, which we can attribute to secular effects on religious attitudes, but we can also see that religious attitudes are having a residual effect, so that change operates in a dialectical fashion. At the level of the individual this implies moral uncertainty and moral doubts; each Catholic spouse is in a difficult moral position when the question of contraception comes up. This moral uncertainty at the individual level is the psychological arena for change in fertility patterns at the population level; where there is no uncertainty and no discussion there will be no change.

What I am suggesting therefore is that we need to understand the relation between religious affiliation and the process of change in fertility patterns in terms of a push–pull process at the level of individual minds. In the above context a couple may be pushed to use mechanical means of contraception in order to limit family size because they no longer trust the rhythm method and are reluctant to risk an unwanted pregnancy; at the same time they may be pulled back to their old beliefs by the power of religious teaching and the desire not to sin, not to have to confess. An opposite example would be a couple who, in order to improve their children's educational opportunities, have taken to using contraceptives in Iraq or Iran before the war between those two countries. As the war reaches fever pitch they become subject to scrutiny by other couples who may want to know why they are not doing their bit for the struggle; religion may cause them to adopt a more pronatalist strategy. This perspective, in which religious considerations are given a causal role in decision-making, is very different from the more usual secular one in which decisions are made rationally on the basis of the costs and benefits of having another child, educating that child, etc.

From looking at things that way, let us return to the concept of adaptation. What would it mean to say that religious rules are adapted to secular environments? It must mean that religious rules provide one aspect of the sphere of discussion from which adaptation eventually arises. We can escape from the tyranny of fertility and reproduction here and consider for a moment the question of food taboos. Harris (1966, 1978) has argued forcefully for the adaptive nature of the religious sanctity of the cow in India, showing how the taboo on eating this animal provides communities with milk, traction, dung for fuel and fertilizer, and leather. He has been criticized for what may be called 'environmental determinism'; it has been argued that political and cultural factors are more relevant than ecological ones, for example that cow sanctity is part of the process by which the priestly (Brahmin) caste obtained and holds on to its dominant position in Hindu society. Naturally, such an argument has no bearing on whether or not the cow taboo is adaptive and tends to relegate the issue of adaptivity, so central to Harris's thesis, to the sidelines. Who is right? If I had to choose one or the other I would choose Harris, but maybe there is an element of truth in both arguments: priests choose to do something for their own interests and it works (perhaps beyond their wildest dreams) because it is adaptive.

So, returning to religions and fertility, it may be that when religions voice pronatalist strategies and these happen to be adaptive, they become established in written doctrines such as the Old Testament and the Koran. When on the other hand such doctrines are painfully at odds with what it would be adaptive to do they fall into disuse and other, more modern forms of words, more liberal policies come into play. In the case of Protestant Christianity we should note that a marriage is conceived of essentially as a relationship of love, trust, and support between a man and a woman; children bless such a marriage but it cannot be dissolved if one of the partners is infertile and no children appear. In many African societies and to a great extent in Islam infertility of either partner is assumed to be the woman's fault and she can be legitimately divorced. Barrenness was a serious impediment to a woman in early Christianity and there is still a slight stigma involved. But the modern Christian career woman is not much affected by all this old-fashioned stuff and may well choose to be child-less. According to Poston (1990) voluntary childlessness in the USA has increased from 12 per cent of ever-married white women 25–29 years old in 1965 to more than 28 per cent in 1986. Bloom and Pebley (1982) projected that for younger cohorts of American women, namely those born in the mid-1950s and later, as many as 30 per cent will never have a child.

In such circumstances, whether these women are Christian or not in terms of formal affiliation, there has clearly been a major shift of thinking about fertility in the USA, a largely Christian country, and it is widely assumed that this change is consequent on the developing image of women as wholly autonomous, career-minded people whose status in society decreasingly depends on being a wife and a mother.

Christianity does, in fact, have a place for the unmarried woman, as a doer of good works and, in its most extreme form, as a Sister in a religious order, a nun. Such women take vows of celibacy and devote themselves to Christ. The single, childless career woman is unlike this; she may have an active contracepting sex life and be unconcerned with doing good in the world. To this extent, and in other respects, religion has declined and can in fact be dispensed with in the modern Western world, and adaptation to modern circumstances can be wholly secular.

The issue of secularization in relation to fertility has been extensively studied in Belgium by Lesthaeghe (1977). He describes the breakdown of the traditional authority of the Catholic church and the process of secularization during the eighteenth and nineteenth centuries. Both the Flemish and Walloon bourgeoisie were anti-clerical, as were the socialist working classes. The decline in religios-ity was measured in this study by declining attendances at Easter confession and communion. Political leaning was obtained from voting for Liberal and Socialist parties. The decline of religiosity was correlated with a decrease in fertility of those concerned. Lesthaeghe does, however, note the existence of 'lags', that is of people still going to church after giving up the faith, for purely secular reasons. We shall return to the phenomenon of 'lags' shortly.

The issue of how, exactly, decreased fertility comes about is discussed further by Lesthaeghe (1980). Here he comes close to the issue of adaptation, and the related issue of whether cultural change is somehow a part of Darwinian evolu-tion, but he rejects the idea. The discussion with which he begins his chapter is interesting, however. Two mechanisms for change have been counterposed to each other. One is the 'invisible hand' as Adam Smith called it, or 'unconscious rationality' as referred to by Wrigley. This is a process by which demographic homeostasis comes about without rational planning by individuals of their own family size. What happens is that families who overshoot or undershoot in terms of the number of offspring they produce are less successful than those who get it right, and as a result their reproductive pattern loses ground. Lesthaeghe disagrees that this is how the change to lower fertility occurs. He considers that demographic homeostasis is a logical ingredient of a social system. For example in Africa where there is gerontocratic control, the post-partum taboo on sexual intercourse is seen as part of a set of short-term goals held by senior lineage members to try and maximize the chances of child survival within their lineage and thus maintain influence. Similarly, in Europe where lineages are less significant and more individualistic patterns of decision-making prevail, individuals make logical decisions about family size and birth spacing in order to maximize their chances of making good use of their resources and achieving good social control of offspring. The decision-making is, however, a logical process not an 'invisible' one. Once again, he refers to 'lags', which come about owing to lack of synchronization of subsystems within society. For example, new forms of economically rational behaviour may not fit with traditional ideas and values. This causes strains for individuals, and he gives the example of a fundamentalist Catholic backlash in the 1860s to combat the growing anti-clericalism and socialism. We could add that such religious backlashes have been very evident in some modern Islamic societies where westernization has proceeded rapidly, too rapidly for the religious authorities and their adherents. Nevertheless, Lesthaeghe would still see the struggle as one of opposing logical ideas and rational beliefs rather than as the workings of an 'invisible hand' that is rearranging the society's fertility schedules in the light of changed environmental conditions.

Small-scale societies

He may well be right, but there remains the possibility that underlying the logical and rational decision-making of individuals and families there is a swell of environmental change which actually is determining the whole discourse. I have discussed the case of the Hutterites and the Kansas–Nebraska Mennonites elsewhere (Reynolds 1988; see also Stevenson *et al.* 1989; Stevenson and Everson 1989, 1990), but it is well to remind ourselves of the lesson from those two groups and also of the Amish of Pennsylvania; they all arrived in the USA as fundamentalist Christian sects. In the case of the Mennonites there was fairly rapid integration with the host community, accompanied by a fall of fertility levels, a rise in educational levels, and an increasing trend to take up professional employment over a 100-year period from 1870 to 1970. In the case of the Hutterites, no such change occurred from their arrival in the USA and Canada until the middle of the twentieth century. During the period of Mennonite adaptation, the Hutterites for the most part did not reduce family size, did not join in the host population's economic and educational ways of life, and in the middle of the twentieth century had an exceptionally high rate of natural increase, 41.5 per 1000 population, and a mean family size of 9.4 (Eaton and Mayer 1953), compared with the Amish figure of 6.8 (Ericksen *et al.* 1979). The Kansas–Nebraska Mennonites, by contrast, show a steadily declining family size during the twentieth century, with values 3.4, 3.5, and 3.6 for women born in 1930–39 in the three communities studied in 1980–81, who would therefore have ceased child rearing (see Table 3.4).

Why did these Mennonites adapt quickly and thoroughly to their environment and the Hutterites not do so, but hold out as a distinct culture for so long? One reason has to do with the land (Stevenson *et al.* 1989). The Hutterites, when they arrived in the New World, bought large tracts of land and were thus able to expand continuously for a long period of time. The Mennonites were not able to buy land, they settled in areas of Kansas and Nebraska where host communities were already thriving and they joined in with them. By contrast, the Hutterites settled in empty lands in South Dakota, Montana, Manitoba, and Alberta where they could maintain their original language and culture, isolated from the host community.

How may this difference have affected the outcome? We can imagine in the first place that orthodox community leaders among the Hutterites were able to command respect and to achieve results. The communes were happy, healthy and flourishing places to live, satisfied with their own way of life. By contrast,

Table 3.4. Mean completed family size, by community, and decade of woman's birth

Decade of woman's birth	Goessel			Henderson			Meridian		
	n	$\overline{X}$	SD	n	$\overline{X}$	SD	n	$\overline{X}$	SD
1870–79	74	8.4	4.34	32	7.3	4.54	7	7.9	3.39
1880–89	54	6.5	4.02	56	6.1	3.08	9	5.9	5.61
1890–99	49	4.8	3.88	37	6.1	3.49	12	9.6	3.40
1900–09	55	4.4	2.89	33	4.3	2.64	5	7.2	5.54
1910–19	57	3.8	1.81	64	3.7	2.13	9	4.2	1.72
1920–29	44	4.0	1.72	56	3.7	1.85	10	5.2	2.20
1930–39	47	3.4	1.51	33	3.5	1.18	7	3.6	1.40
1940–49	26	2.0	0.89	26	2.3	1.34	6	3.8	1.60

From: Stevenson *et al.* (1989).

communal living with shared property and everyone digging for the community as a whole may not have been a viable option for the Mennonites, in which case orthodox community leaders who tried to live by the original principles of the sect would have lost the battle for the minds and affiliation of the people. The Old Order Amish began with exactly the same ideology as the Mennonites but resisted change for much longer on their Pennsylvania farmsteads, albeit in families not communes. Again, availability of land and a commitment to autonomous farming led them to pursue a strategy that deviated from that of the host community just as in the case of the Hutterites.

The resulting population increases were remarkable. The Hutterite population increased from approximately 400 immigrants in 1879 to approximately 22 000 individuals living in 247 colonies in 1977 (Peter 1980). The Amish population growth has been almost as dramatic. For example, between 1945 and 1977 the number of Amish church districts in Lancaster County, Pennsylvania, increased from 19 to 57 (Ericksen *et al.* 1979). In both cases these rates of increase were to prove unsustainable in the long run. In the case of the Hutterites, there was a decline in the crude birth rate from 45.9/1000 in 1950 to 38.4/1000 in 1971 (Laing 1980), brought about by later age at marriage from a mean of 22.0 (1950) to 24.9 (1971) for women and from 23.5 to 26.0 for men. There was also a great increase in the number of never-married women, from 5.4 per cent at the earlier date to 14.8 per cent in 1971. In recent times there may also be some covert use of birth control as well as later marriage and non-marriage (Boldt and Roberts 1980). In the case of the Amish, some families have given up farming and moved over to other occupations, but family size, though lower than that of the Hutterites, is still high. The more liberal Kansas–Nebraska Mennonites, by contrast, practise birth control, with use of contraceptive pills by 40–90 per cent of the population (Stevenson *et al.* 1989).

Lags

We have seen how the question of adaptation raises the question of how change occurs, and we have seen that change may be fairly rapid or very slow. We suggested that where change was slow that was because environmental conditions (in the case of the Hutterites, land) made this possible. The idea developing here is thus one of environmentally determined possibilism: the environment either allows or does not allow a cultural idea (such as that high fertility is a good thing) to flourish. Armed with this idea, let us now look at the question of 'lags' already referred to above. The term 'lags' is used by authors such as Jones (1988) to refer to aspects of a culture that are still present but had their significance in the past and are now useless. Some might say this applied to the British Royal Family! More seriously, the use made by economic historians and others of this idea is to show how lags in economic thinking can slow down or

completely inhibit acceptance of new ideas and hence economic progress generally. China and Japan, for example, both independently held out against westernization for centuries before coming to terms with it in the twentieth century.
India's caste system is a spectacular example of an antique system defying
attempts by successive governments to modernize, for example in the area of the
workplace where occupations could be determined on the basis of merit but are
still largely determined by place in the caste hierarchy.

What is the lesson we learn from lags when applied to the idea of adaptation?
It is that there is a certain cultural inertia present in human societies and it is
partly because of this that adaptation is never perfect. There is, putting it another
way, a pull back to the past which we need to add to the environmental push
referred to above. Adaptation tends to occur when circumstances push people in
certain directions, but it has to contend with the pull of the past, and the outcome
is shaped by the resolution of these two forces.

Let us now look at a puzzling case: that of high fertility in rural and urban
slum dwellers in Latin America and in poor African countries like Uganda. In
these countries, the Pope has, in the course of official visits, reiterated the
Vatican line that any form of artificial contraception is contrary to the rulings of
the church and the Will of God. Poverty is great, and many would argue that
limiting family size is one of the first essentials to break the poverty trap in
which many families find themselves. Such an argument would be that having
to feed and provide for many children prevents families from saving any
money, from moving to a better life-style, from paying for better education for
their children, from improving their own education and hence job opportunities,
etc. Thus the Papal teachings are seen in this view as retrogressive, lagging
behind modern realities. Maybe such teachings had adaptive value when infant
mortality was such that parents needed to have produced large families to have
any surviving children at all. But in the modern world where effective medicine
is available, this no longer applies. And yet such is the hold of Catholicism
over the poor of South America that to disobey the Papal injunction is to many
almost unthinkable. Is this a case where religion is truly out of touch with
modern realities? If so, why are people not 'forced' to change their actual
behaviour patterns as we saw was the case with the Catholics in the
Netherlands or the Mennonites in Kansas and Nebraska? Evidently, the South
American and the other two cases must differ in some very particular way, but
in what way?

In fact the changes seen in Europe and North America are in the context of
full-scale westernization with moderate to high levels of family income, and
there is no real similarity to the absolute poverty of South America or Africa.
This implies that if incomes were higher in real terms in the currently poor countries (which would only happen if they were modernizing generally) then Papal
rulings would lose their hold as the advantages of smaller families began to be
felt. This is the convergence thesis, and for many countries in South America or

Africa it may indeed hold good. The converse of this is that what the Pope is saying today is actually less maladaptive than it might appear. This could be true because mortality rates, especially for children, remain very high, and because there is very little security for old people other than what their children can provide. If this is the case then the argument that the Papal rulings on birth control are a case of lags might be wrong.

However, there is a new element in the situation nowadays, in African countries like Uganda and increasingly world-wide, and that is the presence of AIDS. The only effective protection against AIDS is condom use, and this is not only too expensive for the world's poor but additionally flies in the face of Catholic rulings. We return to the question of adaptation. These days use of contraceptives is not just confined to control of family size but also to control of lethal infection. In such circumstances it must be adaptive to use condoms. It cannot be maladaptive to try and prevent a fatal disease striking oneself, one's spouse and potentially one's children as well. In this latter-day sense I see no case for the Vatican's rulings on contraceptive use. The alternative, abstention from sexual intercourse, seems a foolish counsel given human nature and the inequality of the sexes in most countries. Here, it seems, is a very real lag, and a proof, if proof be needed, that lags are real and do exist.

Islam

In the above, secular environmmental factors (including in the last case disease) were seen as push factors while religion was seen as a conservative pull factor, slowing change. What, then, are we to make of the situation in Islamic countries, as described earlier in this chapter? Why have secular advances not, so far, been correlated with declining fertility and the so-called 'demographic transition' in Islamic countries? Following our earlier analysis it could be that Islamic religion is just very strong. Its pronatalism exerts a decisive pull. Alternatively, it could be argued that the demographic transition is a feature of westernization rather than modernization, and that Islam is modernizing in a non-Western way. If so, its expansion in terms of numbers will be assured for the future, but it will have to content itself with relatively less affluence, for Western levels of affluence are contingent on small family size. It is too early to say what will happen to fertility rates in Islamic countries in the future. The case of Islam does, however, shed a further light on the nature of adaptation.

Ahmed (1984) has argued for a separate, Islamic form of anthropology. He based his argument on the fact that Islam cannot accept any thoroughgoing cultural relativism. Whereas Western anthropology is relativist, Islamic anthropology cannot be, it must put the values of the Koran and of Mohammed first. Here we see an example of the somewhat intolerant nature of Islamic religious thinking. Westernization is based on competition at all levels, between individuals, companies, and states. In Islam there is competition too: some of the fiercest competition occurs between sects with different theoretical orientations to the Koranic texts. But faced with Christianity or secular, profane thinking Islam is united by the Koran, the Word of Allah, which is immutable. The Holy Book of Islam exhorts its subjects to be fruitful and multiply. This is not an exhortation to be lightly dismissed; it is not regarded as a debating point, or an anachronism. Only a change of attitude towards the Koran could see a full blown demographic transition occurring in a Muslim country. The problem is that historically when Western-oriented reformers have made any headway in Islam they have pro-voked a fundamentalist backlash. Whether this must always be the case remains to be seen. Until now, however, Islamic countries remain characteristically pronatalist.

Conclusions

The central question we have been asking in this chapter concerns whether religion can act autonomously in the determination of human fertility, or whether it is dependent upon ecological factors. In the case of Roman Catholics in Europe we saw that Papal rulings on the avoidance of artificial methods of contraception have failed to determine the behaviour of the vast majority of couples, who use a variety of methods of contraception and have low fertility. Here secular factors are more important than religious ones in determining fertility, and we see religion adapting to ecological circumstances. In the case of Islamic countries, pronatalism is still very strong, and the high rates of mortality in the Islamic world indicate that Islamic religious injunctions of a pronatalist kind are adaptive. However, the question of how change in religious attitudes comes about in these countries remains unanswered.

To tackle this question in another context we looked at three Protestant sects, the Hutterites of Canada, and the Amish and Mennonites of the USA, with respect to their fertility schedules. All these groups, at the time of their arrival in the New World, had strongly pronatalist ideologies with a ban on contraception and abortion. In the case of the Hutterites and the Amish we saw persistently high levels of fertility and a lack of change into the twentieth century, but in the case of the Mennonites of the USA there was a fairly rapid transition to low fer-tility. We attributed the difference to prevailing environmental circumstances of the two groups; in particular, to availability of land in the former but lack of such opportunities to maintain a farming tradition in the latter. This was consid-ered as a good example of human adaptation, in this case of reproductive strate-gies, including religious ideas, to prevailing environmental and economic circumstances. After the mid-twentieth century, for much the same reasons, we saw the Hutterites adapting by means of reduced fertility schedules (achieved by later marriage and increased childlessness).

People do not always adapt, even when the need is urgent. Religious ideas can be conservative to the point where they prevent adaptations. We noted the case of the urgent need for people to use mechanical contraception in Uganda in view of the current AIDS epidemic, and the 1992 visit of the Pope to Uganda in which he reaffirmed that contraception was not acceptable in God's eyes. We ended with a consideration of a characteristic of Islam, namely a tendency to revert to fundamentalism and to the words of the Koran after periods of liberalism. This, it seems, is not just a lack of adaptation, it is something different — a conservative determination to achieve a uniquely Islamic pattern of modernization, not modelled on the westernized one. The resulting expansion of Islam, based on the maintenance of high fertility in the modern world, poses a potential long-term population problem as Islamic mortality declines, but for our purposes it suggests that religion can act as an autonomous causal factor underlying reproductive strategies, rather than always being reactive and responsive to environmental and other secular factors.

References

Ahmed, A. (1984). Defining Islamic anthropology. *Royal Anthropological Institute Newsletter*, no. 65.

Bloom, D. E. and Pebley, A. R. (1982). Voluntary childlessness: A review of the evidence and implications. *Population Research Policy Reviews*, **1**, 203–24.

Blurton Jones, N. G. and Reynolds, V. (1978). *Human behaviour and adaptation*. Taylor & Francis, London.

Boldt, E. D. and Roberts, L. W. (1980). The decline of Hutterite population growth: causes and consequences — a critique. *Canadian Ethnic Studies*, **12**, 111–17.

Chamie, J. (1981). *Religion and fertility: Arab Christian Muslim differentials*. Cambridge University Press.

Coale, A. J. and Watkins, S. C. (ed.) (1986) *The decline of fertility in Europe*. Princeton University Press.

Eaton, J. W. and Mayer, A. J. (1953). The social biology of very high fertility among the Hutterites. *Human Biology*, **25**, 206–64.

Ericksen, J., Ericksen, E. P., Hostetler, J. A., and Huntingdon, G. E. (1979). Fertility patterns and trends among the Old Order Amish. *Population Studies*, **33**, 255–76.

Felt, J. C., Ridley, J. C., Allen, G. and Redekop, C. (1990). High fertility of Old Colony Mennonites in Mexico. *Human Biology*, **62**, 689–700.

Harris, M. (1966). The cultural ecology of India's sacred cattle. *Current Anthropology*, **7**, 51–5.

Harris, M. (1978). *Cannibals and kings*. Random House, New York.

Harrison, G. A. (1966). Human adaptability with reference to the IBP proposals for high altitude research. In *The biology of human adaptability* (ed. P. T. Baker and J. S. Weiner), pp. 509–19. Clarendon Press, Oxford.

Hostetler, J. A. and Huntington, G. E. (1967). *The Hutterites in North America*. Holt, Rinehart and Winston, New York.

Hostetler, J. A. and Huntington, G. E. (1971). *Children in Amish society: socialization and community education.* Holt, Rinehart and Winston, New York.

Jones, E. L. (1988). *Growth recurring: economic change in world history.* Clarendon Press, Oxford.

Laing, L. M. (1980). Declining fertility in a religious isolate: the Hutterite population of Alberta, Canada, 1951–71. *Human Biology,* **52,** 288–310.

Landers, J. (1990). Fertility decline and birth spacing among London Quakers. In *Fertility and resources* (ed. J. Landers and V. Reynolds). Cambridge University Press.

Lesthaeghe, R. J. (1977). *The decline of Belgian fertility, 1800–1970.* Princeton University Press.

Lesthaeghe, R. J. (1980). On the social control of human reproduction. *Population and Development Review,* **6,** 527–48.

Lesthaeghe R. J. and Wilson, C. (1986). Modes of production, secularization, and the pace of fertility decline in W. Europe, 1870–1930. In *The decline of fertility in Europe.* (ed. A. J. Coale and S. C. Watkins), pp. 261–92. Princeton University Press.

Mauldin, W. P. and Berelson, B. (1978). Conditions of fertility decline in developing countries, 1965–1975. *Studies of Family Planning,* **9,** 89–147.

Nagi, M. H. (1983). Trends in Moslem fertility and the application of the demographic transition model. *Social Biology,* **30,** 245–62.

Peter, K. A. (1980). The decline of Hutterite population growth. *Canadian Ethnic Studies,* **12,** 97–110.

Poston, D. L. (1990). Voluntary and involuntary childlessness among Catholic and non-Catholic women: are the patterns converging? *Social Biology,* **37,** 251–65.

Reynolds, V. and Tanner, R. E. S. (1983). *The biology of religion.* Longman, London.

Reynolds, V. (1988). Religious rules, mating patterns and fertility. In *Human mating patterns* (ed. C. G. N. Mascie-Taylor and A. J. Boyce), pp. 191–208. Cambridge University Press.

Stevenson, J. C. and P. M. Everson, (1989). Initiation of fertility decline in Kansas–Nebraska Mennonites and North American Hutterites. *Collegium Antropologicum,* **13,** 17–24.

Stevenson, J. C. and Everson, P. M. (1990). The cultural context of fertility transition in immigrant Mennonites. In *Fertility and Resources* (ed. J. Landers and V. Reynolds), pp. 47–61. Cambridge University Press.

Stevenson. J. C. Everson, P. M., and Crawford, M. H. (1989). Changes in completed family size and reproductive span in Anabaptist populations. *Human Biology,* **61,** 99–115.

Westoff, C. F. and Ryder, N. B. (1977). *The contraceptive revolution.* Princeton University Press.

4

The influence of consanguineous marriage on reproductive behaviour in India and Pakistan

A. H. BITTLES

Introduction

Although consanguineous marriages are widely contracted in many major human populations, there still is a remarkable lack of reliable information in the scientific literature with respect to their prevalence and associated biological outcomes. The inter-relationship between inbreeding and reproductive behaviour is a particular problem area, with the widespread belief that marriage between close biological relatives leads to reduced fertility. To permit a more critical assessment of this topic, at least with respect to India and Pakistan, extensive studies conducted into reproductive behaviour during the last two decades have been collated and analysed. By using these data it has been possible to determine the underlying factors, both biological and non-biological, which significantly contribute to the fertility of the populations investigated, with specific attention focused on the influence of consanguinity. As will become apparent, many past generalizations derived from the assumption that fewer children were born to close kin unions appear to lack foundation.

Religious and cultural attitudes to consanguineous marriage

Marriages contracted between persons related as second cousins or closer currently account for 20–50 per cent of the observed total in large regions of South Asia (Bittles 1990). In most South Asian countries Muslims form the majority population, and even in India they comprise approximately 12 per cent of the estimated 883 million inhabitants (Population Reference Bureau 1992). Consanguineous marriages are widely preferred in Islamic society; this is in part because of the desire of Muslims to emulate the words and deeds of the Prophet Muhammad (Basu S. K. and Roy 1974), two of whose wives Khadija and Zaynab bint Jahsh were biological relatives and who married his daughter Fatima to Ali, his ward and son of his paternal uncle Abu Talib (Armstrong 1991). For Muslims the most favoured form of consanguineous marriage is the parallel first cousin father's brother's daughter union, in which the couple share one set of grandparents. But considerable variation in specific patterns of consanguineous marriage is observed, which in South Asia may at least partially be dependent on the degree to which Hindu converts to Islam have retained the customs and preferences of their forebears (Fricke *et al.* 1986). Since first cousins have one-eighth of their genes in common their progeny inherit identical gene copies from each parent at one sixteenth of all loci, which is equivalent to a coefficient of inbreeding (F) of 0.0625. Less frequently, double first cousin marriages ($F = 0.125$) also are reported in Muslim communities, where the spouses have both two sets of grandparents in common.

The preference for consanguineous unions is not restricted to Islamic societies and communities. Although both Hindus and Sikhs in North India generally avoid marriage to biological kin, by tradition searching back in family records seven generations on the paternal side and five generations on the maternal side to preclude the possibility of such a union being arranged (Kapadia 1958; Karve 1990), on average 20–45 per cent of Hindu marriages in the South Indian states of Andhra Pradesh, Karnataka, Kerala, and Tamil Nadu are between close relatives (Bittles *et al.* 1991). Uncle–niece marriages ($F = 0.125$), which are mainly favoured in Andhra Pradesh and Karnataka, are usually restricted to first or occasionally second birth order nieces (Karve 1990; Reddy and Malhotra 1991), but no comparable restriction exists with respect to cross first cousin unions that traditionally are of the mother's brother's daughter pattern. Located between the northern and southern regions with their contrasting patterns of marital preference, the Hindu populations of the states of Maharashtra, Madhya Pradesh, and Orissa exhibit mixed attitudes with respect to consanguinity. In the northern parts of each state the Aryan non-consanguineous pattern of marriage is followed, whereas the Dravidian preference for marriage to close biological kin is more common in southern districts (Goswami 1970; Roychoudhury 1976; Malhotra 1979; Karve 1990).

Within the Muslim and Hindu communities of India adherence to traditional religious marriage prohibitions is, however, often incomplete. For example, although double first cousin and uncle–niece unions represent the same genetic distance, the latter marriage type is prohibited by the *Koran*. Yet despite this ruling a small minority of Muslims do contract uncle–niece marriages in both North and South India (Basu, S. K. and Roy 1974; Puri *et al.* 1978; Roychoudhury 1980; Bittles *et al.* 1991). Similarly, in virtually all northern and eastern states of India a number of Hindu groups, including scheduled tribes, go against the prevailing prohibition on marriage to close kin and sanction cousin unions (Roychoudhury 1976; Karve 1990). The tendency to ignore secular constraints is even more marked, and so although uncle–niece unions were proscribed under the Hindu Marriage Act of 1955 (Kapadia 1958), urban studies conducted in Karnataka during the 1980s showed that 21.0 per cent of all Hindu marriages were between uncles and their nieces (Bittles *et al.* 1991).

Close kin marriage is common among the minority religious communities in South India, including Buddhists (Roychoudhury 1976), Christians (Bittles *et al.* 1991), Parsees (Undevia and Balakrishnan 1978), and Jews (Goldschmidt 1963), presumably indicating their acceptance of prevailing local marriage norms. However, in small religious isolates, such as the Sephardi Jewish community in the city of Cochin, Kerala, an additional contributory factor may be restriction on the number of available marriage partners.

Economic and social determinants of consanguinity

Given the enormous ethnic, religious, and social diversity displayed by the populations of South Asia, hard and fast rules regarding specific determinants of consanguinity tend to be of limited validity. The highest rates of marriage to a close relative have been consistently reported in more traditional rural areas and among the poorest and least educated sections of society (Bittles *et al.* 1991), but first cousin unions also are commonplace in some major land-owning families (Rami Reddy and Chandrasekhar Reddy 1979). It follows that, irrespective of a family's financial status, the maintenance of property is a major determinant in consanguineous marriages, with only token or significantly reduced dowry or bridewealth payments required (Hann 1985; Caldwell *et al.* 1988; Govinda Reddy 1988). Within land-owning groups the preservation of estates and land-holdings is probably the critical factor governing their desire for close kin marriage.

Besides economic considerations, consanguineous marriages are socially accepted because of the comparative ease with which prenuptial negotiations can be conducted. Overall, there is a correlation between consanguinity and marriage distance, but within a specific region each endogamous group has its own scale of marriage distance determined by the spatial distribution and mobility of group members, and in certain artisan castes preference for marriage to a close relative actually may lead to significantly increased marriage distances (Mukherjee 1984). It is believed that consanguineous unions offer the optimum opportunity for compatibility between husband and wife and the bride and her mother-in-law (Dronamraju and Meera Khan 1963), thus benefiting female status (Dyson and Moore 1983) and resulting in significantly less biased tertiary sex ratios in the populations of Andhra Pradesh, Karnataka, Kerala, and Tamil Nadu by comparisons with other Indian states (Bittles *et al.* 1993c). Further indirect support for the claim that marriage to a close relative is supportive of female status is provided by the increasingly reported phenomenon of 'dowry deaths' (Kumari 1988), which are most common in north Indian Hindu communities with rigorous proscriptions against consanguineous unions. A final important, general consideration favouring consanguineous unions is the conviction that, by marrying within the extended family, hidden uncertainties regarding health or other unfavourable family characteristics will effectively be avoided (Bittles *et al.* 1991).

Evidence for a detrimental inbreeding-associated prenatal effect

There are two main avenues by which inbreeding potentially could influence human fertility: by altering the prevalence of primary sterility in a population or by influencing rates of primary and secondary abortion. Both biological and social considerations must be taken into account when assessing the relationship of consanguinity to reproductive behaviour. From a biological viewpoint the sharing by spouses of human leucocyte antigens (HLA), a situation which by definition would be more probable in consanguineous marriages, has been claimed to be a contributory factor in recurrent spontaneous abortion (Thomas *et al.* 1985). Although the proposed relationship between antigen-sharing and fertility is complex, the effect appears to be more significant at HLA-DR loci than at the more commonly investigated HLA-A or -B loci (Gill 1992). In fact the precise mechanism(s) governing recurrent abortion may not be directly associated with the HLA antigens, but rather be caused by HLA-linked recessive lethal or deleterious alleles that interfere with normal development of the embryo (Hedrick 1988); support for this view is provided by studies suggesting that recurrent spontaneous abortion can occur as a familial trait over several generations (Mowbray *et al.* 1991).

With the exception of relatively small-scale clinical studies, much of the reported information on HLA-associated prenatal losses in humans has been derived from the Hutterites, a highly endogamous Anabaptist sect which migrated from Russia in small numbers during the 1850s and 1870s and whose members are now resident in some 300 colonies or communal farms located in the northern USA and Canada (Ober *et al.* 1992). It was observed that couples who shared alleles at the HLA-DR locus had an average completed family size of 6.5 compared with the 9.0 children born to families where the partners were HLA-DR incompatible (Ober *et al.* 1988), the implication being that the difference in numbers of children born in each group was due to excess early spontaneous abortions in the HLA-DR compatible pregnancies. However, the degree of restriction in Hutterite marriage partner choice can be gauged from the records of the Schmiedenleut colony resident in South Dakota, thought to be descended from at most 78 founders and with current members sharing only 45 unique HLA haplotypes (Kostyu *et al.* 1989). Manifestly, the application of data collected on HLA sharing and fertility in communities of this type may be of limited relevance in numerically large human populations with significantly more extensive HLA repertoires. There also is the more general problem of obtaining accurate retrospective data on prenatal losses, with abortions occurring within 6 weeks of conception especially susceptible to faulty recall (Wilcox and

Horney 1984). For this reason, estimates of early post-implantation losses that are not based on sequential human chorionic gonadotrophin (hCG) assays are probably of dubious validity (Wilcox *et al.* 1988).

These factors may explain why, contrary to the Hutterite studies, reports from a number of major populations have consistently shown reduced levels of primary sterility in inbred marriages (Schull *et al.* 1962, 1970; Tanaka *et al.* 1964; Rao and Inbaraj 1977*a*), and there has been no direct evidence linking inbreeding to increased rates of spontaneous abortion or miscarriage (reviewed in Bittles and Makov 1988). Findings of this type have usually been interpreted as reflecting the greater immunological compatibility of the mother and fetus in consanguineous unions, with lower predicted rates of potentially lethal conditions such as rhesus incompatibility (Stern and Charles 1945) and pre-eclamptic toxaemia (Stevenson *et al.* 1976). Indirect indicators of fetal survival, including multiple birth rates and sex ratio at birth, also have failed to show an inbreeding effect (Schull 1958; Freire-Maia *et al.* 1983; Bittles *et al.* 1988). Therefore, unless deleterious recessive genes are operational very early in embryonic/fetal development, in effect before the first missed menstrual period, consanguinity appears not to significantly influence the incidence of prenatal losses in major human populations.

Analysis of data on consanguinity and number of live births

To obtain an overview of the effects of inbreeding on fertility, information was collected on the number of live births produced by consanguineous and non-consanguineous couples. Three simple criteria were adopted for the inclusion of data in the analysis. The study was restricted to surveys conducted within the last two decades, each with a minimum sample size of 750 live births, and with results available from at least three discrete consanguinity classes. The two latter requisites were selected in order to minimize potential problems with small sample sizes and to permit regression analysis on the results. The resultant sample comprised 142 118 marriages drawn from 20 populations in north and south India and Pakistan, with no distinction made between surveys based on completed family size and data derived from cross-sectional studies.

As a working definition, unions contracted between persons related as second cousins or closer, that is with progeny homozygous at 1.56 per cent or more of all loci, were categorized as consanguineous. These arbitrary limits were chosen since the genetic influence in marriages between couples related to a lesser degree would be expected to differ only marginally from that observed in non-consanguineous unions. The consanguinity classes recorded varied, depending on the previously discussed local marital rules, ranging from uncle–niece and/or double first cousin (equivalent to a coefficient of inbreeding in the progeny of $F = 0.125$), first cousin ($F = 0.0625$), first cousin once removed or double second cousin ($F = 0.0313$), second cousin ($F = 0.0156$), and non-consanguineous ($F = 0$). The mean coefficient of inbreeding for each population was calculated as F (or α) $= \Sigma p_i F_i$. Because of the possibility that preference for consanguineous unions may have extended over multiple generations, this calculated value should be regarded as a minimal estimate of the level of inbreeding in each community.

As an initial step, a simple direct comparison was plotted between the numbers of live births in first cousin unions ($F = 0.0625$) and the corresponding non-consanguineous controls ($F = 0$), with the level of statistical significance assessed using the non-parametric sign test. A meta-analysis approach was next adopted, based on the construction of regression models weighted by number for each population (Genstat 5 statistical package, Rothamstead Experimental Station). For meta-analysis the mean numbers of liveborns per consanguinity class were examined in each population as dependent variable, and the equivalent coefficient of inbreeding (F) as independent variable.

The basic demographic characteristics of each population, with percentage inbreeding and mean coefficients of inbreeding (F), are given in Table 4.1. In the nine cities of the Pakistan province of Punjab and the three north Indian communities studied, all marriages were between Muslim couples, both Sunni and Shia. The eight south Indian populations were varied in their composition, with subdivisions on the basis of maternal age, urban/rural status, and religion. Although the patterns of consanguineous marriage in the north Indian and Pakistani Muslim populations differed quite markedly from the Hindu and Christian groups of south India, the range of inbreeding levels and F values in all three study areas showed considerable overlap. With the exception of Karnataka, south India where uncle–niece unions were preferentially contracted by Hindus and Christians (Bittles *et al.* 1992), first cousin marriages ($F = 0.0625$) were the most common form of consanguineous union across all religions. The inbreeding levels cited in Table 4.1 refer to the present generation only and so, as previously noted, the average F values calculated for each locality represent minimal consanguinity estimates in all communities.

In Fig. 4.1 a significant overall association between the number of liveborn children per couple and consanguinity at first cousin level ($F = 0.0625$) is apparent. Of the 20 populations examined, fertility was higher in 18 of the first cousin groups by comparison with their non-consanguineous counterparts, the exceptions being urban Muslims in Rajasthan, north India and in Rawalpindi, Pakistan ($P < 0.01$). On the basis of these findings it is difficult to perceive how the assertion that first cousin unions exhibit reduced fertility (Thornhill 1991) can be justified.

A very similiar picture is seen when the influence of consanguinity on fertility is examined across all levels of inbreeding. The meta-analysis regression plots once again show a negative association between fertility and consanguinity in the urban Muslim communities of Rajasthan and Rawalpindi (Fig. 4.2). In this instance there also was a negative regression value for urban Muslims in Karnataka, caused by the anomalous reduced fertility of uncle–niece unions

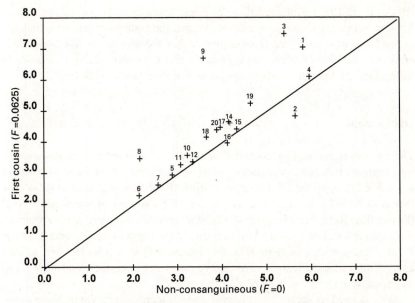

Fig. 4.1 Mean number of livebirths in first cousin and nonconsanguineous unions. (Numbers cited refer to the populations identified in Table 4.1)

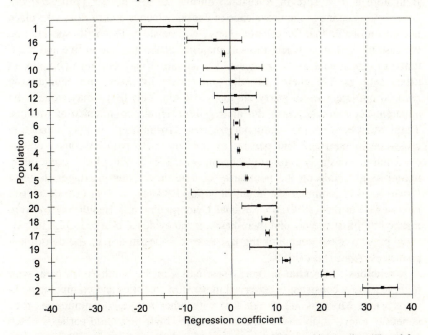

Fig. 4.2 Meta-analysis of the relationship between coefficient of inbreeding (F) and fertility. (Numbers cited refer to the populations identified in Table 4.1)

(Bittles *et al.* 1991). Although these couples, who accounted for 3.7 per cent of Muslim marriages in the Karnataka study, had the youngest mean maternal age at first live birth (19.4 years), subsequently they reported fewer live born deliveries than all other Muslim consanguineous and non-consanguineous classes in the region, yet with no obvious explanation for their low level of fertility.

Discussion

The interest stimulated by countries of the Indian subcontinent in discussions into reproductive behaviour largely derives from their very large population sizes. For example, the combined population of India and Pakistan alone is estimated to be 1004 million, accounting for 18.5 per cent of the world's total (Population Reference Bureau 1992), and in addition there are substantial migrant communities from both countries now resident in Western Europe, North America, and Oceania. For this reason a thorough understanding and appreciation of their varied marriage customs and practices, and how these might influence fertility, is merited.

As evidenced by surveys on consanguineous marriages in Tamil Nadu in the 1970s (Rao and Inbaraj 1977*b*) and the technologically advanced cities of Bangalore and Mysore in Karnataka during the last decade (Bittles *et al.*, 1993*a*), if a decline in the prevalence of consanguineous unions does take place it seems probable that the pace of change will be slow. This will especially be the case in rural areas where the vast majority of the population live and resistance to modernization is strongest. The situation may be more complex in urban settings with their generally smaller family sizes, and equivalently reduced opportunities to marry eligible close kin. This factor may explain the apparent accommodation in the metropolitan Hindu community of Madras, Tamil Nadu between the traditional preference for mother's brother's daughter cross-cousin marriage and partner availability, with parallel cousin unions becoming increasingly common (Ramesh *et al.* 1989). While little recent information is available on the popularity of consanguineous marriages in north Indian Muslim communities, in neighbouring Pakistan 50.3 per cent of women interviewed in the 1990/1991 National Demographic and Health Survey were married to a first cousin, and there has been no evidence of a reduction in consanguinity over the course of the last three decades in any of the constituent provinces (Ahmed *et al.* 1992).

A religious differential in family size exists in the South Asian data, with highest fertility consistently observed in Muslim countries and communities. In areas where Muslims are co-resident with other religious communities they generally marry at an earlier age and produce their first child earliest, which would be expected to facilitate increased levels of fertility by optimizing the reproductive span. This pattern emerged in Karnataka, south India, with Muslim women having a mean age at first liveborn delivery of 20.82 years, by comparison with 21.98 years for Hindus, and 22.86 years among Christians (Bittles et al. 1991). The Karnataka study also showed that the greater fertility of Muslim women was to a lesser extent associated with a larger proportion of live births at more advanced ages, although given the significant decline in fecundity with increasing maternal age (Wood 1989) this prolongation of their reproductive span would not have exerted such a significant effect on family size.

Independent of the religious dimension, the very substantial data sets reproduced in Figs. 4.1 and 4.2 conclusively demonstrate that reproductive behaviour is significantly influenced by consanguinity, a finding replicated in other small-scale south Indian studies (Rami Reddy and Papa Rao 1978; Rami Reddy and Chandrasekhar Reddy 1979; Asha Bai et al. 1981; Govinda Reddy 1987). Younger female age at marriage and first live birth would again appear to be critical factors in the larger family sizes; however, age at marriage alone can be an imperfect indicator of fertility since a longer time to first live birth has been reported for younger mothers owing to adolescent subfertility. The length of the first birth interval may additionally be subject to significant cultural differences (Basu A. K. 1993), or even in some instances the need to complete dowry payments (Ramu 1991), but where dowry payments tend to be low, as in consanguineous unions, socio-economic explanations for an extended time to first birth would be expected to carry less weight. Multicentre studies in Pakistan showed that maternal and paternal ages at marriage were negatively associated with consanguinity (Bittles et al. 1993b), and despite a marginal positive association between consanguinity and time to first delivery, as shown in Figs. 4.1 and 4.2 the net result was a greater number of children born to consanguineous couples in eight of the nine cities investigated. Similarly in Karnataka, and controlling for religion, uncle–niece marriages produced their first child 1.41 years younger, first cousins 1.10 years younger and second cousins 0.84 years younger than non-consanguineous couples, resulting in significantly greater fertility at all levels of inbreeding (Bittles et al. 1991).

It also has been proposed that the larger number of births in consanguineous marriages may represent a reproductive compensation response to increased early postnatal mortality (Schull and Neel 1972), operating via the cessation of lactational amenorrhoea following the death of a breast-fed infant or from a conscious decision by the parents to achieve their desired family size. As yet no direct evidence is available on this topic from India and, for example, the greater fertility observed among consanguineous couples in rural Andhra Pradesh (Reddy 1992) can readily be accommodated in terms of earlier marriage and hence an enhanced reproductive span. Data from Pakistan are rather more persuasive with regard to the operation of reproductive compensation and greater numbers of live births have been reported in families where childhood deaths have occurred (Yusuf and Rukanuddin 1989), especially when the child was male (Rukanuddin 1982). There is, however, less unanimity in terms of the underlying mechanism involved, with both biological (Chowdhury *et al.* 1976) and behavioural (Richter and Adlakha 1989) components specifically identified.

Given the enormous continuing growth in human population sizes, especially in regions where close kin marriage is preferential, the reproductive behaviour of consanguineous couples obviously is a major topic in its own right. But their greater fertility is additionally important in relation to the adverse health effects of inbreeding caused by the expression of deleterious recessive genes inherited from a common ancestor. Frequently, the relationship between the number of children born to a couple who are carriers for an autosomal recessive disorder and the specific expectation that they will conceive an affected child is over-looked or ignored. Yet by definition the more children born to a carrier couple the greater this expectation will be, and so consanguineous couples are more likely to conceive affected infants who will die in infancy or early childhood because of their greater fertility. Viewed solely within the context of the present study, this factor will complicate resolution of the relationship between consanguinity, fertility, and reproductive compensation. Of more primary importance, it may result in significant bias when assessing the overall biological effects of human inbreeding, including the rate at which deleterious recessive alleles can be eliminated from the gene pool of inbred communities.

Acknowledgements

Excellent technical support was provided by Jonathan C. Grant. Generous financial assistance from the Stopes Research Fund and the Wellcome Trust during the course of the study is acknowledged with gratitude.

References

Ahmed, T., Ali, S. M., Aliaga, A., Arnold, F., Ayub, M., Bhatti, M. H., *et al.* (1992). *Pakistan demographic and health survey 1990/91.* Pakistan National Institute of Population Studies and Macro International, Islamabad and Columbia, Maryland.

Armstrong, K. (1991). *Muhammad: a Western attempt to understand Islam.* Gollancz, London.

Asha Bai, P. V., Jacob John, T., and Subramaniam, V. R. (1981). Reproductive wastage and developmental disorders in relation to consanguinity in South India. *Tropical and Geographical Medicine,* **33**, 275–80.

Basu, A. K. (1993). Cultural influences on the timing of first births in India: large differences that add up to little difference. *Population Studies,* **47**, 85–95.

Basu, S. K. (1978). Effects of consanguinity among Muslim groups of India. In *Medical genetics in India* (ed. I. C. Verma), Vol. 2, pp. 173–87. Auroma Enterprises, Pondicherry.

Basu, S. K. and Roy, S. (1974). Change in the frequency of consanguineous marriages among the Delhi Muslims after Partition. *Eastern Anthropologist,* **25**, 21–8.

Bittles, A. H. (1990). *Consanguineous marriage: current global incidence and its relevance to demographic research.* Population Studies Center, Research Report Number 90–186. University of Michigan, Ann Arbor.

Bittles, A. H., Coble, J. M., and Appaji Rao, N. (1993*a*). Trends in consanguineous marriage in Karnataka, South India, 1980–1989. *Journal of Biosocial Science*, **25**, 111–6.

Bittles, A. H., Grant, J. C., and Shami, S. A. (1993*b*). An evaluation of consanguinity as a determinant of reproductive behaviour and mortality in Pakistan. *International Journal of Epidemiology*, **22**, 463–7.

Bittles, A. H. and Makov, E. (1988). Inbreeding in human populations: an assessment of the costs. In *Human mating patterns* (ed. C. G. N. Mascie-Taylor and A. J. Boyce), pp. 153–67. Cambridge University Press.

Bittles, A. H., Mason, W. M., Greene, J., and Appaji Rao, N. (1991). Reproductive behavior and health in consanguineous marriages. *Science*, **252**, 789–94.

Bittles, A. H., Mason, W. M., Singarayer, D. N., Shreeniwas, S., and Spinar, M. (1993*c*). Determinants of the sex ratio in India: studies at national, state, and local levels. In *Urban ecology and health in the Third World* (ed. L. Schell, M. T. Smith, and A. Bilsborough), pp. 244–59. Cambridge University Press.

Bittles, A. H., Radha Rama Devi, A., and Appaji Rao, N. (1988). Consanguinity, twinning and secondary sex ratio in Karnataka, South India. *Annals of Human Biology*, **15**, 455–60.

Bittles, A. H., Shami, S. A., and Appaji Rao, N. (1992). Consanguineous marriage in Southern Asia: incidence, causes and effects. In *Minority populations: genetics, demography and health* (ed. A. H. Bittles and D. F. Roberts), pp. 102–18, Macmillan, London.

Caldwell, J. C., Reddy, P. H., and Caldwell, P. (1988). *The causes of demographic change: experimental research in South India*, p. 239. University of Wisconsin Press, Madison.

Chowdhury, A. K. M. A., Khan, A. R., and Chen, L. C. (1976). The effect of child mortality experience on subsequent fertility: in Pakistan and Bangladesh. *Population Studies*, **30**, 249–61.

Dronamraju, K. R. and Meera Khan, P. (1963). The frequency and effects of consanguineous marriages in Andhra Pradesh. *Journal of Genetics*, **58**, 387–401.

Dyson, T. and Moore, M. (1983). On kinship structure, female autonomy and demographic behavior in India. *Population and Development Review*, **9**, 35–59.

Freire-Maia, N. Chautard-Freire-Maia, E. A., Barbosa, C. A. A., and Krieger, H. (1983). Inbreeding studies in Brasilian schoolchildren. *American Journal of Medical Genetics*, **16**, 331–55.

Fricke, T. E., Syed, S. H., and Smith, P. C. (1986). Rural Punjabi social organization and marriage timing strategies in Pakistan. *Demography*, **23**, 489–508.

Gill, T. J. (1992). Influence of MHC and MHC-linked genes on reproduction. *American Journal of Human Genetics*, **50**, 1–5.

Goldschmidt, E. (1963). Immigrant Jews from Cochin. In *Genetics of migrant and isolate populations* (ed. E. Goldschmidt), pp. 352–3. Willams and Wilkins, New York.

Goswami, H. K. (1970). Frequency of consanguineous marriages in Madhya Pradesh. *Acta Geneticae Medicae et Gemellologiae*, **19**, 486–90.

Govinda Reddy, P. (1987). Effects of consanguineous marriages on fertility among three endogamous groups of Andhra Pradesh. *Social Biology*, **34**, 68–77.

Govinda Reddy, P. (1988). Consanguineous marriages and marriage payment: a study among three South Indian caste groups. *Annals of Human Biology*, **15**, 263–8.

Hann, K. (1985). The incidence of relation marriage in Karnataka, South India. *South Asia Research*, **5**, 59–72.

Hedrick, P. W. (1988). HLA-sharing, recurrent spontaneous abortion, and the genetic hypothesis. *Genetics*, **119**, 199–204.

Kapadia, K. M. (1958). *Marriage and family in India*. Oxford University Press, Calcutta.

Karve, I. (1990). *Kinship organization in India*, 3rd edn. Munshiram Manoharlal Publishers, New Delhi.

Kostyu, D. D., Ober, C. L., Dawson, D. V., Ghanayem, M., Elias, S., and Martin, A. O. (1989). Genetic analysis of HLA in the U.S. Schmiedenleut Hutterites. *American Journal of Human Genetics*, **45**, 261–9.

Kumari, R. (1989). *Brides are not for burning*. Radiant Publishers, New Delhi.

Malhotra, K. C. (1979). Inbreeding among the Dhangar castes of Maharashtra, India. *Journal of Biosocial Science*, **11**, 397–409.

Mowbray, J. F., Underwood, J., and Gill, T. J. (1991). Familial recurrent spontaneous abortions. *American Journal of Reproductive Immunology*, **26**, 17–18.

Mukherjee, D. P. (1984). Changing patterns of marriage in India and genetical implications. *Human Science*, **33**, 201–19.

Ober, C., Elias, S., O'Brien, E., Kostyu, D. D., Hauck, W. W., and Bombard, A. (1988). HLA sharing and fertility in Hutterite couples: evidence for prenatal selection against compatible fetuses. *American Journal of Reproductive Immunology*, **18**, 111–5.

Ober, C., Elias, S., Kostyu, D. D., and Hauck, W. W. (1992). Decreased fecundability in Hutterite couples sharing HLA-DR loci. *American Journal of Human Genetics*, **50**, 6–14.

Population Reference Bureau (1992). *World population sheets*. PRB, Washington, DC.

Puri, R. K., Verma, I. C., and Bhargava, I. (1978). Effects of consanguinity in a community in Pondicherry. In *Medical genetics in India* (ed. I. C. Verma), Vol. 2, pp. 129–39. Auroma Enterprises, Pondicherry.

Ramesh, A., Srikumari, C. R., and Sukumar, S. (1989). Parallel cousin marriages in Madras, Tamil Nadu: new trends in Dravidian kinship. *Social Biology*, **36**, 248–54.

Rami Reddy, V. and Chandrasekhar Reddy, B. K. (1979). Consanguinity effects on fertility and mortality among the Reddis of Chittoor District (A. P.) South India. *Indian Journal of Heredity*, **11**, 77–88.

Rami Reddy, V. and Papa Rao, A. (1978). Inbreeding effects in a coastal village and other parts of Andhra Pradesh. *Acta Genetica et Medica Gemellologiae*, **27**, 89–93.

Ramu, G. N. (1991). Changing family structure and fertility patterns: an Indian case. *Journal of Asian and African Studies*, **26**, 189–206.

Rao, P. S. S. and Inbaraj, S. G. (1977a). Inbreeding effects on human reproduction in Tamil Nadu of South India. *Annals of Human Genetics*, **41**, 87–98.

Rao, P. S. S. and Inbaraj, S. G. (1977b). Inbreeding in Tamil Nadu, South India. *Social Biology*, **24** 281–8.

Reddy, B. M. (1992) Inbreeding effects on reproductive outcome: a study based on a large sample from the endogamous Vadde of Kolleru, Lake, Andhra Pradesh, India. *Human Biology*, **64**, 659–82.

Reddy, B. M. and Malhotra, K. C. (1991). Relationship between birth order of spouses with different degrees of consanguineous relationship. *Human Biology*, **63**, 489–98.

Richter, K. and Adlakha, A (1989). The effect on infant and child mortality on subsequent fertility, *Journal of Population and Social Studies*, **2**, 43–62.

Roychoudhury, A. K. (1976) Incidence of inbreeding in different states of India. *Demography India*, **5**, 108–19.

Roychoudhury, A. K. (1980). Consanguineous marriages in Tamil Nadu. *Journal of the Indian Anthropological Society*, **15**, 167–74.

Rukanuddin, A. R. (1982) Infant-child mortality and son preference as factors influencing fertility in Pakistan. *Pakistan Development Review*, **21**, 297–328.

Schull, W. J. (1958) Empirical risks in consanguineous marriages: sex ratio, malformation and inability. *American Journal of Human Genetics*, **10**, 294–343.

Schull, W. J., Nagano, H., Yamamoto, M., and Komatsu, I. (1970). The effect of parental consanguinity and inbreeding in Hirado, Japan. 1. Stillbirth and prereproductive mortality. *American Journal of Human Genetics*, **22**, 239–62.

Schull, W. J. and Neel, J. V. (1972). The effects of parental consanguinity and inbreeding in Hirado, Japan. V. Summary and interpretation. *American Journal of Human Genetics*, **24**, 425–53.

Schull, W. J., Yanase, T., and Nemoto, H. (1962) Kuroshima: the impact of religion on an island's genetic heritage. *Human Biology*, **34**, 271–98.

Shami, S. A. and Hussain, S. B. (1984). Consanguinity in the population of Gujrat (Punjab), Pakistan. *Biologia*, **30**, 93–109.

Shami, S. A. and Iqbal, I. (1983). Consanguineous marriages in the population of Sheikhupura (Punjab), Pakistan. *Biologia*, **29**, 231–44.

Shami, S. A. and Minha, I. B. (1984). Effects of consanguineous marriages on offspring mortality in the City of Jhelum (Punjab), Pakistan. *Biologia*, **30**, 153–65.

Shami, S. A. and Siddiqui, H. (1984). The effect of parental consanguinity in Rawalpindi City (Punjab), Pakistan. *Biologia*, **30**, 189–200.

Shami, S. A. and Zahida (1982). Study of consanguineous marriages in the population of Lahore (Punjab), Pakistan. *Biologia*, **28**, 1–15.

Stern, C. and Charles, D. R. (1945). The rhesus gene and the effect of consanguinity. *Science*, **101**, 305–7.

Stevenson, A. C., Say, B., Ustaoglu, S., and Durmus, Z. (1976) Aspects of pre-eclamptic toxaemia of pregnancy, consanguinity, and twinning in Ankara. *Journal of Medical Genetics*, **13**, 1–8.

Tanaka, K., Yanase, T., and Furusho, T. (1964). Effects of inbreeding on fertility in man. *Proceedings of the Japanese Academy*, **40**, 852–6.

Thomas, M. L., Harger, J. H., Magener, D. K., Rabin, B. S. and Gill, T. J. (1985) HLA sharing and spontaneous abortion in humans. *American Journal of Obstetrics and Gynecology*, **151**, 1053–8.

Thornhill, N. W. (1991). An evolutionary analysis of rules regulating human inbreeding and marriage. *Behavioral and brain Sciences*, **14**, 247–93.

Undevia, J. V. and Balakrishnan, V. (1978). Temporal changes in consanguinity among the Parsi and Irani communities of Bombay. In *Medical Genetics in India* (ed. I. C. Verma), Vol. 2, pp. 145–50. Auroma Enterprises, Pondicherry.

Wilcox, A. J. and Horney, L. F. (1984) Accuracy of spontaneous abortion recall. *American Journal of Epidemiology*, **120**, 727–33.

Wilcox, A. J. Weinberg, C. R., O'Connor, J. F., Baird, D. D., Schlatterer, J. P., Canfield, R. E. et al. (1988). Incidence of early loss of pregnancy. *New England Journal of Medicine*, **319**, 189–94.

Wood, J. W. (1989). Fecundity and natural fertility in humans. In *Oxford Reviews of Reproductive Biology* (ed. S. R. Milligan), vol. 11, pp. 61–109. Oxford University Press.

Yusuf, F. and Rukanuddin, A. R. (1989). Correlates of fertility behaviour in Pakistan. *Biology and Society*, **6**, 61–8.

5

Human assortative mating: evidence and genetic implications

C. G. N. MASCIE-TAYLOR

Definition and terms

The term assortative mating refers to a departure from random mating or panmixia; when like attracts like the mating is called positive assortative mating or homogamy. If opposites marry then negative assortative mating or heterogamy occurs. Some geneticists use the term assortative mating in the broad sense to include all types of departures from random mating. This definition would include the effects of inbreeding resulting from consanguineous matings (Cavali-Sforza and Bodmer 1971; Jacquard 1970). However, over the last 10–15 years it has become increasingly common to reserve the term assortative mating for unions involving phenotypically similar individuals who are not relatives.

Assortative marriage and assortative mating

Garrison et al. (1968) differentiated between assortative marriage and assortative mating. The latter term implying production of offspring whereas many marriages are childless. Zonderman et al. (1977) proposed a slightly different meaning to assortative mating by defining it as the phenotypic correlation between mates assuming no common environmental contribution while assortative marriage included the common environmental contribution as well as the effects of convergence (the increased similarity between spouses resulting from living together). Since the evidence for convergence is still controversial and it is difficult to separate the common environmental contribution, the terms assortative mating and marriage are used here as defined by Garrison et al. (1968) when referring to phenotypic similarity, that is excluding the effects of inbreeding.

Positive assortative mating rules OK?

Among the theories of mate selection, one which is frequently cited is Winch's theory of complementary needs (Winch 1958). The theory suggests, for example, that a woman high on nurturance is most likely to marry someone high on succurance (the need for nurturance) or a man high on dominance would tend to select a woman low on dominance. Limited evidence for the theory came from studies in American universities where room-mate choices indicated that in stable relationships, complementary needs prevailed, but not so in unstable relationships. However, studies of marital partners and engaged couples provide little or no evidence of opposites attracting and in only four traits has negative assortative mating been reported; these are for albinism (Woolf and Dukepoo 1969), red hair (Stern 1973), pulse rate after work (Smith 1946), and working capacity and movement accuracy (Wolanski 1973).

With so few traits showing evidence of negative assortative mating or marriage it is common to find researchers referring simply to assortative mating when they really mean positive assortative mating. In the rest of this chapter, unless specified otherwise, assortative mating should be interpreted as positive phenotypic assortment.

Empirical studies on assortative mating

The earliest systematic study on human assortative mating can be traced back to the pioneering work of Francis Galton (1869) who studied the psychological and physical characteristics of famous English couples. His data which were statistically analysed by Pearson, revealed, with the exception of measures of temperament, evidence of positive assortment. Subsequently, a great variety of traits have been studied: health, interests, neurosis, truthfulness, neglect of duty, and other unusual traits (Jones 1929; Carter 1932; Richardson 1939). Reviews of more recent research appear in Vandenberg (1972), Roberts (1977), Jensen (1978), Mascie-Taylor (1988), and Susanne and Lepage (1988).

Assortative mating can be broadly measured in terms of propinquity and personal preference. Propinquity includes ethnicity, religion, parental, and own socio-economic status as well as some of its correlates such as education and number of siblings. Personal preference incorporates physical features and attractiveness, personality (including mental illness), and IQ. Factors related to propinquity may cause genetic relatedness with phenotypic similarity as a secondary result, while personal preferences cause phenotypic similarity leading secondarily to genetic relatedness.

Age

Not all variables fit nearly into these two groupings and age at marriage has no obvious genetic consequences, except for the resulting fertility effects. However, there are other variables for which assortative mating occurs which may be affected by age, so that the effect of age should be statistically removed in order not to overestimate or underestimate the effect of the variable under study.

Age at marriage shows the highest positive correlation between spouses. Pearson and Heron (1913) using data from the British Census of 1901 which included over 5 million couples, obtained a correlation of 0.93. Lutz (1905) used records from the Chicago marriage licence office and computed a correlation of 0.76. Roberts (1977) in his review on assortative marriage reported correlations of between 0.51 and 0.94 for age at marriage in Western societies with a weighted mean of 0.85. When childless couples were excluded the lowest correlation was 0.66 with the same upper limit. These data span more than 75 years and suggest some degree of stability in the spousal association for age at marriage over time.

Homogamy for age is a characteristic of dating partners in general (Burgess and Wallin 1943) and is also found in unwed biological parents of adopted children (Plomin *et al.* 1977). The pattern is for the woman to be slightly younger than the man. Kenrick and Keefe (1992) examined the reasons whereby woman marry men slightly older than themselves. They proposed a model whereby the finding of age preferences in mates is the result of sex differences in human reproductive strategies, that is they propose an evolutionary model. This model contrasts with the social psychology model which sees mating preferences as a form of economic exchange (Clark and Reis 1988). Under the evolutionary model, males' preferences for relatively younger females should be minimal during early mating years but should become more pronounced as the male gets older; young females are expected to prefer somewhat older males during the early years and to change less as they age.

On the basis of six studies including classified personal newspaper advertisements they present data on mating preferences in support of their hypothesis. However, the model can be criticized because Kenrick and Keefe present no data on differential reproductive success (only mating preference), only discuss mean effects rather than discuss the wide variation in actual age preferences, and do not explain how similarity in age preferences have been selected for during human evolution.

Assortative mating has also been reported for the length of life. Pearson (1903) made a study of the correlation between husband and wife in two rural areas around Oxford and one limited class (the Society of Friends). In all three groups the correlation was about 0.2 with a mean of 0.22.

Propinquity

Residential and marital distances   For more than 60 years studies have shown that young people tend to marry those who live nearby. The classic study by Bossard (1932) in Philadelphia showed that more than half of the couples lived (residential distance) within two miles (15 blocks) of each other at the time they obtained their marriage licences. Bossard's study has been replicated in other cities in the USA and in Western Europe. There has been an increase in the average distances as Girard's (1964) study of a national sample of 1645 French couples demonstrates. He found that in 60.6 per cent of the couples married prior to 1930, the bride and groom resided in the same commune (township or parish) whereas between 1950 and 1959 the figure had fallen to 53.8 per cent.

Coleman (1982) analysed data from a British national marriage survey of couples married between 1920 and 1960. He found that 76 per cent of men married a woman living in the same place while 50 per cent married a woman born in the same place as himself. Of exogamous marriages, 50 per cent married someone living within 5 miles and born within 20 miles. Spuhler and Clark (1961) studied the medium distance between birthplaces of spouses and the place they married in Ann Arbor, Michigan, USA and found they increased from 40 miles in 1900 to 110 miles in 1950; for more than a third of the sample the distance was only 10 miles. Salzano and Freire-Maia (1970) computed the mean matrimonial radius of Brazilian spouses and showed that they were very low and increased from only 26 to 48 km during the first half of the twentieth century.

Typically the marital distance is shortest for farmers and agricultural workers and longest for the upper classes or professional groups (Girard 1964; Küchemann *et al.* 1974). Figure 5.1 illustrates the findings from the study of the villages in the Otmoor region of Oxfordshire (Harrison *et al.* 1974; Jeffries *et al.* 1976) based on mean marriage distance by birthplace.

Religion   Some religions prohibit marriage to a person from another faith and almost all religions look with some disfavour on such marriages. Although restrictions are weakening there is still a high degree of assortative mating for religion. Burgess and Wallin (1953) in a study of engaged couples calculated the

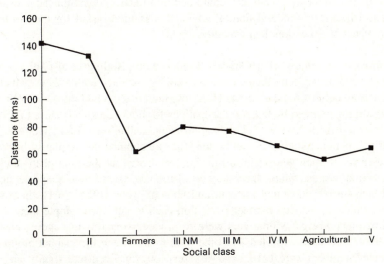

Fig. 5.1   Marital distances by social class, Otmoor villages, Oxfordshire.

chance expectation of the two people of the same faith marrying was 37 per cent while the actual percentage was 79 per cent. Hollingshead (1950) reported a contingency coefficient of 0.77 for religion when studying 1848 couples in New Haven, Connecticut.

Ethnicity   Kennedy (1994) studied intermarriage trends among Catholics of Irish, Polish, and Italian descent, Protestants of British, American, Scandinavian, and German descent, and Jews. Besides replicating the homogamy for religion described above, she also found that Catholic Irish, Italians, and Poles formed separate intermarriage groups, even though the proportions marrying within their own ethnic group had decreased by 1940 to 45, 82 and 53 per cent, respectively. Among so-called 'racial groups' avoidance of intermarriage is even more noticeable and it is unclear to what extent Negro–white marriages in the USA have been increasing. In Hawaii, however, intergroup marriage has had a long history of acceptance and detailed records have been kept. Johnson and Nagoshi (unpublished data) found that intergroup marriages make up nearly 39 per cent of marriages of long-term residents of Hawaii's five major racial/ethnic groups. Even so intergroup marriages are not random and are more likely between individuals of similar income.

Education   Education has consistently been shown to be an important factor in marital choice with up to 70 per cent similarity for years spent in education (Rockwell 1976). For example, Mascie-Taylor (1987) found in a British national sample of 7600 couples that of those husbands who continued into higher education, 82 per cent had wives who had stayed at school beyond the minimum leaving age, and 64 per cent also continued into further education. This result is in accord with the general finding whereby it is more usual for men to have more years of education than women.

Socio-economic status   Early studies (Centers 1949; Hollingshead 1949) showed a tendency much greater than chance for spouses to marry within their own class or one step below or above. In the USA, Warren (1966) found that endogamy for class origins (defined by fathers' occupations for both sexes) was close to 55 per cent when using a three-way classification (white collar, blue collar, and farm). In a British national study Mascie-Taylor (1987) examined the similarity between spouses for women who were in full-time occupation at the time of the child's conception. Using a simple three-way occupational classification into professional and managerial, other non-manual, and manual groups (Table 5.1), there was clear evidence of social homogamy within each group; for example there were 192 matings where both partners were from professional of managerial classes while only 80 were expected. For other non-manuals and the manual group the expected numbers were 1216.5 and 268, respectively. Even so a significant proportion of couples pick a partner from a different social group.

Table 5.1.   Spousal association for occupation in a British National sample

Husband	Wife Professional	Skilled	Unskilled	Total
Professional	192 (80)	375 (367)	68 (188)	635
Skilled	213 (265)	1283 (1216)	612 (627)	2108
Unskilled	47 (107)	415 (490)	387 (252)	849
Total	452	2073	1067	3592

Values in brackets refer to the numbers expected at random.

Personal preference

Physical characters   Extensive reviews of assortative mating with respect to physical characteristics and body measurements can be found in Spuhler (1968), Roberts (1977), and Susanne and Lepage (1988). For instance, Spuhler reviewed the extent of assortative mating for 105 different characteristics including the length and circumference of numerous body parts, lung volume, blood pressure, pulse rate, number of illnesses, eye colour, and hair colour. Excluding age, most of the reported correlations were positive and small, although statistically significant in many cases. For populations of European origin, the median correlation for height and weight was about +0.2 and the median contingency coefficient was also about +0.2 for hair and eye colour. Considering all characteristics about one-third of the correlations fell in the +0.1 to +0.2 range; the second most common range was 0–0.1; and the third range was +0.2 to +0.3. Only two of the 35 observed negative correlations were significant at the 5 per cent level (number of illnesses and pulse after exercise).

Active and passive elements of assortative mating   Mascie-Taylor (1987) attempted to separate the 'active' and 'passive' dimensions of assortative mating for height and weight. In essence he argued that part of the observed association between, for example, spousal heights will be due to similarity in 'background variables' such as educational level, social class and regional propinquity all of which significantly relate to height and weight. Any remaining association between spouses could be ascribed to active choice.

Using a stepwise multiple regression analysis the effects of social class, educational background, region, and age were removed separately from husband's height and weight and wife's height and weight. The correlations between the residual values were calculated and are presented in Table 5.2 together with the original correlations. Although the effects of the background variables were highly significant except for husband's weight, the change in correlation coefficient between spouses was very small. Thus in this sample assortative mating levels for height and weight remained essentially unchanged after taking

Table 5.2. Correlations before and after controlling for background variables

	Before	After
Height	0.287	0.268
Weight	0.109	0.115

into account the background variables. This suggests that most of the observed spousal associations for height and weight are the result of active choice and not a consequence of other factors. However, it must be borne in mind that the 'background variables' used in these analyses comprised only a few of the large number which also correlate with height and weight.

Psychometric characters

About 30 or more studies have reported on the overall IQ spousal association (see reviews by Jensen 1978; Mascie-Taylor 1988). The median correlation reported by Jensen was 0.44 with a range between 0.12 and 0.76. Bouchard and McGue (1981) in reviewing the extent of familial associations calculated a weighted mean correlation of +0.33 based on a total sample of 3817 couples.

There has been some discussion of whether the extent of assortative mating for IQ has declined over time (Johnson *et al.* 1980) but the use of less representative samples and unstandardized tests in the early studies makes direct comparisons impossible. Specific cognitive abilities have been examined less frequently and no consistent pattern emerges except verbal tests tend to show the highest spousal association and spatial tests the lowest.

Personality test results have been reviewed by Spuhler (1967), Vandenberg (1972), Murstein (1976), and Kephart (1977). Most of the samples were small and a wide variety of tests have been used and so definitive conclusions cannot be drawn. The best one can say is that there is evidence for at most low to moderate homogamy. One of the most cited studies is that of Cattell and Nesselroade (1967) who divided marriages into 'stable' and 'unstable' ones. Stable marriages showed low positive associations while there was evidence of negative assortative mating in unstable marriages for outgoingness (–0.50), enthusiasm (–0.40), self-sufficiency (–0.32), and self-opinionated (–0.33).

Assortative mating and convergence   Critics of the observed spousal correlations for IQ and personality argue that the associations are not a consequence of the initial similarity between partners at the time of their marriage, but the result of living together over some years (convergence). Most studies measure the realized assortment (Price and Vandenberg 1980), which is the degree of similarity present after some years of marriage. Furthermore, there might be attrition because dissimilar couples will separate and divorce.

Ideally, longitudinal studies are needed which examine couples prior to and during marriage to answer this criticism. In their absence a number of researchers have examined the indirect effects of convergence to see if couples married for a longer period show greater similarity than those married for a shorter period. Most of these studies find little or no evidence for convergence except for highly plastic variables such as alcohol consumption and amount of social activity (Price and Vandenberg 1980; Mascie-Taylor *et al.* 1987).

Assortative mating and education

Eckland (1970) suggested that the most likely reason for the observed spousal associations for IQ were because of the strong tendency for couples with similar education to marry (see later for discussion of the extent of educational homogamy). Support for this view came from the IQ study of Johnson *et al.* (1980) who showed 'near zero' (their term) spouse correlations after educational level had been partialled out, that is there appears to be very little spousal similarity for that part of cognitive ability which is independent of attainment. Johnson *et al.* used partial correlation analysis to statistically remove the effects of educational level and such an approach is likely to overcorrect the spousal IQ association. Even so, significant correlations ($r = 0.12$) for perceptual speed and verbal factor scores remained.

Watkins and Meredith (1981) found the correlation for verbal reasoning factor was initially 0.4 in their sample of newly weds. The coefficient fell to 0.3 after education was accounted for and it fell slightly further after eight other socio-economic variables had been taken into account but was still significant. Mascie-Taylor *et al.* (1987) studied the IQ similarity (using the WAIS IQ test) between 150 couples living in the Otmoor villages of Oxfordshire. After removing the effects due to occupation, years of education, type of school attended, family size, birth order, birthplace (local to Otmoor or not) and social class, the spousal correlation remained significant for the verbal IQ component although falling from +0.46 to +0.16 (Table 5.3), while the spousal correlations between residuals for visuospatial IQ and total IQ were not significant. In addition the residuals for the vocabulary subtest remained significant and those for the similarities and block design subtests bordered on significance.

Mascie-Taylor and Vandenberg (1988) examined the spousal associations for IQ and personality based on 193 couples from a Cambridge urban locality (Mascie-Taylor 1977; Mascie-Taylor and Gibson 1979). They found, using both partial correlation coefficients and multiple regression analysis, evidence of significant residual IQ association between spouses after taking into account school type, family size, birth order, locality, social class (parent and marriage), personality, and years of education. The partial correlation coefficients were between half and two-thirds the magnitude of the zero-order correlations. Both the Oxford and Cambridge studies indicate that the greater part of the spousal IQ

Table 5.3. Spouse correlations for seven subtests of the WAIS based on 150 couples from the Otmoor region

	Zero order r	P	Residual r	P
Comprehension	+ 0.287	< 0.001	+ 0.06	NS
Similarities	+ 0.442	< 0.001	+ 0.13	NS
Digit span	+ 0.097	NS	+ 0.03	NS
Vocabulary	+ 0.406	< 0.001	+ 0.15	< 0.05
Block design	+ 0.321	< 0.001	+ 0.12	NS
Object assembly	+ 0.162	< 0.05	+ 0.06	NS
Digit symbol	+ 0.130	NS	+ 0.01	NS
Verbal IQ	+ 0.462	< 0.001	+ 0.16	< 0.05
Visuospatial IQ	+ 0.155	NS	+ 0.06	NS
Total IQ	+ 0.372	< 0.001	+ 0.09	NS

association can be statistically accounted for by social class, education, and other background variables.

Heath and Eaves (1985) put forward ways of resolving the degree to which phenotypic assortment and social homogamy independently influence assortative mating. They suggest collecting data on monozygotic and dizygotic twins and their spouses, but sibling pairs and their spouses will also suffice. If homogamous assortative mating results solely from social homogamy then siblings, who have for the most part shared the same social environment, should resemble one another's spouse as much as they do their own. Since siblings differ from one another, they should resemble their own spouse more than the spouse of their sib to the degree that phenotypic assortment influences marital choice.

The method was tested by Nagoshi *et al.* (1987) used 47 sibling pairs from the Hawaii Family Cognition Study. Comparing sibling correlations, spousal correlations, and correlations between the spouse of one sibling and the spouse of the other sibling as well as the results of model fitting analyses they found that the observed spousal verbal IQ association is mostly due to social homogamy. They also studied education and occupational attainment and came to the view that the spousal correlation for education results from both phenotypic assortment and social homogamy while occupational attainment is mainly due to phenotypic assortment.

Psychiatric characters

Assortative mating for psychiatric disorders and illness has been reviewed by Merikangas (1982) who found a tendency for spouses of mentally ill individuals to be at increased risk of being ill themselves. One way of summarizing the risk

Table 5.4.   Studies of assortative mating for psychiatric illness

Study	Date	Assortative mating rate	Risk ratio
Penrose	1944	36%	9.0
Gregory	1959	64%	8.7
Kreitman	1962	29%	1.5
Nielsen	1964	38%	1.4
Kreitman	1968	42%	not available
Hall *et al.*	1971	not available	2.0
Weissman *et al.*	1984	62%	not available

of someone also having the same illness as their spouse is the assortative risk ratio (the risk of having the spouse's disease over the general population prevalence). Table 5.4 provides an overview of a number of studies of psychiatric illness and the risk ratios.

Studies of schizophrenia do not suggest any clear evidence of assortative mating but more recent work based on the idea of a schizophrenia spectrum does provide limited evidence of assortative mating. Alcoholism has been widely studied. Spouses of alcoholics of both sexes are more prone to drinking problems themselves than would be expected by chance. Although the rate of alcoholism is consistently higher in male spouses of female alcoholics than it is among female spouses of male alcoholics (Jacob and Bremer 1986), this difference is accounted for by the higher prevalence in males.

Lewis *et al.* (1976) found no evidence for criminal men to marry criminal women but they did find a significant increase in the amount of psychiatric illness in the wives of criminal men. This finding reinforces the work of Guze *et al.* (1970) who showed that 40 per cent of convicted felons' wives had psychiatric disturbance.

Assortative mating and differential fertility

Education

Kiser (1968) examined differences in fertility in relation to assortative mating for education using US census data by comparing observed fertility levels with those expected under random mating. He found that assortative mating for education in white people led to modest increases in fertility at most educational levels while in non-white people there was evidence of decreases in fertility at most levels. Garrison *et al.* (1968) also used US census data and showed that positively assortative marriages for educational attainment produced more children than negatively assortative marriages, mostly because a larger percentage of negatively assortative marriages were childless (Table 5.5).

Table 5.5. The relationship between educational attainment and fertility

Husband's educational level compared with his wife's level	Number of couples	Children per couple	% Childless
5 levels higher	4531	2.45	19.02±0.58
4 levels higher	25 068	2.35	16.72±0.24
3 levels higher	148 370	2.53	12.58±0.09
2 levels higher	787 716	2.53	11.54±0.04
1 level higher, lower or the same	7 172 501	2.63	10.51±0.01
2 levels lower	879 528	2.59	11.83±0.03
3 levels lower	286 589	2.47	13.80±0.06
4 levels lower	33 681	2.20	17.88±0.21
5 levels lower	6111	1.85	26.10±0.56
Totals	9 344 095	2.61	10.92

Mascie-Taylor (1986) using a British national sample also examined the relationship between educational homogamy and fertility; no childless couples were included because the survey was set up to examine all children born in a specific week of March 1958. The children and aspects of the family life were re-examined at regular intervals, in 1965, 1969, 1974, and 1982. The fertility data were collected in 1974 when the mothers' average age was 44 years and every woman would have had at least one child born 16 years previously; at that time the data would reflect completed fertility for nearly all mothers. Each parent provided information on the number of years spent in full-time education. The absolute difference in years of education was calculated. Very few couples differed by more than 3 years in the number of years of full-time education and those that did were included in the 3-year category. The mean fertility by educational difference (4 categories, 0, and 1–3) are presented in Table 5.6. The results show that increasing similarity in education is associated with more children.

Table 5.6. Relationship between educational attainment and fertility in a British national sample

Educational similarity	Difference in fertility from overall mean	
	Uncorrected	Corrected for confounding variables
No difference	+0.13	+0.07
1 year	−0.11	−0.04
2 years	−0.31	−0.23
3+ years	−0.44	−0.26

These findings could be confounded by the effects of age, social class, and education. Consequently, the analyses were re-run after removing (by multiple regression) their effects. The results are also presented in Table 5.6; they show, even after allowing for the confounding variables, educationally more similar couples have more offspring than educationally more dissimilar matings.

Psychometric and anthropometric studies

Thiessen and Gregg (1980) in their review on assortative mating incorrectly state that Spuhler (1967) showed a relationship between assortative mating and fertility. Spuhler showed in his Ann Arbor sample that there was: (a) significant assortative mating and (b) a relationship between IQ score and fertility in mothers, but not fathers; however, he did not relate the extent of assortative mating and fertility.

However, Spuhler in association with Clark (Spuhler 1962; Spuhler 1968; Clark and Spuhler 1959) did relate physical similarity of couples to their fertility and showed for one measurement, wrist circumference, a significant correlation with fertility ($r = +0.175$, $P < 0.05$). In total 29 traits were studied and only one was significant, which is of course close to chance expectations! Part of the failure to show any 'significant relationship' between similarity of couples and fertility lies in the measure of similarity used by Spuhler and Clark. They computed a similarity index, which was the ratio of the husband's measurement to the sum of the husband's and wife's measurements, that is

$$\text{Similarity index} = \frac{H}{H + W}$$

The similarity indices for five imaginary couples are presented in Table 5.7. Couples with exactly the same height have a similarity index of 0.50. When husbands are taller than their wives the index is above 0.5 (couples 1 and 2) and when wives are taller than their husbands the index is below 0.5 (couples 4 and 5). Spuhler and Clark computed, in effect, the linear relationship between fertility and this index and found, in general, no significant effect. What should have been

Table 5.7. Computation of Spuhler's Similarity Index for Stature

Couple	Husband	Wife	Sum of statures	Similarity index
1	180	150	330	0.55
2	170	165	335	0.51
3	165	165	330	0.50
4	160	165	325	0.49
5	160	180	340	0.47

plotted or fitted was a curvilinear relationship because couples further away from 0.5 (either above or below) should have fewer children and those closer to 0.5 should have more children. Thus the significant relationship between wrist circumference and fertility purported by Spuhler is not correct; in reality Spuhler found that as the husband's wrist circumference became larger relative to their wife's wrist circumference, so fertility increased.

There are a number of more realistic measures of similarity which can be used. For instance, the absolute difference between spouses' scores or dimensions would provide a crude estimate, assuming there was no sex difference in mean values. Alternatively, the normalized difference could be calculated which corrects for disparity between means and variances. Mascie-Taylor and Boldsen (1988) computed the difference (d) between spouses using the normal deviate formula shown here:-

$$d = \frac{\left[\left(H - \left(\overline{H} / SD_H\right)\right) - \left(W - \left(\overline{W} / SD_W\right)\right)\right]}{\sqrt{2 - 2r_{HW}}}$$

where H and W refer to the husband's and wife's heights, $\overline{H}$ and $\overline{W}$ to the corresponding sample averages and SD_H and SD_W to the estimated standard deviations and r_{HW} is the correlation coefficient.

They used this measure to examine the relationship between stature and fertility in the British national cohort described earlier. Since fertility shows social class (occupation), regional differences, and family size correlates with age of the parents, the effects of these three variables were removed before determining the relationship between the absolute value of d and fertility. The results showed a small but highly significant association between husband–wife stature difference and fertility; increasing spousal similarity for height was associated with increasing number of liveborn children.

In addition, Mascie-Taylor and Boldsen (1988) examined the relationship between d and abnormal pregnancy outcome. The proportion of couples having experienced an abnormal pregnancy outcome prior to 1958 (when the index child was born) was 0.208. A polynomial regression of the form, $Y = a + bX + cX^2$, was used where Y is the frequency of abnormal pregnancies and X is equal to d. The analyses revealed a significant quadratic term and an insignificant linear term. The polynomial curve is presented in Fig. 5.2 and clearly demonstrates that as the husband–wife stature difference increases so does the probability of having an abnormal pregnancy outcome.

Genetic and evolutionary effects

The genetic and evolutionary effects of Mascie-Taylor and Boldsen's (1988) results are that selection is acting against couples whose children would show

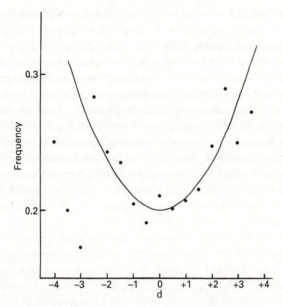

Fig. 5.2 The relationship between pregnancy loss and the differences in husband–wife stature (d).

increased levels of heterozygosity; this is assuming that the phenotypic similarity is a true measure of the underlying genotypic similarity for stature. This mode of selection, which has been demonstrated in plants and animals, is called disruptive selection (Mather 1953). The long-term effects of disruptive selection are that it will increase the variance of a trait and can lead to sympatric speciation (Thoday 1972). However, its role in the evolution of human populations remains unclear especially since the correlations with fitness observed by Mascie-Taylor and Boldsen may be the result of transient social or cultural factors and not some inherent species attribute.

The effect of assortative mating on the genetic composition of populations has been discussed by Crow and Felsenstein (1968). For polygenic systems (and as we saw earlier there is little evidence for assortative mating for characters determined by single genes) there are five potential effects: (a) no change in gene frequencies will occur; (b) the frequency of genotypes giving rise to more extreme phenotypes will increase; (c) there will be a concomitant decline in heterozygosity; (d) there will be an increase in population variance; and (e) parent–child and sib–sib associations will increase.

There have been a number of attempts to explain the evolutionary significance and importance of assortative mating. The Genetic Similarity Theory based on kin selection was first put forward by Rushton *et al.* in 1984. A fuller version of this theory was published in *Brain and Behavioural Sciences* (Rushton 1989) together with commentaries from specialists in a number of fields including zoology, psychology, and biological anthropology. The theory posits that a gene ensures its own survival by acting so as to bring about the reproduction of any organism in which copies of itself are to be found. The theory has been widely criticized for a large number of reasons and rather than laboriously detail them here, readers are requested to look at the commentary following Rushton's 1989 article.

Buss (1989) discussed the evolutionary implications of sex differences in human mate preference. He reported, using data from a wide variety of cultures, that females valued resource acquisition in potential mates more highly than males while characteristics signalling reproductive capacity were valued more by males than females. Reference has already been made to Kenrick and Keefe's (1992) studies on age differences between spouses (see p. 88) and the potential evolutionary consequences of such mating patterns.

Thiessen and Gregg (1980) suggest that there is a compromise between the positive and negative effects of assortative mating. They argue that 'individuals optimize gene transmission by mating with others sharing genes in common. The flow of altruistic behaviours … and the genetic benefits of positive assortative mating are linked to the degree with which interacting individuals share homologous genes'. Thus assortative mating will increase the genetic homology between offspring and parent. The magnitude of the increase above 50 per cent (the value expected under random mating) is dependent upon the level of assortative mating. The negative aspect is that very high levels of homozygosity can lead to inbreeding depression. Consequently, for characters with a high additive variance component one would expect to see low levels of assortative mating (e.g. height and IQ), and for traits with low additive genetic variance the expectation would be for high levels of assortative mating (e.g. social class).

There is some evidence from human populations that this compromise between assortative mating and inbreeding occurs. Crognier (1977) studied the Sara Madjingay tribe from southern Chad in Africa and found that the assortative mating for 33 anthropometric characters was higher among unrelated couples than among related couples. Among unrelated couples no negative correlations were found, but among related couples one-third were negative. Crognier concluded that 'when marriages are arranged in relation to kinship, assortative mating with respect to physical features seems to become if not non-existent, at least of secondary importance. As we have seen, the results obtained from the ordinary unrelated pairs, give, on the contrary, strong evidence for such assortative mating'.

Conclusions

This chapter has provided a brief review of the empirical evidence for assortative mating in humans. The results suggest low to moderate levels of assortative mating for anthropometric and psychometric characters, such as height, IQ, and personality traits and moderate to high levels of assortative mating for characters with little or no heritability such as educational attainment, social class, and smoking habit.

Hardly any data are available on couples prior to marriage and many of the spousal associations are measured at some arbitrary point during the marriage. Consequently, it is very difficult to know whether or not the observed spousal association represents the result of mate selection *per se* or the result of convergence. In addition a random sample of couples may well exclude the more dissimilar pairs who will have separated or divorced. Longitudinal studies of couples would provide answers to these doubts.

Many studies have reported significant spousal correlations for a large number of characters, but there is statistical evidence that much of the observed association, particularly for psychometric traits results from propinquity and not active mate choice. Studies must be devised which separate propinquity from active mate choice.

Although there is some evidence for a relationship between positive assortative mating for educational attainment and differential fertility, there is little or no evidence for most anthropometric and all psychometric traits. Further studies are needed to test whether increasing spousal similarity and differential fertility are correlated.

The genetic consequences of assortative mating have been well documented theoretically and in non-human species. However, the practical impact and evolutionary consequences of assortative mating in humans is still under very active discussion and it is too early to draw definitive conclusions.

References

Bossard, H. S. (1932). Residential propinquity as a factor in marriage reflection. *Marriage and Family Living,* **23**, 234–40.

Bouchard, T. J. and McGue, M. G. (1981). Familial studies of intelligence: a review. *Science,* **212**, 1055–9.

Burgess, E. W. and Wallin, P. (1953). *Engagement and marriage.* J. P. Lippincott, New York.

Buss, D. M. (1989). Sex differences in human mate preferences: evolutionary hypotheses tested in 37 cultures. *Behavioral and Brain Sciences,* **12**, 1–49.

Carter, H. D. (1932). Family resemblances in verbal and numerical abilities. *Genetic Psychology Monographs,* **12**, 1–104.

Cattell, R. B. and Nesselroade, J. R. (1967). Likeness and completeness theories examined by 16PF measures on stably and unstably married couples. *Journal of Personality and Social Psychology,* **7**, 351–61.

Cavalli-Sforza, L. L. and Bodmer, W. F. (1971). *The genetics of human populations.* Freeman, San Francisco.

Centers, R. (1949). Occupational endogamy in marital selection. *American Journal of Sociology,* **54**, 530–5.

Clark, A. C. and Spuhler, J. N. (1959). Differential fertility in relation to body dimensions. *Human Biology,* **31,** 121–37.

Clark, M. S. and Reis, H. T. (1988). Interpersonal processes in close relationships. *Annual Review of Psychology,* **39,** 609–72.

Coleman, D. A. (1982). The population structure of an urban area in Britain. (ed. M. H. Crawford and J. H. Mielke), *Current developments in anthropological genetics,* **2:** Ecology and population structure, pp. 467–506. New York.

Crognier, E. (1977). Assortative mating for physical features in an African population from Chad. *Journal of Human Evolution,* **6,** 105–14.

Crow, J. F. and Felsenstein, J. (1968). The effect of assortative mating on the genetic composition of a population. *Eugenics Quarterly,* **15,** 85–97.

Eckland, B. K. (1970). New mating boundaries in education. *Social Biology,* **17,** 269–77.

Galton, F. (1869). *Hereditary genius.* Macmillan, London.

Garrison, R. J., Anderson, W. E., and Reed, S. C. (1968). Assortative marriage. *Eugenics Quarterly,* **15,** 113–27.

Girard, A. (1964). *Le choix du conjoint.* Presses Universitaires de France, Paris.

Gregory, I. (1959). Husbands and wives admitted to mental hospital. *Journal of Mental Science,* **105,** 457–562.

Guze, S. B., Goodwin, D. W., and Crane, J. B. (1970). A psychiatric study of the wives of convicted felons: an example of assortative mating. *American Journal of Psychiatry,* **126,** 115–18.

Hall, D. J., Baldwin, J. A., and Robertson, N. C. (1971). Mental illness in married pairs: problems in estimating incidence. In *Aspects of the epidemiology of mental illness: studies in record linkage,* Vol. 8 (ed. J. A. Baldwin), pp. 24–39. Little, Brown and Co., Boston.

Harrison, G. A., Gibson, J. B., Hiorns, R. W., Wrigley, J. M., Hancock, C., Freeman, C. A., *et al.* (1974). Psychometric, personality and anthropometric variation in a group of Oxfordshire villages. *Annals of Human Biology,* **1,** 365–81.

Heath, A. C. and Eaves, L. J. (1985). Resolving the effects of phenotype and social background on mate selection. *Behavior Genetics,* **15,** 15–30.

Hollingshead, A. B. (1949). Class and kinship in a Middle Western community. *American Sociological Review,* **14,** 469–75.

Hollingshead, A. B. (1950). Cultural factors in the selection of marriage mates. *American Sociological Review,* **15,** 619–27.

Jacob, T. and Bremer, D. A. (1986). Assortative mating among men and women alcoholics. *Journal of Studies in Alcohol,* **47,** 219–22.

Jacquard, A. (1970). *The genetic structure of populations.* Springer-Verlag, Heidelberg.

Jeffries, D. J., Harrison, G. A., Hiorns, R. W., and Gibson, J. B. (1976). A note on marital distances and movement, and age at marriage, in a group of Oxfordshire villages. *Journal of Biosocial Science,* **8,** 155–60.

Jensen, A. R. (1978). Genetic and behavioural effects of non-random mating. In *Human variation: the biopsychology of age, race and sex* (ed. C.E. Noble, R. T. Osborne, and E. N. Wekyl), pp. 51–105. Academic Press, New York.

Johnson, R. C., Ahern, F. M., and Cole, R. E. (1980). Secular change in degree of assortative mating for ability. *Behavior Genetics,* **10,** 1–8.

Jones, H. E. (1929). Homogamy in intellectual abilities. *American Journal of Sociology,* **35,** 369–82.

Kennedy, R. J. R. (1944). Single or triple melting pot? Intermarriage trends in New Haven, 1870–1940. *American Journal of Sociology,* **49**, 331–339.

Kenrick, D. T. and Keefe, R. C. (1992). Age preferences in mates reflect sex differences in human reproductive strategies. *Behavioral and Brain Science,* **15**, 75–133.

Kephart, W. M. (1977). *Family, society, and the individual.* Houghton-Mifflin, Boston.

Kiser, C. B. (1968). Assortative mating by educational attainment in relation to fertility. *Eugenics Quarterly,* **15**, 98–112.

Kreitman, N. (1962). Mental disorder in married couples. *Journal of Mental Science,* **108**, 438–46.

Kreitman, N. (1968). Married couples admitted to mental hospital. *British Journal of Psychiatry,* **114**, 699–718.

Küchemann, C. F., Harrison, G. A., Hiorns, R. W., and Carravick, R. J. (1974). Social class and marital distance in Oxford City. *Annals of Human Biology,* **1**, 13–27.

Lewis, D. O., Balla, D., Shanok, S., and Snell, L. (1976). Delinquency, parental psychopathology and parental criminality. Clinical and epidemiological findings. *Journal of the American Academy of Child Psychiatry,* **13**, 663–78.

Lutz, E. E. (1905). Assortative mating in man. *Science,* **22**, 249–50.

Mascie-Taylor, C. G. N. (1977). *Gene flow and divergence in Drosophila and man.* PhD thesis. University of Cambridge.

Mascie-Taylor, C. G. N. (1986). Assortative mating and differential fertility. *Biology and Society,* **3**, 167–70.

Mascie-Taylor, C. G. N. (1987). Assortative mating in a contemporary British population. *Annals of Human Biology,* **14**, 59–68.

Mascie-Taylor, C. G. N. (1988). Assortative mating for psychometric characters. In *Human mating patterns* (ed. C. G. N. Mascie-Taylor and A. J. Boyce), pp. 61–82. Cambridge University Press.

Mascie-Taylor, C. G. N. (1989). Spousal similarity and convergence. *Behavior Genetics,* **19**, 223–7.

Mascie-Taylor, C. G. N. and Boldsen, J. L. (1988). Assortative mating, differential fertility and abnormal pregnancy outcome. *Annals of Human Biology,* **15**, 223–8.

Mascie-Taylor, C. G. N. and J. B. Gibson (1979). Assortative marriage and IQ components. *Annals of Human Biology,* **6**, 1–16.

Mascie-Taylor, C. G. N. and Vandenberg, S. G. (1988). Assortative mating for IQ and personality due to propinquity and personal preference. *Behavior Genetics,* **18**, 339–43.

Mascie-Taylor, C. G. N., Harrison, G. A., Hiorns, R. W., and Gibson, J. B. (1987). Husband-wife similarities in different components of the WAIS 1Q test. *Journal of Biosocial Science,* **19**, 149–55.

Mather, K. (1953). The genetical structure of populations. *Symposium of the Society of Experimental Biology,* **7**, 66–97.

Merikangas, K. R. (1982). Assortative mating for psychiatric disorders and psychological traits. *Archives of General Psychiatry,* **39**, 1173–80.

Murstein, B. I. (1976). *Who will marry whom? Theories of research in marital choice.* Springer Verlag, New York.

Nagoshi, C. T., Johnson, R. C., and Ahern, F.M. (1987). Phenotypic assortative mating vs. social homogamy among Japaneses and Chinese parents in the Hawaii Family Study of Cognition. *Behavior Genetics,* **17**, 477–85.

Nielsen, J. (1964). Mental disorders in married couples (assortative mating). *British Journal of Psychiatry,* **110**, 683–97.

Pearson, K. (1903). Assortative mating in man. *Biometrika,* **2**, 481–98.

Pearson, K. and Heron, D. (1913). On theories of association. *Biometrika,* **8,** 159–315.

Penrose, L. S. (1944). Mental illness in husband and wife: a contribution to the study of assortative mating in man. *Psychiatric Quarterly,* **18**, (suppl.). 161–6.

Plomin, R., DeFries, J. C., and Roberts, M. K. (1977). Assortative mating by unwed biological parents of adopted children. *Science,* **196**, 449–50.

Price, R. A. and Vandenberg, S. G. (1980). Spouse similarity in American and Swedish couples. *Behavior Genetics,* **10**, 59–71.

Richardson, H. M. (1939). Studies of mental resemblance between husbands and wives and between friends. *Psychological Bulletin,* **36**, 104–120.

Roberts, D. F. (1977). Assortative mating in man: husband and wife correlations in physical characteristics. *Bulletin of the Eugenics Society,* Supplement 2.

Rockwell, R. C. (1976). Historical trends and variation in educational homogamy. *Journal of Marriage and the Family,* **38**, 83–95.

Rushton, J. P. (1989). Genetic similarity, human altruism, and group selection. *Behavioral and Brain Sciences,* **12**, 503–559.

Rushton, J. P., Russell, R. J., and Wells, P. A. (1984). Genetic similarity theory: beyond kin selection. *Behavior Genetics,* **14**, 179–93.

Salzano, F. M. and Freire-Maia, N. (1970). *Problems in human biology, a study of Brazilian populations.* Wayne State University Press, Detroit.

Smith, M. (1946). A research note on homogamy of marriage partners in selected physical characteristics. *American Sociological Review,* **11**, 226–228.

Spuhler, J. N. (1962). Empirical studies on quantitative human genetics. In *The use of vital and health statistics for genetic and radiation studies,* pp. 241–68. United Nations, New York.

Spuhler, J. N. (1967). Behavior and mating patterns in human populations. In *Genetic diversity and human behavior* (ed. J. N. Spuhler). Aldine, Chicago.

Spuhler, J. N. (1968). Assortative mating with respect to physical characteristics. *Eugenics Quarterly,* **15**,128–40.

Spuhler, J. N. and Clark, P. J. (1961). Migration into the human breeding population of Ann Arbor, Michigan 1900–1950. *Human Biology,* **33**, 223–36.

Stern, C. (1973). *Principles of human genetics.* Freeman, San Francisco.

Susanne, C. and Lepage, D. Y. (1988). Assortative mating for anthropometric characters. In *Human mating patterns* (ed. C. G. N. Mascie-Taylor, and A.J. Boyce), pp. 83–99. Cambridge University Press.

Thiessen, D. and B. Gregg (1980). Human assortative mating and genetic equilibrium: an evolutionary perspective. *Ethology and Sociobiology,* **1**, 111–40.

Thoday, J. M. (1972). Disruptive selection. *Proceedings of the Royal Society B,* **182**, 109–42.

Vandenberg, S. G. (1972). Assortative mating or who marries whom? *Behavior Genetics,* **2**, 127–58.

Warren, B. L. (1966). A multiple variable approach to the assortative mating phenomenon. *Eugenics Genetics,* **13**, 285–90.

Watkins, M.P. and Meredith, W. (1981). Spouse similarity in newlyweds with respect to specific cognitive abilities, socio-economic status, and education. *Behavior Genetics,* **11**, 1–21.

Weissman, M.M., Kidd, K. K., and Prusoff, B. A. (1984). Variability in the rates of affective disorders in the relatives of severe and mild major non-bipolar depressives and normals. *Archives of General Psychiatry,* **39**, 1397–403.

Winch, R. F. (1958). *Mate selection, a study of complementary needs.* Harper Bros. New York.

Wolanski, N. (1973). Assortative mating in the Polish rural population. *Studies in Human Ecology,* **1**, 182–194.

Woolf, C. M. and Dukepoo, F. C. (1969). Hopi Indians, inbreeding and albinism. *Science,* **164**, 30–7.

Zonderman, A. B., Vandenberg, S. G., Spuhler, K. P., and Fein, P. R. (1977). Assortative marriage of cognitive abilities. *Behavior Genetics,* **7**, 261–71.

6
Using within-populational variability to measure environmental optimality and adaptability

L. H. SCHMITT

Understanding the nature and significance of variability within and between human populations is a primary concern of biological anthropology. A difficult but commonly encountered problem is trying to determine the influence of genes and environment on interpopulational differences. Biometrical genetic models are concerned with assessing variability within populations and are not designed for determining the origins of differences between populations. This chapter illustrates that, by making an assumption about the nature of genetic variability within populations, the effects of the environment on population differences can be assessed.

Genetic data of a populational nature are often analysed from the perspective of the quantity and pattern of variability within populations. There is considerable literature on the degree of heterozygosity in populations and differences between populations, species, and higher taxonomic ranks. Morphological and other metric characters on the other hand are less frequently considered from a within-population variability perspective, with some obvious exceptions, especially heritability studies. This, of course, does not deny the use of character variances to estimate standard errors, but here the interest is primarily in measuring accuracy and making inferences about means rather than in the biological interpretation of the variances themselves. Some other studies that do focus on the level of within-population metrical variability include investigations of its relationship with levels of heterozygosity, and studies of fluctuating asymmetry to measure the effects of environmental perturbation.

The level of morphometric variability within populations is usually considered through the quantitative genetic models that partition the variance into genetic and non-genetic or environmental determinants, and interactions and correlations between these effects. It has been argued elsewhere (Hiernaux 1963; Harrison 1987; Schmitt 1989) that the absolute genetic contribution to the total phenotypic variance of a trait will not usually vary greatly among populations. Hence differences between populations in the level of variability found within them will largely be due to environmental effects, in particular the level of environmental diversity. In addition, the quality or optimality of the environment will influence the level of phenotypic diversity within a population, since a poor environment will make the maintenance of homeostasis and homeorhesis difficult, leading to greater variability among individuals.

This chapter describes three examples where the comparative analysis of anthropometric variances within populations is used to gain an insight into the optimality of the environment and the significance of physiological changes associated with extreme environmental conditions. Two of these analyses are concerned with birthweight and growth velocity variability in Aboriginal Australians, a group of people who are experiencing a rapid acculturation process. In a third analysis, variances are used to assess the adaptive significance of haematological changes associated with altitude.

Growth velocity variability in Aboriginal Australians

As part of an intervention trial into the effects of zinc supplementation on growth, Smith and Spargo measured the stature of about 700 Aboriginal Australian children living in the Kimberley region of Western Australia. This is a remote region in the most northerly part of the State with an Aboriginal population of about 15 000. Many Aboriginal people live in isolated communities ranging in size from about 50 to 400 individuals, while others live in or near the larger regional towns. Since the European settlement of Australia, Aboriginal people have experienced a series of transitions in their life-styles. In recent years, especially in remote communities, this transition has been particularly rapid, fuelled by changes in State and Commonwealth Governmental policies and practices, and resulting in the adoption of many aspects of a 'Western' life-style. Associated with this rapid acculturation process have been dramatic changes in health. Morbidity and mortality rates for Aboriginal Australians are much higher than for non-Aboriginal Australians and this is particularly true of the so-called life-style diseases. This is a picture seen in other parts of the world where traditional peoples have had their land colonized by Europeans.

Relative to non-Aboriginal Australians, the growth of Aboriginal people is typified by low birthweight, followed by a high weight gain in the first 6 months of life and lower than normal growth thereafter (Kettle 1966). This growth pattern is usually interpreted as the result of malnutrition and the poor living conditions experienced by many Aboriginal people. However, it has always been difficult to eliminate the possibility that genetic differences contribute substantially to the differences in growth.

Most of the children who participated in the zinc trial were measured on more than one occasion between 1981 and 1984, and all measurements were taken by one person, Dr R. M. Smith, who kindly provided the raw data. The zinc trial was double-blind and there was no evidence that zinc supplementation influenced growth (Smith *et al.* 1985). The measurements used here were taken in June–July 1981, September 1982, October–November 1983, and December 1984. Annual stature velocities were calculated for those consecutive measurements that were within 2 months of exactly 1 year apart. All velocity measurements were calculated from periods greater than 12 months. Linear interpolation was used to compute exact 12-month velocities for each individual. Each velocity was assigned to an age class according to the age of the individual at the mid-point of the two measurements that contributed to the velocity. Age classes were centred on integer values: for example 6 years includes 5.5–6.5 years. The mean and standard deviation of each age class were then computed.

Figure 6.1 shows the standard deviation of stature velocity for Aboriginal males and for comparative purposes, three other data sets used by Harrison and

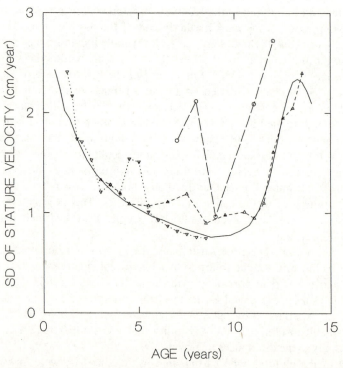

Fig. 6.1 Plot of standard deviation of yearly stature velocity (cm/year) against age in Australian Aboriginal (— — —), British (—), Indian (– – –), and Thai (·····) children.

Schmitt (1989). These are the British standards of Tanner *et al.* (1966*a,b*), rural Thailand data of Bailey *et al.* (1984), and semi-urban Indian data of Hauspie *et al.* (1980). Only standard deviations based on sample sizes greater than 30 are plotted. For the Australian data, the sample size for each age category varied between 32 and 40. At comparable ages the Australian values are larger than those found in any of the other studies and the female data show a similar pattern.

There are statistical factors that could contribute to this difference. Variances are usually correlated with their mean and so some standardization for mean differences is desirable. Unfortunately, there is no entirely satisfactory way of making this standardization. The coefficient of variation has often been used in such circumstances, but its valid use relies on assumptions that are difficult to test. In particular, it assumes that the relationship between the mean and standard deviation is linear and that the regression of standard deviation on the mean passes through the origin. For the Australian data analysed here, the mean annual velocity is, perhaps surprisingly, greater than either of the three comparative data sets. However, the coefficient of variation shows a similar pattern to the standard deviation, with the Australian values generally being considerably greater then those observed in the other three studies. It seems unlikely that the differences in standard deviation are due to differences in the means.

Another source of variance in these data is an effect of age 'classes': the grouping of ages into whole year bins such that each bin contains children varying in age up to 6 months either side of the class mid-point. Since velocity is changing, this pooling creates a greater variance for a given class than would be observed if all individuals were of exactly the same age, which occurs, for example, when they are all measured on or near their birthday. Healy (1962) defined the correction required for the variance of achieved growth and this has been adapted and applied to the Australian velocity data on the assumption that the changes in velocity are linear within a yearly age group. This correction reduces the variance by a trivial fraction, usually affecting only the second or third decimal place of the estimate of the standard deviation.

Seasonal variation in growth can also influence the velocity variances (Goldstein 1979). The measurements used in the Australian study were taken over 4 years and observations were recorded in six different months in the different years. Any additional variance due to one set of measurements being made at a time of particularly rapid growth will be averaged out by times when growth was less rapid and therefore less variable. Thus these data should, in this regard, be comparable with other studies where measurements were made throughout the calender year.

There is at least one factor which leads to an underestimate of the variability in these Australian data. For all the measurements analysed here, the time difference between measurements from which velocity is estimated is greater than 1 year. This reduces the contribution of periods of rapid or slow growth to velocity variability. Velocities calculated from observations taken over short periods lead to higher variances than those taken over longer periods (Tanner *et al.* 1966*b*). For the velocities calculated from the first period, 1981–82, the mean number of days elapsing between the two measurement times was 412.5 days (minimum 411 and maximum 414). For the second period, 1982–83, the mean was 414.5 days (411–420) and for the third period, 1983–84, the mean was 399.4 days (395–403). Furthermore, the reported standard deviations were computed by pooling the variances obtained in the three periods when velocities were estimated. Pooling did not substantially alter the results obtained, nor did it change substantially if the analysis was made on velocities calculated from time differences of 10–12 months.

Is it high environmental variability or adversity or both that contribute to the high Kimberley growth variance? The area is located in the wet–dry tropics. One striking feature of this physical environment is its apparent constancy over the short- and medium-term but a marked contrast between the two seasons. This raises the possibility that longer-term environmental fluctuations (i.e. twice yearly) may be adding to the growth variance. This possible effect could be tested by comparing growth variability over shorter times during the different seasons and at the seasonal changes. However, even more striking than this variation, is the adverse public health environment in which most Aboriginal people of the Kimberley live. The standards of housing, primary health care and nutrition are mostly far below that experienced by other Australians.

Finally, the number of observations on which these analyses are based, is barely adequate for anything but the most simplistic approach used here. Despite this, they show a quite marked effect and, perhaps more importantly, the potential for similar analyses on more extensive data for detecting environmental impacts on growth differences.

Birthweight variability in Western Australia

The use of growth velocity variability to assess environmental optimality is hampered by a paucity of appropriate data. In the study described above, over 700 children in the Kimberley region were measured and this provided just a few 1-year age classes for each sex that had sample sizes between 30 and 40. Furthermore, variances are far more difficult to measure accurately than means; for a normally distributed character, the variance of the estimate of the variance is proportional to the true variance squared.

Growth velocity reflects an individual's recent environmental history. Birthweight, like growth velocity, has determining factors that have acted in the very recent past, and is sensitive to environmental disturbance. Birthweight has the added advantage that records are often kept and collated by government instrumentalities and therefore recordings of substantial numbers can sometimes be obtained. Furthermore, these often extend over long periods of time, so that secular trends may be observed. Birthweight data have the distinct disadvantage that the recordings are not usually taken by the same individual, nor always with the same experimental accuracy.

The Health Department of the State Government of Western Australia supervises a Midwives' Notification System which records all births of a gestational age of 20 weeks or more in the State. It is a statutory requirement that information on all births is recorded and it is believed that the system collects information on nearly all births in the State. Kliewer and Stanley (1989) tabulated the distribution of birthweight by gestational age, sex, and race (of the mother) of all live births for the period 1980–86. This represented a total of 158 729 births, about 5 per cent of which were to Aboriginal mothers and will be referred to as 'Aboriginal', the others as 'non-Aboriginal' (largely European ancestry), although the degree of admixture in each group is undetermined. The sample sizes for females are presented in Table 6.1.

Aboriginal births at term (37–41 weeks gestation) are characterized by a lower mean birthweight than that found in the non-Aboriginal group. However, there is an interesting gestational-age pattern, with Aboriginal live births prior to about 35 weeks gestation being heavier than non-Aboriginal live births, while the opposite is true for longer gestational times. This may be due to between-group bias in the recall of the date of the last menstrual period, which was used to estimate gestational length. Similar differences between groups have been observed in US statistics (Wilcox 1981). While the accuracy of the gestational age determinations in the two groups has been questioned (Lancaster 1989), it seems clear that, at term, female Aboriginal liveborns are smaller than their non-Aboriginal counterparts and a similar pattern is seen in males.

A second marked difference between the two groups is that pre-term births were more frequent for Aboriginal than non-Aboriginal mothers. Indeed, Aboriginal births constituted about 13 per cent of all live births up to about 33 weeks gestation and this value gradually declined to less than 5 per cent at term (Fig. 6.2). There also appears to be a clear difference between the sexes in this trend.

The interpretation of such data is, of course, problematical. It was argued by Kliewer and Stanley (1989) that both environmental and genetic factors may be responsible for the differences between the groups. Similar difficulties are experienced when interpreting the lower Aboriginal postnatal growth rates (with the exception of about the first 6 months of life) compared with Europeans, which is particularly evident in remote Kimberley communities (Gracey *et al.* 1983). An examination of the variance of birthweight provides a different perspective. The standard deviation of birthweight for females by gestational age is shown in Fig. 6.3. The plot for males is very similar. It is clear in these graphs that for term births, the standard deviation of birthweight is considerably greater for Aboriginal than non-Aboriginal live births. At other gestational ages, the difference is not as marked. Indeed for births between 31 and

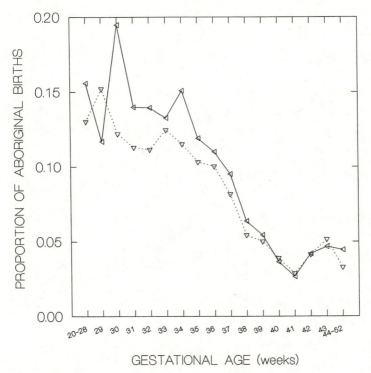

Fig. 6.2 The proportion of Aboriginal births by gestational age in Western Australia, 1980–86 (adapted from Kliewer and Stanley 1989). Females, ◁; males, ▽.

36 weeks gestation, non-Aboriginal female variances are the greater, but this trend is not seen in males, where, with the exception of 35 weeks gestation, the non-Aboriginal values are lower in this period.

The differences in variance for term births could be the result of greater accuracy in determining gestational age in non-Aboriginal mothers. Lancaster (1989) has questioned the validity of gestational-age determination in Aboriginal mothers and casts serious doubts on the utility of these gestational-age estimates. To overcome this difficulty the variances of birthweight have been computed for all live births, irrespective of gestational age and for term births only (Table 6.2). For all live births, Aboriginal birthweight variances are about 30 per cent greater than those for non-Aboriginals of the same sex. For term births, which constitute the large majority of all live births, the difference is about 15 per cent. These variance ratios are statistically significant (all $P <$ 0.001, using a two-tailed F-test). The proportionately greater variance of birthweight for all Aboriginal births compared with term births only, is probably at least partly due to the smaller proportion of pre-term births in non-Aboriginal

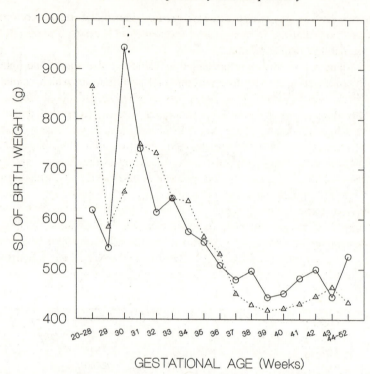

Fig. 6.3 The standard deviation of birthweight (g) of Aboriginal (O) and non-Aboriginal (△) female livebirths in Western Australia.

Table 6.2. Variance ($g^2 \times 10^{-3}$) of birthweight for sex and population group

	Females		Males	
Gestational age range (weeks)	37–41	20–52	37–41	20–52
Aboriginal	231	346	247	387
Non-Aboriginal	199	261	217	296

mothers. However, since the term births constitute the large majority of all births it seems unlikely that the difference arises solely from difficulties in assessing gestational age. In this data set, correcting the variances for mean differences would simply increase the populational differences, since the non-Aboriginal means are greater than the Aboriginal values. It is not known if factors such as parity and maternal age are confounding this difference. These data support the conclusion that the environmental variance contributing to

Aboriginal birthweight is considerably greater than that for non-Aboriginal birthweight and that the former group experience, on average, a more adverse set of pre-natal growth conditions.

The variances of birthweight presented in Table 6.2 also shed some light on sex differences in sensitivity to environmental perturbation, which cannot be due to difficulties in assessing gestational age. In both populational groups, for term births, males have a variance that is about 8 per cent greater than that of the females. When all gestational ages are considered, the male variance is about 12 per cent greater than females and again this is similar in both populational groups. These differences are statistically significant at the 0.1 per cent level, using a two-tailed *F*-test, with the exception of Aboriginal births at term ($P < 0.1$). This greater variability in males is expected if males are less able to maintain homeorhesis than females.

There is another aspect of these data that deserves consideration. Whereas in non-Aboriginal live births, the sex ratio is higher in the pre-term group than those at term, the ratio in Aboriginal live births appears relatively independent of gestational age at birth (Fig. 6.4). This very marked phenomenon may be due

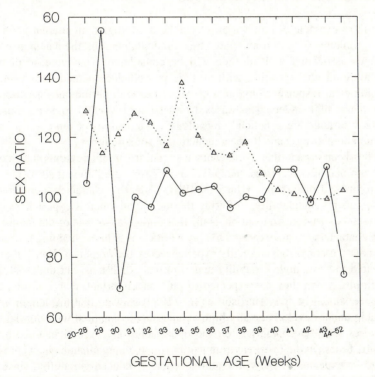

Fig. 6.4 The sex ratio by gestational age for Aboriginal(○) and non-Aboriginal(△) live births in Western Australia.

to several factors, including population-specific differences in primary sex ratio. Alternatively, or in addition, it may be due to a higher sex ratio in undetected Aboriginal losses very early in development, than in the non-Aboriginal group. There may be a subset of males in all populations who are particularly sensitive to suboptimal environmental conditions. If the developmental conditions for Aboriginal fetuses are, on average, poorer than for non-Aboriginal fetuses, then among this sensitive subset, more undetected losses may be expected to occur in the very early developmental period for Aboriginal than non-Aboriginal fetuses. This would have two effects. The secondary (live birth) sex ratio would be higher in non-Aboriginal births, since that population would be expected to experience a smaller proportion of undetected very early development male losses. Aboriginal births have a secondary sex ratio of 1.02 compared with 1.07 for non-Aboriginal births. In addition though, it may leave proportionately more non-Aboriginal male fetuses susceptible to later and detectable pre-term birth compared with the Aboriginal group, as is observed.

Haemoglobin variability at altitude

As a third example of how variances can be used to gain an alternative insight into problems of environmental stress and adaptation, the haematopoietic changes associated with altitude will be considered. The increase in mean haemoglobin concentration with altitude is well documented. However, the physiological response to hypoxia of visitors to high altitude differs markedly from native highlanders. This raises the question of whether some responses to living at altitude are beneficial physiological adaptations or represent a break-down in homeostasis and hence a reduction in somatic fitness.

It has been argued that some characters can, in simplistic terms, be categor-ized into one of two classes, 'adaptive' or 'fitness' based upon their response to environmental disturbance (Harrison 1963). Adaptive characters contribute to an organism's adaptability, buffering the individual when it experiences envi-ronmental extremes. An example is the thermoregulatory role of the mouse tail. Such characters are not expected to play a critical role in maintaining homeosta-sis under the conditions normally experienced by the organism. Hence they are expected to show high variability under normal conditions, but under stressful conditions, when they are expected to play an important adaptive role, their variance should be low. Harrison *et al.* (1959) showed that tail length is less variable under developmentally high temperatures compared with normal tem-peratures. Fitness characters, on the other hand, are crucial in maximizing somatic fitness in the usual environment in which an organism lives, where they would be expected to show low non-genetically induced variability, since any significant deviation from the optimal setting would lead to decreased viability. These characters can be considered to be specialized to the normal environment and under abnormal conditions the ability of the organism to maintain these characters at their optimal setting may break down, leading to an increase in their variability.

Polycythaemia is usually considered to be an adaptive character at high altitude, in the sense that it represents a physiologically beneficial response to low oxygen tension. Haemoglobin concentration is also, undoubtedly, a fitness character at or near sea level oxygen levels and this is a good example of the difficulty of assigning characters to only one or the other class. None the less, migrants to high altitude experience an increase in their haemoglobin concentration. Recently, the adaptive nature of this response has been questioned (e.g. Ballew *et al.* 1989), since native populations at altitude show only a modest level of polycythaemia. If the response reflects a breakdown in homeostasis and is not beneficial, then the variability of haemoglobin concentration should increase with altitude.

In a review of the published data for permanent residents of high altitude localities, Frisancho (1988) tabulated haemoglobin levels in 29 Andean and Himalayan groups. A plot (Fig. 6.5) of the standard deviation of haemoglobin concentration against altitude shows a strong positive trend ($r = 0.53$, $P = 0.01$).

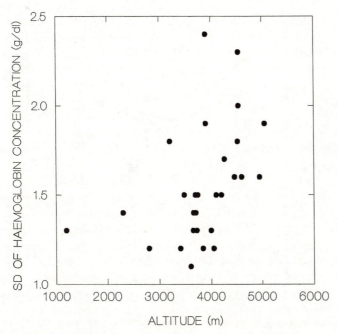

Fig. 6.5 The standard deviation of haemoglobin concentration (g/dl) by altitude for 29 Andean and Himalayan native populations (data from Frisancho 1988).

However, there is a strong relationship between the mean haemoglobin concentration and altitude ($r = 0.76$) as shown in Fig. 6.6. Does the variability relationship with altitude reflect the breakdown in control of a 'fitness' character or is it simply the result of an increasing mean value? A multiple regression (weighted by the square root of the sample size) of the standard deviation on both altitude and mean revealed that the partial regression coefficient for altitude was not significant. Using the partial pressure of oxygen in the inspired air rather than altitude gave almost identical results. Furthermore, there is no difference in the standard deviations of Himalayan and Andean populations. Because mean corrected variability of haemoglobin levels remain unchanged with increasing altitude, polycythaemia appears to be acting as both a fitness and an adaptive character in these populations.

The data analysed included two types of communities: mining and non-mining. Since many individuals who live in mining communities live under extreme conditions, as exemplified by an increased incidence of respiratory disease, they are more likely to experience a breakdown in homeostasis and a concomitant increase in variability compared with non-mining communities. While multiple regressions revealed that, on average, mining communities do

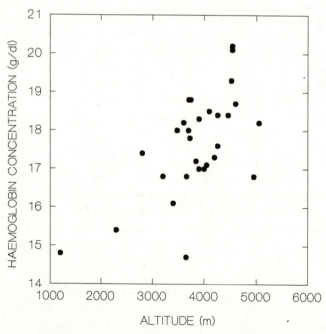

Fig. 6.6 The mean haemoglobin concentration (g/dl) by altitude for 29 Andean and Himalayan native populations.

have greater standard deviations of haemoglobin concentration, when corrections are made for altitude and the mean concentration, this difference does not reach statistical significance.

Similar analyses of recent immigrants could be undertaken to ascertain the mode of their response. If this response reflects a breakdown in homeostasis then, as a group, these newly arrived individuals would be expected to show high levels of variability.

Conclusions

The primary aim of this chapter has been to demonstrate the benefits of examining character variances within populations to an understanding of the impact of the environment on the developmental and homeostatic processes. Variances offer a distinctive and alternative view of the process of individual adaptation.

This methodology is predicated on the assumption that the genetic contribution to phenotypic variance is much the same in all human populations or, at least, that differences between populations in the absolute value of the genetic component are small compared with the environmental component. For such analyses to be effective, substantial sample sizes are required because, for a given sample size, the true variance is estimated with far less accuracy than the mean. Perhaps the greatest methodological difficulty is in making an appropriate correction for the effect of the size of the trait on variance. The method, in terms of estimating optimality, works best with characters that are labile and reflect the recent environmental history of the individual. Thus, birthweight and growth velocities are particularly amenable to such analyses. However, even adult values can be used to some effect (e.g. Schmitt and Harrison 1988; Pollard *et al.* 1991). In principle, by statistical control, the method can be made independent of the genetically determined mean differences between populations. Indeed, its value is in being able to distinguish the possible causes of populational differences in means, when these causes are uncertain. For example, the interpretation of interpopulational differences in childhood growth are hampered by the difficulty in distinguishing genetic and environmental causes. Under the assumption of no differences in the magnitude of genetic variability within the populations, variability differences must reflect environmental factors.

It has been proposed by Boyden (1970) that humans are, in some respects, maladapted to a 'Western' life-style. Some features of this maladaptation appear to reach a zenith in groups who have lived a traditional life-style until recently, when they have come in contact with aspects of a Western life-style. During the transitional phase when this life-style is taken up, these groups, of which Aboriginal Australians are one, show some of the deleterious health aspects of a modern life-style to a degree that is much more extreme than that shown by 'traditional' Western societies. This may be partly due to the rate of social and cultural change, since they have moved from an almost complete absence of these diseases to reach this state over a very short time, about one generation. The exploitation of variance differences between populations should provide a different perspective on the aetiology of these changes and the effects of a marginal environment on biological diversity.

Acknowledgements

R. M. Smith (Division of Human Nutrition, CSIRO) generously provided the original data for the Kimberley growth study and M. Gracey (Health Department of Western Australia) directed me to the study by Kliewer and Stanley. I am grateful to Robert Attenborough for comments on the manuscript.

References

Bailey, S. M., Gershoff, S. N., McGandy, R. B., Nondasuta, A., Tantiwongse, P., Suttapreyasri, D., Miller, J., and McCree, P. (1984). A longitudinal study of growth and maturation in rural Thailand. *Human Biology*, **56**, 530–57.

Ballew, C., Garruto, R. M., and Haas, J. D. (1989). High-altitude hematology: paradigm or enigma? In *Human population biology: a transdisciplinary science* (ed. M. A. Little and J. D. Haas), pp. 239–62. Oxford University Press, New York.

Boyden, S. V. (ed.) (1970). *The impact of civilization on the biology of Man*. Australian National University Press, Canberra.

Frisancho, A. R. (1988). Origins of differences in hemoglobin concentration between Himalayan and Andean populations. *Respiratory Physiology*, **72**, 13–18.

Goldstein, H. (1979). *The design and analysis of longitudinal studies*. Academic Press, London.

Gracey, M., Murray, H., Hitchcock, N. E., Owles, E. N., and Murphy, B. P. (1983). The nutrition of Australian Aboriginal infants and young children. *Nutrition Research*, **3**, 133–47.

Harrison, G. A. (1963). Temperature adaptation as evidenced by growth of mice. *Federation Proceedings*, **22**, 691–8.

Harrison, G. A. (1987). *Adaptability, fitness, and health*. The first Paul T. Baker Lecture. The Pennsylvania State University.

Harrison, G. A. and Schmitt, L. H. (1989). Variability in stature growth. *Annals of Human Biology*, **16**, 45–51.

Harrison, G. A., Morton, R. J., and Weiner, J. S. (1959). The growth in weight and tail length of inbred and hybrid mice reared at two different temperatures. I. Growth in weight. II. Tail length. *Philosophical Transactions of the Royal Society B*, **242**, 479–516.

Hauspie, R. C., Das, S. R., Preece, M. A., and Tanner, J. M. (1980). A longitudinal study of the growth in height of boys and girls of West Bengal (India) aged six months to 20 years. *Annals of Human Biology*, **7**, 429–41.

Healy, M. J. R. (1962). The effect of age-grouping on the distribution of a measurement affected by growth. *American Journal of Physical Anthropology*, **20**, 49–50.

Hiernaux, J. (1963). Heredity and environment: their influence on human morphology. *American Journal of Physical Anthropology*, **21**, 579–90.

Kettle, E. S. (1966). Weight and height curves for Australian Aboriginal infants and children. *Medical Journal of Australia*, **2**, 972–7.

Kliewer, E. V. and Stanley, F. J. (1989). Aboriginal and white births in Western Australia, 1980–1986. Part I: birth weight and gestational age. *Medical Journal of Australia*, **151**, 493–502.

Lancaster, P. A. L. (1989). Birth weight percentiles for Aborigines? *Medical Journal of Australia*, **151**, 489–90.

Pollard, T. M., Brush, G., and Harrison, G. A. (1991). Geographic distributions of within-population variability in blood pressure. *Human Biology*, **63**, 643–661.

Schmitt, L. H. (1989). Determinants of anthropometric variation within contemporary populations. In *The growing scope of human biology*. Proceedings of the Australasian Society for Human Biology, 2. (ed. L. H. Schmitt, L. Freedman, and N. W. Bruce), pp. 113–20. Centre for Human Biology, University of Western Australia, Nedlands.

Schmitt, L. H. and Harrison, G. A. (1988). Patterns in the within-population variability of stature and weight. *Annals of Human Biology*, **15**, 353–64.

Smith, R. M., King, R. A., Spargo, R. M., Cheek, D. B., Field, J. B., and Veitch, L. G. (1985). Growth-retarded Aboriginal children with low plasma zinc levels do not show a growth response to supplemental zinc. *Lancet*, **i**, 923.

Tanner, J. M., Whitehouse, R. H., and Takaishi, M. (1966*a*). Standards from birth to maturity for height, weight, height velocity, and weight velocity: British children, 1965. Part I. *Archives of Diseases in Childhood*, **41**, 454–71.

Tanner, J. M., Whitehouse, R. H., and Takaishi, M. (1966*b*). Standards from birth to maturity for height, weight, height velocity, and weight velocity: British children, 1965. Part II. *Archives of Diseases in Childhood*, **41**, 613–35.

Wilcox, A. J. (1981). Birth weight, gestation, and the fetal growth curve. *American Journal of Obstetrics and Gynecology*, **139**, 863–7.

7

Growth variation and comparative growth homeostasis

G. BRUSH

Introduction

This chapter is a summary of recent attempts to analyse variation in growth. The purpose is not to tabulate variance nor to use it to quantify statistical uncertainty, but to describe how variation accumulates during the process of growth. The results will indicate that a portion of the environmental contribution to growth variation is expected to accumulate in a distinctive pattern. This pattern will be modelled in an attempt to quantify the interaction between environmental conditions which disrupt growth and the ability of homeostatic mechanisms to compensate.

Simple models of length growth variation

Simple models have been devised that describe how components of length variance accumulate with growth (Brush and Harrison 1990). The models make use of increments known as 'accumulated increments'. Consider a cohort of children measured at an arbitrary time, t_0, and then at times t_1, t_2, ..., t_n. For each child, accumulated increments are computed as growth increments over the intervals t_0 to t_1, t_0 to t_2, ..., t_0 to t_n. As an example, if length were measured monthly from birth, the accumulated increments would be the gains in length from birth to 1 month, birth to 2 months, and so on. The method uses the starting point to set the mean and variance of a trait to zero. Observations on the subsequent accumulated increments allow for an examination of the relationship between mean and variance with growth. This relationship depends on the processes underlying growth and is different for the different components of growth. The following sections describe these patterns for the genetic, environmental, and measurement error components.

Genetic component

In an ideal world where the environment does nothing to hinder growth, and in which growth is a smooth process, that is, it is not pulsatile and is measured without error, the only variation present among children is that of the genetic potential for growth. Because each child is on and stays on its genetic growth track the monthly growth increments have a correlation of 1 from one to the next. This correlation ensures that the relationship between mean and the genetic variance, *G*, of the subsequent accumulated increments is that of a quadratic function in which the variance increases in proportion to the square of the mean (Brush and Harrison 1990), as in

$$G_t = g\overline{X}_t^2$$

In this equation, *g* represents the genetic variance of a unit accumulated increment. This implies that as long as the mean of the accumulated increments continues to increase so too will the variance, and at a rate which is faster than that of the mean. If growth were to stop the variance would not be lost but would be fixed at the level of the mean.

Environmental components

The environmental variance has been modelled in two forms, one which is controlled by homeostasis and another which is not. Homeostasis by definition is a control mechanism which attempts to remove deviations from normal variation. For height, growth deviations result from environmental insults that 'knock' a child off its growth track. Catch-up growth is the well-known homeostatic response. The former adds to the phenotypic variance and the latter removes it. With complete catch-up growth any enviromental variance in the population is eventually removed.

If there were no catch-up growth, environmentally caused variation would accumulate without check. If each insult were unrelated to all others, variance would increase in an additive, or linear relationship with mean growth, as in

$$E_{a,t} = e_a\overline{X}_t,$$

where $E_{a,t}$ is the additive environmental component of variance. The coefficient *e* is the amount of variance added when the mean accumulated increment equals 1. For length growth, this component is probably not very large because of the known control that homeostasis has on height. However, for traits such as skinfold, an additive component of environmental variation is hypothesized to comprise a larger proportion of the total.

With homeostasis, increases in enviromental variance are kept in check. However, because of the time lag between insult, growth retardation, and catch-up, some environmentally induced variation is always present. This variance is modelled as a constant that reflects an equilibrium between the input and removal of variation. The magnitude of this 'homeostatic constant' depends on the length of time a child spends in the 'homeostatic cycle', the period of time

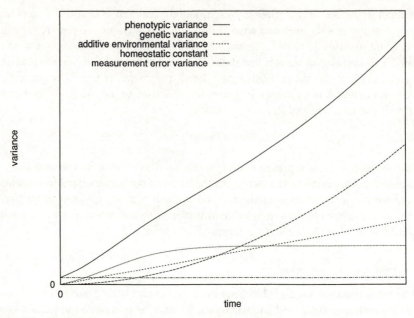

Fig. 7.1 Modelled components of length growth variation.

from the initial growth disturbance to full catch-up (Harrison and Brush 1990). The longer the homeostatic cycle, the larger the constant and, as such, the homeostatic constant is a measure of the quality of the environment and the efficiency of the homeostatic control.

When observing accumulated increments, the constant must be generated from the arbitrary starting point, t_0, which has zero variance. The exact nature of the accumulation of variation to the constant is not known because of the uncertainty about the statistical nature of the homeostatic cycle. However, a logistic curve can be used as a first approximation (Brush and Harrison 1990), as is illustrated in Fig. 7.1.

If environmental insults are correlated, that is, the environment is stratified, the pattern of the increase in variance is identical to that of the genetic component in having a quadratic relationship with mean growth. Variance resulting from environmental stratification is indistinguishable from the genetic component.

Measurement error

Measurement error variance, M, is assumed to be independent and constant, and therefore has no relationship with mean growth.

Phenotypic variance

On the assumption that the components of variance are independent of each other, the phenotypic variance, P_t, is equal to their sum,

$$P_t = G_t + E_t + M,$$

where G_t and E_t are the genetic and total environmental components of variance at time t, and M is the measurement error variance. The phenotypic variance and the various forms of its component variances are shown in Fig. 7.1. Although this is only a schematic representation, it is assumed that the additive and home-ostatic environmental components of the phenotypic variance are larger at first in comparison with the genetic component. The latter, however, because of its quadratic rate of increase, eventually overtakes the environmental variance and comes to account for an ever greater proportion of the total. The relationship predicts an increase in hereditability with growth.

Graphical analysis

The accumulation of growth variance can be visualized through the behaviour of the coefficient of variation (CV) with respect to mean accumulated incre-ment. Table 7.1 and Fig. 7.2 display the relationship of the CV of the accumu-lated increment with respect to the mean. The simplest pattern is that of the constant CV which arises if genetic variation is the sole component of the vari-ance. The remaining three traces display the CV when genetic and non-genetic components are combined. The two common features of these latter traces are

Table 7.1. Relationship to mean accumulated increment, at time t, of the vari-ance and coefficient of variation of components of length growth variation

Variance component	Relationship of variance to the mean	Relationship of CV to the mean
Measurement error	m	$100\sqrt{m} / \bar{X}_t$
Additive environmental	$a\bar{X}_t$	$100\sqrt{a\bar{X}_i} / \bar{X}_t$
Homeostatic constant (logistic)	$\dfrac{he^{r(\bar{x}_t+c)}}{1+e^{r(\bar{x}_t+c)}}$	$100\sqrt{\dfrac{he^{r(\bar{x}_t+c)}}{1+e^{r(\bar{x}_t+c)}}} / \bar{X}_t$
Genetic	gX_t^2	$100\sqrt{g\bar{X}_t^2} / \bar{X}_t = 100\sqrt{g}$

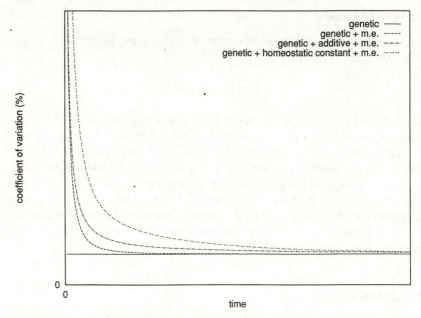

Fig. 7.2 Example of the relationship between mean accumulated length increment and its coefficient of variation, for different models of growth variation.

the rapid decline in CV over short increments of growth and the asymptotic approach to the CV of the genetic component. These traces allow for some general statements concerning the pattern of the phenotypic CV of accumulated increments:

1. Holding all parameters constant, the CV decreases to an asymptote. This asymptote is equal to that of the CV of the genetic component of the variance (which can be equal to zero). The decline in CV arises from the additive, homeostatic, and measurement error components of variance which, when expressed as a standard deviation, do not keep pace with the mean. Only the standard deviation of the genetic-stratified component is linearly related to the mean, and therefore becomes an increasingly larger proportion of the total variance as the other components fall behind.

2. Holding all parameters constant, the CV can never increase with respect to the mean. The most rapid accumulation of variance arises from growth increments perfectly correlated from interval to interval. This is modelled by the genetic component of variation. Its standard deviation has a

linear relationship with the mean that generates the constant ratio. There can be no faster accumulation of variance than this. A CV that is observed to increase therefore implies some kind of temporal heterogeneity, such as a sudden injection of environmental variance, a growth pulse, or a shift to a different set of genetic controls.

The figure is suggestive that the three traces which include the non-genetic components are distinguishable by the speed at which they approach the asymptote. Unfortunately, this is more a consequence of the parameters chosen for the graph than any particular feature of the components. However, measurement error is assumed to be the smallest of the non-genetic components and on its own will produce a rapid approach to the genetic constant.

Estimating parameters

Graphical inspection of the coefficient of variation gives a broad view of the pattern of variance accumulation but provides fewer opportunities for analysing the contributions of the various components. The latter requires estimating the parameters of the component models described in the preceding sections. The one model which has fitted most consistently with length data and agrees with the notions of genetic, stratified environmental, and homeostatic contributions to growth variance involves two terms,

$$VAR_t = g\bar{X}_t^2 + \frac{he^{r(\bar{x}_t+c)}}{1+e^{r(\bar{x}_t+c)}}, \qquad (7.1)$$

where VAR_t and X_t are, respectively, the variance and mean of the accumulated increment at time t. The quadratic term, $g\bar{X}_t^2$, subsumes the variances arising from genetic differences and environmental stratification. The second term is a logistic equation modelling both the generation of the homeostatic constant and the constant of measurement error. The model is fitted using non-linear regression (SAS Institute Inc. 1989), to a series of mean-variance pairs, each pair being the mean and variance of the accumulated increment at time t. The estimated parameters are h, the homeostatic constant, r, the rate of increase in variance, c, an offset, and g, the coefficient of the genetic-stratified component of the variance. A few examples are now provided from data collected on infants from Hong Kong (Field and Baber 1973) and Sudan (Zumrawi *et al.* 1987*a,b*) In both cases, length was measured at birth and thereafter at monthly intervals for 10–12 months. The similarity of the data collection provided an opportunity to compare the patterns of variation of the two groups.

Hong Kong

The Hong Kong infants and their growth have been described in Field and Baber (1973) and Brush *et al.* (1992). Briefly, the sample is fully longitudinal with 131 infants measured for supine length at birth and then at monthly intervals during the first year of life.

Figure 7.3 displays the variance and CV of length growth in relation to mean accumulated increment of the infants. The variance demonstrates the expected increase and the CV the expected decrease with mean accumulated increment.

The fitted model and its components are shown in Fig. 7.4. Points 6, 7, and 8 were omitted from the sample of means and variances, as they appear to be an example of a brief perturbation of the variance which is unrelated to the general trend. The figure demonstrates a reasonably good fit considering the unknown nature of the generation of the homeostatic constant. The environmental variance as modelled rises from a value of a little over 0.2 to that approaching a constant of $h = 1.17$. The initial variance near 0.2 is an estimate of the sum of all components of measurement error, including variation in measurement interval. Note, however, that the estimate is an extrapolation of the data which depends on the suitability of the logistic curve to model adequately the generation of the homeostatic constant. More data between birth and 1 month are required to investigate the need for a better fitting model.

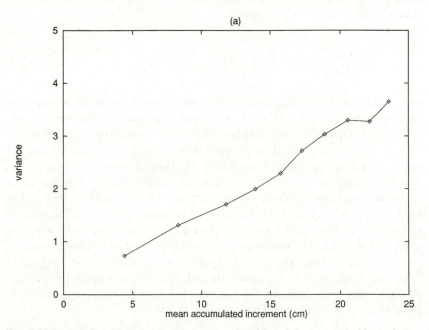

Fig. 7.3(a)   Relationship between mean accumulated length increment and its variance.

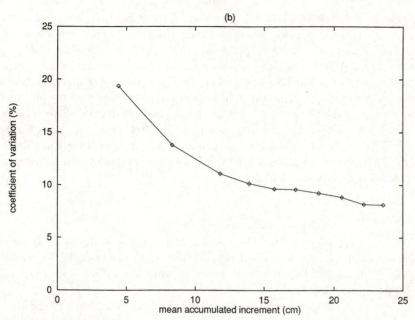

Fig. 7.3(b) Relationship between mean accumulated length increment and its coefficient of variation in Hong Kong infants.

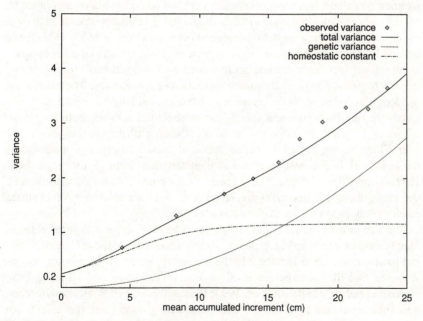

Fig. 7.4 Fitted genetic and homeostatic components of the variance of accumulated length increment in Hong Kong infants.

Figure 7.4 illustrates how the genetic-stratified component, modelled by the quadratic curve, eventually overtakes the environmental variance and comes to account for an ever increasing proportion of the total variance. The value of g, estimated at 0.0044, represents at least the amount of genetic variance gained in the first unit of accumulated increment. This is equivalent to a genetic CV of approximately 7 per cent (Brush and Harrison 1990), and thus the projected asymptote of the CV in Fig. 7.3. This estimate is high in comparison with the CV of 3.6 per cent reported by Schmitt and Harrison (1988) for adult height. The difference probably arises from additional variation in Hong Kong due to environmental stratification. Even the value of 3.6 per cent may be an overestimate because of such stratification.

Khartoum

The Sudanese infants came from poor urban families in the three towns of Khartoum province. Longitudinal measurements were taken monthly for the first year of life on 199 infants of both sexes. A more detailed account is given in Zumrawi *et al.* (1987*a,b*).

Figure 7.5 compares the variance of accumulated increments of the Hong Kong and Sudanese infants. The two groups are clearly different in the variance of their length growth from birth. However, all attempts at fitting the variance model to the Khartoum data failed. Further analyses of the Khartoum children revealed a much greater complexity than could have been accounted for by the model. The Sudanese infants displayed a strong postnatal pattern of catch-up/catch-down growth that extended over the first year of life. This is evidenced by strong negative correlations between birth length and all subsequent accumulated increments; some infants who were long at birth tended subsequently to grow slowly while some short infants grew quickly. The pattern was echoed in correlations between birth and subsequent lengths, which showed a steady decline from an initial correlation of about 0.8 between birth length and length at 1 month, to a correlation of 0 between birth length and length at 1 year. Thus, having passed through a period of growth adjustment, the length of the infants at 1 year was unrelated to their length at birth (Brush *et al.* 1992; Harrison and Brush 1993). These correlational patterns contrast with those of the Hong Kong infants, who displayed little outward evidence for postnatal catch-up/catch-down growth (Brush *et al.* 1992).

The situation in the Khartoum infants is, however, more complicated than a simple case of catch-up/catch-down growth. Overlain are the effects of household attributes such as income and the housewife status of the mother, and the weaning and illness experience of the infant (Zumrawi and Dimond 1988; Harrison *et al.* 1992; Brush *et al.* 1993; Harrison *et al.*1993). Housewife status and income relate to both pre-and postnatal growth, but the effects are reversed. Infants born to families with low household incomes tend to be

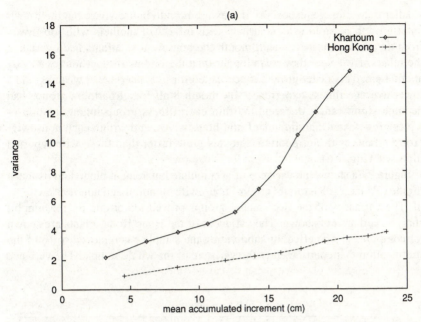

Fig. 7.5(a)   Relationship between mean accumulated length increment and its variance.

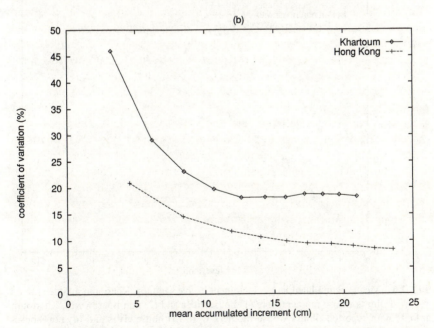

Fig. 7.5(b)   Relationship between mean accumulated length increment and its coefficient of variation in Khartoum and Hong Kong infants.

smaller than average, especially if they are born to housewives, but their postnatal growth is rapid in comparison with infants of mothers with jobs away
from the home. By the seventh month the housewives' infants had overtaken
the others. By 1 year they were longer than the infants of non-housewives by
about 4 cm. This faster growth is accounted for by a later age at weaning and a
lower average illness experience. By month 8 all four Khartoum groups had
become significantly different. Within each illness group infants of housewives grew faster than infants of non-housewives, and within each housewife
group infants with no reported illnesses grew faster than those with reported
illnesses (Fig. 7,6).

Figure 7.7a shows the variance of accumulated increment plotted on its mean
for the two largest Khartoum groups, housewife — not ill and non-housewife —
ill. The variances of the two smaller groups proved too erratic for meaningful
analysis and are not shown. The variances of the Hong Kong infants are shown
for comparison. The effect of subdividing the sample has removed some of the
stratification that contributed to the variance of the whole sample. The variance

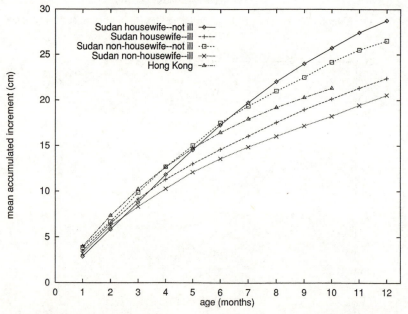

Fig. 7.6 Mean accumulated length increment in five samples: Khartoum infants with no
reported illness whose mothers were (1) housewives and (2) non-housewives, Khartoum
infants with reported illness whose mothers were (3) housewives and (4) non-housewives, and (5) Hong Kong infants.

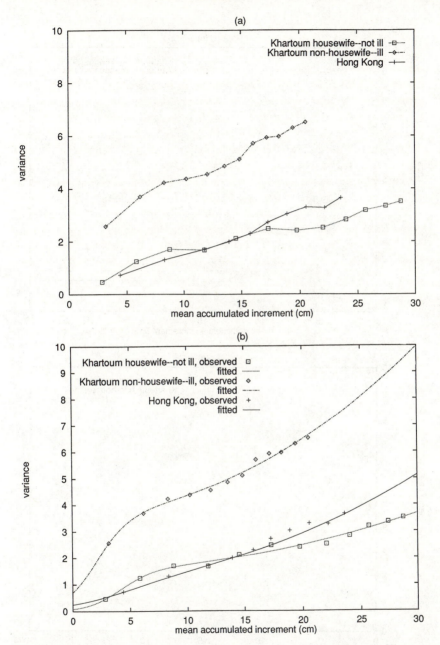

Fig. 7.7 Variances in accumulated length increments in three samples, (1) Khartoum infants with no reported illness whose mothers were housewives, (2) Khartoum infants with reported illness whose mothers were non-housewives, and (3) Hong Kong infants: (a) observed total variances, (b) fitted and observed total variances.

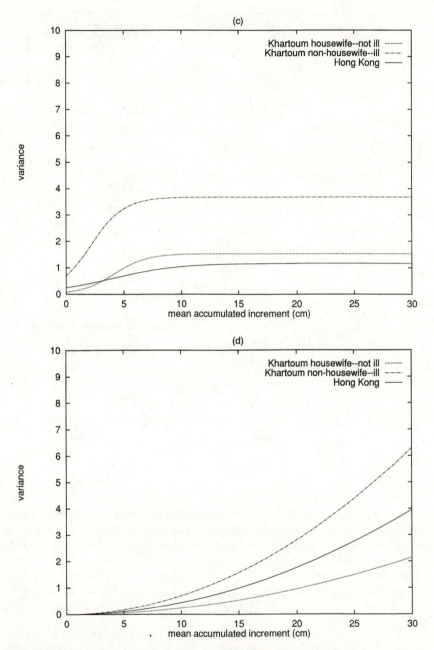

Fig. 7.7 (c) fitted homeostatic constants, (d) fitted quadratic components.

of the housewife — not ill group is now similar to that of the Hong Kong infants. The non-housewife — ill group is still much more variable than the Hong Kong infants and the Khartoum housewife — ill group. These differences are significant from month 4 onwards.

The variance model (eqn 7.1) was fitted to the two Khartoum samples as is shown in Fig. 7.7b. This time the model fitted reasonably well. Figure 7.7c displays the estimated homeostatic constants of the two Khartoum samples in comparison with the infants from Hong Kong. The homeostatic constant of the Khartoum housewife — not ill sample is similar to that of the Hong Kong infants, both of which contrast sharply with the large constant of the Khartoum non-housewife — ill group. The fitted quadratic components of the variance are shown in Fig. 7.7d. The two Khartoum groups were again clearly distinct, the housewife — not ill group having a smaller quadratic increase in variance than did the non-housewife — ill group. The Hong Kong infants were positioned midway between the two Khartoum groups.

The analysis of the growth variances reveals that the two Khartoum groups show two different patterns of variation. The ill infants of non-housewives are considerably more variable than the healthy infants of the housewives. The variance model suggests that this difference is accounted for in both the greater size of the homeostatic constant and of the greater quadratic accumulation of growth variance of the non-housewives' infants. Comparing the two Khartoum groups with the Hong Kong infants reveals that the healthy infants of the Khartoum housewives have a similar homeostatic constant to those of the Hong Kong infants, but a lower increase in the quadratic component. The non-housewife group shows greater variation than the Hong Kong sample in both homeostatic constant and quadratic component.

Discussion

The model of growth variation presented in this chapter is based on the assumption that environmental variance, generated from the disruption of growth, would increase indefinitely if it were not for homeostatic mechanisms that remove variance. Because children are in different phases of disruption and catch-up the environmental variance is assumed to reach a constant that reflects the input and removal of variance. Small constants represent little disruption with quick recovery and large constants greater disruption with slow recovery.

A second component of variance stems from recurrent influences on growth. At a minimum this accounts for variance arising from genetic differences in growth rates but will also include the effects of any environmental stratification, assuming that the effects of the stratification are constant over the period of observation. This type of variation increases without check (at least over short periods) at a rate proportional to the square of mean growth.

Two populations were used to examine the ability of the model to explain the increase of variance of accumulated increments of length growth in infants from birth to 1 year. While the model fitted the variance pattern of the Hong Kong infants, initial attempts at fitting the data from the Khartoum sample failed. In the latter, the complicated pattern of growth rates relating to the housewife status of the mother and illness history of the children prevented the model from adequately fitting the data. However, when the sample was subdivided by house-wife status of the mother and the illness history of the infant the model was found to fit the data for those strata with sample sizes large enough to analyse.

The infants in the two strata had opposite average rates of growth, as was expected from the definitions of the samples. The total variance of the slower growing group (ill infants of non-housewives) was significantly greater than the variances of the faster growing, healthy infants of housewives. The slower growing group also had a large homeostatic constant, suggesting that it had a greater difficulty in recovering from environmental insults than did the healthy infants of the housewives. Both the average and the variance suggest a poor environment for growth.

The magnitude of the quadratic component is predicted to be equal in the two Khartoum groups, under the assumption that the quadratic term is measuring only the genetic variance and that the two groups are independent samples of the same gene pool. Assuming that the observed differences are significant (a significance test is yet to be devised) the observed differences in the quadratic component might reflect greater genetic variation in one group over the other. However, the difference could easily be accounted for through greater environmental stratification in the ill infants of the non-housewives as compared with the healthy infants of the housewives.

Comparing Hong Kong with Khartoum reveals that the Hong Kong infants grow faster than the ill infants of the non-housewives, suggesting that the Hong Kong infants are growing up in a better environment. That the Hong Kong infants have a smaller homeostatic constant is in agreement with this conclusion. In comparison with the healthy infants of the Khartoum housewives, the Hong Kong infants have a slower growth rate, suggesting here that the Hong Kong infants are growing up in a relatively poorer environment. However, the evidence from the homeostatic constant does not support this latter conclusion. The similarity of the two homeostatic constants indicates that the two groups live in similar environmental conditions with respect to growth. As growth rates must always include genetic and environmental determinants, perhaps the slower growth of the Hong Kong infants reflects a genetic difference. Further work needs to be done to confirm this suggestion.

References

Brush, G. and Harrison, G. A. (1990). Components of growth variation in human stature. *IMA Journal of Mathematics Applied in Medicine & Biology*, **7**, 77–92.

Brush, G., Harrison, G. A., Baber, F. M., and Zumrawi, F. Y. (1992). Comparative variability and interval correlation in linear growth of Hong Kong and Sudanese infants. *American Journal of Human Biology*, **4**, 291–9.

Brush, G., Harrison, G. A., and Zumrawi, F. Y. (1993). A path analysis of some determinants of infant growth in Khartoum. *Annals of Human Biology*, **20**, 381–7.

Field, C. E. and Baber, F. M. (1973). *Growing up in Hong Kong*. Hong Kong University Press.

Harrison, G. A. and Brush, G. (1990). On correlations between adjacent velocities and accelerations in longitudinal growth data. *Annals of Human Biology*, **17**, 55–7.

Harrison, G. A. and Brush, G. (1993). Growth during the first year of life. In *New perspectives in Anthropology* (ed. P. K. Seth and S. Seth), pp. 193 – 201.

Harrison, G. A., Brush, G., and Zumrawi, F. Y. (1992). Interrelations between growth, weaning and disease experience in Khartoum infants. *European Journal of Clinical Nutrition*, **46**, 273–8.

Harrison, G. A., Brush, G., and Zumrawi, F. Y. (1993). Motherhood and infant health in Khartoum. *Bulletin of the World Health Organization*, **71**, 529–33.

SAS Institute Inc. (1989). *SAS/STAT user's guide, version 6*, 4th edn, Vol. 2. SAS Institute Inc, Cary, NC.

Schmitt, L. H. and Harrison, G. A. (1988). Patterns in the within-population variability of stature and weight. *Annals of Human Biology*, **15**, 353–64.

Zumrawi, F. Y. and Dimond, H. (1988). Determinants of growth in the first 6 months of life among the urban poor of Sudan. *Journal of Tropical Medicine and Hygiene*, **91**, 139–46.

Zumrawi, F. Y., Dimond, H., and Waterlow, J. C. (1987a). Effects of infection on growth in Sudanese children. *Human Nutrition: Clinical Nutrition*, **41C**, 453–61.

Zumrawi, F. Y., Dimond, H., and Waterlow, J. C. (1987b). Faltering in infant growth in Khartoum Province, Sudan. *Human Nutrition: Clinical Nutrition*, **41C**, 383–95.

8

Mother's morale and infant health in Ethiopia

A. M. ALMEDOM

Introduction

Previous studies have examined infant health in relation to nutritional status and physical growth performance. Studies which demonstrated the complexities of the relationships, particularly those between nutrition and morbidity, some more than two decades ago, continue to influence current research (Scrimshaw et al. 1968, 1969; Mata et al. 1977, Mata 1978; Tomkins 1981; 1986; Black et al. 1984; Tomkins and Watson 1988; Aaby 1988; Ulijaszek 1990). Malnutrition makes infants susceptible to infection and infection leads to the failure to make effective use of nutrients and thus leads to malnutrition.

The 'malnutrition-infection complex' is mediated by environmental factors including economic deprivation and also by a whole set of factors that constitute what has been termed 'maternal technology' within a deprived environment. Mata (1979) chose the term maternal technology to describe a multitude of characteristics of the mother related to disease management (including feeding patterns during illness and choice of medicine), hygiene (food handling, preparation, storage; handling of drinking water; bathing and personal hygiene; disposal of wastes), and patterns of socializing her child (see also Mata 1980). Variations in mothers' management of the limited resources available to low-income households are often reflected in the differential well-being, growth, and ultimate survival of infants and young children.

In many parts of the tropics, malnutrition coupled with infection renders the growth performance of the majority of infants and young children inadequate. However, there is great variability in growth performance and some individuals seem to thrive despite the hazards of infection and malnutrition associated with socio-economic deprivation. Such individuals have been identified as 'positive deviants' because they seem to thrive against the odds (Zeitlin and Ghassemi 1986). It is often pointed out that the reason why some individuals thrive while others do not has much to do with maternal technology.

How then is maternal technology related to child health? This is a multifaceted question. The various components of maternal technology that may contribute to positive deviance do not lend themselves to quantitative measurement. A recent review has highlighted the limitations of standard epidemiological research methods to address the question (Zeitlin 1991). It is therefore necessary to adopt a holistic approach, involving a mix of both qualitative and quantitative methods if the problem is to be tackled satisfactorily.

This chapter presents data from a prospective study in which enquiry into the prevalence of infection among infants was conducted in the home taking into account the feeding regimen, the mother's health, her management of disease including her preference of medicine, the quality of the home environment in terms of water supply, refuse disposal and sanitation facilities, and other relevant factors. The objectives of the study were first to explore the determinants of health and physical growth of suckling and weanling infants in Ethiopia under 'normal' conditions (i.e. in the absence of widespread acute food shortage/famine); and second to identify the key issues that need to be addressed in order to promote a better understanding of maternal and child health. The situation is assessed from the perspectives of anthropology and human ecology. Some of the components of 'maternal technology' which influence the well-being of infants and young children are focused on. In particular, the role of the mother's morale in maintaining a home environment that is conducive to her infant's well-being is explored.

Study site

Fieldwork was carried out in Addis Ababa, the Ethiopian capital. The choice of study site was chiefly influenced by two factors: theoretical and practical/logistical. First, in order to collect data that would address the research questions posed (the study aim and objectives), a location was sought where food shortage was not widespread and where there was little or no intervention in terms of health care and/or nutritional supplementation. Second, the prevailing adverse political situation in the country was a serious limiting factor that had to be taken into account. The investigator's nationality seemed to invite a negative response from the various government ministries to whom requests were made for permission to conduct research. In the end, authorization was obtained by indirect means through the Save the Children Fund (UK), a non-governmental organization which was on good terms with the Ethiopian government. The investigator was required to limit her choice of field sites to Addis Ababa.

Addis Ababa is the most permanent capital of Ethiopia. Prior to 1886, when the Emperor Menelik conquered the local Oromo population and moved his court to Finfine (later renamed Addis Ababa), Ethiopian kings had traditionally moved their capitals from one place to another depending on which king gained utmost political power and which place was best for him in militarily strategic terms. Power changed hands every time a king defeated all the other kings in battle and became king of kings, Emperor. King Menelik had moved his court four times before he finally settled in Addis Ababa. Addis Ababa was at first merely a glorified military camp. However, when the Emperor Yohannes of Tigray died and Menelik became Emperor in 1889, he built a palace in it. Menelik's army Generals stationed their encampments around him. These encampments grew into villages and gradually merged into what is now the city of Addis Ababa.

From the point of view of human ecology, Addis Ababa was an unmanageable disarray: as the population grew, the absence of sewage and refuse disposal systems translated into the spread of water/sanitation-related diseases such as typhoid fever and trachoma. In contrast to other cities in the region such as Asmara, there has been no co-ordinated municipal central planning in Addis Ababa (Teka 1993).

After the 1974 Revolution, Addis Ababa was divided into 25 *keftegna*s, districts, each of which was further divided into smaller units known as *kebele*s. The origin of the *kebele*s, housing associations, was the old *idir*, a traditional burial association which consisted of neighbourhood organizations which provided both moral and economic support to their members, for example, at the time of mourning the loss of relatives. However, the *kebele*'s function was significantly different. In contrast to the *idir*, the *kebele*'s primary purpose was to enforce political control, with the secondary role of implementing economic centralization. At the time of data collection, in 1987–88, when Colonel Menghistu's highly repressive socialist and military government was in power, each *kebele* in Addis Ababa had a prison, where countless 'counter-revolutionaries' were detained and a great many of them had perished over a total period of 13 years. Each *kebele* also had a 'cooperative' shop where basic food items could be purchased upon presentation of the household ration coupons.

A pilot study involving direct observations and unstructured interviews/discussions was carried out in Addis Ababa during October 1987. Subsequently, *Kebele* 11 *Keftegna* 24, located in the western periphery of the city was selected as a suitable study site.

Subjects and methods

The data presented here were collected as part of a mixed longitudinal study of the health and growth of suckling and weaning infants in low-income households. A mixed longitudinal study is one in which the subjects (in this case the infants) are of different ages when data collection begins. A selected sample of 113 mother–infant pairs were visited in their homes every month for a period of 6 months from November 1987 to April 1988. Selection criteria, including the household income level, age of the infant(s), and the mother's willingness to participate in the study were applied in recruiting the sample. Exact birth dates were obtained from each infant's vaccination card and checked against the mother's report, often supported by other documented records such as christening cards. A more detailed description of the sample and methods may be found elsewhere (Almedom 1991*a* or *c*).

At each visit data on infant illnesses were collected using a longitudinally designed structured interview schedule. The mother was asked whether her infant had been ill with diarrhoea, coughing, fever, and vomiting for 2 consecutive days or more, over the previous 4 weeks. The interval between visits was 29 ± 2 days, the time that it took the investigator and assistant to complete a round of visits to all 113 households. Ensuring that all data (interview, observational and anthropometric) were collected by the same investigator (with an assistant) had the advantage of eliminating inter-observer bias and the disadvantage of longer intervals between visits than might have been desired.

In accordance with standard anthropological methods, local terms for illnesses and associated symptoms were identified and used in the design of the structured interview schedule employed for eliciting and recording data. Diarrhoea (Amharic, *teqmat*) was defined as frequent loose stools (more than three times a day) for 2 or more consecutive days; fever (Amharic, *tikoussat*) was defined as noticeably high temperature; coughing (Amharic, *saal*) was defined as persistent cough; and vomiting (Amharic, *makleshlesh*) was defined as the persistent bringing-up of food and/or drink over the same duration of time. Data on symptoms were missing if the mother was absent at the time of visit. No questions were asked of alternative carers or minders.

At the same time, the mother was interviewed about her own health. An attempt was made to specify mothers' reports of ill-health that fell in the categories of 'aches and pains' and 'other'. For instance, a large number of mothers reported that they suffered from constant '*ye-menfäs chinquet*' (Amharic), which literally translates as 'oppression of the soul'. This variable, entered in the analysis as mother's morale was found to have a significant influence on infant well-being as will be shown below. Data on environmental sanitation, domestic hygiene, and personal hygiene were collected by means of direct observation (spot check) and informal interviews. Questions were addressed to the mother on the frequency of washing and/or bathing of her infant, often while observing her performing this activity and matching her answers with observations of the infant's personal hygiene prior to weighing him/her in the nude. Data obtained by observing the cleanliness of the homestead at each visit complemented the interview data. Bathing or giving the infant a wash once a day was coded as adequate personal hygiene. Constant litter including faecal contamination observed in and around the home, and signs of poor infant-care and personal hygiene such as persistent body and clothing odours were recorded as indicators of inadequate hygiene. Other information gathered includes data on infant feeding, weaning (Almedom 1991*a,b*); and physical growth (Harrison *et al.* 1990).

Cross-sectional surveys of ethnicity, religion, mother's education, household water-supply, waste disposal system, sanitation, occupation of household head, mother's education and occupation, and other details, were carried out at different stages during the study period.

The conduct of interviews was informal, following a conversational manner rather than a strict question and answer format. The Amharic language was used in all cases apart from the few cases (four sample women from Tigray) in which Tigrinya was used. Data were collected by the author and a female assistant. In the absence of major cultural, linguistic, and gender barriers, good relations with the study sample were established and easily maintained.

The data were checked, re-checked, and entered into micro-computer files. All analyses were carried out on the Oxford University mainframe computers using the BMDP (Dixon 1988, 1990) and SAS (SAS Inc. 1985) statistical packages.

The statistical techniques used in the analysis include log-linear modelling and logistic regression. There are two reasons for choosing to use log-linear analysis rather than two by two chi-square contingency tables or a multi-way analysis of variance model. First, log-linear modelling allows multivariate analysis with a mixture of categorical and metric data (although the application of this is not included in this chapter), whereas conventional multivariate methods would be inappropriate because of their built-in assumptions of metric qualities: linearity and additivity. Second, log-linear modelling enables one to look at all possible associations (statistically termed 'effects'). The relative importance of effects in log-linear models is assessed by computing two *ad hoc* statistics for each effect. These are the chi-square statistic (χ^2) and the log-likelihood ratio chi-square (G^2). The first statistic measures the 'marginal' association, that is, the association between two factors without controlling for other factors. The second statistic measures the 'conditional' association, that is, the association between two terms when other factors are controlled for. These tests indicate the order of magnitude of the change in the goodness-of-fit produced by entering a given effect into the model. The primary use of log-linear models is exploratory and descriptive. Associations between categorical variables relating to symptoms of illness, household socio-economy, and maternal characteristics were first explored and described using log-linear models (see Almedom 1991*c*, pp. 154–5 and 174–81 for more details). Meaningfully significant associations were then further confirmed by using logistic regressions.

Results

There was no public health care service for *Keftegna* 24. However, in *Kebele* 11 there was a small clinic set up by the Mekane Yesus Church, a protestant denomination. This clinic opened one morning a week and offered basic medication for young children such as cough mixtures, soluble aspirin for febrile illnesses, and eye ointments for the treatment of conjunctivitis, free of charge. This clinic also provided mothers with advice on how to prepare and administer oral rehydration solution. Some of the Christian mothers and one or two Muslim ones, mostly the ones who lived in close proximity to it frequented this clinic. The rest of the inhabitants of *Kebele* 11 could, in theory, be served by Kolfe clinic in neighbouring *Keftegna* 25 which was about 40 min walk uphill from *Kebele* 11. In practice, however, very few of the mothers in the sample reported visits to this clinic other than for the purposes of immunization.

The mothers studied represented various ethnic groups including Oromo, Gurage, Amara, Sidama, Tigrawai and Dorze. Eighty-one per cent of the women were Christian and 23 per cent Muslim. Motherhood was the sample women's main occupation. However, the majority of mothers were also engaged in domestic labour (28 per cent), in making handcrafts for sale (22 per cent), and in petty trade, most commonly the sale of fruit and vegetables on the main road that crossed *Kebele* 11 (17 per cent). If the mother's work took her out of her home, her infant and toddler(s) would accompany her so that patterns of breast feeding and child care did not change significantly as a result of the maternal occupation. As far as education is concerned, 65 per cent of the sample women had achieved basic literacy (resulting from the adult literacy campaign which was launched after the 1974 Revolution); 5 per cent had completed primary education; 3 per cent had primary education plus some vocational training such as dress-making or machine-knitting; and 27 per cent had no formal education and could not read and write.

The majority of the mothers interviewed used home-prepared traditional medicines consisting mostly of herbs such as *damakisse* (genus *Origanum*), rue (*Ruta graveolens*), and eucalyptus leaves and twigs for common infant ailments. These same traditional medicines were also offered by the sample mothers to the investigator and assistant who were advised to use them in order to ward off the many possible diseases they might encounter while frequenting areas of *Besheta* (Amharic for disease, often equated with bad smells and unsanitary conditions) such as *Kebele* 11. The number of mothers who reported having given their infants modern medicine was very small. Many of the mothers reported that they could not afford to buy medicine from the pharmacies. However, they would use modern medicine if it was given free of charge but not exclusively. Very few mothers visited the Mekane Yesus clinic.

Figures 8.1 and 8.2 show the prevalence of symptoms by month and by age group, respectively. Some of the characteristics of the physical environment and their association with the symptoms recorded are summarized in Tables 8.1 and 8.2.

Table 8.2 demonstrates the use of log-linear modelling to distinguish between marginal and conditional associations. It can be seen that significant marginal associations between some of the environmental and morbidity variables, probably mediated by the significant conditional associations between the environ-

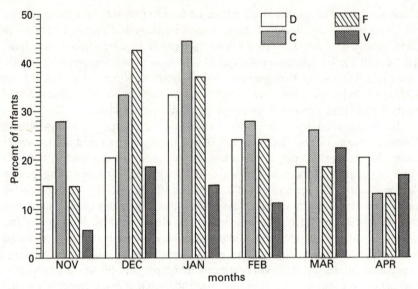

Fig. 8.1   Prevalence of symptoms, by month. D = diarrhoea; F = fever; C = coughing; V = vomiting.

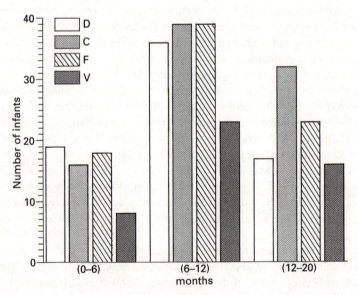

Fig. 8.2   Prevalence of symptoms, by age group. D = diarrhoea; F = fever; C = coughing; V = vomiting.

Table 8.1. Water source, sanitation, and waste disposal facilities ($n = 113$)

Variable	Category	n	%
Water source	private tap	16	14.16
	shared tap	68	60.18
	public tap	21	18.58
	shared tap + river	4	3.54
	no information	4	3.54
Sanitary facility	private pit latrine	22	39.82
	shared pit latrine	45	19.47
	none	39	34.51
	no information	7	6.19
Disposal of refuse	thrown into river	39	34.51
	collected and burned	21	18.58
	thrown off cliff	20	17.69
	collected by van	17	15.04
	no effort made	7	6.19
	no information	9	7.96

Table 8.2. Association of symptoms with the variables in Table 8.1

		Association				
		Conditional			Marginal	
Effect	d.f.	Likelihood ratio (G^2)	P <		Pearson χ^2	P <
wdisp. x diarrhoea	4	1.88	NS		7.82	NS
wdisp. x fever	4	4.14	NS		12.64	0.013
wdisp. x coughing	4	5.63	NS		15.17	0.004
wdisp. x vomiting	4	4.15	NS		14.16	0.007
wsup. x diarrhoea	4	4.56	NS		16.63	0.002
wsup. x fever	4	2.35	NS		13.84	0.008
wsup. x coughing	4	7.42	NS		20.97	0.001
wsup. x vomiting	4	3.09	NS		5.09	NS
san.. x diarrhoea	2	0.71	NS		2.25	NS
san. x fever	2	1.78	NS		3.34	NS
san. x coughing	2	0.33	NS		0.87	NS
san. x vomiting	2	0.20	NS		1.76	NS
wdisp. x wsup.	16	43.40	0.012		50.94	0.001
wdisp. x san.	8	18.31	0.019		17.91	0.022
wsup. x san.	8	24.69	0.002		25.63	0.001

BMDP — 4F (Dixon 1988).
wdisp., waste disposal system;
wsup., water supply;
san., sanitary facility;
d.f., degrees of freedom;
NS, not significant.

mental variables, lose their significance when these factors are controlled for (in the conditional test).

A great majority of the mothers, 83 per cent, reported that they suffered from constant *ye-menfäs chinquet*, Amharic for 'oppression of the soul'. There was little variation in the reasons given for this complaint: 90.1 per cent of the mothers reported that the cause was related to the current laws of mass conscription; prolonged absence of a son who had been forcibly conscripted, or a husband who has been in the army for some time. A small number, 6.4 per cent, attributed *ye-menfäs chinquet* to family/marital disharmony, and 3.5 per cent reported that they did not know. This variable was entered in the analysis as 'mother's morale'.

Table 8.3 summarizes the results of log-linear analysis in which selected maternal variables were examined against diarrhoea in the infant. A full account of associations between maternal variables and infant morbidity variables may be found elsewhere (see Almedom 1991*c*, pp. 175–8).

Table 8.3.   Association of infant's diarrhoea with maternal variables

		Association			
		Conditional		Marginal	
Effect	d.f.	Likelihood ratio (G^2)	P <	Pearson χ^2	P <
First-order association					
locw. x diarrhoea	1	6.36	0.012	8.38	0.004
twb. x diarrhoea	1	2.73	NS	4.40	0.036
educ. x diarrhoea	3	8.94	0.030	10.17	0.017
hyg. x diarrhoea	1	4.34	0.037	2.99	NS
mor. x diarrhoea	1	3.43	NS	1.15	NS
locw. x twb.	1	260.03	0.001	276.31	0.001
hyg. x mor.	1	68.12	0.001	68.57	0.001
hyg. x educ.	3	12.80	0.005	12.68	0.005
educ. x mor.	3	29.27	0.001	33.87	0.001

BMDP — 4F (Dixon 1988)
twb., mother's time spent with infant (all day or part of the day only);
locw., location of mother's work for earnings (within the home or outside);
hyg., domestic and personal hygiene (adequate or poor);
educ., mother's education (no literacy, basic literacy, primary school and/or vocational training);
mor., mother's morale (presence or absence of 'oppression of the soul');
NS, not significant.

Location of the mother's work and the amount of time she spent with her infant (whether she spent all day or only part of the day) were strongly correlated. Similarly, the level of domestic and personal hygiene observed was highly significantly associated with maternal education and morale. Maternal education and morale were in turn highly significantly related. All of these strong associations between maternal variables remained significant in the conditional test.

A higher prevalence of diarrhoea was found among infants whose mothers worked outside the home in order to generate income. It was found that the infants of mothers who were engaged in petty trade, selling vegetables, fruit, and charcoal by the roadside, were minded by older siblings or relations. These infants had significantly more incidence of diarrhoea than the infants who accompanied their mothers to work (in the case of domestic labour in better-off households) and those who stayed at home.

Significantly higher prevalence of diarrhoea was found among the infants of non-literate mothers compared with those whose mothers had achieved basic literacy, primary schooling, and primary schooling plus some vocational training. Entering all of the above variables into graphical log-linear analysis yielded the model presented in Fig. 8.3 below as model with the best goodness-of-fit. Re-examining these associations with logistic regression provided further confirmation of the links between mother's morale and education, the level of domestic and personal hygiene, and diarrhoea in the infants (see Table 8.4).

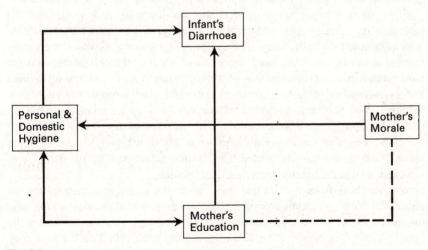

Fig. 8.3

Table 8.4. Logistic regression equations for diarrhoea (dependent variable) ($n = 70$)

Reg.	Variable	Regression coefficient	Standard error	F	P <
1	hygiene	−0.61	0.28	4.54	0.034
2	morale	0.30	0.39	0.57	NS
	education	0.47	0.28	2.78	NS
	hygiene	−0.66	0.32	4.14	0.043
3	morale	0.44	0.53	−	−
	hygiene	−0.45	0.33	−	−
	morale x hygiene	−0.34	0.79	24.75	0.001
4	education	−0.52	0.51	−	−
	hygiene	−1.60	0.49	−	−
	education x hygiene	1.39	0.61	5.22	0.023
5	education	0.10	0.26	−	−
	morale	0.15	0.52	−	−
	education x morale	0.88	0.75	1.38	NS
	morale x education	1.51	0.85	3.06	NS

BMDP — LR (Dixon 1990).
NS, not significant.

Discussion

Although *Kebele* 11 was selected for this study because it had no intervention programmes, the under-fives immunization programme was a significant intervention, averting major causes of morbidity and mortality such as measles and tuberculosis. Immunization programmes are of particular importance in areas with high infant mortality rates such as Ethiopia. However, diseases averted by immunization are often 'replaced' by others of which childhood diarrhoea is the most prominent one (Hirschhorn *et al.* 1989). In Addis Ababa, almost all *kebeles* had been reached either through regular clinics or through outreach programmes. Vaccines were administered to every child against tetanus, diphtheria, polio, whooping cough, tuberculosis, and measles starting from the age of 3 months. Cases of the above diseases were rare in the sample. One example was a 1 month-old baby who died from tetanus infection after his uvula were removed, as was customary, by a traditional doctor.

None of the infants studied had been taken to a clinic or a hospital for the treatment of the symptoms recorded. The data presented thus relate to the day-to-day incidence of symptoms of mild or moderate illness, based on the mother's own assessment. The mothers' reports were relied on because they were in close contact with their suckling and weanling infants: infants were breast-fed exclusively for 9 months on average, and breast feeding did not terminate until a median age of 20 months (see Almedom 1991a). A recent study has noted that mothers can recognize their children's ill health and can describe it as accurately as clinicians regardless of their educational and socio-economic background (Roy *et al.* 1993). Moreover, breast feeding mothers are most likely to notice slight changes in their infants' health status (Winikoff 1981). The fact that mothers were asked to report infants' symptoms over a period of 4 weeks poses the problem of recall. However, the longitudinal study design has meant that mothers were asked the same questions repeatedly and the data have shown internal consistency, minimizing the effect of possible recall error.

The quality of the environment in which the sample infants lived was poor in terms of income level, characteristics of housing, hygiene, and sanitation. However, food supply was good during the first 3 months of the study period for seasonal reasons: in November, when data collection began, it was the end of the harvest in the surrounding rural areas and food crops were sold at relatively low prices in Addis Ababa. Many of the sample infants were reported to have been introduced to weaning foods in December owing to the seasonal availability of food. The situation deteriorated gradually during the second 3 months of the study, largely due to cultural factors: as is customary for most Ethiopian Orthodox Christians, the sample women 'fasted' throughout Lent. The cost of the reduced availability of food in the sample households during this period of time is thought to have been borne largely by the mothers, but would no doubt have affected their suckling and weanlings as well (see Almedom 1991*c*).

The main severe health hazard that occurred during the study period was an epidemic of cerebrospinal meningitis (CSM) in February and March. Meningitis epidemics have been known to occur almost every year during the dry season (peaking in March) in the endemic parts of Ethiopia, the north-western regions in relation to Addis Ababa (Tekle *et al.* 1988). The symptoms of developed CSM are fever, convulsions, headache, and stiffness of the neck and back. Two children from the sample households died, having had these symptoms for a day or two. In both cases, the cause of death was clinically confirmed as CSM. One of these fatalities was a 13-year-old boy whose younger brother was in the study and the other was a 20 months old boy who was in the study, from a different household. More than 50 per cent of the fatalities reported from the 1987–88 CSM epidemic were below the age of 14 years (Tedla 1993).

While there were no significant monthly variations in the incidence of diarrhoea, fever, and coughing showed significant variation, both with peaks in December (Fig. 8.1). The prevalence of vomiting also showed significant increases in December and in April. However, these changes were not significant when the presence of other symptoms was controlled for (see Almedom 1991*c*, p. 169). The data on fever and vomiting, as reported by the mother, were found to be difficult to interpret, mainly due to the huge variation in the way mothers recognized and defined these symptoms (see Almedom 1991*c*). The symptom that was focused on in the analysis, and has shown interesting associations with a range of environmental/ecological as well as maternal variables is diarrhoea.

Significantly more diarrhoea was reported for infants in the age group 6–12 months (Fig. 8.2). The most likely explanation for this seemed to be the infants' increased development of motor skills. From the age of about 6 months onwards, infants who were previously protected from the hazards of low levels of hygiene by being carried around and exclusively breast-fed became exposed to significant doses of diarrhoeal pathogens when they began to crawl and walk, putting dirty fingers in the mouth, ingesting contaminated food and water, and so forth. As infant age was not found to be a major factor in the weaning process for this sample, this phenomenon could more appropriately be called 'developmental diarrhoea' rather than weanling's diarrhoea (Almedom 1991*b,c*, p. 172).

The quality of the physical environment of the sample households was more or less homogeneous (Table 8.1). All households visited had access to piped water supply and most used it exclusively although some used 'stream' water as well. Interviews with the mothers revealed that the Amharic term *'wänz'* was used indiscriminately to refer to freshwater streams and rivers as well as sewage canals. Bacteriological analysis of samples of water from both upstream and downstream of the Kataba, a stream that runs along the eastern boundary of *Kebele* 11, revealed high levels of faecal contamination with a coliform count of over 161/100 ml during the dry season. All households visited were characterized by poor housing and sanitary conditions. The waste-disposal and sanitation system was poor: 35 per cent of sample households had no latrines. Thus the benefits derived from access to piped water to all households in minimizing infection, were negated by the widespread lack of safe waste disposal and sanitation.

Very few studies have looked at the relationships between ecological and behavioural factors with childhood diarrhoea in the same way as the *Kebele* 11 study did. In one study which explored the ecology of child health in Addis Ababa, variables such as the quality of housing, level of crowding, source of water-supply and 'hygiene and sanitation' were isolated as powerful predictors of childhood diarrhoeal disease (Freij and Wall 1979). This study assessed hygiene and sanitation by looking at the availability of latrines in the sample households that represented all income levels. The Kirkos study was conducted in 1972–74 by an Ethio-Swedish team, with the aim of exploring the ecology of infant/child morbidity in a socio-economically mixed sample of 600 households in Addis Ababa. The investigators provided Kirkos, the study site, with a primary health-care clinic in which diagnoses of illness were carried out in addition to home visits by non-medical enumerators who conducted structured interviews with adult household members. The most important contribution of the Kirkos study was that it employed a multifactorial approach to the investigation of child health. It also pioneered the use of a statistical technique for examining interactions in a multifactorial framework of analysis. The technique called 'Theta Automatic Interaction Detector' (THAID), now superseded by log-linear models, was applied in order to screen interaction effects between variables

(Freij *et al.* 1976; Freij and Wall 1977, 1979). Compared with the Kirkos study, the *Kebele* 11 study has approached the problem in a more focused way, with a more detailed and in-depth approach, using a smaller sample. In the *Kebele* 11 study, mothers were specifically targeted as the source of information on their infants' illnesses, rather than any adult household member as was the case in the Kirkos study. Such methodological advantages have contributed positively to the results of the *Kebele* 11 study.

Mothers who suffered from 'oppression of the soul' exhibited behaviours of demoralized resignation on a day-to-day basis. They also tended to practise significantly less adequate domestic and infants' personal hygiene. These mothers had lost their *joie de vivre* due to the distress caused by the notorious *afessa*, press-gang mass conscription. The absence of their sons and/or husbands, of whom they had no news, resulted in a resigned attitude towards hygiene and child care. The magnitude of the mass conscription under the previous regime in Ethiopia is corroborated by recent reports from human rights organizations (Africa Watch 1991). However, its effect on the psychological well-being of the population, particularly that of women has not been looked at. It is disappointing that a recent publication on the ecology of health and disease in Ethiopia, which includes a chapter on 'mental health' in its revised edition, makes no mention of war-related trauma as a possible cause of psychological disorders in the community (Kloos and Ahmed Zein 1993).

The association of hygiene with diarrhoea detected by log-linear analysis (Table 8.3) was consistent in magnitude and direction with the result of logistic regression of hygiene with diarrhoea as the dependent variable (Table 8.4). Clearly, the carer's hygiene behaviours and activities have a significantly strong bearing on diarrhoeal infection in the child. The association between mother's education and hygiene may be interpreted in two different ways. Basic literacy may help mothers to achieve better standards of hygiene. Alternatively, mothers who already maintain reasonable standards of hygiene may be the ones who are more likely to attend literacy classes.

The graphical model (see Fig. 8.3) summarizes the interactions between the most significant predictors of infant health in the study population. The model was selected by downward stepping from a saturated hierarchical model (Edwards and Kreiner 1983), using the microcomputer program for graphical log-linear modelling called MIM (Edwards 1988). Stepwise regression technique in which less significant effects are removed step-by-step is more reliable than upward stepping, in which effects are added at each step (Feinberg 1980).

In conclusion, while the association between mother's education and child health has been commonly observed (e.g. Caldwell 1979; Cleland and Wilson 1987) and should thus come as no surprise, the association of low morale with domestic hygiene is more unexpected. This precise causal sequence is probably unique to Ethiopia, but mothers in other societies where civil violence and political repression are the norm may be presumed to suffer in similar ways.

It was recommended at the end of the *Kebele* 11 study that while the provision of psychological assistance in the form of counselling and medication might improve the mothers' morale, the restoration of their *joie de vivre* is probably best achieved through political reforms which would remove the underlying causes of 'oppression of the soul' (see Almedom 1991*c*). Fortunately, for the mothers in *Kebele* 11 at least, the Menghistu government fell shortly after the completion of this study, and so some of the underlying causes of low morale have been removed. However, the domains of maternal morale and psychological well-being in regions of conflict and post-conflict, and their influence on child health still remain to be explored and studied more thoroughly.

Acknowledgements

This study was conducted as part of my doctoral thesis under the supervision of Geoffrey Harrison. The fieldwork was financed by the Wenner-Gren Foundation for Anthropological Research and the Royal Anthropological Institute. The Save the Children Fund (UK) provided logistical support in Addis Ababa.

References

Aaby, P. (1988). Malnutrition and overcrowding/intensive exposure in severe measles infection. *Reviews of Infectious Diseases*, **10**, 478–91.

Africa Watch (1991). *Evil days: thirty years of war and famine in Ethiopia*. Human Rights Watch, New York.

Almedom, A. M. (1991*a*). Infant feeding in urban low-income households in Ethiopia: I. the weaning process. *Ecology of Food and Nutrition*, **25**, 97–109.

Almedom, A. M. (1991*b*). Infant feeding in urban low-income households in Ethiopia: II. determinants of weaning. *Ecology of Food and Nutrition*, **25**, 111–21.

Almedom, A. M. (1991*c*). *Aspects of the health and growth of the suckling and weanling infant in Ethiopia*. D. Phil. thesis. University of Oxford.

Black, R. E. (1984). Diarrhoeal diseases and child morbidity and mortality. *Population and Development Review*, **10**, (Suppl.), 141–61.

Black, R. E., Brown, K. H., and Becker, S. (1984) Malnutrition is a determining factor in diarrhoeal duration, but not incidence among young children in a longitudinal study in rural Bangladesh. *American Journal Clinical Nutrition*, **391**, 87–94.

Caldwell, J. C. (1979). Education as a factor in mortality decline: an examination of Nigerian data. *Population Studies*, **23**, 395–413.

Cleland, J. and Wilson, C. (1987). Demand theories of the fertility transition. An iconoclastic view. *Population Studies*, **41**, 5–30.

Dixon, W. J. (ed.) (1988). *BMDP Statistical software manual*. University of California Press, Berkeley.

Dixon, W. J. (ed.) (1990). *BMDP statistical software manual*. University of California Press, Berkeley.

Edwards, D. (1988). *MIM: a program for hierarchical models. A computer software package,* Version 4.1, Copenhagen.

Edwards, D. and Kreiner, S. (1983). The analysis of contingency tables by graphical models. *Biometrika,* **70**, 553–65.

Feinberg, S. E. (1980). *The analysis of cross-classified data.* MIT, Cambridge, Massachusetts.

Freij, L. and Wall, S. (1977). Exploring child health and its ecology: the Kirkos study in Addis Ababa — an evaluation of procedures in the measurement of acute morbidity and a search for causal structure. *Acta Paediatrica Scandinavica,* (Suppl.), 267.

Freij, L. and Wall, S. (1979). Quantity and variation in morbidity, THAID-analysis of the occurrence of gastroenteritis among Ethiopian children. *International Journal of Epidemiology,* **8**, 313–25.

Freij, L., Kidane, Y., Sterky, G., and Wall, S. (1976). Exploring child health and its ecology: the Kirkos study in Addis Ababa. *Ethiopian Journal of Development Research,* **11** (Suppl.)

Harrison, G. A., Brush, G., Almedom, A., and Jewell, T. (1990). Short term variation in stature growth in Ethiopian and English children. *Annals of Human Biology,* **17**, 407–16.

Hirschhorn, N., Grabowsky, M., Houston, R., and Steinglass, R. (1989). Are we ignoring different levels of mortality in the primary health care debate? *Health Policy and Planning,* **4**, 343–53.

Kloos, H. and Ahmed Zein, Z. (1993). *The ecology of health and disease in Ethiopia.* Westview, Boulder.

Mata, L. J. (1978). *The children of Santa Maria Cauque: a prospective study of health and growth.* MIT, Cambridge, MA.

Mata, L. J. (1979). The malnutrition-infection complex and its environmental factors. *Proceedings of the Nutrition Society,* **38**, 29–40.

Mata, L. J. (1980). Child malnutrition and deprivation — observations in Guatemala and Costa Rica. *Food and Nutrition,* **6**, 7–14.

Mata, L. J., Kromal, R. A., Urrutia, J. J., and Garcia, B. (1977). Effect of infection on food intake and the nutritional state: perspectives as viewed from the village. *American Journal of Clinical Nutrition,* **30**, 1215–27.

Roy, K. S., Rahman, M. M., and Mitra, A. K. (1993) Can mothers identify malnutrition in their children? *Health Policy and Planning,* **8**, 143–9.

Scrimshaw, N. S., Taylor, C. E., and Gordon, J. E. (1968). *Interactions of nutrition and infection.* World Health Organization Monograph Series, No. 57, Geneva.

Scrimshaw, N. S., Behar, M., Guzmán, M. A., and Gordon, J. E. (1969). Nutrition and infection field study in Guatemalan villages, 1959–1964 II. *Archives of Environmental Health,* **18**, 51–62.

Statistical Analysis System (1985). *SAS Users guide: statistics* Version 5, SAS Institute Inc., Cary, NC.

Tedla, T. (1993). Meningococcal meningitis. In *The ecology of health and disease in Ethiopia* (ed. H. Kloos and Z. Ahmed Zein), pp. 285–93. Westview, Boulder.

Teka, G. A. (1993). Water supply and sanitation. In *The ecology of health and disease in Ethiopia* (ed. H. Kloos and Z. Ahmed Zein), pp. 179–90. Westview, Boulder.

Tekle, E., Habte-Gabr, E., and Gebre-Yohannes, A. (1988). Meningococcal meningitis. In *The ecology of health and disease in Ethiopia.* (ed. H. Kloos and Z. Ahmed Zein), pp. 273–80. Ministry of Health, Addis Ababa.

Tomkins, A. M. (1981). Nutritional status and severity of diarrhoea among pre-school children in rural Nigeria. *Lancet*, **i**, 860–2.

Tomkins, A. M. (1986). Protein–energy malnutrition and risk of infection. *Proceedings of the Nutrition Society*, **45**, 289–304.

Tomkins, A. M. and Watson F. (1988). *Interaction of Nutrition and Infection*. World Health Organization, Rome.

Ulijaszek, S. J. (1990). Nutritional status and susceptibility to infectious disease. In *Diet and disease in traditional and developing societies* (ed. G. A. Harrison and J. C. Waterlow), pp. 137–54. Cambridge University Press.

Winikoff, B. (1981). Issues in the design of breastfeeding research. *Studies in Family Planning*, **12**, 177–83.

Zeitlin, M. F. (1991). Nutritional resilience in a hostile environment: Positive deviance in child nutrition. *Nutrition Reviews*, **49**, 259–68.

Zeitlin, M. F. and Ghassemi, H. (1986) Positive deviance in nutrition: adequate child growth in poor households. In *Proceedings of the XIIIth international congress of nutrition* (ed. T. G. Taylor and N. K. Jenkins), pp. 158–61. J. Libby, London.

9

Living with schistosomes: adaptation, accommodation, or severe ill-health?

M. PARKER

Introduction

More than 200 million people world-wide live with schistosomes. Academics and public health professionals generally equate schistosomal infection with ill-health and, until recently, it has been sufficient to cite epidemiological data documenting the prevalence of infection to show that schistosomiasis presents a major public health problem in the tropical and subtropical world. This chapter draws attention to our limited understanding of the relationship between infection, intensity of infection, and ill-health and raises the following questions: are there any data to suggest that people adapt or accommodate to life with schistosomes? Is it appropriate for governments and international agencies to continue to allocate scarce resources to control schistosomiasis in the absence of information documenting severe ill-health for the majority of people harbouring schistosomes?

This chapter is divided into four parts. Part one discusses the extent to which *Schistosoma mansoni* affects reproductive success and part two explores the relationship between *S. mansoni* and some of the parasitological, pathological, and clinical indicators of morbidity. The third part of the chapter examines the relationship between schistosomes and daily activities and the fourth and final part discusses the implications of this large body of work for public health policy. The chapter focuses on *S. mansoni*, but the questions raised are applicable to other species of schistosome, especially *S. haematobium*, *S. intercalatum* and, to a lesser extent, *S. japonicum*.

Mortality and fertility

Demographic indicators of mortality and fertility convey useful information about reproductive success. Unfortunately, there are no studies monitoring the effects of *S. mansoni* on mortality and fertility among large populations over prolonged periods of time; it is thus unclear whether schistosomal infection influences reproductive success.

A limited amount of research examining the effects of *S. mansoni* on fertility has been carried out and may be summarized as follows: Weisbrod *et al.* (1973) studied the effects of *S. mansoni* (and four other parasitic diseases) on the birth rate in St Lucia, and found no significant relationships. Parker (unpublished results, 1984) examined the effects of *S. mansoni* on the number of live births and the number of miscarriages, as well as infant and child mortality in two village populations in Gezira Province, Sudan. As with Weisbrod *et al.* (1973) no significant relationships were recorded in this cross-sectional study. However, it cannot be concluded from either of these studies that schistosomal infection does not affect fertility. In both studies little, if any, information could be obtained concerning a subject's past infective history; and it would be erroneous to relate current egg loads to past reproductive events without knowledge of the duration and intensity of infection experienced by each subject.

With reference to mortality, research investigating the relationship between schistosomiasis and stillbirths, neonatal deaths and subsequent deaths up to and during the reproductive life-span has been minimal. This work has been undertaken by Weisbrod *et al.* (1973), Kloetzel (1964) and Ongom and Bradley (1972*a*). Weisbrod *et al.*'s (1973) research in St Lucia found no significant relationship between *S. mansoni* and mortality among children and adults in the surveyed villages. The intensity of infection was defined as 'moderate' in this cross-sectional study as egg loads ranged from 1 to 105 eggs/g.

The prevalence and intensity of infection was heavier in the populations surveyed by Kloetzel (1964) in Gameleira, Brazil and by Ongom and Bradley (1972*a*) in West Nile, Uganda. The data collected in these two studies, in combination with Weisbrod *et al.*'s (1973) findings, suggest that considerable mortality may occur up to and during the reproductive years in certain hyperendemic areas of *S. mansoni*. Kloetzel documented a crude mortality of 38 in those with hepatosplenic disease (23 of which were due to schistosomiasis); and Ongom and Bradley's study suggested that at least 25% of the mortality observed over 2 years in the selected village was of schistosomal origin. However, the investigators point out that none of the patients were seen by a doctor at death and their conclusions are necessarily tentative. It would be useful to undertake longitudinal studies of large populations over prolonged periods of time to assess the validity of these provisional data and, ultimately, to assess the effects of *S. mansoni* on reproductive success.

The current difficulties of establishing a relationship between *S. mansoni*, fertility, and mortality and the possibility that some of the clinical and pathological sequelae of infection may underlie causes of death ascribed to other conditions accounts for the widely held view that 'morbidity due to schistosomiasis represents in numerical terms a profound burden on the public health and therapeutic services in countries where transmission is endemic' (WHO 1980, p. 38).

It is interesting that there are few data to support this view. Indeed, there is a growing body of biomedical and behavioural research which suggests that in areas where *S. mansoni* is endemic it is inappropriate to equate infection with ill-health as the majority of people appear to live with schistosomes without impairment to their health and well-being. The following two sections discuss the key findings emerging from this pathological, clinical, epidemiological, and behavioural research.

Morbidity

Biomedical research examining the relationship between infection with schistosomes and subsequent morbidity is extensive and contrasts with the limited and tentative nature of information on demographic indicators of reproductive success. Most of this research has been undertaken by pathologists, clinicians, epidemiologists, and physiologists. Some of the most important findings include the following: first, autopsy studies undertaken by Cheever (1968), Cheever *et al.* (1975, 1977), and Kamel *et al.* (1978) established a clear relationship between the presence of schistosomal disease and worm burden for *S. mansoni* and *S. haematobium*. Second, these studies also showed that worm burden is related to the excretion of eggs in faeces (for *S. mansoni*) and urine (for *S. haematobium*). Third, these findings suggest excretion of eggs in the urine and faeces may be a useful measure of intensity of infection in living people. Fourth, a multitude of studies have examined the relationship between infection, intensity of infection (as assessed by egg output), and clinical indicators of morbidity in hospital and community settings. These studies have documented the prevalence of hepatomegaly and splenomegaly and, to a lesser extent, pulmonary hypertension, cor pulmonare, and colonic polyposis for *S. mansoni* (e.g. Ongom and Bradley 1972*b*; Cook *et al.* 1974; Arap Siongok *et al.* 1976; Lehman *et al.* 1976; Salih *et al.* 1979; Smith *et al.* 1979; Sukwa *et al.* 1986); and haematuria, proteinuria, and bacterial infections of the urinary tract for *S. haematobium* (e.g. Wilkins 1977; Laughlin *et al.* 1978; Wilkins *et al.* 1979; Mott *et al.* 1983; Tanner *et al.* 1983). They have suggested that there is an increased probability of developing these clinical signs of infection with heavy infestations of schistosomes.

The findings generated by these studies have encouraged health planners to allocate substantial resources to control schistosomiasis in regions where it is endemic. They have also influenced the type of control strategies which have been formulated. For example, selective chemotherapy (for individuals with heavy infections) or targeted mass chemotherapy (usually aimed at children and young adults as they tend to be more heavily infected) has been advocated by several investigators (Jordan and Webbe 1982; Mahmoud *et al.* 1983; Jordan 1985) as well as international organizations such as the World Health Organization (World Health Organization 1985) and the Rockefeller Foundation.

This is unfortunate as it is difficult to interpret many of the clinical, pathological, and parasitological data which have been collected as functional impairment is not necessarily associated with these signs of infection. In the case of schisto-somiasis *mansoni*, for example, decompensated portal hypertension due to peri-portal liver fibrosis is the most important pathology to be prevented as some of the clinical consequences may be fatal. However, research undertaken by Gryseels and Polderman (1987), Gryseels (1988), and Gryseels and Nkulikyinka (1990) suggests that while hepatomegaly (and splenomegaly) may be positively associated with infection few if any cases lead to decompensated portal hyper-tension or other forms of functional morbidity. The autopsy studies undertaken by Cheever (1968) and the ultrasound studies undertaken by Homeida *et al.* (1988) have also suggested that hepatomegaly was not related to the presence of periportal liver fibrosis or to any other functional pathology. It is thus possible that hepatomegaly is not a reliable indicator of severe morbidity.

In addition, the research undertaken by Gryseels and Polderman (1987) in Zaire and Homeida *et al.* (1988) in Sudan suggests that intense infections (assessed by egg output) are insufficient to cause severe pathology although the extent to which regional differences in schistosomal strains, host susceptibility, nutritional factors, and concomitant parasitism influence the outcome of infec-tion is unclear. It is also unclear whether there is any relationship between infec-tion, intensity of infection, and reduced resistance to other infections as this has not been studied systematically.

The relationship between infection, intensity of infection, and morbidity cannot, of course, be understood by relying upon a small number of pathological, clinical, and parasitological indicators. Several hospital-based clinicians and clin-ical epidemiologists have thus attempted to document the experience of infection by enquiring about the symptoms associated with schistosomal infection. In the case of *S. mansoni*, for example, investigators such as Arap Siongok *et al.* (1976), Lehman *et al.* (1976), Omer *et al.* (1976), Cline *et al.* (1977), Smith *et al.* (1979), Hiatt (1976), Pope *et al.* (1980), Guimaraes *et al.* (1985), Sleigh *et al.* (1985) and Gryseels and Polderman (1987) have enquired about the presence or absence of one or more of the following symptoms: abdominal pain, fatigue, diarrhoea, and blood in the stool. The results generated from these studies suggest that there is no demonstrable relationship between symptoms associated with *S. mansoni* and the presence or intensity of infection (Parker 1989). However, the methods and approaches employed to elicit symptoms are so faulty that it is difficult to know whether or not these findings accurately reflect the lack of a clear symptomatology associated with *S. mansoni* or whether alterna-tive methods would enable rather different conclusions to be drawn.

One of the most striking limitations of this type of research is that it betrays a biomedical conception of the body, illness, and affliction. Moreover, biomedical investigators assume that their knowledge and ideas are shared, or at least under-stood, by those participating in their research. It is thus not problematic to enquire about the presence or absence of blood in the stool, abdominal pain, and fatigue by putting pre-designed questions in a set format to the study population.

Investigators simply ask direct questions such as 'do you have abdominal pain?', 'do you feel tired', and 'have you had diarrhoea in the last 24 hours?'

Unfortunately, terms such as 'abdominal pain', 'fatigue', and 'diarrhoea' are rarely defined by the investigators; and it is impossible to tell whether respondents have interpreted the question in the way intended by the investigator. Anthropological research suggests these data should be treated with caution as many ethnic groups identify different types of abdominal pain, fatigue, and diarrhoea. Among the Nankani in northern Ghana, for example, there are more than 10 words to describe different types of diarrhoea. These diarrhoeas are generally identified according to colour, texture, and perceived aetiology (rather than 'the number of loose motions passed in the last 24 hours'); and there is no single word which describes them all. Enquiries about the presence or absence of diarrhoea will thus elicit different responses according to the investigator's choice of word.

Similarly, it is usual for ethnic groups to employ a variety of words and phrases to describe different aspects of tiredness. The Hasaneeya in Gezira Province, Sudan, for example, have a large vocabulary to describe different aspects of tiredness. Some of these words have perjorative overtones like lazy while others may absolve an individual from their daily responsibilities, as they are associated with severe ill-health. Questions such as 'do you feel tired?' or 'have you felt tired in the last 24 hours?' can be interpreted in a multitude of ways as they do not enable respondents to differentiate between lethargy, malaise, weakness, exhaustion, etc.

Indeed, respondents may interpret questions about the experience of pain, exhaustion, etc. in ways that bear no relation to the investigator's understanding of the question. To ask a man if he is tired in parts of India, for example, is a delicate way of enquiring whether or not he is impotent (H. Lambert, personal communication). It goes without saying that a survey enquiring about the presence or absence of tiredness in this part of the world would generate different responses from men, whatever their infective status!

Linguistic issues aside, there is a tendency by those with a biomedical training to discount anthropological research demonstrating the different ways in which social, cultural, and economic processes influence the conceptualization and manifestation of illness, affliction, and health. This is unfortunate as there is a substantial body of work which demonstrates that prevailing approaches to the study of symptomatology are inadequate (e.g. Constantinides 1985; Frankel 1986; Morsy 1978).

In sum, the difficulties of interpreting hospital and community based data describing the symptoms associated with *S. mansoni* are considerable and it is currently not clear whether most people infected with *S. mansoni* are asymptomatic or symptomatic as the data which have been collected are of questionable validity. The following section discusses the behavioural responses to infection and, once again, challenges the assumed relationship between schistosomal infection and ill-health.

Behavioural responses to infection with *S. mansoni*

There is very little research describing the effects of *S. mansoni* (or any other species of schistosome) on daily behaviour. This is unfortunate as many people will never receive treatment and will probably live with parasitic infestations for considerable periods of time. In the case of *S. mansoni* the mean life-span has been variously estimated as being between 3–5 years (Hairston 1965; Goddard and Jordan 1980) and 5–10 years (Warren *et al.* 1974), although records indicate that schistosome worms can live for as long as 20–32 years (Wallerstein 1949; Berberian *et al.* 1953; Harris *et al.* 1984). Moreover, many individuals living in areas where schistosomiasis is endemic may acquire additional infections during their lifetime and thus be infected for the greater part of their life.

It would be helpful to know how, if at all, infection alters their daily activities as this will shed light on the extent to which it is possible to accommodate or adapt to life with schistosomes. It is particularly important to address this question in view of the dearth of information about reproductive success; the difficulties of identifying whether there is a relationship between infection, intensity of infection, and ill-health (according to clinical, pathological, and parasitological indicators of morbidity); the chronic nature of infection and the difficulties of examining the relationship between infection and well-being among populations who do not identify or know about the invading pathogen.

Parker (1989, 1992, 1993) is the only investigator to have documented some of the behavioural responses to schistosomal infection. This research focused on women engaged in domestic and agricultural activities in Omdurman aj Jadida, a village in the Gezira/Managil irrigation scheme, Sudan. Biomedical and continuous observational data were collected over a period of 14 months between 1985 and 1986. These data were interpreted in the light of ethnographic information acquired during two previous field trips to Gezira in 1981 and 1983 as well as this 14-month period of fieldwork. The following questions were addressed: does *S. mansoni* influence the nature and extent of activities undertaken by women nursing newborn infants and engaged in domestic work? Is there a relationship between a mother's infective status, her daily activities, and the subsequent growth and development of her infant? To what extent does *S. mansoni* influence the nature and extent of activities undertaken by women in the fields during the cotton picking season? Is there a relationship between a woman's infective status, daily activity patterns, and her productivity in the cotton fields?

The methods employed to address these questions (and detailed information about the study site) have been described elsewhere (Parker 1989, 1992). They may be summarized as follows: 24 women participated in research exploring the links between *S. mansoni*, domestic activities, and infant growth; and 22 women participated in research exploring the relationship between *S. mansoni*, agricultural activities, and productivity. Both studies were characterized by a paired design. That is, the 12 most heavily infected women nursing infants and engaged in domestic activities were paired with 12 women free from infection but also nursing infants and engaged in domestic activities. Similarly, the 11 most heavily infected women engaged in agricultural activities were paired with 11 women free from infection but also engaged in agricultural activities. Infective status aside, women were matched for a wide range of social, economic, and biological variables that might otherwise have affected their daily activities. These included estimated age, household composition, ethnicity, parity, available domestic labour, selected indicators of socio-economic status and, for the women engaged in domestic activities, care was taken to ensure that their infants were exclusively breast-fed and tightly matched for age. Stool and urine samples were also analysed to ensure that women participating in these studies were free from other parasitic infections such as *S. haematobium*, ascaris, and hookworm; and blood samples were analysed to monitor haemoglobin levels. Observations were conducted on a minute by minute basis in order to detect the effects of *S. mansoni* on female activity patterns in the domestic and agricultural spheres. The following two sub-sections describe the methods and results employed in these two studies.

The impact of S. mansoni on domestic activities and infant growth

Every woman nursing an infant and engaged in domestic work was observed for 2 consecutive days and her pair, where possible, was observed on the following 2 days. These observations were undertaken for a minimum of 5 continuous hours between 0800 and 1300 and every activity attempted by a woman — with or without her newborn infant — during this period of time was recorded. The time engaged in these activities was subsequently related to anthropometric, parasitological, and haematological indicators of ill-health.

Some of the most important findings include the following: first, women infected by *S. mansoni* had an arithmetic mean egg load of 860 eggs/g. Second, paired *t*-test analyses showed that women infected by *S. mansoni* did not spend significantly different amounts of time engaged in domestic work (such as food preparation, sweeping, washing-up) or infant and child-care activities (such as breast feeding, supplementary feeding, cleaning the infant, holding the infant, caring for other children within the household). These results are presented in Table 9.1.

Third, the type of domestic work undertaken by women did not significantly vary by infective status during the period of observation. However, an enormous variety of domestic activities are attempted by women and these activities require different amounts of energy and effort to be expended. Drawing upon the author's observations and lay perceptions of the effort required to attempt different types of domestic work, it was possible to group these activities according to those requiring 'heavy' effort, 'moderate' effort, and 'light' effort.

Living with schistosomes

Table 9.1. Paired *t*-tests showing whether or not infective status affects the time engaged in domestic work, infant and child care, social activities, non-essential activities, and rest (uninfected–infected)

	n	n Missing	Mean	SEM	t	P
Activities between 0800 and 1300 h						
Domestic work	12	0	−6.3	18.0	−0.35	0.734
Infant/child work	12	0	9.8	14.6	0.67	0.518
Social activities (log10)	8	4	−0.2	0.3	−0.62	0.555
Non-essential acts (log10)	10	2	0.3	0.2	1.47	0.177
Rest	12	0	−0.1	0.1	−1.37	0.198

The results from paired *t*-test analyses are presented in Table 9.2 and suggest that *S. mansoni* did not significantly affect the amount of time engaged in these three activity groups.

Fourth, women infected by *S. mansoni* did not spend significantly different amounts of time engaged in the five main types of infant and child-care activities than women free from infection. The results from paired *t*-test analyses are presented in Table 9.3. In common with domestic work activities, the energy and effort expended to attempt these activities varies and they were thus divided into three groups: activities involving 'very active and active', 'passive', and 'very passive' behaviour by a mother towards her infant. There were no significant results (see Table 9.3).

Fifth, the time engaged in social activities (such as attending circumcision ceremonies and visiting friends and relatives), non-essential activities (such as plaiting hair), and rest (such as sleeping, lying down, and sitting) did not vary with infective status. The results from paired *t*-test analyses are presented in Table 9.1.

Table 9.2. Paired *t*-tests showing whether or not infective status affects the time engaged in heavy, moderate, and light domestic work (uninfected–infected)

	n	n Missing	Mean	SEM	t	P
Activities between 0800 and 1300 h						
Domestic work						
Heavy domestic work (log10)	9	3	0.16	0.23	0.70	0.505
Moderate domestic work	12	0	−11.75	13.71	−0.86	0.410
Light domestic work	12	0	2.96	6.25	0.47	0.645

Table 9.3 Paired *t*-tests showing whether or not infective status affects the time engaged in different types of infant and child activities and the effort expended in very active, active, passive, and very passive activities (uninfected–infected)

	n	n Missing	Mean	SEM	t	P
Activities between 0800 and 1300 h						
Infant and child care						
Holding infant	12	0	7.33	15.0	0.49	0.634
Breast feeding	12	0	6.25	4.9	1.27	0.231
Supplementary feeding	12	0	0.04	1.2	0.04	0.972
Cleaning infant (log10)	9	3	0.32	1.5	2.16	0.063
Other child care (log10)	8	4	–0.09	0.3	–0.35	0.735
Effort expended						
Active + very active (log10)	12	0	0.11	0.06	1.71	0.115
Passive	12	0	–5.40	12.57	–0.45	0.663
Very passive	12	0	–1.00	10.88	–0.09	0.928

The analyses of continuous observational date from 24 women thus suggest that infection with *S. mansoni* does not influence the nature and extent of activities in the domestic sphere. These data do not quantify the energy and effort required to perform a particular task and the long-term consequences of harbouring schistosomes for physiological well-being cannot be assessed. However, anthropometric, parasitological, and haematological data were collected from the 24 women participating in this piece of observational work and their infants at 5-weekly intervals over a period of 5–8 months in 1985. These data document some of the biological responses to infection among women and they provide a crude measure of the success with which infected women were able to care for their infants compared with women free from infection.

The results from paired *t*-test analyses are presented in Tables 9.4 and 9.5. Table 9.4 suggests that infection by *S. mansoni* did not affect anthropometric and haematological indices of nutritional well-being among nursing women over time; and Table 9.5 suggests that maternal infective status did not significantly affect the rate of growth and development of their nursing infants.*

*See M. Parker (1989: 267–95) for a detailed discussion of the techniques employed to analyse these data and the issues concerning the interpretation of these data.

Table 9.4. Paired *t*-tests showing whether or not a woman's infective status affects average weekly anthropometric and haematological indices over time (uninfected–infected)*

		n	n Missing	Mean	SEM	t	P
Haemoglobin	(g/l)	11	1	0.264	0.24	1.08	0.304
Weight	(kg)	12	0	0.022	0.03	0.82	0.428
Upper arm circ	(cm)	12	0	0.009	0.02	0.61	0.553
Biceps	(mm)	12	0	−0.007	0.01	−0.82	0.429
Triceps	(mm)	12	0	−0.021	0.01	−1.45	0.176
Subscapular	(mm)	12	0	−0.031	0.03	−1.43	0.181
Suprailiac	(mm)	11	1	0.004	0.03	0.15	0.887

* Measurements were taken from nine pairs of women between July 1985 and February 1986 and three pairs of women between October 1985 and February 1986.

Table 9.5. Paired *t*-tests showing whether or not a woman's infective status affects the average weekly incremental rate of growth of her infant (unifected–infected)*

		n	n Missing	Mean	SEM	t	P
Supine length	(cm)	12	0	−0.10	0.04	−0.28	0.784
Weight	(kg)	12	0	0.00	0.01	0.08	0.937
Upper arm circ	(cm)	12	0	−0.02	0.01	−1.21	0.252
Head circ	(cm)	11	1	0.02	0.01	1.44	0.181
Biceps	(mm)	11	1	0.01	0.02	0.54	0.603
Triceps	(mm)	11	1	−0.01	0.03	−0.26	0.797
Subscapular	(mm)	10	2	0.00	0.04	0.09	0.926
Suprailiac	(mm)	10	2	0.02	0.02	0.72	0.488

* Measurements were taken from nine pairs of infants between July 1985 and February 1986 and three pairs of infants between October 1985 and February 1986.

The analyses of biomedical and continuous observational data thus suggest that women infected with *S. mansoni* and engaged in domestic work were able to accommodate schistosomes without altering their daily activities. They experienced few, if any, biological costs over the period of observation and infective status did not appear to alter the physical growth and development of their infants. This finding casts further doubt on the assumed relationship between infection, intensity of infection, and ill-health; and it is particularly interesting when it is considered in the light of the data presented in the following.

The impact of S. mansoni on agricultural activities and productivity in the cotton fields

Twenty-two women (11 pairs) participated in research documenting the effects of *S. mansoni* on daily activities and productivity in the cotton fields. Every woman infected with *S. mansoni* was observed for 1 day and, wherever possible, observations were undertaken with a woman's uninfected pair the next day. The following information was collected during each day's observation by the same observer: the total amount of time spent in the cotton fields; the type and duration of activities undertaken in the cotton fields; and the amount of cotton picked in the morning and afternoon. Domestic and social activities undertaken by women when they were not working in the fields were also recorded at the end of the day.

Observations were undertaken on a minute by minute basis to monitor the type and duration of activities undertaken in the cotton fields. Every activity attempted by a woman in the morning and/or afternoon was recorded. These observations took place for periods of fifteen minutes starting at 0730, 0800, 0830, 0900, 0930, 1000, 1500, 1530, 1600, 1630, 1700, and 1730.

The activities attempted during these time intervals were subsequently divided into the following five groups: female posture while picking cotton; work activities associated with picking cotton (such as putting cotton in sacks); other agricultural activities undertaken in the fields (such as gathering up weeds to feed goats); types of rest (such as sleeping, lying down, and sitting); and other activities undertaken in the cotton fields that did not directly affect a woman's daily productive output.

The most important findings emerging from this study may be summarized as follows: first, women infected with *S. mansoni* had an arithmetic mean egg load of 1958 eggs/g. Second, every woman participating in this research went to the fields in the morning to pick cotton. Third, women infected by *S. mansoni* spent less time in the fields in the morning than woman free from infection and results from a paired *t*-test (see Table 9.6) showed this difference to be highly significant ($P = 0.008$).

Paired *t*-tests were also performed on the continuous observational data which were collected in the morning; and they showed that women infected by *S.*

Table 9.6. Paired *t*-test showing whether or not there is a difference in the amount of time (min) women spend in the cotton fields (uninfected–infected)

	n	n Missing	Mean	SEM	t	P
Time difference, am:	7	4	+28.3	7.3	+3.96	0.008

mansoni utilized their time in the fields in different ways from women free from infection. That is, women spent significantly less observed time picking cotton ($P = 0.009$) but they did not pick significantly less cotton ($P = 0.620$). These results are presented in Tables 9.7 and 9.8, respectively.

A similar pattern emerged in the afternoon among those women who were infected with *S. mansoni* and returned to the fields to pick cotton. They spent significantly less observed time picking cotton ($P = 0.034$) but they did not pick significantly less cotton ($P = 0.803$). However, they spent significantly less observed time engaged in other agricultural activities ($P = 0.054$). These results are also presented in Tables 9.7 and 9.8. The statistical analyses of continuous

Table 9.7. Paired *t*-tests showing whether or not there are differences by infective status in the time engaged in six main activities — as a proportion of total observed time (minutes) spent in the cotton fields (uninfected–infected)

Main activities	n	mean	SEM	t	P
a.m.					
Picks cotton	11	+14.2	4.4	+3.24	0.009
Other cotton work	11	+01.4	1.8	+0.77	0.461
Other agricultural work	11	+01.5	1.5	+1.06	0.315
Organizational work	11	0.0	0.0	–	–
Rest	11	–02.7	2.0	–1.31	0.219
Non-productive work	11	+00.1	0.1	+1.00	0.341
p.m.*					
Picks cotton	7	+17.9	6.6	+2.73	0.034
Other cotton work	7	+02.7	1.8	+1.51	0.181
Other agricultural work	7	+03.3	1.4	+2.39	0.054
Organizational work	7	0.0	0.0	–	–
Rest	7	–04.9	2.9	–1.67	0.146
Non-productive work	7	–01.6	1.6	–0.99	0.364

* Four women infected with *S. Mansoni* did not go to the fields in the afternoon. They were excluded from the analyses of continuous observational data in the afternoon along with their uninfected pairs.

Table 9.8. Paired *t*-tests showing whether or not there are differences by infective status in the total amount of cotton picked (uninfected–infected)

Cotton picked (kg)	n	n Missing	Mean	SEM	t	P
Total picked, a.m.	11	0	+0.4	0.7	+0.51	0.620
Total picked, p.m.	7	4	+0.2	0.7	+0.26	0.803
Total picked, p.m.	11	0	+1.6	0.8	+2.12	0.061

observational data collected in the morning and afternoon suggest, overall, that women working in the fields and infected by *S. mansoni* attempted to pick as much cotton as possible in the shortest time period feasible.

This finding should be interpreted in the light of additional data recording the number of women who returned to work in the afternoon and the type of activities undertaken by women between cotton picking sessions. Two results are particularly interesting: first, four of the 22 women (18.18 per cent) did not go to the fields in the afternoon. These women all said they were too tired to attempt any work and they were all infected with *S. mansoni*. The Fisher exact probability test (one-tail) showed this difference to be significant at the 0.045 level. Second, infected women were less likely to participate in 'personal care' activities between cotton picking sessions than women free from infection. These activities included combing and plaiting hair and using *halawa* (an ointment which removes body hairs) to clean their bodies. Fisher's exact probability test (one-tail) showed this difference to be significant at the 0.010 level. These two findings, in combination with continuous observational data monitoring the nature and extent of activities undertaken in the cotton fields, suggest that infection by *S. mansoni* (at recorded egg loads) altered daily activity patterns among women engaged in agricultural work.

Living with schistosomes: a range of experiences

Research monitoring the effects of *S. mansoni* on daily activities in Omdurman aj Jadida suggests that women respond to infection with schistosomes in a variety of ways. That is, women engaged in domestic work were able to live with schistosomes without altering their daily regime; and the physical growth and development of their nursing infants was not impaired. By contrast, women engaged in agricultural work altered their activities in the fields by trying to pick as much cotton as possible in the shortest time period feasible. A significant number of women were too tired to sustain this regime and they did not, therefore, return to the fields in the afternoon. The results generated from these two studies raise an interesting question: is there any evidence to suggest that women accommodate or even adapt to heavy infestations of schistosomes?

This is a difficult question to answer as both studies are characterized by small samples and each woman in each study was observed on a minute by minute basis for a maximum of 2 days. It would certainly be helpful to know whether the results could be replicated by undertaking two similar studies with larger samples of women monitoring each woman's activities for a greater number of days. Moreover, a number of important questions remain unanswered. These include the following: does infection with *S. mansoni* exert a constant effect (or lack of) on female activities or does it become progressively debilitating over time? How many women become progressively debilitated to the point where they are too sick to work? To what extent would similar results have been obtained in the agricultural sphere by pairing women with light or moderate infections (rather than heavy infections) with women free from infection? Do infected women think they expend more energy and/or effort on their activities in the domestic or agricultural sphere than women free from infection?

Research addressing these questions would help to develop a detailed understanding of the effects of *S. mansoni* on daily activities. It is also necessary to explore the links between biomedical indicators of morbidity, daily activities, survival, and reproductive success as this would enable a detailed assessment of the extent to which individuals or populations accommodate or even adapt to infection.

Unfortunately, the biomedical, behavioural, and demographic data are currently too few to do this in a rigorous way but there are a few indications from the data collected in Omdurman aj Jadida which suggest that some of the behavioural responses to infection promote survival and fitness. For example, women infected with *S. mansoni* and engaged in agricultural work spent less time in the fields and significantly less observed time picking cotton but they did not pick significantly less cotton than women free from infection. In other words, women with limited energy and debilitated by infection utilized their time in the fields by picking as much cotton as possible in the shortest time period feasible. In so doing, they generated income which they could subsequently use to safeguard their own health and well-being. Their children's health and welfare could also be promoted as some of this income could be used to pay for medical consultations, drugs to alleviate illness, essential household items, clothes, and occasionally food.

The cotton picking session is one of the few times in the year when large numbers of women are able to earn some money. They are usually reliant on their husbands, fathers, and brothers to purchase food and the opportunity to earn some money is valued by women (and particularly those in polygamous unions) as it enables them to put money aside to cover the costs of consultations with healers, and to purchase essential household items, clothes, etc.

Some of the other findings emerging from the analyses of continuous observational data support this view. For instance, women spent less time engaged in other agricultural activities such as collecting weeds to feed goats, and this variable was significantly different in the afternoon. Collecting weeds for goats is an important activity as it affects the amount of milk produced by goats. Milk, in turn, affects the nutritional well-being of household members and it is revealing that women infected with *S. mansoni* did not feel able to participate in these activities as frequently as their uninfected pairs. Accepting the responsibility of male members of their household to ensure adequate provisions of food throughout the year, infected women channelled their energy and effort into earning sufficient income to meet other needs. In so doing, they helped to safeguard their own health and well-being as well as that of their children.

The proposed links between infection, behaviour, income, and subsequent survival and fitness are tentative and it is, of course, difficult to quantify the extent to which daily work regimes in the cotton fields promote survival and fitness. Indeed, it would be useful to corroborate these data by documenting the amount of income infected women generated during the cotton picking season compared with their uninfected pairs.

The fact that the majority of women infected with *S. mansoni* were able to accommodate heavy worm burdens by altering their working regime should not deflect attention from the fact that a significant number of infected women felt too weak to sustain this work regime. It is not known whether other members of the household covered for these women by spending more time in the cotton fields and/or generating income from other sources. The long-term economic consequences are difficult to gauge and it is difficult to predict the extent to which schistosomal infection impairs survival and fitness.

In sum, the biomedical, behavioural, and ethnographic information collected from women engaged in domestic and agricultural work suggests that the impact of *S. mansoni* is complex and variable. Women engaged in domestic work were protected from intense solar radiation as they undertook their activities in their houses and/or enclosed cooking areas. These activities required energy and effort to be expended for relatively short periods of time and detailed observational data suggest that women were able to live with schistosomes without altering their daily regime in this type of environment. By contrast, infected women engaged in cotton picking activities were exposed to intense solar radiation in the fields and the work required energy and effort to be expended over longer periods of time. It was necessary, under these conditions, for women to alter their work regimes and for the majority of women this may not have had any economic ramifications.

Conclusions

The biomedical and behavioural data presented in this chapter suggest that ill-health does not necessarily follow from infection with schistosomes. Indeed, it is possible that the majority of people infected with schistosomes are able to accommodate heavy worm burdens sufficiently well for key aspects of their lives to remain unaffected. It would, of course, be helpful to monitor the long-term consequences of harbouring schistosomes as this would enable a detailed and accurate assessment of the proportion of people who remain free from ill-health to be acquired. In the meantime, health planners are left with an awkward question: is it appropriate for international agencies (such as USAID, GTZ) and governments to allocate substantial resources to reduce the transmission of schistosomiasis in the absence of information documenting ill-health from schistosomes?

Many of the countries where schistosomiasis is endemic also experience a high prevalence of malaria, diarrhoeal diseases, acute respiratory infections, measles, AIDS, etc. The mortality rate for these diseases is high and the burden on health services considerable. It seems inappropriate to continue to channel resources into the control of schistosomiasis when at least some of these resources could otherwise be used to control these more serious diseases. It is a matter of some urgency that health planners working for governments and international agencies explain the rationale for their policies and, failing that, support research exploring the biomedical, behavioural, and socio-economic consequences of infection. They could do a lot worse.

Acknowledgements

This chapter is based upon ideas and data presented as a doctoral thesis at the Department of Biological Anthropology, University of Oxford. I am grateful to Tim Allen, Ahmed Babiker, Gerry Brush, Asim Daffalla, Alan Fenwick, Ahmed el Gadal, David Evans, Robert Sturrock, and Nick Mascie-Taylor for helping with different parts of this research. I am particularly grateful to Geoff Harrison whose encouragement and insights played a central role in the development of this work. The Royal Anthropological Institute, the Medical Research Council, the Rockefeller Foundation and the Health and Population Division of the UK Overseas Development Administration have funded various parts of this work. I thank them all.

References

Arap Siongok, T. K., Mahmoud, A. A. F., Ouma, J., Warren, K. S., Muller, A. S., Handa, A. K., and Hauser, H. B. (1976). Morbidity in schistosomiasis mansoni in relation to intensity of infection: study of a community in Machakos, Kenya. *American Journal of Tropical Medicine and Hygiene*, **25**, 273–84.

Berberian, D. A., Paquin, H. O., and Fantauzzi, A.(1953). Longevity of *Schistosoma mansoni*. Observations based on a case study. *Journal of Parasitology*, **39**, 517–19.

Cheever, A. W. (1968). A quantitative post-mortem study of schistosomiasis mansoni in man. *American Journal of Tropical Medicine and Hygiene*, **17**, 38–64.

Cheever, A. W., Torky A. H., and Shirbiney, M. (1975). The relation of worm burden to passage of *Schistosoma haematobium* eggs in the urine of infected patients. *American Journal of Tropical Medicine and Hygiene*, **24**, 284–88.

Cheever, A. W., Kamel, I. A., Elwi, A. W., Mosimann, J. E., and Danner, R. (1977). *Schistosoma mansoni* and *S. haematobium* infections in Egypt. II. Quantitative parasitological findings at necropsy. *American Journal of Tropical Medicine and Hygiene*, **26**, 702–16.

Cline, B. L., Rymzo, W. T., Hiatt, R. A., Knight, W. B., and Berrios-Duran, L. A. (1977). Morbidity from *Schistosoma mansoni* in a Puerto Rican community: a population based study. *American Journal of Tropical Medicine and Hygiene*, **26**, 109–17.

Cook, J. A., Baker, S. T., Warren, K. S., and Jordan, P (1974). A controlled study of morbidity of schistosomiasis in St Lucian children, based on quantitative egg excretion. *American Journal of Tropical Medicine and Hygiene*, **23**, 625–33.

Constantinides, P. M. (1985). Women heal women: spirit possession and sexual segregation in a muslim society. *Social Science and Medicine*, **21**, 685–92.

Frankel, S. (1986). *The Huli response to illness*. Cambridge University Press.

Goddard, M. J. and Jordan, P. (1980). On the longevity of *Schistosoma mansoni* in man on St Lucia, West Indies. *Transactions of the Royal Society of Tropical Medicine and Hygiene*, **74**, 185–91.

Gryseels, B. (1988). The morbidity of schistosmiasis mansoni in the Rusizi Plain (Burundi). *Transactions of the Royal Society of Tropical Medicine and Hygiene*, **83**, 582–7.

Gryseels, B. (1989). The relevance of schistosomiasis for health. *Tropical Medicine and Parasitology*, **40**, 134–43.

Gryseels, B. and Nkulikyinka, L. (1990). The morbidity of schistosomiasis mansoni in the highland focus of Lake Cohoha, Burundi. *Transactions of the Royal Society of Tropical Medicine and Hygiene*, **84**, 542–7.

Gryseels, B. and Polderman, A. M. (1987). The morbidity of schistosomiasis mansoni in Maniema (Zaire). *Transactions of the Royal Society of Tropical Medicine and Hygiene*, **81**, 202–9.

Gryseels, B. and Polderman, A. M. (1991). Morbidity, due to schistosomiasis mansoni, and its control in subsaharan Africa. *Parasitology Today*, **7**, 244–8.

Guimaraes, M. D. C., de Barros, H. L., and Katz, N. (1985). A clinical epidemiologic study in a schistosomiasis endemic area. *Revista do Instituto de Medicina Tropical Sao Paulo*, **27**, 123–31.

Hairston, N. G (1965). On the mathematical analysis of schistosome populations. *Bulletin of the World Health Organization*, **33**, 45–62.

Harris, A. R. C., Russel, R. J., and Charters, A. D. (1984). A review of schistosomiasis in immigrants in Western Australia demonstrating the unusual longevity of *Schistosoma mansoni*. *Transactions of the Royal Society of Tropical Medicine and Hygiene*, **78**, 385–8.

Harrison, G. A. (1982). Adaptation and well-being. *Human Genetics and Adaptation*, **2**, 165–71.

Harrison, G. A. (1991). The ecological analysis of human behaviour. *Journal of the Indian Anthropological Society*, **26**, 31–5.

Hiatt, R. A. (1976). Morbidity from *Schistosoma mansoni* infections: An epidemiological study based on quantitative analysis of egg excretion in two highland Ethiopian villages. *American Journal of Tropical Medicine and Hygiene*, **25**, 808–17.

Homeida, M., Ahmed, S., Daffalla, A., Suliman, S., El Tom, I., Nash, T., and Bennett, J. (1988). Morbidity associated with *Schistosoma mansoni* infection as determined by ultrasound: a study in Gezira, Sudan. *American Journal of Tropical Medicine and Hygiene*, **39**, 196–201.

Jordan, P. (1985). *Schistosomiasis — the St Lucia Project*. Cambridge University Press.

Jordan, P. and Webbe, G. (1982). *Schistosomiasis: epidemiology, treatment and control*. Heinemann Medical, London.

Kamel, I. A., Elwi A. M., Cheever A. W., Mosimann J. E., and Danner, R. (1978). *Schistosoma mansoni* and *S. haematobium* infections in Egypt. IV. Hepatic lesions. *American Journal of Tropical Medicine and Hygiene*, **27**, 939–43.

Kloetzel, K. (1964). Natural history and prognosis of splenomegaly in schistosomiasis mansoni. *American Journal of Tropical Medicine and Hygiene*, **13**, 541–4.

Laughlin, L. W., Farid, Z., Mansour, N., Edman, D. C., and Higashi, G. I. (1978). Bacteriuria in urinary schistosomiasis in Egypt: a prevalence survey. *American Journal of Tropical Medicine and Hygiene*, **27**, 916–18.

Lehman, J. S., Mott, K. E., Morrow, R. H., Muniz, T. M., and Boyer, M. H. (1976). The intensity and effects of infection with *Schistosoma mansoni* in a rural community in North east Brazil. *American Journal of Tropical Medicine and Hygiene*, **25**, 285–94.

Mahmoud, A. A. F., Siongok, T. A., Ouma, J., Houser, H. B., and Warren, K. S. (1983). Effect of mass treatment on intensity of infection and morbidity in schistosomiasis mansoni: three year follow-up of a community in Machakos, Kenya, *Lancet*, **i**, 849–51.

Morsy, S. A. (1978). Sex roles, power and illness in an Egyptian village. *American Ethnologist*, **5**, 137–50.

Mott, K. E., Dixon, H., Osei-Tutu, E., and England, E. C. (1983). Relation between intensity of *Schistosoma haematobium* infection and clinical haematuria and proteinuria. *Lancet*, **i**, 1005–7.

Omer, A. H. S., Hamilton, P. J. S., de C. Marshall, T. F., and Draper, C. C. (1976). Infection with *Schistosoma mansoni* in the Gezira area of the Sudan. *Journal of Tropical Medicine and Hygiene*, **79**, 151–7.

Ongom, V. L. and Bradley, D. J. (1972*a*). The epidemiology and consequences of *Schistosoma mansoni* infection in West Nile, Uganda. 1. Field studies of a community at Panyagoro. *Transactions of the Royal Society of Tropical Medicine and Hygiene*, **66**, 835–51.

Ongom, V. L. and Bradley, D. J. (1972*b*). The epidemiology and consequences of *Schistosoma mansoni* infection in West Nile, Uganda. II. Hospital investigation of a sample from the Panyagoro community. *Transactions of the Royal Society of Tropical Medicine and Hygiene*, **66**, 852–63.

Parker, M. (1989). The effects of *Schistosoma mansoni* on female activity patterns and infant growth in Gezira Province, Sudan. D. Phil. thesis, University of Oxford.

Parker, M. (1992). Re-assessing disability: the impact of *S. mansoni* on female activities in Gezira Province, Sudan. *Social Science and Medicine*, **35**, 877–90.

Parker, M. (1993). Bilharzia and the boys: questioning common assumptions. *Social Science and Medicine*, **37**, 481–92.

Pope, R. T., Cline, B. L., and El Alamy, M. A. (1980). Evaluation of schistosomal morbidity in subjects with high intensity infections in Qalyub, Egypt. *American Journal of Tropical Medicine and Hygiene*, **29**, 416–25.

Salih, S. Y., de C. Marshall, T. F., Radalowicz, A., (1979). Morbidity in relation to the clinical forms and to intensity of infection in *Schistosoma mansoni* infection in the Sudan. *Annals of Tropical Medicine and Parasitology*, **73**, 439–49.

Sleigh, A. C., Mott, K. E., Hoff, R., Barreto, M. L., Mota, E. A., Maguire, J. H., *et al.* (1985). Three-year prospective study of the evolution of Manson's schistosomiasis in north-east Brazil. *Lancet*, **ii**, 63–6.

Smith, D. H., Warren, K. S., and Mahmoud, A. A. F. (1979). Morbidity in schistosomiasis mansoni in relation to intensity of infection: study of a community in Kisumu, Kenya. *American Journal of Tropical Medicine and Hygiene*, **28**, 220–9.

Sukwa, T. Y., Bulsara, M. K., and Wurapa, F. K., (1986). The relationship between morbidity and intensity of *Schistosoma mansoni* infection in a rural Zambian community. *International Journal of Epidemiology*, **15**, 248–51.

Tanner, M. (1989). Evaluation of public health impact of schistosomiasis. *Tropical Medicine and Parasitology*, **40**, 143–8.

Tanner, M., Holzer, E., Marti, H. P., Saladin, B., and Degremont, A. A. (1983). Frequency of haematuria and proteinuria among *Schistosoma haematobium* infected children of two communities from Liberia and Tanzania. *Acta Tropica*, **40**, 231–7.

Wallerstein, R. S. (1949). Longevity of *Schistosoma mansoni*: observations based on a case. *American Journal of Tropical Medicine and Hygiene*, **29**, 717–22.

Warren, K. S., Mahmoud, A. A. F., Cummings, P., Murphy, D. J., and Houser, H. B. (1974). Schistosomiasis mansoni in Yemeni in California: duration of infection, presence of disease and therapeutic management. *American Journal of Tropical Medicine and Hygiene*, **23**, 902–9.

Weisbrod, B. A., Andreano, R. L., Baldwin, R. E., Erwin, H. E., and Kelley, A. C. (1973). *Disease and economic development. The impact of parasitic diseases in St Lucia*. University of Wisconsin Press, Madison.

Wiley, A. S. (1992). Adaptation and the biocultural paradigm in medical anthropology: a critical review. *Medical Anthropology Quarterly*, **6**, 216–36.

Wilkins, H. A. (1977). *Schistosoma haematobium* in a Gambian community. III. The prevalence of bacteriuria and of hypertension. *Annals of Tropical Medicine and Parasitology*, **71**, 179–86.

Wilkens, H. A., Goll, P., Marshall, T. F. C., and Moore, P. (1979). The significance of proteinuria and haematuria in *Schistosoma haematobium* infection. *Transactions of the Royal Society of Tropical Medicine and Hygiene*, **73**, 74–80.

World Health Organization (1980). *Epidemiology and control of schistosomiasis*. Report of a WHO expert committee. Technical Report Series, No. 643. World Health Organization, Geneva.

World Health Organization (1985). *The control of schistosomiasis*. Report of a WHO expert committee. Technical Report Series, No. 728. World Health Organization, Geneva.

10

Child-care strategies in Nepal: responses to ecology, demography, and society

C. PANTER-BRICK

Introduction

Child-care strategies are a fundamental component of human behaviour, for they have significant consequences for maternal and child health and vary enormously within and between populations. Thus many studies from the fields of social and biological anthropology, sociology, demography, psychology, or evolutionary biology have taken child-care patterns as a focus of enquiry. Arguably, the particular contribution of biological anthropology is to document the range of human life-styles and explain patterns of population variation, adopting an interdisciplinary and comparative approach to data collection, and applying the concept of adaptation to explain behaviours as responses to specific natural or social environments.

From the above perspective, a study of child care requires an evaluation of the extent to which behaviour may vary as a consequence of human choice or environmental necessity. What choices and what constraints underlie the diversity of child-care patterns? And what consequences follow, which help to evaluate the appropriateness of observed behaviours? To examine child-care strategies through the theoretical and methodological lens of human adaptability is to examine how a range of alternative behaviours are adopted in response to cultural choice and environmental constraints.

A review of cross-cultural patterns of child care is a vast undertaking, and this chapter will focus on a population in north-west Nepal for whom fine-grained anthropological data are now available. The Tamang agropastoralists of Nepal present an interesting case for a number of reasons. First, women assume two potentially conflicting responsibilities, namely full participation in the subsistence economy and prime responsibility for child care. Second, the time spent working outside the home shows significant seasonal variation between the winter and the monsoon seasons, which has implications for child care (Panter-Brick 1993a). Lastly, the Tamang live sympatrically with other ethnic groups who espouse different roles for women, distinct modes of subsistence and strategies for child care. Comparison with other populations helps to contrast behaviour patterns and highlight essential Tamang attributes. This chapter examines the role played by ecological, demographic, socio-economic, and cultural factors in shaping child-care strategies.

Ecology

While many studies emphasize the degree to which cultural beliefs affect child-care patterns, relatively few stress the fact that child-minding behaviours are often finely tuned to environment (Draper 1976; Blurton-Jones 1986). Child-care responsibilities must be fitted in the general organization of a household's activities, which itself is a response to environmental constraints (Whiting and Whiting 1975).

A brief description of the Tamang's subsistence economy will help identify how ecological factors may constrain family life. The Tamang, the single largest ethnic group of Nepal, exploit diverse land, animal, and natural resources to subsist as agropastoralists in the foothills of the Himalaya. In Salme village (1870 m), for example, a community of 335 households lives half-way up a steep mountainside rising from 1350 to 3800 m over an area of 30.7 km², of which 69 per cent are forests, 25 per cent are terraced fields, 5 per cent are pastures, and 1 per cent are paths and settlements. Five main cereal crops are grown on narrow terraces staggered at different altitudes, and a large herd of animals is maintained, whose manure fertilizes the fields. The monsoon rains from late June to mid-September signal a peak in agricultural work-loads for transplanting irrigated and rain-fed crops. Thus the Tamang, like many other mountain communities, make a living by exploiting to full advantage the spatial and temporal variation in their environment; indeed, they can only be self-sufficient by sustaining a diversified economy.

Each household strives to achieve a measure of self-sufficiency, and this generates both constraints of time and shortages of labour. During the monsoon, paddy rice and finger-millet must be planted with the very first rains in order to catch the best of the growing season, and this requires intense work effort on the part of all able-bodied adults. Tamang women of Salme average 8.2 h/day in subsistence activities outside the home (as measured by minute-by-minute focal observations), and the young and old, the pregnant or lactating and non-child-bearing women assume equal work-loads (Panter-Brick 1993a). In contrast during the winter, there is no urgent work pressure (women average only 5.4 h/day outdoors but there are multiple subsistence tasks to complete in different locations (planting one crop, harvesting or processing another, tending cattle, cutting fodder and firewood), which keep all family members employed (Fig. 10.1). To save both time and effort in daily travel, the Tamang often stay overnight close to the workplace, transporting shelters from terrace to terrace on the mountainside.

Thus intense work effort is required in the monsoon, while a flexible labour force is needed in the winter. The relevant constraints for child-minding are time

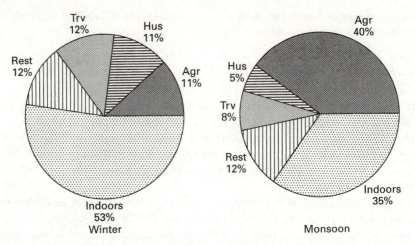

Fig. 10.1 Time-allocation for Tamang women: outdoor subsistence (agriculture, husbandry or forest-work, travel, rest) and indoor activities in the winter and monsoon season (per cent of 11.4 and 12.7 of daylight observation hours, respectively).

shortages in the monsoon, and the dispersion of family members in the winter. Since the household cannot afford the loss of female labour during a woman's child-bearing years, the mother must either carry children to the place of work, or leave them behind for extended periods of time. In sum, ecological factors, requiring full use of adult labour and high mobility away from home, are important constraints on child-care patterns. One can expect a degree of seasonal variation in Tamang child-care strategies if indeed they emerge as a response to environmental constraints.

Demography

The importance of demographic factors in shaping child-care strategies has begun to receive emphasis in the anthropological literature, as child-minding behaviours were shown to vary with measures of household density (Munroe and Munroe 1984; Borgerhoff Mulder and Milton 1985), availability of alternative caretakers (Weisner and Gallimore 1977; Engle 1992), and rates of fertility and mortality (LeVine 1980; Hewlett 1991).

Consider patterns of residence, fertility, and child mortality, three variables which influence the availability of subsistence labour and the allocation of child-care responsibilities. The Tamang in north-west Nepal live in small family units within large nucleated settlements, as shown in Table 10. 1 for two separate vil-

Table 10.1. Residence patterns in two Tamang villages of Nepal

	Salme (1870 m)*	Timling (1980 m)†
No. inhabitants	1540	639
No. households	335	132
Mean household size	4.91	4.84
Household type		
nuclear	62%	67%
stem (one married son)	21%	24%
joint/extended	11%	5%
other	6%	4%

* From Dobremez (1986; 83).
† From Fricke (1994; 65).

lages. Nuclear households predominate, at least if one takes the population in cross-section, because families reside for only a short time as extended units with married sons. Fricke, studying the process of Tamang household formation in the village of Timling, shows that, on average, a son marries at 23 years of age and establishes his own household at age 27, 'after his unit proves its viability by producing a child' (Fricke 1994, p. 152). This viability rests upon having a positive ratio of producers to consumers, which is rapidly achieved since both spouses and adolescent children participate actively in food production (in contrast to agropastoralist communities in Iran, for example, where women make no significant economic contribution; Irons 1986, p. 233). While extended households sport an even better ratio, they are vulnerable to fission when conflicts develop between in-laws, as Tamang wives, who exercise considerable independence, may return to their nearby natal home. Thus nuclear residence predominates, and married sons soon build their own house, alongside their father's. Tamang villages are thus constituted by rows of adjoining houses facing the valley, inhabited by families related by a common ancestor (patrilines). Because of relative geographical isolation and a cultural preference for cross-cousin marriages, these villages are highly endogamous nucleated settlements (Salme has 1540 inhabitants and a rate of endogamy of 81 per cent).

Turning to levels of fertility, Tamang women give birth, on average, to only five children (completed fertility rates are 4.7 in Salme and 5.4 in Timling). This low fertility for a non-contracepting population results from both social and biological variables, including late age at first birth (mean 23 years; Fricke 1994), unstable marriages (with late cohabitation until the birth of the first child, intermittent spouse separation related to subsistence activities, and frequent divorce), frequent nursing for 3 years post-partum which prolongs amenorrhea (Panter-Brick 1991), and seasonal suppression of ovulation for women who lose body-weight during the monsoon season (Panter-Brick *et al.* 1993a). One expects

Table 10.2. Mortality rates for children 0–5 years of age for Nepal, selected countries in the 1976 World Fertility Survey, and two Tamang villages

	Infant 0–1 year/1000	(%)	Child 1–5 years/1000	(%)	Total under-fives/1000	(%)
Bangladesh (WFS 1976)	141[2]	(66)	74[3]	(34)	215[3]	(100)
Senegal (WFS 1976)	123[6]	(43)	164[1]	(57)	287[1]	(100)
Nepal (WFS 1976)	166[1]	(64)	93[2]	(36)	259[2]	(100)
Tamang (Salme)	175	(65)	96	(35)	271	(100)
(Timling)	204	(74)	72	(26)	276	(100)

Superscripts are rankings among 28 Third-World countries, World Fertility Survey 1976 from Hobcraft (1984). Tamang data for Salme from Koppert (1988: 195) and for Timling from Fricke (1994: 116).

birth intervals, which for the Tamang average 37.7 months, to strongly influence the behaviour of women who must manage both outdoor subsistence and child-care responsibilities.

Levels of mortality also influence child-care behaviour (Hewlett 1991). Rates of childhood mortality were high for Nepal in the 1976 World Fertility Survey: the country was ranked as having the highest infant mortality and the second highest child mortality among 28 Third-World countries (Hobcraft *et al.* 1984). While in Senegal mortality is associated with weaning between the ages of 1 and 5 years, in Nepal and Bangladesh it occurs mostly in the first year of life (Table 10.2). The Tamang show the same pattern of mortality, with two-thirds of childhood deaths occurring in infancy in both the villages of Salme and Timling. Thus the first year is the most dangerous time of life for children. One might expect child-care strategies to vary from infancy to late childhood if mothers adapted their behaviours to the prevailing risks of mortality and child vulnerability.

In sum, living in small family units exacerbates the shortages of time and labour generated by the mixed subsistence economy and limits the availability of potential caretakers within the household. However, limited births and well-spaced pregnancies help women retain their mobility on the mountainside and cope with both an infant and its older siblings. Thus demographic factors both constrain and facilitate Tamang patterns of child care. They also specify different mortality risks for children before and after infancy. Thus child-care behaviours might well vary in response to household density, birth spacing, and child age.

Society

Child-care patterns are, culturally, extremely diverse. Much of the demographic and sociological literature in this field has focused on the 'value of children' and associated patterns of fertility and mortality in countries undergoing a demographic transition (Cain 1977; Fricke 1994), and has reviewed the impact of women's work on child care and child health (Leslie and Paolisso 1989; Engle 1992; Dettwyler and Fishman 1992). One simple but important contribution of anthropologists has been to show that parental goals governing child-care behaviours are not uniform across societies but range from those aiming to secure basic health and survival to those aiming to foster emotional as well as physical well-being (LeVine 1980; Cassidy 1987).

Thus R. A. LeVine (1980) emphasized that attitudes to child care in the Third World need not be like those in the West, while Cassidy (1987) and Engle and Nieves (1993) made the logic of different world views and child-minding strategies explicit. For instance, many parents do not consider that a special time should be allocated to child care, nor that special foods should be given to growing infants (Engle and Nieves 1993). In the high-altitude community of Humla in Nepal, N. E. Levine (1988, pp. 235 and 247) reports that women view child care as demanding very little special attention, a task 'manageable even by children', and will leave infants behind when working in the fields. The Tamang women of Salme will take infants to the fields but also emphasize subsistence responsibilities over and above child care. Unlike the Tamang, the blacksmith Kami, who live sympatrically in Salme and derive income from the craft of men in the smithy, emphasize a different role for women as wives and mothers principally. Acharya and Bennett (1981) contrasted the Tibetan–Burman communities such as the Tamang in Nepal, for whom the role of the worker is emphasized more strongly than the role of mother, and Indo-Aryan groups such as the Kami, for whom the emphasis is the reverse.

Child-care strategies

Ecological, demographic, and cultural factors combine in the Tamang case to create the following situation: a relatively small labour force within the household, whose adult members are intensively engaged in subsistence activities and extensively disperse on the mountainside; a large pool of consanguineous and affinal kin as neighbours, who also work in subsistence and are unavailable for child care at the home base; a long interval between births, with children on average 3 years older than their younger sib; and an emphasis on the role of women as a provider for the household, having to fit child-care responsibilities within daily subsistence activities. Under these conditions, one expects mothers to take prime responsibility for their children only if they carry them to the place of work, and alloparental care if they leave them at home.

In essence, Tamang women adopt the strategy of 'child care at the place of work', but in reality several strategies are observed, geared to the age and vulnerability of the child, the seasonal demands for labour, and the availability of alternative caretakers. The mother takes chief responsibility for her infant, carrying it to the work-place in a cot supported by a head strap, which leaves her hands free for work. The alternative, leaving the infant at home or in shelters on the mountainside, is difficult without a dependable pool of child-minders. This arrangement is no longer adopted when the infant grows older and less portable. Children who are too heavy to carry or too slow to walk long distances are left behind, particularly if the mother is absent only a few hours or must carry back a load.

In the winter, workers disperse on the mountainside and few adults, teenagers, or older people remain in the village (many reside in the cattle shelters). Older children are left in the village to join their peers, or left in a shelter where they may stay with sibs and a dog to guard them. This is not a particularly dangerous environment, except at high altitudes where 'panthers' are known to devour sheep. Moreover, the fact that shelters are moved every few days on the mountainside, to be close to the place of work, considerably reduces travel time and parental absence from the child. In the monsoon, however, family members work very long hours in the fields, joining forces to work in mixed male/female labour groups. Such team-work is an adaptive strategy to complete work swiftly and efficiently, as workers in a group divide tasks among themselves (men plough or dig the field, women transplant after them) and cooperate in the use of scarce or disputed resources (such as oxen for ploughing, or rotas for irrigation canals). Group labour also helps in minding children, as neighbours and kin in the labour group are at hand to help in child care, either directly by intervening when a baby cries, or indirectly, by providing two meals for all present in the fields thereby saving individual mothers extra cooking tasks. It is essential for mothers to have babies with them, since they must stay away from home from early morning to late evening and their labour cannot be spared at home. However, they may leave 3–6 year olds behind in the village, to eat cold left-overs and look after themselves until they return.

It is useful to look beyond general patterns of child-care supervision to examine nursing and feeding behaviours in more specific detail. How much time do working mothers actually devote to their children? How much food do they allocate to each child, and how does this vary by household composition? A detailed time-allocation study shows that maternal work-loads do not prejudice the care of young infants, although older children above 3 years of age receive less maternal attention; conversely, child-care responsibilities at the work-place do not significantly reduce maternal inputs in subsistence (Panter-Brick 1991, 1993a). Tamang children 0–38 months old average eight nursing sessions during daylight observation, each lasting 6 min at 1.9 h interval (the nursing pattern is age-dependent). While subsistence activity does constrain nursing patterns, mothers retain enough flexibility of work schedule to accommodate their infant's demands, because different tasks make different demands upon their time, and afford different opportunities for child care. In the winter, mothers undertake a mixture of activities during the day, some of which constrain child care (e.g. carrying loads) while others facilitate it (e.g. herding animals), and can schedule nursing intervals in ways to integrate both work and child-care responsibilities. In the monsoon, mothers focus day-long on agricultural tasks, but minimize child interference by breast feeding during the time labour groups normally allocate to rest and eat meals in the fields; surprisingly, they do not reduce overall lactation time when working intensively in the monsoon relative to the winter, in contrast to Gambian and Bangladeshi women (Huffman *et al.* 1980; Lunn *et al.* 1981). Thus while the Tamang child is truly breast-fed 'on demand', mothers organize themselves such that feeds are not 'random' but structured by 'opportunity', which is determined by the schedule and nature of maternal activity (Panter-Brick 1991).

Food surveys in Nepal have shown that children receive poor quality and infrequent meals even though they benefit from preferential food allocation within the household (Gittelsohn 1991; Panter-Brick 1993b). In Salme, supplementary foods consist of maize, millet, wheat/barley flour boiled to a thick paste, or more occasionally rice, and are no different from the normal adult meal except that ghee is sometimes added. The cereal gruel has an energy density of 1.4 kcal/g, but excessive cellulose and fibre content makes it difficult to digest, while accompanying vegetable or spicy sauces, more easily absorbed, have a calorific value of less than 0.6 kcal/g (Koppert 1988, p. 71). Proteins (85 per cent of which derive from cereals) are also limited relative to children's needs for rapid growth. Furthermore, the mother's absences from home and the unavailability of other care-takers severely constrain the number of meals available to older children who stay behind in the village. Although meat and milk are generously given to young children, they are in short supply; buffalo milk is only available through regular visits to cattle shelters which contain lactating she-buffaloes. Children aged 3–6 years, whose total intake is only 860 kcal/day or two-thirds of FAO/WHO/UNU (1985) recommended allowances, have the most compromised nutritional status in terms of weights and heights (Koppert 1988, p. 97).

Evaluation

What are the specific consequences of child-care strategies for child well-being? In the case of this hard-working poor rural community, the costs of parental behaviour to child's health include inappropriate feeding, slow growth, and high morbidity and mortality, especially during the monsoon season. Yet such costs are no doubt reduced by the behaviour of women who take infants to the workplace and prolong 'on demand, opportunity nursing' for 3 years until the integration of work and child care is constrained by the child's age and lack of portability. Costs are also reduced by low fertility and long birth intervals, which are behaviour-dependent in being related to work-loads, temporary marital separation, lactation schedules, and energy balance (Panter-Brick 1992).

The Tamang show slow growth in response to insufficient food intakes and periodic illnesses, with recurrent difficulties in the monsoon season when children lose significant bodyweight (Koppert 1988; pp. 165–7). But while the growth pattern of children appears fairly difficult, the anthropometric status of adults indicates relatively good health. Adults are small in height (men are 158 cm, women 150 cm, about 1.2 cm taller than the Bakola Pygmees of equatorial Cameroun) but of medium corpulence (Koppert 1988, p. 152). Women are able to withstand heavy work-loads with only slight seasonal changes in body mass, and able to carry heavy loads averaging 84 per cent of body mass downhill and 65 per cent of body mass uphill with slopes up to 40 per cent incline (Panter-Brick 1992, 1993a).

These growth and health statistics are well illustrated by the case of three Tamang children who had achieved very different heights and weights but were of the same age (according to the local calendar of Tibetan years and Nepali months, they were born under the sign of the monkey, (hence in 1980) in September). In July 1983, one boy, the fifth child from a family of well-spaced birth, was in good health (79 cm tall and weighing 11 kg). The second boy, the third child of a woman who neglected him and was pregnant again, showed severe growth stunting (70.5 cm and 7 kg) and clinical signs of malnutrition such as oedema and hair discoloration. The third child, a girl with no other sib-lings, receiving lavish maternal attention, was the tallest and heaviest of the three (85 cm and 12.5 kg) even though she currently experienced such severe diarrhoea that her bowel had protruded outside the anus. Seven years later, a time coinciding with another spell of fieldwork, all three children were alive, even the second boy who had recovered from all signs of nutritional and emo-tional stress. Comparison of the photographs taken of the three children in 1983 and 1990 (see Frontispiece) first made obvious what anthropometric measure-ments then confirmed, that the growth differentials had been maintained. The important point from a parental perspective is that all had survived.

High death rates for the Tamang lead to two important considerations: first, why infant mortality should not be low given that babies are the focus of mater-nal attention; and, second, what biological and behavioural variables underlie variability in mortality. In the first place, poor socio-economic conditions, sani-tation, and lack of medical care contribute to elevate both infant and child mor-tality in Nepal, one of the poorest countries in the world, particularly in remote regions where the Tamang live. Deaths are due principally to upper respiratory infections in the first year of life, and to diarrhoea which becomes increasingly prevalent in late childhood. The monsoon season is obviously the most difficult period of the year for all children, when there is a significant peak of both infant (0–1 year old) and child (1–5 years old) mortality (Koppert 1988, pp. 203–4; see also Nabarro 1984). Mortality rates, however, would be higher still if infants were left behind by working mothers (see Levine 1987).

Moreover, childhood mortality rates are significantly higher when birth inter-vals are less than 36 months (296/1000) relative to intervals longer than 36 months (185/1000 or 1.6 times lower). Since birth spacing is likely to be short in the event of sibling death, it is necessary to differentiate cases where the older sib died or survived. In both these cases, there is excess infant mortality (0–1 year old) with short birth intervals, especially if the older sibling is alive (Koppert 1988). Child mortality (1–5 years old) is less strongly affected, proba-bly because the 'fittest' have already survived infancy, the most critical period of life when two-thirds of the under-fives will die. The mechanisms whereby child spacing lowers mortality are commonly attributed to maternal nutritional depletion with repeated pregnancies, which affects a child's birthweight and subsequent chances of survival, and sibling competition for scarce food or maternal attention (Hobcraft *et al*. 1983, 1985).

The following example illustrates the benefits of longer birth intervals — ensuring that sibs do not compete severely for the mother's attention, and facilitating the enlistment of older siblings to look after an infant (Weisner and Gallimore 1977). Two sons were born in January 1979 and September 1982. The eldest was 33 months old when his brother was born, the age at which most mothers will wean. To allow the mother to focus on the newborn, the oldest was handed over to the charge of his grandmother, and allowed to suckle her dry breasts in consolation for the loss of maternal breast-milk. Within 8 months, this child was old enough to be assigned the role of sibling caretaker. During the winter, the mother often left both children alone in the shelter on the mountainside, while she fetched a harvest, fodder, or firewood. The baby was wedged in his bamboo cot, and the older child, without peers to play with and distract him, just stood by. They appeared to be safe, as no accidents were reported to children thus left behind, and social or emotional stimulation of children was simply not a parental priority during daylight working hours. Given the work-load of rural Nepali women, one agrees with Gubhaju that 'previous birth interval stands out as the most important factor affecting infant mortality; the next most important factor is the survival of the preceding child' (Gubhaju 1986, p. 435).

Conclusions

The data presented for the Tamang show how families vary their child-care strategies according to the exigencies of their environment, family structure, caretaker availability, and child's age and vulnerability. It is useful to compare this case with child-care strategies in other communities where the contribution of women to the household economy requires high mobility and long absences from home. The anthropological literature on hunter–gatherers, horticulturalists, and pastoralists has shown that the particular choices adopted to resolve the potential conflict between work and child-care responsibilities are structured by the interaction of ecological, demographic, and social factors.

Draper (1976) describes the constraints which influence child-care strategies for the hunter–gathering !Kung in Botswana. Mothers often carry children when they travel to work, even when this entails a walk of 16 km per day carrying both plant foods and a child. However, adults have considerable free time from subsistence work and live in very small settlements with open spaces, which facilitate a high degree of communal child-care supervision at the home base. Draper (1976, p. 200) concludes that 'the major constraints on child life derived from the nature of adult work and from the organization of people in space', namely the subsistence economy and settlement patterns. This statement concurs well with the situation observed for the Tamang.

Tamang organization differs from the !Kung, however, in that adults rarely stay at home. Tamang mothers seem more like the Hadza, whose range of movement is spatially more restricted than the !Kung, and who carry babies to work but leave toddlers behind. Hawkes *et al.* (1989) note that Hadza nursing mothers manage to reduce the interference of infant care surprisingly well by enlisting older children as baby-sitters at the work-place, but will curtail the more energy-demanding subsistence tasks such as digging tubers because grandmothers work particularly hard to help them. Among the Ache hunter–gatherers of Amazonia, an environment hazardous for unattended children due to the prevalence of insects and reptiles, nursing mothers will curtail economic productivity to focus upon child-care responsibilities, relying on socially sanctioned food-sharing to obtain extra produce (Hurtado *et al.* 1985). Again, ecological, demographic, and social factors account for the unusual case of the Agta of Papua New Guinea, where women participate fully in hunting activities, carrying babies to the hunt, and leaving toddlers in the care of family members (Goodman *et al.* 1985). Hunting in groups and with dogs, close to base camp, and child-care cooperation make this option possible.

In Salme, Tamang women vary the balance of priorities between outdoor work and child care according to the seasonal demands for labour and the age of a child (Panter-Brick 1992), while the Kami blacksmiths face a different situation as they assume lighter work-loads. And since infancy is the most critical period of life, Tamang mothers will concentrate attention on small infants, possibly to the detriment of older children; however, the latter should by then be fit to survive (Panter-Brick 1992). Scheper-Hughes (1991) also documents how women vary child-care attention with the age of a child; in the case of Brazilian slum-dwelling women, emotional bonds are withheld until weak infants have demonstrated a will to survive.

Levine describes alternative child-care strategies in Nepali communities in high-altitude Humla, north-west Nepal. As in the case of the Tamang, Humla 'women place great emphasis on productive labour and arrange childcare around it' (Levine 1988, p. 235). The usual arrangement is for women to leave both infants and toddlers at home in the care of other household members, including children, while they work in the fields. The costs of this strategy are clear from the extremely high infant and child mortality (about 255/1000 and 317/1000), which results, at least in part, from the contamination of supplementary foods given to babies left behind (Levine 1987). Women perceive agricultural labour to be incompatible with child care, as travel on steep paths is difficult and the mountain environment is associated with mystical danger. Levine remarks that the only Humla hamlet where women customarily take infants to the field is in a less rugged area, where transport of a child poses fewer problems and where family members divide their responsibilities between two homes near low and high altitude fields, which reduces the availability of substitute caretakers. In comparing three different ethnic groups living in Humla, she concludes that 'existing variations [in childcare patterns] appear to have their source in systems of labor management, the exigencies of local resource use, and relative prosperity' rather than the very different cultural systems and ethnic backgrounds of the communities studied (Levine 1988, p. 247). In this demanding environment, ecological constraints shaping child-care patterns are more powerful than cultural prescriptions.

There is a substantial literature on the importance of household structure, caretaker availability, nature of the economy, women's work, and value of children (Whiting and Whiting 1975; Weisner and Gallimore 1977; Nag *et al.* 1978; LeVine 1980; Katz and Konner 1981; Weisner 1982; Munroe and Munroe 1984; Borgerhoff Mulder and Milton 1985; Hewlett 1991; Dettwyler and Fishman 1992; Engle 1992). The Tamang are a specific example of how mothers manage to integrate subsistence and child-care responsibilities, and how ecological, demographic, and social factors constrain child-care patterns. The data show how families vary their child-care strategies according to the exigencies of a seasonal environment, child's age, and presence of older siblings. The nature of women's work, high infant mortality, and long birth spacing emerge as the most important variables influencing Tamang child-care practices (Panter-Brick 1992).

References

Acharya, M. and Bennett, L. (1981). *The rural women of Nepal*. CEDA, Tribhuvan University, Kathmandu, Nepal.

Blurton Jones, N. (1986). Bushman birth spacing: a test for optimal interbirth interval. *Ethnology and Sociobiology*, **7**, 91–105.

Borgerhoff Mulder, M. and Milton, M. (1985). Factors affecting infant care in the Kipsigis. *Journal of Anthropological Research*, **41**, 231–62.

Cain, M. (1977). The economic activities of children in a village in Bangladesh. *Population and Development Review*, **3**, 201–27.

Cassidy, C. M. (1987). World-view conflict and toddler malnutrition: Change-agent dilemmas. In *Child Survival* (ed. N. Scheper-Hughes), pp. 294–324. Reidel, Dordrecht.

Dettwyler, K. A. and Fishman, C. (1992). Infant feeding practices and growth. *Annual Review of Anthropology*, **21**, 171–204.

Dobremez, J. F. (ed.) (1986). *Les collines du nepal central. II*. INRA, Paris.

Draper, P. (1976). Social and economic constraints on child life among the !Kung. In *Kalahari hunter–gatherers* (ed. R. Lee and I. DeVore), pp. 199–217. Harvard University Press, Cambridge, MA.

Engle, P. L. (1992). Care and child nutrition. Paper presented at the International Conference of Nutrition, Rome. UNICEF, 3 United Nations, Plaza, New York, NY 10017.

Engle, P. L. and Nieves, I. (1993). Intra-household distribution among Guatemalan families in a supplementary feeding program; behavior patterns. *Social Science and Medicine*, **36**, 1605–12.

FAO/WHO/UNU Expert Consultation (1985). Energy and protein requirements. Technical report series no. 724. World Health Organisation, Geneva.

Fricke, T. E. (1994). *Himalayan households: Tamang demography and domestic processes*. Book Faith India, Delhi.

Gittelsohn, J. (1991). Opening the box: intrahousehold food allocation in rural Nepal. *Social Science and Medicine*, **33**, 1141–54.

Goodman, M., Griffin, P., Estioko-Griffin, A., and Grove, J. (1985). The compatibility of hunting and mothering among the Agta hunter–gatherers of the Philippines. *Sex Roles*, **12**, 1199–209.

Gubhaju, B. B. (1986). Effect of birth spacing on infant and child mortality in rural Nepal. *Journal of Biosocial Science*, **18**, 435–47.

Hawkes, K., O'Connell, J., and Blurton-Jones, B. (1989). Hardworking Hadza grandmothers. In *Comparative socioecology — the behavioural ecology of humans and other mammals* (ed. R. Foley and V. Standen), pp. 341–66. Blackwell Scientific Publications, Oxford.

Hewlett, B. S. (1991). Demography and childcare in preindustrial societies. *Journal of Anthropological Research*, **47**, 1–37.

Hobcraft, J. N., McDonald, J. W., and Rutstein, S. O. (1983). Child-spacing effects on infant and early child mortality. *Population Index*, **49**, 585–618.

Hobcraft, J. N., McDonald, J. W., and Rutstein, S. O. (1984). Socioeconomic factors in infant and child mortality: a cross-national comparison. *Population Studies*, **38**, 193–223.

Hobcraft, J. N., McDonald, J. W., and Rutstein, S. O. (1985). Demographic determinants of infant and early child mortality: a comparative analysis. *Population Studies*, **39**, 363–85.

Hurtado, A. M., Hawkes, K., Hill, K., and Kaplan, H. (1985). Female subsistence strategies among the Ache hunter–gatherers of eastern Paraguay. *Human Ecology*, **13**, 1–28.

Huffman, S. L., Chowdhury, A. K. M. A., Chakraborty, J., and Simpson, N. K. (1980). Breast-feeding patterns in rural Bangladesh. *American Journal of Clinical Nutrition*, **33**, 144–54.

Irons, W. (1986). Yomut family organization and inclusive fitness. *Proceedings of the International Meetings on Variability and Behavioral Evolution, Roma*, pp. 227–36. Accademia Nazionale dei Lincei, Rome.

Katz, M. M. and Konner, M. J. (1981). The role of the father: an anthropological perspective. In *The role of the father in child development* (ed. M. Lamb), pp. 189–222 (2nd ed.). New York, Wiley.

Koppert, G. J. A. (1988). Alimentation et culture chez les Tamang, les Ghale et les Kami du Népal. Thèse de 3ème cycle, Faculté de Droit et de Science Politique, Aix-Marseille, juin.

Leslie, J. and Paolisso, M. (ed.) (1989). *Women, work, and child welfare in the Third World*. Westview Press, Boulder, CO.

Levine, N. E. (1987). Differential child care in three Tibetan communities: beyond son preference. *Population and Development Review*, **13**, 281–304.

Levine, N. E. (1988). Women's work and infant feeding: a case from rural Nepal. *Ethnology*, **28**, 231–51.

LeVine, R. A. (1980). A cross-cultural perspective on parenting. In *Parenting in a multicultural society* (ed. M. Fantini and R. Cardenas), pp. 17–26. Longman, New York.

Lunn, P. G., Watkinson M., Prentice, A. M., Morrell, P., Austin, P., and Whitehead, R. G. (1981). Maternal nutrition and lactational amenorrhea. *Lancet* (i): 1428–1429.

Munroe, R. L. and Munroe, R. H. (1984). Health and wealth in four societies. *Journal of Social Psychology*, **123**, 135–6.

Nabarro, D. (1984). Social, economic, health and environmental determinants of nutritional status. *Food and Nutrition Bulletin*, **6**, 18–32.

Nag, M., White, B., and Peet, R. C. (1978). An anthropological approach to the study of the economic value of children in Java and Nepal. *Current Anthropology*, **19**, 292–306.

Panter-Brick, C. (1991). Lactation, birth-spacing and maternal work-loads among two castes in rural Nepal. *Journal of Biosocial Science*, **23**, 137–54.

Panter-Brick, C. (1992). Women's working behaviour and maternal–child health in rural Nepal. In *Physical activity and health* (ed. N. Norgan), pp. 190–206. Cambridge University Press.

Panter-Brick, C. (1993a). Seasonality and levels of energy expenditure during pregnancy and lactation for rural Nepali women. *American Journal of Clinical Nutrition*, **57**, 620 –8.

Panter-Brick, C. (1993b). Mother–child food allocation and levels of subsistence activity in rural Nepal. *Ecology of Food and Nutrition*, **29**, 319–33.

Panter-Brick, C., Lotstein, D. S., and Ellison, P. T. (1993). Seasonality of reproductive function and weight loss in rural Nepali women. *Human Reproduction*, **8**, 684–90.

Scheper-Hughes, N. (1991). Social indifference to child death. *Lancet*, **337**, 1144–7.

Weisner, T. S. (1982). Sibling interdependence and child caretaking: a cross-cultural view. In *Sibling relationships: their nature and significance across the lifespan* (ed. M. E. Lamb and B. Sutton-Smith), pp. 305–27. Erlbaum, Hillsdale.

Weisner, T. S. and Gallimore, R. (1977). My brother's keeper: child and sibling caretaking. *Current Anthropology*, **18**, 169–90.

Whiting, B. B. and Whiting, J. W. M. (1975). *Children of six cultures*. Harvard University Press, Cambridge, MA.

11

Change and variability in Papua New Guinea's patterns of disease

R. D. ATTENBOROUGH AND M. P. ALPERS

Introduction

Modernization — whatever that may be [1]— increases life expectancy through a shift away from infectious, mainly early-acting causes of ill-health and death, towards non-infectious, mainly degenerative and later-acting causes. Versions of this statement have been advanced by many researchers and are widely accepted (e.g. Trowell and Burkitt 1981; Boyden 1987; Caldwell *et al.* 1990; Landers 1992). Western societies — where the historical process is now more or less complete, though not irreversible (Fenner 1990) — are the paradigm cases. A similar or partly similar transition is currently under way to varying degrees in non-Western, including Third-World developing countries, and amongst Fourth-World indigenous minorities such as Aboriginal Australians.

Our aim in this chapter is not to dispute the general thrust of this argument about health and mortality transition, but to examine some of the complexity and variability in disease patterns that are concealed by statements as bald as our opening sentence. The setting in which we shall pursue this exploration is the Third-World nation of Papua New Guinea (PNG). Though not very much larger than Sweden in land area or Greater Manchester in population, PNG is a remarkable microcosm of human and environmental diversity, well-suited in principle to the demonstration of epidemiological variety where that prevails. The health of Papua New Guineans has indeed been highly diverse, both over time and in space, and we shall try to conjure up briefly some impression of this variety.

Geoffrey Harrison's outstanding contribution to human population biology has included substantial research in and on PNG (Harrison and Walsh 1974; Harrison *et al.* 1975, 1976 *a,b,c*; Boyce *et al.* 1976, 1978 *a,b*; Panter-Brick and Harrison 1982; Brush *et al.* 1983, 1989) and searching analyses of human variability, biosocial interactions, fitness in its different senses, and disease and health and the shady area between them (e.g. Harrison 1970, 1973, 1987, 1990).

---

[1] Ulijaszek (in press) discusses definitions of this vexed term. King and Collins (1989) propose an index.

Our task is, however, not an altogether easy one. For all its advantages and attractions as a research environment, PNG also presents daunting research problems. The challenge of mounting studies of a scale and design to do justice to multifarious diversity is often compounded by logistical difficulties, and by the observer effect whereby the very presence of outsiders competent to make written descriptions is associated with factors likely to bias those descriptions. Below we use some national and provincial data, and some from studies concentrating on specific groups. Among other sources we shall draw on contributions to Attenborough and Alpers (1992), where much of the available material is more fully reviewed. But despite the substantial information now available, shortage of detailed studies remains a frequent constraint.

Since the concept of a health transition is one of secular change, we shall take a broadly chronological view of health patterns in PNG. As we approach recent decades, this picture will be amplified by comparing health patterns in populations living under different environmental, climatic, economic, and social conditions. A plausible view of the contrasts among contemporaneous groups is that they represent different stages along a broadly similar trajectory of change, that is, modernization; but we shall attempt to bear in mind that this is potentially too restrictive a model, which may not fit a complex reality. There is no implication here that epidemiological diversity is a novel phenomenon in PNG — undoubtedly it is not — but the data shortage is most acute for the earliest periods.

Highlands, highlands fringes, and lowlands

PNG is mountainous and situated wholly within the humid tropics, so that the most salient single measure of its complex climatic and ecological contrasts is altitude. Altitudinal contrasts in human populations are arguably starker in PNG than anywhere else, in spite of the fact that PNG's highland valley populations are scarcely high-altitude ones at all by international standards (Baker 1978). Physiological hypoxia, if relevant at all, is secondary to a host of other altitude- and thus temperature-related impacts, especially on the ecology of disease and nutrition. Above all, transmission of malaria, perhaps PNG's most important infection, is intense in the warm wet lowlands and becomes less stable with altitude, shading out between 1300 and 2500 m: except in lower-lying swampier areas, malaria in the highland valleys occurs mainly as isolated cases and restricted outbreaks, often related to human movement from the lowland and thus more frequent in the post-war period (Cattani 1992).

The often rugged highland fringes, the zones at intermediate altitude (600–1200 m) surrounding the central cordillera, are the most sparsely populated of the altitudinal zones. The populations there appear particularly vulnerable both to growth deficit (Heywood and Jenkins 1992), and to epidemic malaria, in populations immunologically and probably also genetically ill-prepared for it. Malaria may be a key determinant of the sparseness of highland fringe populations (Riley 1983), and there are abundant accounts of highland groups moving into the fringes but withdrawing on encountering sickness probably due to malaria. The fringes thus appear to have had a crucial historical role in keeping highland and lowland populations to some degree apart, and thus in accounting for their contrasts.

Palaeopathology

Palaeopathology supplies the only direct evidence on the health of prehistoric populations anywhere. In the case of PNG, this amounts so far to rather little. Most notably, studies (summarized by Hope *et al.* 1983) of skeletal remains from Motupore Island and Nebira, both in the Port Moresby area and both dated between c. 1000 and c. 300 years BP suggest the presence of osteoarthritis, tuberculosis, treponematosis (specifically yaws), leprosy, iron-deficiency anaemia, and thalassaemia major in one or both of these populations, and extensive caries and periodontal disease in the former (probably associated with higher dietary intake of sago).

Sociodemographic factors and infectious disease

For perhaps the first 40 of the 50 or so millennia that people have lived on the island of New Guinea, they did so as hunter–gatherers, probably in small scattered groups with 'faint archaeological signatures', occupying the lowlands first and taking maybe ten millennia to settle the highlands (Lilley 1992). Generalizing about hunter–gatherers is fraught with dangers of false extrapolation, but it is likely that the main causes of morbidity and mortality among low-latitude hunter–gatherers not interacting with agriculturalists were infection and maybe accidental trauma, violence, snakebite, and so forth, with no more than a minor role for degenerative disease or perhaps for overt malnutrition (Dunn 1968; Truswell and Hansen 1976).

Within a context dominated by infectious disease, however, many salient infections of the modern world would have been absent or unimportant. Many of the major infections of modern Europe probably originated zoonotically from the animals with which people had closest contacts, i.e. domesticated animals, and/or were able to persist endemically only in quite large populations (Cockburn 1977). For cases such as measles, where acute infective disease is rapidly followed by death or recovery with long-term immunity, models and empirical data on island populations suggest a minimum community size of between 300 000 and 1 000 000, below which transmission cannot be indefinitely sustained through natural increment of new susceptibles (McKeown

1988). Given such thresholds, the conclusion that such diseases were absent from prehistoric hunter-gatherer societies is robust even if we greatly under-estimate their sizes and over-estimate their isolation.

Only infections which can escape this demographic constraint are likely to have persisted endemically in prehistoric hunter–gatherer communities, even once introduced. Two main categories of viral diseases would have been capable of this: actively zoonotic infections such as arboviruses spread from wild animal reservoirs which effectively increase host population size, and chronically per-sistent or latent infections such as chickenpox-zoster not characterized by the full immunity acquired after measles (Fenner 1980; Garruto 1981). Mycobacterial, treponemal, streptococcal, staphylococcal, fungal, protozoal and some helminth and bacterial enteric infections could also have sufficient chronicity and recurrent infectivity to persist in small communities. Biogeographic as well as demographic factors — especially the effectiveness of sea barriers around and rugged terrain within the main island — would have been influential in determining which of these pathogens in fact have a long prehistory in New Guinea. It is hard today to say which these were, beyond the fact that palaeopathological studies (see above) indicate the presence of tubercu-losis, leprosy, yaws, and streptococcal dental disease, at least in coastal areas in late prehistory.

From studies of ancient drainage systems in the Wahgi valley swamps, it appears that horticulture was developed in highland New Guinea about 9000 years ago, based probably on cultivation of endemic species (Golson 1991). Staple root crops such as taro (of South-East Asian origin if not endemic to New Guinea) were incorporated from perhaps 6000 years ago, though South American sweet potato, now the staple of highlands horticulture, probably not till about 400 years ago (Lilley 1992). Although cassowaries and other native fauna are sometimes reared, the native fauna has not proven an important source of domesticates, nor apparently of zoonoses. The main animal domesticates, chickens, dogs and, above all, pigs (Groves 1981), were apparently introduced from South-East Asia, probably (since claims otherwise have yet to be confirmed) not before the mid-Holocene. It is debatable to what extent the horticultural intensification which sustained population growth in the highlands was related to the particular properties either of pig husbandry or of sweet potato cultivation. Hence, it is unclear how long highlands populations had been as dense as they were when first described by outsiders, but it may not have been very long.

Even in recent times population densities have been far from high by contemporary world standards. In 1966 the only major concentrations of rural populations at densities over 30 persons per km^2 were in parts of the highlands (up to 190 locally), the Sepik River basin (up to 150 locally), and the Gazelle Peninsula of East New Britain (over 60, after recent rapid population growth) (Ward and Lea 1970). Even where density was relatively high, traditional settlements were usually quite small — tending towards 70–300 residents in tuber-dependent areas — a finding which Forge (1972) related to the reliance of traditional egalitarian institutions in Melanesia on face-to-face interactions. In some regions, notably the Sepik basin and the Papuan Gulf where sago was a staple food and water transport was important, villages were often larger. In the Sepik, villages of over 1000 residents were able, Forge argued, to cohere in response to military necessity through their formalized systems of interrelationships which complemented face-to-face interactions. In many parts of pre-colonial New Guinea, settlements would presumably have been isolated from one another to a certain extent, not only by formidable topography but also by enmities and cultural and linguistic differences — though none of these, probably, were barriers quite as effective as outsiders have often thought.

While they leave much uncertain, these points suggest some epidemiological inferences. First, people lived in New Guinea for a very long period before they first incurred the infectious and nutritional risks brought by horticulture and domestication (Cohen and Armelagos 1984), which, as in most parts of the world, are recent on a scale of millennia. Second, at least in certain periods of Holocene prehistory, there was sufficient interaction between human communities for plant and animal domesticates to have been passed from South-East Asia to New Guinea, and from the New Guinea coasts through the interior lowlands and highland fringes to the highlands. Zoonotic and other infectious micro-organisms could probably have been transmitted along the same routes. But third, while horticulture no doubt brought increases in sedentism, community size, and inter-community contact to many parts of New Guinea, community life generally remained on a relatively small scale. Thus, the demographic constraints on the range of infections which horticultural New Guinea communities — unlike some rural agricultural societies elsewhere — could sustain would not have been greatly different from those outlined for hunter–gatherers above.

The last two points are both illustrated by observations made when acute infections were introduced. Adels and Gajdusek (1963), for example, describe a 'virgin-soil' epidemic of measles in the Asmat area of Irian Jaya in 1961: contact between villages was sufficient to permit the infection a 'snake-like pattern of progression over a map of these scattered villages', but not so intensive as to introduce it to all villages in the area or to link the area together as part of a single effective population that might sustain it endemically. Indeed, neither Port Moresby itself (McMurray 1985) nor the largest language group in PNG (Foley 1992) at the present time, let alone any traditional community, reaches even the lower estimate of the threshold for the persistence of measles. But measles is endemic in PNG (and has recently become a much more lethal disease, associated with a very young age at infection). Hence the increase in movement of people must have created sufficiently large regional populations in PNG which are effectively above this threshold.

Genetic factors and malaria

Besides palaeopathology and sociodemographic organization, there remains a further basis for inference about prehistoric disease in New Guinea: genetics. Only for one infectious disease — malaria — is genetic evidence yet very informative for this purpose. World-wide, malaria is unique in the range of genetic variants demonstrated or strongly suspected to have been sustained at polymorphic frequencies by the natural selection it has exerted (Flint *et al.* 1993).

While no histocompatibility antigens are yet identified as having played such a role in New Guinea populations and some well-known haemoglobin variants such as sickle-cell do not occur there, the range of other genetic variants associated with malaria is as striking as any in the world: α- and β-thalassaemia, glucose-6-phosphate-dehydrogenase deficiency, ovalocytosis, and Gerbich-negative blood group are reviewed by Serjeantson *et al.* (1992). All of these are common and widespread in the northern and some in the southern lowlands of mainland PNG, but they are diverse in their genetic and evolutionary mechanisms. Alpha-globin has two loci, G6PD is X-linked, and β-thalassaemia is the most complex of all the haemoglobinopathies. Absence of homozygotes for a 27bp deletion associated with ovalocytosis suggests a biological cost more severe even than for sickle-cell (K. K. Bhatia and M. P. Alpers, unpublished), but it is uncertain whether there is a biological cost to Gerbich-negative blood group. It is unclear which, if any, of these variants has reached equilibrium and how they interact where they co-occur. Nonetheless, together they constitute strong evidence that these populations' ancestors have had a long exposure to malaria.

Quite for how long, at what intensity, and where that exposure has taken place, are open to debate. The speed with which a mutant gene could reach the frequencies observed depends on the intensity of selection (Rendel 1970), which for malaria might be high. For Africa, Livingstone (1958) hypothesized that agriculture had made malaria a much more important disease than before, through increased breeding opportunities for *Anopheles* mosquitos and increased human population density; and Wiesenfeld (1967) estimated that, on reasonable assumptions about selection intensity, the sickle-cell haemoglobin variant might have stabilized close to observed frequencies in as few as 1000–1500 years. If these arguments are even broadly correct, there would be no difficulty in supposing that malaria as a holo- or hyperendemic disease, and the rise of the genetic variants associated with it, may be no older in lowland PNG than horticulture is. This date is essentially unknown, but, indications of forest tree management apart, there is little at present to put it earlier than island Melanesia's Lapita archaeological tradition, that is about 3600 years ago (Spriggs 1993).

Groube (1993) has recently reviewed the antiquity of malaria in Melanesia. He concludes that malaria due to *Plasmodium vivax* and *P. malariae* was present in Pleistocene New Guinea, perhaps within a few millennia of initial settlement, and would rapidly have become endemic in lowland environments favourable to it; that the most lethal malaria due to *P. falciparum* is a post-Pleistocene avian zoonosis of African origin unlikely to have reached Melanesia much before a thousand years ago, to which the present populations are still adjusting; that endemic malaria has constituted a significant brake on population growth and has properties which make it an effective regulator of population distribution (cf. Riley 1983); and that from its first appearance malaria would have imposed a number of unconscious 'choices' in relation to settlement, subsistence and use of the environment which would have amounted to 'learning to live with malaria'. Clark and Kelly (1993), on the other hand, consider that malaria may or may not have been present in the region before the Lapita diffusion brought Austronesian-speaking horticultural groups of South-East Asian origin to coastal Melanesia; but that in any case, these groups would have brought with them not only cultural but also biological adaptations to coastal lowlands, in the form of certain Gm haplotypes favourably selected in malarial environments, which would have resulted in demographic advantages over any Papuan-speakers living there.

Groube's hypothesis that malaria has been present in New Guinea nearly for as long as human beings, but has undergone important changes over that time, is not inconsistent with the possibility that some malaria-related genetic variants were already polymorphic in sea-faring groups which only reached Melanesia in Lapita times. But when the full range of genetic variants related to malaria is considered, some of which do not occur outside the New Guinea area or occur only in forms distinguishable from the New Guinean ones, the probability seems low that all stem from relatively late introductions or mutations, and correspondingly Groube's model appears still more plausible.

The New Guinea highlands have much lower prevalences of malaria than the lowlands, and most parts were essentially malaria-free at colonial contact (Riley and Lehmann 1992). The Wahgi swamps which provide the earliest indications of highlands horticulture are, however, among the areas within reach of malaria now; and the puzzling use-abandonment cycles of the ancient drainage systems (Lilley 1992) might be intelligible on a hypothesis involving epidemic malaria. The near-absence of any of the well known malaria-related genes from the New Guinea highlands (Serjeantson *et al.* 1992) — in contrast to malaria-free Polynesia where polymorphic α-thalassaemia testifies to ancestral migrations through malarial zones as well as to drift (Flint *et al.* 1993) — raises a further question. The ancestors of present highland populations evidently passed through the New Guinea lowlands at some stage. These populations either once had the variant genes and lost them in the absence of malaria-directed selection, or they never had them in the first place (irrespective of whether malaria was then present on the coast). For each particular genetic polymorphism one or other of these two possibilities might have occurred. At present it would be hard to decide between them.

Although it is possible that deterministic models, for example based on past population density, have a role to play in explaining the widely varying frequencies of malaria-protective alleles across the now malarial lowlands, it is also possible, even likely, that the explanation is essentially one of historical contingency. The Sepik–Ramu basin in the north, for example, was a large inland sea until its infill within the last 6000 years (Swadling and Hope 1992), and its peopling may have chanced to introduce polymorphisms there which never were introduced to the populations to the south of the cordillera.

Outside explorers and colonial authorities

Although there is a history of foreign contact going back some centuries, most PNG communities probably had their first significant contacts with non-Melanesian outsiders at periods ranging from the mid-nineteenth to the mid-twentieth centuries (Allen 1992). Exploration and colonization naturally began earlier in more accessible areas than in the interior. Remote outsiders brought 'acculturation'[2], the novel aspect of which was not culture contact or historical change *per se*, but the magnitude of the differences in beliefs and worldview, in material resources and technology, and in a host of sociodemographic and biomedical factors affecting disease risk. Some also brought a European scientific approach (of the period) to bear on New Guinea's disease patterns even as their own presence played a part in changing those patterns. An early scientifically trained visitor was the Russian Mikloucho-Maclay (1975), who travelled mainly near the present town of Madang, and whose diary for 1872 includes several accounts of people with elephantiasis, smallpox pockmarks and various skin diseases.

By 1886 the Netherlands had claimed the territory that is now Irian Jaya (the western portion of the main New Guinea island), Germany and Britain between them the territories that now, after Australian control for much of the twentieth century, constitute the nation of PNG (the eastern portion, plus many large and small islands) (Allen 1992). Although for several decades the colonizers had no knowledge of the more remote populations in the lands they had claimed, and vice versa, in more accessible areas plantations, missions, mines, trading centres, administrative centres, agencies of law and order, and so forth were rapidly established, in some cases even before formal governmental claims.

Concerns for the health of both colonizer and colonized were evident from early on. The Annual Reports for Papua (the South-Eastern portion of New Guinea) for the years before the first World War already document persistent attention to the laying out of cemeteries and the prohibition of traditional disposal practices such as exposure and burial within villages. There was a smallpox vaccination campaign, as the Dutch had undertaken earlier, stimulated by an epidemic in Australia in 1914. Other measures followed in the third and

---

[2]A term whose primary meaning is culture change through culture contact. It does not refer solely to contact with modern global culture, but frequent use in this restrictive sense has rendered the term problematic as noted by Alpers and Attenborough (1992: 30)

fourth decades of the twentieth century, including: sanitation, with directions to villagers to construct latrines where existing practices were not approved (though in Nakanai, New Britain, precautions against sorcery already resulted in very acceptable latrines); mass hookworm and yaws treatments even of the uninfected; legal constraints to reduce the spread of venereal disease, antimalarial measures including swamp drainage, kerosening and gauzing of tanks and clearing of jungle; collection and incineration or sea disposal of nightsoil; dietary recommendations to overcome beriberi; and systems of quarantining and of inspecting slaughtered meat and food preparation premises. Many of these measures would clearly have been very local (e.g. around Rabaul and Port Moresby) and/or temporary in their effect, though some affected tens of thousands. A pneumococcal vaccine was mooted early on (e.g. 1922–3 New Guinea Annual Report), though none was put into practice for another half-century, or is indeed yet routine (Riley *et al.* 1992). Denoon *et al.* (1989) describe in detail the evolution of medical policies; and contributors to Burton-Bradley (1990) review the history of medicine in PNG.

The Annual Reports of the colonial authorities constitute a written, sometimes quantitative record of the health problems faced by indigenous Papua New Guineans, which does indicate variability over time and from place to place. For several reasons, however, these records are difficult to interpret systematically. Data collection systems follow no single scheme across the series; and indeed medical concepts, even of malaria, tuberculosis, etc. were still rapidly evolving in the early colonial period. The geographical scope of administrative control was incomplete for most of the colonial period, and even where hospitals, clinics and field patrols were operating, their case-finding must often have been very partial, and their demographic base poorly known. For 1920–1, the New Guinea and Papua Annual Reports list 5 medical officers in each territory, and those few would have given disproportionate attention to the non-native population and to communities in and near Rabaul, Port Moresby and other urban centres. We make a few salient points here, mainly from the British and Australian reports up to 1927. What emerges with most clarity from the reports is the judgment of those on the spot as to which were the outstanding health problems of the moment and locality, usually on account of their high prevalence or case-fatality or their predicted capacity to spread. Even purely qualitative descriptions of outbreaks and epidemics probably do correspond to peaks of prevalence or incidence. Whether the earliest outbreaks recorded for specific infections are the earliest to have occurred is generally hard to determine, since even exotic infections may have been introduced by pre-colonial sea-voyagers (see under palaeopathology) or at least have spread ahead of the frontier of direct colonial contact (as smallpox in Australia). But in certain cases the pattern observed is suggestive either of established endemicity at colonial contact or of a 'virgin-soil' epidemic, that is at least a lifetime since any previous outbreak.

Rubella is first recorded in Papua as an outbreak on board ship in the South-Eastern Division in 1903, which then spread to labourers; and it reappears in 1912, 1916, and 1926–7, without apparently causing serious mortality. In 1894 measles was recorded in the Western Division and was noted to have occurred earlier, and it reappeared in 1902–4, 1913, 1921 and 1925–7; mortality directly attributable to measles was generally not as great as in Fiji in 1875, and the contrast drew comment at the time. Smallpox was feared on several occasions, and after Mikloucho-Maclay's observations it was again introduced into German New Guinea in the 1890s wreaking much havoc; but it never became endemic or spread very far (partly due to intergroup hostilities blocking transmission), and despite fears of reintroduction especially from Dutch New Guinea which spurred on major vaccination efforts, it has not recurred in PNG this century (Fenner *et al.* 1988). Influenza was first reported in the Northern Division in 1904, and again in 1908, 1911, and yearly on some scale 1919–27, although many of the outbreaks are described as relatively mild and localized. There was apparently no catastrophic mortality attributable to 'Spanish flu' of the post-First World War pandemic, and although there seems no obvious block to its introduction from Dutch New Guinea or across Torres Strait, it is unclear whether influenza of that antigenic type did arrive. Whooping cough and chickenpox were imported from Cooktown in Australia in 1900 and 1902, but whereas the latter's progress appears to have been successfully arrested, the former spread rapidly along the coast and somewhat into the interior. It appears to have been a novel infection at this time and caused severe mortality across Papua in the years up to 1912: by the 1920s, however, outbreaks appear to have become milder, affecting children more particularly and causing less mortality overall.

Dysentery caused heavy, often epidemic, mortality nearly every year from first records in 1897 for nearly 20 years, before outbreaks became less dramatic and a more endemic pattern predominated, and its overall impact apparently declined. Accounts vary as to its presence before outsider contact, but historical reviews within the Annual Reports attribute its spread to the activities of planters and recruiters in New Guinea around 1875–80 and those of early pearl-fishers in Papua. The additional range of human movements induced under colonial rule appeared to have been very effective in dysentery transmission, and disastrous epidemics recurred in association with mining, for example on the Papuan goldfields in 1906 and 1909–10 and the New Guinea goldfields in 1926–7, though with a much lower case-fatality in the latter. In 1914 there was no epidemic either in Central or South-Eastern Division, and the contrast with preceding years drew remark. From that time dysentery appears to have declined from its position as a prime cause of illness, death and public health concern, regaining that status only during the highlands epidemic during the Second World War (Burton 1983). The reasons for its decline, and for the generally lower salience of gastrointestinal disease in PNG today are hard to determine but seem likely to include effective public health measures, low population densities, and the acquisition of immunity.

Any heavy or steeply rising rates of death were naturally apparent to the populations affected, and there are repeated cases in the Annual Reports where epidemics of infection, sometimes on unprecedented scales, were accompanied by outbreaks of violence as villagers applied the explanations available in their worldviews — often of murder by sorcery — to these events.

From 1887, sexually transmitted diseases (STDs) are frequently discussed in the Annual Reports, but often generically or with caution as to the possible confusions amongst them and with yaws. After four decades of intense control and treatment campaigns but also of conditions such as labour migration favourable to them, some areas appeared to be free but total eradication seemed a remote prospect. There appear to have been several introductions before 1898, and STDs appear to have been widespread by an early date. Prevalence appears to have been higher in the Trobriand Islands and other eastern island regions of both Papua and New Guinea, and also in the Western Division of Papua, than in the central regions. Donovanosis, probably a recent introduction, was apparently responsible for many of the cases, as it was between 1920 and 1950 amongst the Marind-Anim across the border in Dutch New Guinea, where customary sexual mores contributed to the extraordinary scale of the epidemic (Vogel and Richens 1989).

Gonorrhoea is much the most frequent of the STDs mentioned specifically. Prevalence was up to 80 per cent in one remote village in the Talasea region of New Britain in 1926. It was reported to have spread ahead of the frontier of direct foreign contact, with returning labourers from Manumbo (behind Bogia, New Guinea coast) at least to Ambunti (Sepik plain). Syphilis, on the other hand, is consistently noted as rare or non-existent in these reports, a phenomenon attributed to cross-immunity from endemic yaws, as in the highlands more recently (Gajdusek 1990).

What appears to be underemphasized in the reports is the role of disease whose toll was more or less constant or was thought to be more on morbidity than mortality: especially malaria, also filariasis, tropical ulcer, cough, intestinal helminths, tinea, scabies etc. There are fewer observations on these than might be expected, but they often include a remark as to their ubiquity. Malaria was most often discussed as a risk to the expatriate population but was clearly very common in low-lying areas. Filariasis was noted as widespread and fairly common in places, but observers who had seen it in the island Pacific did not think its PNG manifestations very severe. Yaws drew more attention than most chronic infections, and appears widespread and common in many places from the earliest records, mainly in children, but was considered mild and rarely responsible for hospital admissions even in areas served by hospitals; though in some isolated areas (e.g. the D'Entrecasteaux Islands in 1911) introduction appeared to be recent in view of the wide age range of patients. A report in 1898 suggests that scabies had been introduced only 3–4 years previously, but within

Table 11.1. Major diseases in colonial Papua and New Guinea

(a) Table of important* diseases, Papua, 1917–18 n = 1629 cases	%
Ulcers	31.8
Granuloma inguinale (i.e. donovanosis)	25.1
Gonorrhoea	17.0
Malaria	9.9
Beriberi	3.8
Dysentery	3.6
Yaws	3.1
Venereal (unspecified)	2.5
Ulcerated mouth (scurvy)	1.6
Venereal warts	0.9
Phthisis (i.e. tuberculosis)	0.6
Varicella	0.06
Pertussis	0.06

Source: Dr W. M. Strong (Territory of Papua, Annual Report 1917–18, p. 60)

*Dr Strong notes that these 'have come under my notice officially or have been reported to me' and 'have been selected because, for one reason or another, they appear to me to be such as to require watching from a public health point of view'. His original table also includes 80 European cases, predominantly of (uncomplicated) malaria but including three conditions not reported to occur amongst New Guineans — blackwater fever, dengue fever, and syphilis.

(b) Chief causes of death, New Guinea, 1922–39 n = 1436 autopsies	%
Pneumococcal infections	26.9
Tuberculosis	19.6
Bacillary dysentery	12.7
Septic infections	6.6
Tropical ulcer and sequelae	6.5
Enteric fever	2.1
Miscellaneous causes	25.5

Source: Dr T. C. Backhouse (Territory of New Guinea, Annual Report 1938–9, p. 59)

Note: Sampling design, population base and age structure are not stated in either table.

a few decades it seems to have been its absence rather than its presence that drew remark. Otherwise there is little to indicate that any of these more chronic conditions were new.

Pneumonia (sometimes grouped with pleurisy, bronchitis, etc.) is consistently prominent in the early reports, and was clearly both common and an important cause of death often as a complication of influenza or other acute respiratory infections, with sufficient epidemicity (sometimes seasonal) to draw more attention than malaria. All divisions seem to have been similarly affected and the figures where available speak for themselves: for example, 142 deaths in a Bainings (New Britain) population of 817 in 2 months in 1927.

In 1918 Dr W. M. Strong, Chief Medical Officer in Papua, summarized the important diseases in the territory (Table 11.1, left), in a way which, though it could hardly mirror exactly the situation on the ground, states concisely the contemporary informed view of the population's health problems around that time, broadly applicable in both territories. A more rigorous picture emerges from a summary in 1939 (Table 11.1, right) of the autopsy experience of Dr T. C. Backhouse in Rabaul since 1922. Backhouse's findings reinforce the conclusion that infectious diseases were overwhelmingly the most important causes of death up to this date (i.e. in the pre-antibiotic era) in PNG. This series was, however, not analyzed by age. It was also drawn from the Rabaul area, so that the findings reflect, for example, a level of malaria control not achieved elsewhere in the lowlands of PNG.

Since the Second World War

Relatively few Papua New Guinean villagers died in the fighting of the Pacific War on their soil, but concurrent epidemic disease and disrupted agricultural production caused much death and illness. After the war, during which many Papua New Guineans had travelled extensively, there was a period of rapid change in both Papua New Guinean and Australian expectations of how life in the colony should be ordered. Like many other developments in the colonial era and since, these changes affected different parts of the country differentially, and so in some respects accentuated pre-existing economic inequalities and cultural differences, while introducing a new level of uniformity in other respects to the regions most affected (Allen 1992).

Economic development, increased internal migration and since 1975 national independence have formed parts of the continually changing context for changing health patterns in the post-war period. For this period too there is much fuller information available than previously to describe patterns of epidemiological diversity in PNG. A few exceptional studies trace epidemiological changes in the same population over a significant length of time. For example, large reductions in infant mortality, splenomegaly, hepatomegaly and malaria prevalence, but significantly increased blood pressure and surprisingly ambivalent changes in nutritional anthropometry were found amongst the Wopkaimin, as the Ok Tedi mining development and the associated economic changes and health programmes got under way in their previously very remote part of Western Province (Lourie 1987). A few studies also integrate evidence from studies conducted over a long period in specific areas, e.g. Allen (1989) for the Torricelli foothills north of the Sepik river.

But most studies present profiles of the health of particular groups at particular times, and here we shall be fairly ahistorical in selecting a few of these to explore contrasts in health patterns. This is not because historical trends are unimportant, but because even where they are in similar directions, they are highly desynchronized. The disparities between provinces, between urban and rural sectors, and between local communities can be seen as a moving frontier of socioeconomic change and health care provision, with different starting times, different speeds of movement, and assuming somewhat varying characters, progressively reaching more remote areas.

By the start of the post-war period, prehistoric and recorded outside impacts had had a considerable time depth in the coasts and lowlands especially, and had brought changes of many kinds. None the less, in many areas the rural population (a large majority even nowadays) was still made up mainly of small-scale communities, in which people had to make their living with limited involvement in the cash economy, had access to quite basic health care and prevention at best, and lived lives in which indigenous norms, beliefs and practices continued to play a large part.

Successive censuses indicate considerable and progressive declines in mortality through the post-war period; and substantial increases in life expectancy between the 1971 and 1980 censuses are consistent across all provinces (Allen 1992; Riley and Lehmann 1992). At this level the demographic evidence is clearly in keeping with the health transition model. The controversy whether 'acculturation' (see footnote, p. 196) has negative or positive effects on health (Wirsing 1985; Dennett and Connell 1988) appears resolved in favour of the latter — though if the different phases of the process and the different causes of ill-health are more finely dissected, evidence in both directions can be found. The causes of improving life expectancies are probably not uniform across the nation. Health care measures (if only chloroquine and penicillin) are probably very important. Dietary change and diversification related to economic development have been thought influential too, though working for money may also bring less positive impacts on subsistence activities and breast feeding patterns. Nutritional changes over the post-war period are reviewed in more detail by Heywood and Jenkins (1992) and Ulijaszek (in press), and given the importance of the malnutrition-infection synergism these are clearly very relevant.

Beyond the general alleviation of mortality, what is also very striking is how much the scale of mortality and (it can safely be assumed) morbidity varies across PNG throughout this period. The above-mentioned census data show a wide range in expectancies of life at birth at the province level in 1980, from 59.6 years in North Solomons Province to 42.1 years in West Sepik Province, with corresponding differences in infant and child mortality (Allen 1992). The magnitude and persistence of differences amongst provinces are illustrated by the fact that, despite trends in similar directions, West Sepik in 1980 had yet to reach the level of North Solomons in 1971. More localized studies show a more extreme range of variation as might be expected, ranging to extremes such as amongst the Saniyo-Hiyowe of the East Sepik Province highland fringes, only 51 per cent of whose children survive to age 5 years owing mainly to treatable infectious diseases, especially respiratory diseases and malaria (Townsend 1985), or of the Abelam of the East Sepik lowlands, esti-mated in one study to have had an infant mortality rate of 570 per 1000 (Forge, summarized by Peters 1960).

There are no diseases, signs or symptoms which all Papua New Guineans are at equal risk of contracting. Ubiquitous variation according to age, sex, nutri-tional status, and pre-existing disease states alone suffices to ensure individual variation in disease susceptibility within each population. It is also hard to find conditions which, when individuals' risks are aggregated into a group measure, occur with equal frequency in all populations studied. Perhaps the nearest to such a condition is cough which, though seldom remarked on in daily life, is common and widespread throughout PNG, and exhibits surprisingly similar, though in each case strongly age-related, prevalences even in contrasting settings (Anderson and Woolcock 1992).

Riley and Lehmann (1992) compare a rural highlands (Tari, Southern Highlands Province) and a rural lowlands (Anguganak, West Sepik Province) population. In Tari, with life expectancies of 50.0 and 51.0 years (males and females respectively), respiratory infections accounted for more than half the deaths under one year and were the leading cause at all ages listed, jointly with accidents and violence at 15–44 years. Neonatal and congenital factors were the only other major cause of infant death (< 1 year), and diarrhoeal disease the only other major cause of child death (1–4 years). In Anguganak, with lower life expectancies of 44.6 and 40.6 years, respiratory diseases and malaria were jointly the prime causes of infant death, with neonatal and congenital factors the only other major cause. Malaria accounted for an even larger proportion of child deaths, making it much the predominant cause of death in this age group, but respiratory infections were less important at this age. Amongst the contrasts between Tari and Anguganak, the higher overall mortality and vastly greater importance of malaria in the lowlands are crucial; whilst respiratory diseases (mainly bacterial pneumonia in PNG generally) take a relentless toll in both.

In a broader based survey, Vines (1970) compared Highlands (i.e. the high-land provinces), Mainland (i.e. the northern lowland provinces) and Islands (i.e. the large island provinces). The findings on cause of death (Table 11.2) show

Table 11.2.   Causes of death and diseases, sample survey 1962–6, PNG

(a)   Leading causes of hospital death

Cause	Highlands region (*n* = 1949) %	Mainland region (*n* = 2530) %	Islands region (*n* = 1098) %
Pneumonia	45.4	15.8	12.3
Gastroenteritis	11.5	6.4	3.1
Tuberculosis	0.3	8.0	13.8
Meningitis	7.7	5.4	5.9
Immaturity	6.7	5.2	3.7
Dysentery	9.7	3.6	1.6
Malignant neoplasms	3.2	3.8	10.3
Malaria	4.5	6.2	2.1
Malnutrition	5.0	5.2	1.2
Nephritis	2.4	3.6	5.6

(b)   Period prevalence of certain diseases in one month prior to survey (by recall)

Disease	(*n* = 1034) %	(*n* = 943) %	(*n* = 1066) %
Upper respiratory tract infection	11.1	14.8	21.5
Headache	5.4	14.4	16.2
Fever	5.2	16.8	13.4
Acute bronchitis/ pneumonia/pleurisy	1.9	2.9	2.7
Chronic bronchitis/emphysema	0.9	3.9	2.7
Diarrhoea/gastroenteritis	1.0	2.0	2.5
Burns to skin	1.5	1.3	0.8
Dysentery	0.3	0.1	0.2
Congestive cardiac failure	0.1	0.1	–

Source: Vines (1970), Tables 6(B) and 9

that the Tari and Anguganak populations, though only two of very many, are representative to a degree of the highland–lowland contrast. Respiratory infections are the most prominent everywhere, and in the lowland samples gastrointestinal infections more salient and malaria less so than at Anguganak. Some lowland areas are indeed less malarial than Anguganak, but malaria deaths may have been underrepresented in Vines' sample through his reliance on hospital data and lack of control for age. Certainly his malaria survey data show much higher parasitaemia rates, more steeply declining with age, in the Mainland sample than in the Highland one (Vines 1970: Table 8.19).

Malaria is a major risk not only in lowland PNG but also at intermediate altitudes, whose populations appear peculiarly vulnerable to its complication hyperreactive malarious splenomegaly syndrome, with a high risk of death in mid-life from ill-defined causes (Crane 1986). Other diseases where risk decreases with altitude include other vector-borne infections, in particular filariasis, which also leads to splenomegaly (Schuurkamp 1992), and skin infections such as tinea imbricata (Serjeantson *et al.* 1992), where warmth and humidity appear to be important for the survival and direct person-to-person transmission of the microorganism. Although it is clear that malaria risk declines with altitude, it is not clear whether pneumonia risk actually increases with altitude as might be hypothesized on behavioural or physiological grounds, because of the difficulties of confirming diagnoses in the field and of separating pneumonia from its statistical and causal interactions with malaria.

Altitude and the nutritional and/or health care correlates of socioeconomic development are then amongst the factors which can explain the regional diversity still apparent in the health profiles of rural Papua New Guineans. Another such factor of great importance is cultural difference, which though often transformed by the events of the past century has not been abolished by them. Kuru in the Fore region of the eastern highlands (Alpers 1992), pigbel in the highlands generally (Lawrence 1992), and donovanosis in the southern lowlands (see above: still above average prevalence in Western Province) are perhaps the clearest cases where epidemiological diversity within PNG can be related to cultural practices which, serendipitously from the viewpoint of the infectious agent, have been favourable to transmission. Subtler cultural differences which affect the vulnerability of particular groups are probably legion, especially when nutritional deficiencies, conditions with a psychological component, trauma, and violence are considered alongside infections, but are hard to identify as definitely. Cultural practices yet to be identified may, for example, play a part in explaining the localized occurrence of the highly lethal swollen belly syndrome associated with massive intestinal infections of *Strongyloides fuelleborni kellyi* in young babies (Barnish 1992). Traditional practices intended to reduce mosquito bites (for example, the use of basketware mosquito nets) or with a likely effect of doing so (for example, siting of villages on ridges etc., more probably for defensive reasons) may have had some impact on malaria transmission. Traditional residence practices as well as simple demographic factors were formerly conducive to small settlement size in most parts of the country, and thus formed some protection against many acute infections until their semi-isolation was broken down (see above); though it is not certain whether even the largest and densest of these was at that stage large enough to be any more vulnerable — e.g. to malaria — than the others. Risks associated specifically with urban settlements are discussed further in a later section.

Community studies

A few studies consider the health profiles of specific groups sufficiently broadly to convey the range of conditions commonly experienced, and the impact they have on the daily lives of those groups. Maddocks (1978) reported on patterns of attendance at a permanent clinic established in the Motu village of Pari in the National Capital District, 3 km from suburban Port Moresby. There were 3.9 reported sickness episodes, resulting in 8.7 attendances, reported per person per year. Children under 5 years attended much more often than adults, but major illness (tuberculosis, influenza if leading to repeated attendances, etc.) formed an increasing proportion of all illness episodes with increasing age. Lewis (1975) described the health of the Gnau of Lumi Sub-Province, West Sepik Province, and Frankel (1986) that of the Huli of Tari, Southern Highlands Province (two provinces already compared earlier in this chapter). Lewis and Frankel both worked as anthropologists in areas further from medical facilities, but used different methods to compile their records. Lewis, working in a small community, recorded all illnesses that came to his attention through direct contact with patients or news of them, except that only some of the more trivial ones (transient fevers, minor cuts and skin infections, vague aches, conjunctivitis, and colds) were included; and he simply enumerates these episodes. Frankel, working with Huli research assistants in a larger, more scattered community, questioned each member of the sample fortnightly, and he enumerates the results as symptom-days per person per year, separately by age group and sex. He found the 5–39 year old age groups in both sexes to have the lowest symptom frequencies overall, with higher rates in the 0–4, and much higher rates in the 40+ age groups, especially the males of both. The main epidemiological findings of these three studies are summarized as similarly as possible in Table 11.3. Frankel's data have been converted to a form closer to the other two (that is, a form not adjusted for age/sex structure); but the method differences cannot be entirely removed. Thus, their findings are comparable only in the approximate sense that the relative proportions in each community convey some impression of the burden of illness there.

Nonetheless, some intelligible patterns emerge. It is in keeping with expectation, for example, that respiratory disease and symptoms are prominent in all three cases, most of all in the highlands; that malaria is most important in the rural lowlands, and least in the peri-urban area where it is amenable to control; and that gastrointestinal disease has some prominence everywhere. But some less obvious points also arise. The illnesses which are probably the leading causes of death among the Gnau as they are at Anguganak nearby, lower respiratory tract infections and malaria, account only for 10 per cent (when respiratory disease is subdivided) of the morbidity episodes. Among the Huli of the Tari basin, likewise, severe symptoms, presumably often due to lower respiratory tract infections, account for no more than 30 per cent and in most age–sex

Table 11.3. Selected community health studies in PNG

	Motu 1969–74 (coastal peri-urban)* % of disease episodes $n = 20\ 615$	Gnau 1968–9 (inland lowlands)† % of disease episodes (excluding some minor ones) $n = 274$	Huli 1977–9 (highlands)‡ % of symptom-days (estimated from graphs) $n =$ approx. 31 049/year
Skin trauma	27.4	12.0	7.5
Skin infections	20.1	19.0	13.2
Acute/severe respiratory disease	20.1	15.7	23.1
Cough	–	–	15.5
Diarrhoeal disease/ abdominal pain/vomiting	7.1	6.2	4.2
Eye/ear infection	6.2	1.8	–
Diagnosed/suspected malaria	–	9.9	3.1
Other infections (e.g. filariasis, meningitis, urinary tract infection)	–	9.5	–
'Rheumatic' pains, joint and back pains	–	8.0	11.9
Head pains	–	4.4	6.1
Body and chest pains (not respiratory)	–	–	8.9
Disturbed behaviour; attempted suicide etc.	–	3.3	–
Other conditions (incl. heart failure, severe arthritis, gynaecological disease)	–	5.5	–
Undiagnosed malaise	–	2.2	–
Deaths from undiagnosed cause	–	2.6	–

Notes: Some assumptions and approximations have been used here to derive illness categories as comparable as possible across the different studies: consequently comparability is at a crude level only. Entries marked – indicate that the conditions in question were not listed in the source, and were probably recorded infrequently (< 2% each) or not at all. The different recording methods need to be borne in mind in interpreting the figures: e.g. Lewis notes that he omitted some minor cases; and uncomplicated cough undoubtedly occurred among all three communities as Huli people said when questioned, but would not have been seen as a reason to seek medical attention and therefore does not emerge in the Motu and Gnau cases.

* Maddocks (1978), table 2.4
† Lewis (1975), table 8
‡ Frankel (1986), figs.11–36

groups less than 15 per cent of all symptom-days recorded. Thus, even though Lewis notes that his figures underestimate less serious complaints, skin lesions outnumber the major infections amongst the Gnau and are also frequent amongst the Motu and to a lesser extent (despite the method difference) the Huli. A variety of aches and pains are prominent amongst the Gnau and especially amongst the Huli, where Frankel relates them to patterns of everyday work and to the effects of violence. Vines' prevalence data (Table 11.2) also illustrate the importance of non-fatal morbidity.

Frankel's breakdown according to age and sex reveals some further patterns not detailed in Table 11.3: for example, the high prevalence of minor cutaneous lesions (sores, cuts, burns) in children aged 12 years, especially males; the high prevalence of aches and pains in adults over 40 years, especially backache in females (who spend much time carrying heavy loads and stooping over in their gardens) and arthritic knee pain in males (who often walk long distances over treacherous tracks and sometimes still suffer the effects of arrow wounds in warfare); and the extremely high frequencies of cough and severe respiratory symptoms of males over 40 years, probably attributable to tobacco smoking (traditionally discouraged in many areas in females, who experience a much slighter rise with age in severe respiratory symptoms and none in cough). Across the highlands generally it is sometimes men, sometimes women, who have been found to have the higher chronic lung disease rates (Anderson and Woolcock 1992), and smoking behaviour also varies substantially.

Lewis categorized the disease episodes he observed according to his judgment of their pathological severity; and he found, for example, that serious illness constituted some 13 per cent of the total, affecting the sexes similarly but much more, as expected, infants and adults over 45 years than children or younger adults. To obtain a clearer picture of the degree of incapacity imposed by illness, Lewis also considered patterns of behaviour during illness, patterns which reflect a complex combination of absolute physiological restriction, individuals' perception of their own situation, and cultural conventions about how a sick person is expected to behave, in the context that daily life involves demanding physical work outside the village for everyone. He found that in 34 per cent of illness episodes (no sex difference), patients carried on with their usual routine; in 30 per cent of episodes (more in males), they confined themselves to the village but otherwise behaved as usual; in 11 per cent of episodes (more in females), they were severely debilitated and recumbent; and in 13 per cent of episodes (for complex reasons more in younger women and older men, very rare in children), they were again recumbent and did not eat or converse, to an extent out of keeping with their clinical signs. Lewis reports that the Gnau themselves would not make this last distinction, since 'time lost by illness or by fears that this was illness, which I judged unwarranted, were equally to the Gnau time lost through illness' (p. 112). Recalculating to omit a further category of ill babies, 61 per cent of illness episodes recorded thus had an observable effect on the daily life of the Gnau, registered in ways that are meaningful in the context of their environment, daily duties, and beliefs about illness. With some exceptions that are hard to explain, this behavioural impact was in accordance with Lewis' judgment of their clinical severity.

What emerges from studies such as these three, then, is a picture which extends the bare mortality and cause of death statistics to show firstly, the extent of and variation in the burden of morbidity even from causes with a very low case-fatality; secondly, some complexities in the uneven distribution of this burden amongst the different age/sex subgroups; and thirdly, something of its translation according to the context into varying levels and kinds of impairment of capacity to function. A variety of factors lead us frequently — and justifiably from a European viewpoint, though Papua New Guineans might have a different perspective — to emphasize mortality as a measure of population health: the finality of death, its shocking frequency in many PNG societies, and the simple availability of data. But even in high-mortality societies, non-fatal infections, traumas, and stresses can impose a heavy burden on human wellbeing; and it is a burden which must not be overlooked, as Harrison (1987, 1990) has argued in other contexts. That is a lesson which is now more widely heeded in Western society (low back pain, arthritis etc.), and is being extended to some major infections of the developing world. Perhaps these are areas which now need further attention in PNG, too.

The effects of modern living

Though obstetric complications, snake- and invertebrate-bites, nutritional deficiencies, cancers, metabolic, genetic and psychiatric illness, and most particularly, accidents and violence were all undoubtedly responsible for some morbidity and mortality in pre-outsider and early contact times, the main burden of illness in PNG has clearly been from infection. Health transition models suggest that modernization brings a decline in infectious disease[3] and a rise in non-infectious disease. In addition to the simple arithmetical fact of more people surviving long enough to experience degenerative disease are the 'effects of modern living' (Harrison 1973). Environmental, dietary, behavioural, and social changes that typically accompany modernization elsewhere and carry some increased disease risks include: increased intakes of refined carbohydrate, animal fats, salt, cows' milk and many artificial additives, usually without acute food shortages, but with decreased intake of fibre and earlier weaning; air pollution and numerous chemical substances in cosmetics, pleasure-promoting substances and antidotal drugs; more controlled ambient temperatures, longer exposure to visible light and ionizing radiation, and higher noise levels; higher population densities with consequences for both infection and social relationships, especially the need to deal with strangers; complex

[3]Ulijaszek (in press), however, reports national statistics suggesting that diarrhoeal disease has increased and child nutritional status worsened since 1975, and that PNG's decline in infectious disease is specific to infections effectively tackled by immunization programmes.

changes in time-budget usually including more regular eating and sleeping and lower exercise levels with little need for physical activity to acquire food; occupational monotony; increased spatial and marital mobility and its correlate in a new range of traumas, the traffic accident; and socioeconomic stratification.

Such changes have struck PNG's citizens, mainly those of them who live in urban and periurban environments, with especial speed. Their epidemiological effects are nowadays open to well-grounded predictions in many cases, and the evidence is now available to show that indeed there has been a dramatic impact on blood pressure (Lourie *et al.* 1992), ischaemic heart disease since the first fully documented case in 1971 (Sinnett *et al.* 1992), and non-insulin-dependent diabetes and impaired glucose tolerance in the populations of the northern and southeastern coasts, among whom modernizing lifestyle changes have been at work longest and who, it has been hypothesized, may additionally be genetically more susceptible (King 1992). Carrad (1987) supplies further evidence of the growth in hospital admission for conditions such as peptic ulcer, appendicitis, and traffic accidents. Thus, superimposed on pre-existing epidemiological patterns is a new axis of variation, the rural–urban. As urban populations grow, as permanent migrants to the towns increase in proportion to temporary ones despite the lack of jobs for them, and as urban children grow up with their first language a *lingua franca* rather than their parents', new patterns of health and disease emerge with some force from the problems and advantages of urban life. Except as offset by public and personal health measures, intended and unintended, these include both the non-infectious risks previously mentioned and the infectious risks of living in larger and more cosmopolitan settlements.

Not all of PNG's 'new diseases' are readily attributed to one of the causes already listed, or to urbanism. The rise in asthma, for example, is poorly understood. While its frequency in urban PNG, as in many modern urban settings, is substantial enough to cause concern, it is in rural areas, especially amongst the Fore and some other Eastern Highlands groups, that atopic asthma, related to the abundance of house-dust mites, has recently emerged on an epidemic scale (Anderson and Woolcock 1992). Asthma seems to illustrate the continuing importance of ecological and biogeographical factors alongside those of modernization and urbanism.

Conclusions

We have attempted to review some of the key features of PNG's changing and varying patterns of disease in relation to the concept of health transition. Unsurprisingly, with its predominantly rural population, PNG's most important health problems are still those of infectious disease, but a modernizing shift towards a greater impact of the non-infectious causes of major and minor morbidity is clearly under way, and its end not yet in sight. This is broadly in keeping with the prevailing health transition models. But the PNG evidence has a wider value in reminding us that there is a continuing high toll and recurrent risk from infection; that in the long term, changes in infectious morbidity and mortality (like fertility: Wood 1992) have been more complex than simply a transition from high to low; that there is persistently high regional and local variation in disease patterns, increasingly attributable to socio-economic factors, modernization, and urbanism, but also still to cultural, demographic, and environmental ones; and that the burden of non-fatal illness, which can be very high in both rural and urban situations, will demand increasing attention as mortality continues — we hope — to be alleviated. The continuing changes ahead will no doubt remind us how much we all can fruitfully learn from the microcosm of many of the world's problems and opportunities that is Papua New Guinea.

Acknowledgements

Many thanks to Peter Bellwood, Don Gardner, Robin Hide, Mary-Jane Mountain, Linc Schmitt, Stan Ulijaszek and the editors for their suggestions and critical readings of part or whole of this chapter in draft.

References

Adels, B. R. and Gajdusek, D. C. (1963). Survey of measles patterns in New Guinea, Micronesia and Australia. *American Journal of Hygiene*, **77**, 317–43.

Allen, B. J. (1989). Infection, innovation and residence: illness and misfortune in the Torricelli foothills from 1800. In *A continuing trial of treatment: medical pluralism in Papua New Guinea*, (ed. S. Frankel and G. Lewis). Culture, Illness and Healing, **14**, pp. 35–68. Kluwer, Dordrecht.

Allen, B. J. (1992). The geography of Papua New Guinea. In *Human biology in Papua New Guinea: the small cosmos*, Research Monographs on Human Population Biology, **10**, pp. 36–66, (ed. R. D. Attenborough and M. P. Alpers). Clarendon Press, Oxford.

Alpers, M. P. (1992). Kuru. In *Human biology in Papua New Guinea: the small cosmos*, Research Monographs on Human Population Biology, **10** (ed. R. D. Attenborough and M. P. Alpers). Clarendon Press, Oxford.

Alpers, M. P. and Attenborough, R. D. (1992). Human biology in a small cosmos. In *Human biology in Papua New Guinea: the small cosmos*, Research Monographs on Human Population Biology, **10**, pp. 1–35, (ed. R. D. Attenborough and M. P. Alpers). Clarendon Press, Oxford.

Anderson, H. R. and Woolcock, A. J. (1992). Chronic lung disease and asthma in Papua New Guinea. In *Human biology in Papua New Guinea: the small cosmos*, Research Monographs on Human Population Biology, **10**, pp. 289–301, (ed. R. D. Attenborough and M. P. Alpers). Clarendon Press, Oxford.

Attenborough, R. D. and Alpers, M. P. (ed.) (1992). *Human biology in Papua New Guinea: the small cosmos*. Research Monographs on Human Population Biology **10**, Clarendon Press, Oxford.

Baker, P. T. (ed.) (1978). *The biology of high-altitude peoples*. International Biological Programme, **14**. Cambridge University Press, Cambridge.

Barnish, G. (1992). The epidemiology of intestinal parasites in Papua New Guinea. In *Human biology in Papua New Guinea: the small cosmos*, Research Monographs on Human Population Biology, **10**, pp. 345–54, (ed. R. D. Attenborough and M. P. Alpers). Clarendon Press, Oxford.

Boyce, A. J., Harrison, G. A., Platt, C. M., and Hornabrook, R. W. (1976). Association between PTC taster status and goitre in a Papua New Guinea population. *Human Biology*, **48**, 769–73.

Boyce, A. J., Attenborough, R. D., Harrison, G. A., Hornabrook, R. W., and Sinnett, P. (1978a). Variation in blood pressure in a New Guinea population. *Annals of Human Biology*, **5**, 313–19.

Boyce, A. J. Harrison, G. A., Platt, C. M., and Hornabrook, R. W., Serjeantson, S., Kirk, R. L., and Booth, P. B. (1978b). Migration and genetic diversity in an island population: Karkar, Papua New Guinea. *Proceedings of the Royal Society of London B*, **202**, 269–95.

Boyden, S. (1987). *Western civilization in biological perspective: patterns in biohistory*. Clarendon Press, Oxford.

Brush, G., Boyce, A. J., and Harrison, G. A. (1983). Associations between anthropometric variables and reproductive performance in a Papua New Guinea highland population. *Annals of Human Biology*, **10**, 223–34.

Brush, G., Harrison, G. A., Boyce, A. J., and Lourie, J. A. (1989). Parotid gland enlargement and female reproductive performance in a Papua New Guinea highland population. *Annals of Human Biology*, **16**, 437–41.

Burton, J. (1983). A dysentery epidemic in New Guinea and its mortality. *Journal of Pacific History*, **18**, 236–61.

Burton-Bradley, B. G. (ed.) (1990). *A history of medicine in Papua New Guinea: vignettes of an earlier period*. Australasian Medical Publishing Company, Kingsgrove, New South Wales.

Caldwell, J., Findley, S., Caldwell, P., Santow, G., Cosford, W., Braid, J., and Broers-Freeman, D. (ed.) (1990). *What we know about health transition: the cultural, social and behavioural determinants of health*. Health Transition Centre, Australian National University, Canberra.

Carrad, E. V. (1987). *Review of disease patterns in Papua New Guinea*. University of Papua New Guinea Press, Port Moresby.

Cattani, J. A. (1992). The epidemiology of malaria in Papua New Guinea. In *Human biology in Papua New Guinea: the small cosmos*, Research Monographs on Human Population Biology, **10**, pp. 302–12, (ed. R. D. Attenborough and M. P. Alpers). Clarendon Press, Oxford.

Clark, J. T. and Kelly, K. M. (1993). Human genetics, paleoenvironments and malaria: relationships and implications for the settlement of Oceania. *American Anthropologist*, **95**, 612–30.

Cockburn, A. (1977). Where did our infectious diseases come from? The evolution of infectious disease. In *Health and disease in tribal societies*, Ciba Foundation Symposium (New York Series), **49** (ed. Ciba Foundation), pp. 103–13. Elsevier, Amsterdam.

Cohen, M. N. and Armelagos, G. J. (ed.) (1984). *Paleopathology at the origins of agriculture*. Academic Press, New York.

Crane, G. G. (1986). Recent studies of hyperreactive malarious splenomegaly (tropical splenomegaly syndrome) in Papua New Guinea. *Papua New Guinea Medical Journal*, **29**, 35–40.

Dennett, G. and Connell, J. (1988). Acculturation and health in the highlands of Papua New Guinea. *Current Anthropology*, **29**, 273–99.

Denoon, D., Dugan, K., and Marshall, L. (1989). *Public health in Papua New Guinea: medical possibility and social constraint, 1884–1984*. Cambridge University Press, Cambridge.

Dunn, F. L. (1968). Epidemiological factors: health and disease in hunter–gatherers. In *Man the hunter*, (ed. R. B. Lee and I. DeVore), pp. 221–28. Aldine, New York.

Fenner, F. (1980). Sociocultural change and environmental diseases. In *Changing disease patterns and human behaviour*, (ed. N. F. Stanley and R. A. Joske), pp. 7–26. Academic Press, London.

Fenner, F. (1990). Emerging virus diseases. In *Is our future limited by our past?* Proceedings of the Australasian Society for Human Biology, **3**, pp. 287–95, Centre for Human Biology, University of Western Australia, Perth, Western Australia.

Fenner, F., Henderson, D. A., Arita, I., Jezek, Z., and Ladnyi, I. D. (1988). *Smallpox and its eradication*. History of International Public Health, **6**, World Health Organization, Geneva.

Flint, J., Harding, R. M., Clegg, J. B., and Boyce, A. J. (1993). Why are some genetic diseases common? Distinguishing selection from other processes by molecular analysis of globin gene variants. *Human Genetics*, **91**, 91–117.

Foley, W. A. (1992). Language and identity in Papua New Guinea. In *Human biology in Papua New Guinea: the small cosmos*, Research Monographs on Human Population Biology, **10** , pp. 136–49, (ed. R. D. Attenborough and M. P. Alpers). Clarendon Press, Oxford.

Forge, A. (1972). Normative factors in the settlement size of neolithic cultivators (New Guinea). In *Man, settlement and urbanism*, (ed. P. J. Ucko, R. Tringham, and G. W. Dimbleby), pp. 363–76. Duckworth, London.

Frankel, S. (1986). *The Huli response to illness*. Cambridge Studies in Social Anthropology, **62**. Cambridge University Press, Cambridge.

Gajdusek, D. C. (1990). Raymond Pearl Memorial Lecture, 1989: Cultural practices as determinants of clinical pathology and epidemiology of venereal infections: implications for predictions about the AIDS epidemic. *American Journal of Human Biology*, **2**, 347–351.

Garruto, R. M. (1981). Disease patterns of isolated groups. In *Biocultural aspects of disease*, (ed. H. R. Rothschild), pp. 557–97. Academic Press, New York.

Golson, J. (1991). Introduction: transitions to agriculture in the Pacific region. *Indo-Pacific Prehistory Association Bulletin*, **11**, 48–53.

Groube, L. M. (1993). Contradictions and malaria in Melanesian and Australian prehistory. In *A community of culture: the people and prehistory of the Pacific*. Occasional Papers in Prehistory, **21**, pp. 164–86, (ed. M. Spriggs, D. E. Yen, W. Ambrose, R. Jones, A. Thorne, and A. Andrews). Department of Prehistory, Research School of Pacific Studies, Australian National University, Canberra.

Groves, C. (1981). *Ancestors for the pigs: taxonomy and phylogeny of the genus* Sus. Technical Bulletin, **3**. Department of Prehistory, Research School of Pacific Studies, Australian National University, Canberra.

Harrison, G. A. (1970). Human variation and its social causes and consequences. *Proceedings of the Royal Anthropological Institute*, **1970**, 5–13.

Harrison, G. A. (1973). The effects of modern living. *Journal of Biosocial Science*, **5**, 217–28.

Harrison, G. A. (1987). *Adaptability, fitness and health: the first Paul T. Baker lecture*. Pennsylvania State University, Philadelphia.

Harrison, G. A. (1990). The biology of human well-being. In *Is our future limited by our past?* Proceedings of the Australasian Society for Human Biology, **3**, pp. 3–10, (ed. L. Freedman) Centre for Human Biology, University of Western Australia, Perth, Western Australia.

Harrison, G. A., Boyce, A. J., Hornabrook, R. W., and Craig, W. J. (1976a). Associations between polymorphic variety and anthropometric and biochemical variation in two New Guinea populations. *Annals of Human Biology*, **3**, 557–68.

Harrison, G. A., Boyce, A. J., Hornabrook, R. W., and Craig, W. J. (1976b). Associations between polymorphic variety and disease susceptibility in two New Guinea populations. *Annals of Human Biology*, **3**, 253–67.

Harrison, G. A., Boyce, A. J., Hornabrook, R.W., Serjeantson, S., and Craig, W. J. (1976c). Evidence for an association between ABO blood group and goitre. *Human Genetics*, **32**, 335–7.

Harrison, G. A., Boyce, A. J., Platt, C. M., and Serjeantson, S. (1975). Body composition changes during lactation in a New Guinea population. *Annals of Human Biology*, **2**, 395–8.

Harrison, G. A. and Walsh, R. J. (ed.) (1974). A discussion on human adaptability in a tropical ecosystem: an I. B. P. human biological investigation of two New Guinea communities. *Philosophical Transactions of the Royal Society of London B*, **268**, 221–400.

Heywood, P. F. and Jenkins, C. (1992). Nutrition in Papua New Guinea. In *Human biology in Papua New Guinea: the small cosmos*. Research Monographs on Human Population Biology, **10**, pp. 249–67, (ed. R. D. Attenborough and M. P. Alpers). Clarendon Press, Oxford.

Hope, G. S., Golson, J., and Allen, J. (1983). Palaeoecology and prehistory in New Guinea. *Journal of Human Evolution*, **12**, 37–60.

King, H. (1992). The epidemiology of diabetes mellitus in Papua New Guinea and the Pacific: adverse consequences of natural selection in the face of sociocultural change. In *Human biology in Papua New Guinea: the small cosmos*, Research Monographs on Human Population Biology, **10**, pp. 363–72, (ed. R. D. Attenborough and M. P. Alpers). Clarendon Press, Oxford.

King, H. and Collins, A. M. (1989) A modernity score for individuals in Melanesian society. *Papua New Guinea Medical Journal*, **32**, 11–22.

Landers, J. (ed.) (1992). *Historical epidemiology and the health transition*. Health Transition Review, **2**, (Supplement). Health Transition Centre, Australian National University, Canberra.

Lawrence, G. (1992). Pigbel. In *Human biology in Papua New Guinea: the small cosmos*, Research Monographs on Human Population Biology, **10**, pp. 335–44, (ed. R. D. Attenborough and M. P. Alpers). Clarendon Press, Oxford.

Lewis, G. (1975). *Knowledge of illness in a Sepik society: a study of the Gnau, New Guinea*. London School of Economics Monographs on Social Anthropology, **52**, Athlone Press, University of London, London.

Lilley, I. (1992). Papua New Guinea's human past: the evidence of archaeology. In *Human biology in Papua New Guinea: the small cosmos*, Research Monographs on Human Population Biology, **10**, pp. 150–71, (ed. R. D. Attenborough and M. P. Alpers). Clarendon Press, Oxford.

Livingstone, F. B. (1958). Anthropological implications of sickle-cell gene distribution in West Africa. *American Anthropologist*, **60**, 533–62.

Lourie, J., Budd, G., and Anderson, H. R. (1992). Physiological adaptability in Papua New Guinea. In *Human biology in Papua New Guinea: the small cosmos*, Research

Monographs on Human Population Biology, **10**, pp. 268–80, (ed. R. D. Attenborough and M. P. Alpers). Clarendon Press, Oxford.

Lourie, J. A. (ed.) (1987). *Ok Tedi Health and Nutrition Project Papua New Guinea 1982–1986: final report.* University of Papua New Guinea and Ok Tedi Mining Limited, Port Moresby and Tabubil.

Maddocks, I. (1978). Papua New Guinea: Pari village. In *Basic health care in developing countries: an epidemiological perspective,* (ed. B. S. Hetzel), pp. 38–62. Oxford University Press, Oxford.

McKeown, T. (1988). *The origins of human disease.* Blackwell, Oxford.

McMurray, C. (1985). *Recent demography of Papua New Guinea.* Working paper 85/5. National Centre for Development Studies, Australian National University, Canberra.

Mikloucho-Maclay, N. N. (1975). *New Guinea Diaries, 1871–1883.* Translated by C. L. Sentinella. Kristen Pres, Madang (PNG).

Panter-Brick, C. and Harrison, G. A. (1982). Interrelationships between anthropometric and serum biochemical variables in children in Papua New Guinea. *Annals of Human Biology,* **9**, 337–42.

Peters, W. (1960). Studies on the epidemiology of malaria in New Guinea. *Transactions of the Royal Society of Tropical Medicine and Hygiene,* **54**, 242–60.

Rendel, J. M. (1970). The time scale of genetic change. In *The impact of civilisation of the biology of man,* (ed. S. V. Boyden), pp. 27–47. Australian National University Press, Canberra.

Riley, I. D. (1983). Population change and distribution in Papua New Guinea: an epidemiological approach. *Journal of Human Evolution,* **12**, 125–32.

Riley, I. D. and Lehmann, D. (1992). The demography of Papua New Guinea: migration, fertility and mortality patterns. In *Human biology in Papua New Guinea: the small cosmos,* Research Monographs on Human Population Biology, **10**, pp. 67–92, (ed. R. D. Attenborough and M. P. Alpers). Clarendon Press, Oxford.

Riley, I. D., Lehmann, D., and Alpers, M. P. (1992). Acute respiratory infections. In *Human biology in Papua New Guinea: the small cosmos*, Research Monographs on Human Population Biology, **10**, pp. 281–88, (ed. R. D. Attenborough and M. P. Alpers). Clarendon Press, Oxford.

Schuurkamp, G. J. T. (1992). *The epidemiology of malaria and filariasis in the Ok Tedi region of Western Province, Papua New Guinea.* Ph.D. thesis, University of Papua New Guinea.

Serjeantson, S. W., Board, P. G., and Bhatia, K. K. (1992). Population genetics in Papua New Guinea: a perspective on human evolution. In *Human biology in Papua New Guinea: the small cosmos,* Research Monographs on Human Population Biology, **10**, pp. 198–233, (ed. R. D. Attenborough and M. P. Alpers). Clarendon Press, Oxford.

Sinnett, P. F., Kevau, I. H., and Tyson, D. (1992). Social change and the emergence of degenerative cardiovascular disease in Papua New Guinea. In *Human biology in Papua New Guinea: the small cosmos,* Research Monographs on Human Population Biology, **10**, pp. 373–86, (ed. R. D. Attenborough and M. P. Alpers). Clarendon Press, Oxford.

Spriggs, M. (1993). Island Melanesia: the last 10 000 years. In *A community of culture: the people and prehistory of the Pacific,* Occasional Papers in Prehistory, **21**, pp. 187–205, (ed. M. Spriggs, D. E. Yen, W. Ambrose, R. Jones, A. Thorne, and A. Andrews). Department of Prehistory, Research School of Pacific Studies, Australian National University, Canberra.

Swadling, P. and Hope, G. (1992). Environmental change in New Guinea since human settlement. In *The naive lands: prehistory and environmental change in Australia and the Southwest Pacific* (ed. J. Dodson), pp. 13–42. Longman Cheshire, Melbourne.

Townsend, P. K. (1985). Infant mortality in the Saniyo–Hiowe population, Ambunti District, East Sepik Province, *Papua New Guinea Medical Journal*, **28**, 177–82.

Trowell, H. C. and Burkitt, D. P. (ed.) (1981). *Western diseases: their emergence and prevention*. Edward Arnold, London.

Truswell, A. S. and Hansen, J. D. L. (1976). Medical research amongst the !Kung. In *Kalahari hunter–gatherers: studies of the !Kung San and their neighbours*, (ed. R. B. Lee and I. DeVore), pp. 166–94. Harvard University Press, Cambridge (Massachusetts).

Ulijaszek, S. J. (in press) . Development modernisation and health intervention. In *Health intervention in less developed countries* (ed. S. J. Ulijaszek). Oxford University Press, Oxford.

Vines, A. P. (1970). *An epidemiological sample survey of the highlands, mainland and islands regions of the territory of Papua and New Guinea*. Department of Public Health, Territory of Papua and New Guinea, Port Moresby.

Vogel, L. C. and Richens, J. (1989). Donovanosis in Dutch South New Guinea: history, evolution of the epidemic, and control. *Papua New Guinea Medical Journal*, **32**, 203–18.

Ward, R. G. and Lea, D. A. M. (ed.) (1970). *An atlas of Papua and New Guinea*. University of Papua and New Guinea and Collins–Longman, Port Moresby and Glasgow.

Wiesenfeld, S. L. (1967). Sickle-cell trait in human biological and cultural evolution. *Science*, **157**, 1134–40.

Wirsing, R. (1985). The health of traditional societies and the effects of acculturation. *Current Anthropology*, **26**, 303–22.

Wood, J. W. (1992). Fertility and reproductive biology in Papua New Guinea. In *Human biology in Papua New Guinea: the small cosmos*, Research Monographs on Human Population Biology, **10**, pp. 93–118, (ed. R. D. Attenborough and M. P. Alpers). Clarendon Press, Oxford.

12

Population genetics of the α-globin complex in Oceania

A. J. BOYCE, R. M. HARDING, AND J. J. MARTINSON

Introduction

The techniques of molecular genetics now make it possible to study genetic variation at the level of the DNA and the application of these techniques has greatly enhanced our understanding of the causes of genetic diversity within and between human populations (Devor 1992). One of the most extensive surveys of DNA variation has been of the α-globin complex. The analysis of this diversity has provided new evidence for the importance of malaria as a selective agent. In addition to selection, genetic diversity results from the interaction of genetic drift and migration, and present day distributions of DNA markers are providing information about population movements and affinities. The purpose of this chapter is to review some of the recent population genetics analyses of the α-globin complex, drawing on the extensive data which have been accumulated for South-East Asia and the Pacific.

The α-globin complex

The human α-globin complex lies at the end of the short arm of chromosome 16. It includes two adult ($\alpha2$ and $\alpha1$) genes and one embryonic ($\zeta 2$) gene, separated by three inactive pseudogenes ($\psi\zeta1$, $\psi\alpha2$ and $\psi\alpha1$), in the order 5' $\zeta2-\psi\zeta1-\psi\alpha2-\psi\alpha1-\alpha2-\alpha1$ 3' (Fig. 12.1). Diversity in this region has arisen through a variety of mutational processes, from single base changes to more extensive deletions and duplications of DNA. Complete characterization of this diversity will only be possible when individual chromosomes are fully sequenced, but the use of restriction enzymes enables a number of single base changes to be recognized. Higgs *et al.* (1986) in a systematic search for polymorphic markers in the α-globin complex identified a total of 203 restriction sites, 14 of which are polymorphic, giving an estimate of nucleotide diversity in this region of 1 in 80 base pairs (bp). In addition to single base changes, variation also arises through changes in the number of tandemly repeated sequences (HVR: hypervariable regions), probably as a result of non-homologous recombination. Four such regions have been identified in the α-globin region to date,

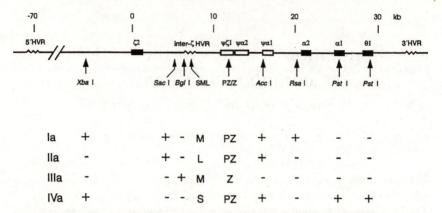

Fig. 12.1 The α-globin cluster. Functional genes are shown by solid boxes; pseudo-genes by open boxes; zig-zag lines show the location of hypervariable loci. The locations of the polymorphic loci which make up the α-globin haplotype, together with the restriction enzymes with which they are detected, are shown below the map. Examples of four common haplotypes are shown at the bottom of the figure.

one lying approximately 70 kilobases (kb) 5′ to the ζ2 gene (the 5′ HVR, consisting of repeats of a 57-bp unit), one lying between the ζ2 and ψζ1 genes (the inter-ζ HVR, IZHVR, 36 bp unit), one located in the first intron of the ζ-like genes (ζIVS1 HVR, 14 bp unit), and one situated just 3′ to the region (3′ HVR, 17–21 bp unit).

Haplotypes

Restriction site and HVR polymorphisms in a limited region of DNA such as those in the α-globin complex do not segregate independently of one another but show linkage disequilibrium. Such groups of linked polymorphisms allow the identification of *haplotypes* and this permits diversity to be studied at a higher level than that of the individual sites. Such haplotypes can be considered as multi-allelic loci. Their study in the α-globin complex has been invaluable in understanding the population genetics processes affecting population diversity in this complex.

In their survey, Higgs *et al.* (1986) used the common polymorphisms (ones in which the frequency of the less common allele is greater than 5 per cent) to define multi-marker haplotypes for the α-globin region (Fig. 12.1). The haplotypes identified were assigned to eight major groups (I–VIII) according to their 3′ haplotype (Z/PZ, *Acc*I, *Rsa*I, *Pst*I, *Pst*I). These were then subdivided according to their 5′ haplotypes (*Xba*I, *Sac*I, *Bgl*I, IZHVR — small, medium, or large), into a number of subgroups (Ia, Ib, etc.). Using all possible combinations of individual alleles in the cluster, 768 possible haplotypes could occur but, in their initial survey, Higgs *et al.* (1986) found only 29 distinct haplotypes, with a small number of haplotypes predominating. In a summary of world-wide surveys of the α-globin haplotypes, Flint *et al.* (1993*b*) identified 30 haplotypes and showed that more than half of the 2021 chromosomes studied belonged to one of the following haplotypes: Ia (25.4 per cent), IIIa (13.7 per cent), IIa (9.1 per cent), IVa (7.7 per cent).

α^+ thalassaemia

The genetic diversity that has been revealed through haplotype analysis does not appear to be associated with any obvious phenotypic effects. For these to occur mutations which affect gene expression are required, and the α-globin complex provides many examples of mutations which give rise to clinical conditions — those of α-thalassaemia. Unlike the mutations which produce polymorphic restriction sites, many of the mutations which lead to α-thalassaemia are due to more extensive deletions of DNA. The thalassaemias are divided into α^0 and α^+ according to whether the underlying mutation abolishes or only reduces the production of functional protein. α^0-thalassaemia is due to the inactivation or loss of both α-globin genes from one chromosome. Deletions of a single α gene result in α^+-thalassaemia. Homozygotes for this condition have two α genes ($-\alpha/-\alpha$) and heterozygotes three α genes ($-\alpha/\alpha\alpha$). Deletion of the linked pair of α genes results in α^0-thalassaemia. Heterozygotes ($-/\alpha\alpha$) have a mild hypochromic anaemia indistinguishable from homozygous ($-\alpha/-\alpha$) α^+-thalassaemia. Heterozygotes for the single and doubly deleted chromosomes ($-\alpha/--$) have haemoglobin H (HbH) disease. Homozygotes ($--/--$) have no α-globin genes and are generally stillborn.

The characterization of these mutations, particularly those giving rise to α^+-thalassaemia, has been greatly helped by molecular techniques. Sequencing studies have shown that the α-globin cluster has three blocks of homology (the X, Y, and Z boxes) separated by regions of non-homologous DNA. Recombination between misaligned Z and X boxes can give rise to extensive areas of DNA duplication and deletion (Fig. 12.2). If two X boxes misalign and a cross-over occurs, then 4.2 kilobases (kb), the distance from the first to the second X box, are deleted from one chromosome and duplicated on the other, giving rise to chromosomes with one or three α genes. The products are referred to as $-\alpha^{4.2}$ and $\alpha\alpha\alpha^{\text{anti4.2}}$ chromosomes. The products of recombination between the Z boxes involve the deletion and duplication of a 3.7 kb segment and give rise to $-\alpha^{3.7}$ and $\alpha\alpha\alpha^{\text{anti3.7}}$ chromosomes. Because the cross-overs can occur in different places in the Z boxes, three different deletions can be detected. The length of the homologous segments which have undergone misalignment and cross-over differs among the three mutations: 1436 bp for $-\alpha^{3.7}$I; 171 bp for $-\alpha^{3.7}$II; and 46 bp for—$\alpha^{3.7}$III (Higgs *et al.* 1984).

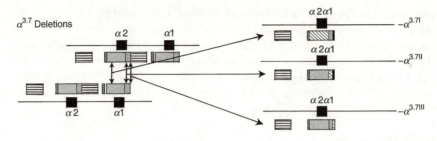

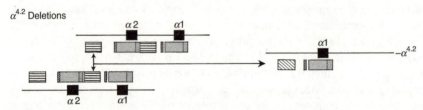

Fig. 12.2 Origin of the common α-thalassaemia deletions. Misalignment of regions of homology (shown as shaded boxes) and subsequent unequal cross-over (indicated by the double-headed arrows) lead to the deletion of either 3.7 or 4.2 kb of DNA. Crossing over can occur anywhere within the regions of homology. One of the homology boxes, where misalignment results in the 3.7 kb deletions, consists of three stretches of identity (indicated by differences in shading), and deletions can be subdivided into three types, according to where within the box they occur. The three deletions result in a composite gene with a 5′ α2 and a 3′ α1 sequence. Diagonal shading shows where the cross-over has taken place.

The role of selection

The proposal that the distribution of β-thalassaemia might be understood in terms of increased resistance to malaria in heterozygotes was first made by Haldane (1948). There is convincing support for the malaria hypothesis in the case of sickle cell disease (Allison 1954) and more limited evidence in support of this hypothesis in the case of β-thalassaemia (Siniscalco *et al.* 1961, 1966). Selection through increased resistance to malaria also offers an explanation of the distribution of α-globin variants which give rise to α-thalassaemia.

Figure 12.3 shows the distribution of α⁺-thalassaemia in the Pacific. Three patterns are visible: in Papua New Guinea there is a striking contrast between highland and coastal populations, with frequencies of less than 5 per cent in the highlands and over 70 per cent in the northern coastal populations. A similar

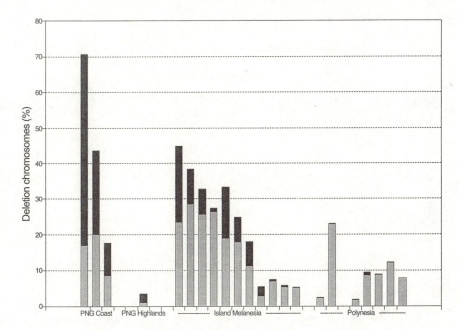

Fig. 12.3 α-thalassaemia gene frequencies in the Pacific, divided into $-\alpha^{3.7}$ and $-\alpha^{4.2}$ subtypes. Data from Flint *et al.* (1993*a*, table 1). ⊡, 3.7 kb; ■, 4.2 kb.

contrast is found in malarial endemicity. Surveys of malarial prevalence reveal that before eradication campaigns, malaria was endemic below 2500 m in Papua New Guinea. In island Melanesia, the variation in frequency of α^+-thalassaemia is with latitude rather than with altitude. When the overall data on the deletion chromosome frequencies are plotted against level of malarial endemicity (Fig. 12.4), a highly significant correlation is found, with nearly 88 per cent of the variation in gene frequency accounted for by the variation in malarial endemicity. Other, unlinked, polymorphisms show no such correlation with malarial endemicity (Flint *et al.* 1986).

Figure 12.3 also shows that different mutations give rise to α^+-thalassaemia in the Pacific: in parts of Papua New Guinea, the $-\alpha^{4.2}$ deletion predominates, while in island Melanesia, $-\alpha^{3.7}$ is more common. The use of molecular techniques makes it possible to characterize these mutations in more detail: by subtyping the $-\alpha^{3.7}$ deletions and by examining the α-haplotypes on which the mutations occur. This analysis shows that both $-\alpha^{3.7}$I and $-\alpha^{3.7}$III deletions occur; that the $-\alpha^{4.2}$ deletion occurs on three different haplotypes, and the $-\alpha^{3.7}$I on at least two. The haplotypes bearing identical mutations cannot easily be related to one another by recombination or mutation, and this implies that each deletion has arisen more than once. This additional analysis confirms the

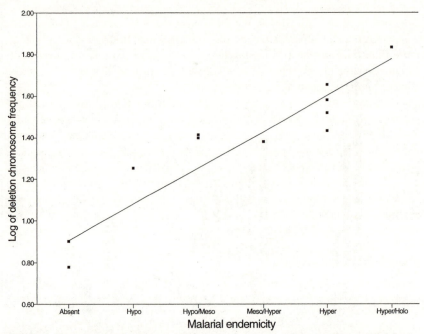

Fig. 12.4   Relationship between α-thalassaemia and malarial endemicity in Melanesia. The frequency of the single deletion chromosome (−α) is shown on a logarithmic scale. Data from Flint *et al.* (1986, table 2).

regional specificity of the mutations. The -$\alpha^{4.2}$ deletion common in Papua New Guinea is on a different haplotype to that on which the −$\alpha^{4.2}$ deletion found in South-East Asia occurs. Although the −$\alpha^{3.7}$ deletion is found in both Papua New Guinea and island Melanesia, in the former it is prominently −$\alpha^{3.7}$I while in island Melanesia the commonest deletion is −$\alpha^{3.7}$III. The haplotype with which these mutations is most frequently associated, the IIIa haplotype, is the commonest haplotype in Melanesia and rare outside the Pacific. This evidence that mutations have arisen locally, and that different mutations predominate in different Melanesian populations that are otherwise very similar makes their alternative explanation based on population movements virtually impossible to sustain.

The data shown in Fig. 12.3 also indicate that α^{+}-thalassaemia occurs in parts of the Pacific which have never been subject to malaria. The frequency of the deletion chromosome varies considerably from island to island, in an apparently random manner. Furthermore, there are fewer mutations and they are more widely distributed. In Polynesia, for example, where malaria has never been present, over 95 percent of the α^{+}-thalassaemia is of the subtype −$\alpha^{3.7}$III, and when the haplotypes on which this deletion is found are examined, they are found to be exclusively IIIa. Because the recombinational event presumed to have produced the $-\alpha^{3.7}$III deletion involves a much shorter length of homologous DNA than the alternative deletions, the likelihood of the deletion occurring more than once on the IIIa haplotype is small. Gene flow is the most likely explanation for the presence of α^+-thalassaemia in parts of the Pacific which have never experienced malaria.

Two microevolutionary processes thus underlie the distribution of α^+-thalassaemia in the Pacific. Where the frequency of α^+- thalassaemia is very high there are multiple gene deletion variants, each regionally specific and associated with a single or a small number of local haplotypes. This pattern occurs where selection has elevated the frequency of these genotypes. Where the frequency of α^+-thalassaemia is low and variable, a single mutation is found, and occurs entirely on one haplotype. This pattern is best explained as a result of gene flow combined with genetic drift.

The dynamics of selection

Although the associations found in Melanesia provide strong evidence for the action of selection, much remains to be learnt about the way in which selection operates. Not only is the physiological basis of the protection afforded by α-thalassaemia against malaria poorly understood, it is uncertain whether the protection is in the heterozygote or homozygote or both. Basic models in population genetics offer some insight into which of these possibilities is most likely. Haldane's original hypothesis was that malarial selection acted on the heterozygote leading to a balanced polymorphism. In the case of α-thalassaemia, the fittest genotype may be the homozygote $-\alpha/-\alpha$ rather than the heterozygous carrier, in which case the polymorphism is a transient one with the $-\alpha$ chromosome, in the presence of malaria, moving to fixation. The highest frequencies in the Pacific are found in the coastal populations of Papua New Guinea and it is assumed that these frequencies have been achieved within a time span of a few thousand years since the introduction of malaria into Melanesia. Figure 12.5a indicates that a mutation with an initial frequency of 10^{-4} could reach the frequency observed in Papua New Guinea (70 percent) within 5000 years through either heterozygote or homozygote advantage. However, for this to be achieved by homozygote advantage it is also necessary for the heterozygote ($-\alpha/\alpha\alpha$) to have a greater fitness than the 'normal' homozygote ($\alpha\alpha/\alpha\alpha$). Even if chance factors had led to higher initial frequencies of the deletion chromosome (e.g. 1 per cent as in Fig. 12.5b) present day frequencies could not be achieved through selection in favour of the homozygote alone; although smaller fitness differentials among the genotypes are required to achieve the present day frequencies.

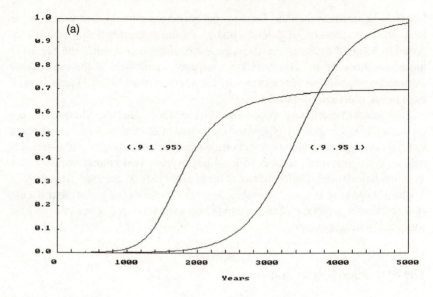

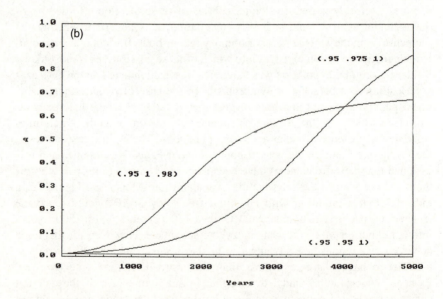

Fig. 12.5(a&b)   Change in frequency of −α chromosomes under selection. (a) Initial frequency of −α chromosome 0.0001; (b) Initial frequency of −α chromosome 0.01. Figures in parentheses show fitness of homozygote (αα/αα), deletion heterozygote (−α/αα), and deletion homozygote (−α/−α) respectively.

Although in Melanesia the present situation is one in which only the single gene deletion chromosome is found, chromosomes can arise in which both α genes have been deleted. The full dynamics of α-thalassaemia are therefore those of a three-allele rather than a two-allele system. Wills and Londo (1981) explored representative sets of fitnesses for genotypes involving normal, single, and doubly deleted chromosomes and showed that three outcomes are possible: the single deletion chromosome is fixed, the single and normal chromosomes form a stable polymorphism or the normal and doubly chromosomes form a stable polymorphism. However, the third outcome is sensitive to the introduction of sufficiently large numbers of single gene chromosomes, which may force fixation of the single chromosomes.

The dynamics of the three allele system can be displayed on a triangular plot. Figure 12.6a and b show two possible pathways followed by a population in which a small number of single and doubly deleted as well as normal chromosomes are initially present. From this starting position, the population moves towards a situation in which only the normal and the singly deleted chromo-

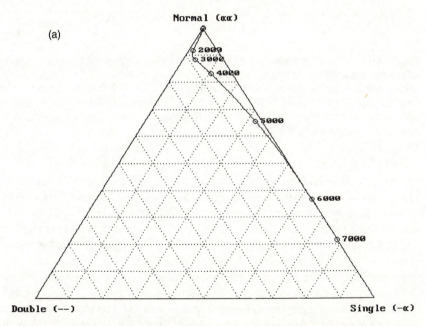

Fig. 12.6(a) Change in frequency of single and doubly deleted chromosomes under selection. In addition to a single $-\alpha$ chromosome at a frequency of 0.0001, a doubly deleted chromosome is also present at a frequency of 0.00001. (a) Initial chromosome frequencies: $\alpha\alpha = 0.99989; -\alpha = 0.00010; -- = 0.00001$. Fitnesses: $\alpha\alpha/\alpha\alpha = 0.90; -\alpha/\alpha\alpha = 0.95; -\alpha/-\alpha = 1.00; \alpha\alpha/-- = 0.95; -\alpha/-- = 0.70; --/-- = 0.00$. Time scale in years assumes a generation length of 20 years.

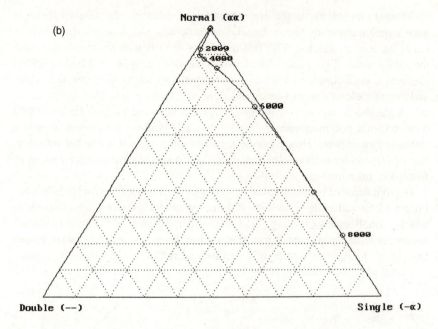

Fig. 12.6(b)   Change in frequency of single and doubly deleted chromosomes under selection. In addition to a single $-\alpha$ chromosome at a frequency of 0.0001, a doubly deleted chromosome is also present at a frequency of 0.00001. Initial chromosome frequencies: $\alpha\alpha$ = 0.99989; $-\alpha$ = 0.00010; $--$ = 0.0001. Fitnesses: $\alpha\alpha/\alpha\alpha$ = 0.90; $-\alpha/\alpha\alpha$ = 0.95; $-\alpha/-\alpha$ = 1.00; $\alpha\alpha/--$ = 0.95; $-\alpha/--$ = 0.60; $--/--$ = 0.00. Time-scale in years assumes a generation length of 20 years.

somes occur and eventually reaches fixation for the single deletion chromosome. The figures show first that the time to fixation of the single deletion chromosome is longer than that shown in the simple two-allele model (Fig. 12.5a) and furthermore that the time to fixation is sensitive to assumptions about the extent to which the fitness of the heterozygote for the singly and doubly deleted chromosomes $-\alpha/--$ is reduced (i.e. the severity of HbH disease).

Further insights into the dynamics of selection and α-thalassaemia will be obtained by models which explore more fully possible ranges of fitnesses and which incorporate assumptions about population size and structure. Yokoyama's model (Yokoyama 1983) which incorporates the effect of genetic drift with selection is an example of such an approach; although in his model he assumed that the deletion of an α gene from a chromosome reduces rather than increases fitness, and with remarkable prescience he drew attention to the need to consider the possibility of the deletion chromosome either in the heterozygote or homozygote enhancing rather than reducing fitness.

Haplotype diversity in Oceania

The study of α-thalassaemia in Melanesia shows how selection can play a crucial role in determining patterns of genetic diversity. In the absence of selection, the similarities and differences between populations are the result of migration operating against a background of founder effect and genetic drift. In this case the patterns of genetic diversity provide clues to population affinities. Extensive data are now available on the distribution of the α-globin haplotypes among the peoples of South-East Asia and Oceania and these are being examined to see what they reveal about the relationships of the peoples of this region.

Table 12.1 summarizes data on α-globin haplotypes for South-East Asia, Micronesia, Melanesia, and Polynesia. The pattern of diversity is most easily studied through the use of genetic distance and ordination analyses. Figure 12.7 shows the results, in two dimensions, of a multidimensional scaling analysis (Kruskal 1964*a,b*) of Nei's distance between pairs of populations (Nei 1972). The patterns of diversity emphasize the genetic links among the peoples of South-East Asia, characterized by high frequencies of haplotypes from groups I and II, especially Ia and IIa. Furthest in terms of genetic distance from the peoples of South-East Asia are the inhabitants of Papua New Guinea, characterized by high frequencies of groups III, IV, and V, especially IIIa, IVa, and Vc. The inhabitants of Papua New Guinea show close links with Australian Aborigines, confirming previous studies (Chen *et al.* 1992; and see Hill and Serjeantson 1989) and providing a picture which is consistent with what is known of the prehistory of the region; which suggests that groups of genetically related populations had spread across Sahul-land, the single Pleistocene landmass of Australia and New Guinea more than 40 000 years ago.

Micronesia shows close links with the peoples of South-East Asia. Of particular interest is the position of the peoples of Polynesia. These are characterized by haplotypes from all five groups. Although close to Micronesia and South-East Asia, which reveals the contribution of the peoples of Asia to the founders of Polynesia, the haplotype distribution in Polynesia links these populations through Fiji and Vanuatu with the coastal populations of Papua New Guinea. These data suggest that the haplotypes in groups III–V found in Polynesia are derived from Melanesia. This is in keeping with the evidence of α-thalassaemia in Polynesia

Table 12.1. Normal α-globin haplotypes in South-East Asia and Oceania (%)

| Haplotype | South-East Asia | | | | | | | Micronesia | | | | | |
	Thailand	Burma	South China	Taiwan	Brunei	Philippines	Total	Tarawa	Ponape	Guam	Palau	Maju	Total
Ia	19.4	31.3	33.3	34.5	11.4	31.8	28.6	24.2	31.0	57.7	36.8	13.9	27.6
Ib				4.8		4.5	1.9						
Ia/b													
Ic			1.8				0.4			15.4			2.1
Id	5.6		5.3	3.6	5.7	9.1	4.5						
IIa	30.6	50.0	28.1	16.7	20.0	9.1	24.8	3.0	21.4		26.3	9.7	11.5
IIb				1.2			0.4		2.4				0.5
IIc	5.6		1.8	7.1	17.1	4.5	6.0	6.1	4.8	7.7		23.6	12.0
IId				3.6		4.5	1.5	6.1		3.8		29.2	12.5
IIe				15.5		18.2	6.4		4.8	3.8	10.5		2.6
IId/e	19.4	9.4	17.5		28.6		11.3						
IIf				2.4			0.8	12.1					2.1
IIg	2.8	3.1	1.8	3.6			2.3				5.3		0.5
IIf/g													
IIIa	16.7	3.1	7.0	4.8	14.3	9.1	8.3	6.1	19.0	7.7	10.5	15.3	13.0
IIIb									3.8				0.5
IIIa/b													
IIIc		3.1	3.5				1.1	12.1	2.4			2.8	3.6
IIIe					2.9	4.5	0.8		2.4				0.5
IIIh				2.4		4.5	1.1						
IVa									21.2	4.8		5.6	6.8
IVb									3.0				0.5
IVa/b													
IVc													
Vb									3.0		5.3		1.0
Vc									3.0	7.1	5.3		2.6
Vd													
Chromosomes	36	32	57	84	35	22	266	33	42	26	19	72	192
Sources	c	c	c	b	c	e		c	c	c	c	c	

Table 12.1. Continued

Australia	Melanesia					West Polynesia			East Polynesia					Grand
Aborigines	PNG Highlands	PNG Coast	Vanuatu	Fiji	Total	Tonga	Samoa	Total	Niue	Cook Islands	Tahiti	Maori	Total	total
14.6			3.7	22.0	5.9	37.9	26.9	27.9	75.9	36.4	28.8	23.2	35.6	23.2
2.2														0.5
2.2														0.2
				1.7	0.2									0.4
				1.7	0.2									0.8
11.7						17.2	4.2	5.3	1.9	3.6	6.4	10.5	6.4	8.5
1.5														0.2
0.7						3.4	2.9	3.0		7.3	4.5		3.1	3.6
			1.0	11.9	2.5		13.0	11.9	5.6			5.3	2.2	5.1
4.4							10.1	9.2	1.9			9.5	2.8	4.1
			11.0		8.1	13.8	4.5	5.3		16.4	17.9		10.3	6.9
				3.4	0.5									0.5
														0.4
										3.2			1.4	0.3
44.5	57.9	60.0	4.3	22.0	13.3	27.6	19.5	20.2	3.7	12.7	2.6	11.6	6.7	14.9
5.8	21.1		1.3		2.9									1.2
2.2		42.7			31.4						9.0		3.9	8.5
											1.9		0.8	0.8
			3.4		0.5		1.6	1.5		7.3			1.1	0.8
							1.6	1.5			0.6		0.3	0.5
8.0	5.3	20.0	5.3	16.9	7.4		14.9	13.6	11.1	5.5	3.2	40.0	14.4	8.9
0.7	5.3		0.3		0.7									0.3
			30.3		22.4						17.3		7.5	6.9
1.5														0.1
			3.4		0.5		0.3	0.3		1.8			0.3	0.4
	5.3	20.0	13.6		2.9		0.3	0.3		9.1	4.5		3.3	1.8
	5.3				0.5									0.1
137	38	10	300	59	407	29	308	337	54	55	156	95	360	1699
d	c,e	e	b,c	c		c	a,c		a	c	b,c	a		

In some cases haplotypes are based on eight rather than nine polymorphic sites and hence haplotype subgroups could not always be resolved. These are shown in the Table as Ia/b, etc.

Sources: (a) Hertzberg *et al.* (1988); (b) Martinson (1991); (c) O'Shaughnessy *et al.* (1990); (d) Tsintsof *et. al.* (1990); (e) Higgs (1986 and pers. comm.).

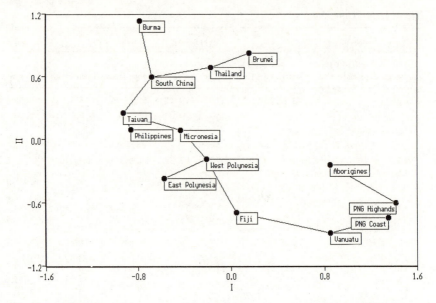

Fig. 12.7 Multidimensional scaling analysis of Nei distances among Oceania populations. The minimum spanning tree (Gower and Ross 1969) is superimposed on the plot.
Data from Table 12.1.

where the great majority of the deletion chromosomes are of the $-\alpha^{3.7}$III subtype,
and found on the IIIa haplotype, the predominant type found in Melanesia. Thus
the haplotype data support the proposal that Polynesians have a hybrid gene pool
derived from Melanesia and South-East Asia, implying significant contact
between Austronesian-speaking proto-Polynesian migrants and Melanesian populations, either in island Melanesia or later in Fiji.

Conclusion

The studies of the α-globin complex have shown how the combination of molecular techniques and population surveys can throw light on the processes which
lead to adaptation and diversity in human populations. Fuller understanding of
these processes will require studies at finer levels of resolution — the use of
more extensive DNA sequencing, and the study of individuals appropriately
sampled in terms of demography, and geography. Not only will such
approaches offer clearer understanding of the origin and fate of human diversity, they will also provide deeper understanding of the relationships of human
populations.

References

Allison, A. C. (1954). Protection afforded by sickle cell trait against subtertian malarial infection. *British Medical Journal*, I; 290–4.

Chen, L. Z., Easteal, S., Board, P., and Kirk, R. L. (1992). Genetic affinities of Oceanic populations based on RFLP and haplotype analysis of genetic loci on three chromosomes. *Human Biology*, **64**, 1–15.

Devor, E. J. (ed.) (1992). *Molecular applications in biological anthropology*. Cambridge University Press.

Flint, J. Harding, R. M., Clegg, J. B., and Boyce, A. J. (1993a). Why are some genetic diseases common? Distinguishing selection from other processes by molecular analysis of globin gene variants. *Human Genetics*, **91**, 91–117.

Flint, J., Harding, R. M., Boyce, A. J., and Clegg, J. B. (1993b). The population genetics of the haemoglobinopathies. *Bailliére's Clinical Haematology*, **6**, 215–62.

Flint, J., Hill, A. V. S., Bowden, D. K., Oppenheimer, S. J., Sill, P. R., Serjeantson, S. W., *et al.* (1986). High frequencies of α-thalassaemia are the result of natural selection by malaria. *Nature*, **321**, 744–50.

Gower, J. C. and Ross, G. J. S. (1969). Minimum spanning trees and single-linkage cluster analysis. *Applied Statistics*, **18**, 54–64.

Haldane, J. B. S. (1948). The rate of mutation of human genes. *Proceedings of the 8th International Congress on Genetics. Hereditas Supple.* **35**, 267–73.

Hertzberg, M. S., Mickleson, K. N. P., and Trent, R. J. (1988). Alpha-globin gene haplotypes in Polynesians: their relationships to population groups and gene arrangements. *American Journal of Human Genetics*, **43**, 971–7.

Higgs, D. R., Hill, A. V. S., Bowden, D. K., Weatherall, D. J., and Clegg, J. B. (1984). Independent recombination events between the duplicated human α globin genes; implications for their concerted evolution. *Nucleic Acids Research*, **12**, 6965–77.

Higgs, D. R., Wainscoat, J. S., Flint, J., Hill, A. V. S., Thein, S. L., Nicholls, R. D., *et al.* (1986). An analysis of the human α-globin cluster reveals a highly informative genetic locus. *Proceedings of the National Academy of Sciences, USA*, **83**, 5165–5169.

Hill, A. V. S. and Serjeantson, S. W. (ed.) (1989). *The colonization of the Pacific*. Clarendon Press, Oxford.

Kruskal, J. B. (1964a). Multidimensional scaling by optimizing goodness of fit to a nonmetric hypothesis. *Psychometrika*, **29**, 1–27.

Kruskal, J. B. (1964b). Nonmetric multidimensional scaling: a numerical method. *Psychometrika*, **29**, 28–42.

Martinson, J. J. (1991). *Genetic variation in South Pacific islanders*. D. Phil. thesis, University of Oxford.

Nei, M. (1972). Genetic distance between populations. *American Naturalist*, **106**, 283–92.

O'Shaughnessy, D. F., Hill, A. V. S., Bowden, D. K., Weatherall, D. J., and Clegg, J. B. (1990). Globin genes in Micronesia: origins and affinities of Pacific island peoples. *American Journal of Human Genetics*, **46**, 144–55.

Siniscalco, M., Bernini, L., Latte, B., and Motulsky, A. G. (1961). Favism and thalassaemia in Sardinia and their relationship to malaria. *Nature*, **190**, 1179–80.

Siniscalco, M., Bernini, L., Filippi, G., Latte, B., Khan, P. M., Piomelli, S., and Rattazzi, M. (1966). Population genetics of haemoglobin variants, thalassaemia and glucose-6-phosphate dehydrogenase deficiency, with particular reference to the malaria hypothesis. *Bulletin of the World Health Organization*, **34**, 379–93.

Tsintsof, A. S., Hertzberg, M. S., Prior, J. F., Mickleson, K. N. P., and Trent, R. J. (1990). Alpha-globin gene markers identify genetic differences between Australian Aborigines and Melanesians. *American Journal of Human Genetics,* **46**, 138–43.

Wills, C. and Londo, D. R. (1981). Is doubly deleted α-thalassaemia gene a 'fugitive' allele? *American Journal of Human Genetics,* **33**, 215–26.

Yokoyama, S. (1983) Equilibrium frequencies of α-globin genes. *Journal of Theoretical Biology,* **100**, 173–80.

13

The Cerdanya, a valley divided: biosocial anthropology in a research project

H. M. MACBETH

Within anthropology the optimism of the early 1970s for greater re-integration of biological and social perspectives on the human sciences (Harrison and Boyce 1972) remains in the 1990s problematic, although still an enthusiasm of many students. This chapter concerns research that owes much to that 1970s optimism in regard to the human sciences.

Introduction

The relevance of barriers to human movement as obstacles to reproduction is well documented in biological anthropology. Isolation and even partial isolation of a group of people behind any obstacle to gene flow is of interest to biological anthropologists because the divergent effects on gene frequencies on either side of such barriers lead to genetic differences. As humans can and do cross all known physical barriers, totally isolated populations do not exist, but obstacles to passage do reduce the likelihood of marriage and mating. Such obstacles can be physical, for example the river Ray on Otmoor (Boyce *et al.* 1968), or social, as humans construct barriers through their perceptions of social affiliation. The biological anthropologists' interest has frequently been directed towards mating patterns either side of that obstacle, when boundaries to biological 'populations' are sought in the genetic, 'Mendelian' sense, but biological diversity can also be caused by non-genetic factors (Harrison 1978). While ecological differences may well be discussed, too often omitted are the differences in culture, even slight, that can affect these non-genetic factors. Where the boundary is socially constructed, this is particularly likely.

My own interest in boundaries and the biological consequences of concepts of identity was first roused in attempts to relate the idea of 'Otmoor folk' to a more biological definition of a 'population' (Macbeth 1985). There existed a certain sense of being 'an Otmoor local', but it was interesting that many residents excluded themselves from this label, and partly because of a lack of boundaries

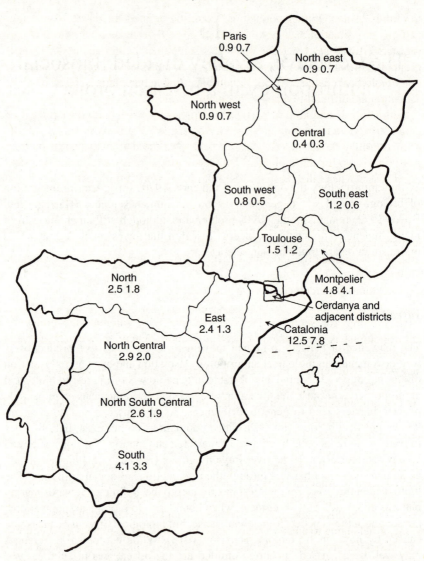

Fig. 13.1 Regions of France and Spain with proportions of birthplaces. Cerdan marriage registers (1915–84): regional distribution of percentages of birthplaces of grooms (first figure) and brides (second figure), excluding Cerdanya and adjacent districts (see Fig. 13.3) 〰〰〰 ...., national border; 〰〰〰〰〰 ..., delineation of region.

the limits of no 'Otmoor population' could be defined. In regard to marriage patterns this situation had been identified in 1967 from research into marriage registers (Boyce *et al.* 1968). What was sometimes being said about Otmoor group definition, therefore, was not likely to be reflected in gene frequencies or other biological characteristics. Without identifiable boundaries, claims of social affiliation are difficult to relate to population biology.

Nationality is one kind of social affiliation, which is legally documented by nation states and the boundaries are known, while for some a so-called 'ethnic' affiliation may be an important distinction from the nationality noted on their passport. Thus, for the biological anthropologist a potentially interesting situation exists where the regional distribution of some ethnic affiliation is not thought by some people to coincide with the border between two nation states. The situation may be considered spatial, social, and political, and the biological interest is not limited to genetic structure because the aetiology of most biological characteristics is multifactorial. Life-styles under cultural control are affected by nationality and ethnicity and provide non-genetic effects on the biology.

In relation to perceived barriers, the decisions about whom to marry from among those within one's vicinity and whom one may not marry are social and a frequent topic for social anthropologists, but what interests the biological anthropologist is the outcome of the decisions. Where they exist, marriage records have been used by biological anthropologists to create models of past gene flow (Küchemann *et al.* 1967). The non-genetic influences consequent upon these choices and decisions affected by socialization are less commonly studied around perceived barriers. The situation is even more interesting where there exists some physical barriers(s) not concordant with any of the social or political boundaries.

Such perspectives on human biology led to research in the Cerdanya, a Catalan valley in the eastern Pyrénees, straddling the Franco-Spanish frontier and adjacent to Andorra (Fig. 13.1). Unlike the mountain valley populations in some other biological studies, the residents of the Cerdanya are not an isolated population. In this chapter the words *national* and *nationality* will be used in the sense of belonging to a nation state. *Ethnicity* will be referred to as an alternative affiliation of a group of people, usually a minority; while this is etymologically incorrect, it is both common and useful. The objective of the ongoing research is to understand the biological effects that division by an international border has on a population geographically united within a mountain valley and, some would argue, ethnically united as Catalans. The central part of this chapter concerns a food intake frequency study, but recent study of marriage registers will be briefly reviewed.

The Cerdanya valley

Although almost entirely surrounded by high mountains, this broad, fertile, and sunny valley has since prehistory provided one of the few reasonably accessible passes across the Pyrenees. It has a long history of human passage frequently military (Sahlins 1989). The head of the valley is on a relatively gentle slope north-east towards Conflent and then Perpignan. To the south-west the River Segre has carved narrow gorges through which passes an ancient route from Seu d'Urgell. Other traditional routes used to be more formidable over high mountain passes, but rail and recent road tunnels take modern traffic north and south more swiftly.

Such is the physical description, but interest lies in the division of this valley between the nation states of France and Spain. Whereas elsewhere the Franco-Spanish border coincides with the physical barrier of high Pyrenean peaks, in the Cerdanya the border meanders across the valley through agricultural fields and rolling foothills (Fig. 13.2). Its generally north-west route crosses the most fertile part of the valley floor along a north–south axis, with both north-facing and south-facing slopes in each country's sector. Over the last couple of centuries there has been a larger population on the Spanish side of the border, but in recent years the numbers have become more similar. Few ecological differences between the sectors are apparent. The position of the border was agreed in 1659 between distant officials of the nation states of France and Spain, which because of their ignorance of the locality and a vocabulary difference between the words for village and town led to the anomaly of the Spanish enclave of Llivia within the French sector. Although more precise demarcation with boundary markers only occurred in the nineteenth century, the seventeenth century decisions remained essentially unchanged (Sahlins 1989). Frequently guarded fiercely, but never with great success, this international border has apparently always been easily crossed by local people, their merchandise and their genes.

Though today divided between France and Spain, this whole valley lies within the Catalonia ruled in the thirteenth century by Jaume I; and these days Catalanism is for some people a strong belief in the contemporary 'nation' of *Catalunya*. An interesting discussion, therefore, can be directed towards the perceptions of social identity, Spanish, French, and Catalan — even Cerdan —, but that discussion belongs elsewhere. It is sufficient here to point out that in the Cerdanya there is an interesting complexity of national and ethnic sentiments. In such a situation the identity claimed by individuals tends to be contextual, that is it would vary to reflect the context within which each statement is made. An example of this is that the researchers found 'our Cerdan' recipes and food habits to be almost identical either side of the valley, whereas both French and Spanish nationals have been heard to claim that their medical facilities were superior.

This incongruence of physical, national, and ethnic boundaries provided the rationale for biological research. Marriage patterns on either side of the border

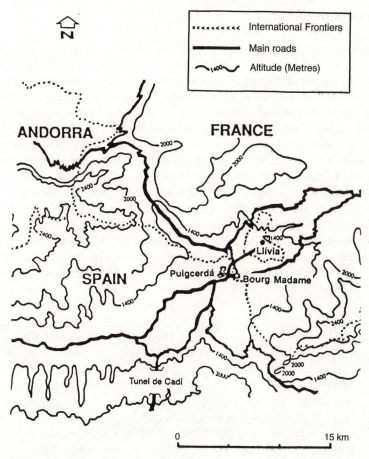

Fig. 13.2 Cerdanya and adjacent districts with main roads and contours.

have been studied (Salvat *et al.* 1992; Vigo *et al.* 1992) and analyses for the whole valley are in preparation. Meanwhile, study of food habits (Macbeth 1992) in adjacent French and Spanish towns has shown significant life-style differences. In this chapter, only brief reference is made to the work on birth-places of brides and grooms to give an indication of the patterns of genetic mobility and local miscegenation, while results on the food intake frequency study will be reviewed to indicate non-genetic effects on biology. The cultural control of such variables is emphasized and a glimpse of socialization in process has been provided by the study of teenage food preferences (Macbeth *et al.* 1990, Macbeth and Green in preparation). The interest in relating these different types of research findings and their cultural control will be explored in the discussion.

Marriage records

In ongoing work, Macbeth, Bertranpetit, Salvat, and Vigo have been analysing marriage records to study distributions of birthplaces of brides and grooms across the regions of the two nation states. On both sides of the border within the Cerdanya the great majority of people are Roman Catholic, and there are no other churches. There is, therefore, a general conformity of parish registers, despite some differences and some changes over time. Marriage registers for every ecclesiastical parish in the Cerdanya were microfilmed and transposed to computer. Although marriage records for a longer period were analysed in the French parishes, the records studied for the Spanish side only coincide with French data for the years 1915–85 and this is the period discussed here; during this time there were 5127 marriages for the larger population in the Spanish parishes and 2717 marriages in French parishes.

An objective of this research was the comparison of physical and political barriers to past marriages and therefore to gene flow. Of all those married anywhere in the valley between 1915 and 1985, Fig. 13.3 shows the proportions

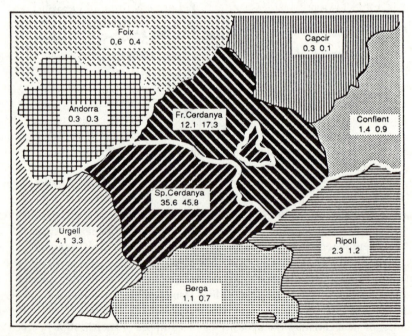

Fig. 13.3 Cerdanya and adjacent districts with percentages of birthplaces of grooms (first figure) and brides (second figure).

born in the Cerdanya and in adjacent districts. When these frequencies are reviewed in relation to topographical contours and main roads (Fig. 13.2), it is not surprising to note that there were more marital partners born in neighbouring districts linked to the Cerdanya by road or rail than across sierras where passage is difficult even in summer. Also shown is the common European pattern that more brides than grooms were born within the region, but this may well not correspond to their future place of residence. These maps also show the border and the enclave of Llivia. The largest numbers were born within the Cerdanya, one side or the other; the proportions born within the Cerdanya who married across the frontier are shown in Table 13.1.

Viewed on this scale, it is clear that within the Cerdanya, more Spanish Cerdans have married in France than vice versa. Analyses of adjacent districts (Macbeth *et al.* in preparation), show that for the period under review the border has been less of a barrier to marriage than have those mountains which no main roads cross.

Furthermore, that the population of the Cerdanya cannot be described as a genetic isolate is clearly supported by the distribution of birthplaces across all France and Spain (Fig. 13.1); taken at this scale, the proportions of transfrontier marriages are even greater because of the mobility across both nations. Table 13.2 shows proportions of brides and grooms from all parts of France and Spain involved in transfrontier marriages in Cerdan parishes in three time periods.

While parish of marriage need not imply future residence, it is obvious that at least one, and perhaps both, partners will have crossed the frontier in these marriages. Macbeth *et al.* (in preparation) discuss such migration elsewhere, but three aspects are clear from Table 13.2: first, that there has been sufficient migration for considerable miscegenation; secondly, that over the last three generations there has been a decrease in transfrontier marriages; and finally, that there has been more migration from Spain to France than vice versa. While it should not be forgotten that over the whole period there has been national endogamy for the majority of people, it seems clear that the population of the Cerdanya is, and for most of this century has been, part of a much wider gene flow system from Andalucia in Spain to Brittany in France.

Table 13.1. Percentages of transfrontier marriages for those born and married within the Cerdanya (1915–84)

| French parishes | | Spanish parishes | |
Spanish grooms	Spanish brides	French grooms	French brides
289 10.3%	246 8.8%	113 2.2%	58 1.1%

Table 13.2. Percentages of transfrontier marriages from all parts of France and Spain

Years	French parishes				Spanish parishes			
	Grooms (Spanish % all)		Brides (Spanish % all)		Grooms (French % all)		Brides (French % all)	
1915–39	380	36%	261	23%	92	6%	36	3%
1940–64	213	21%	188	18%	58	3%	41	2%
1965–85 (20 years)	68	9%	49	7%	26	1%	32	2%
Totals	674	24%	508	18%	176	3%	109	2%

Life-style differences in the Cerdanya

To summarize the ongoing work by Macbeth *et al.* (in preparation) the population of the Cerdanya valley, far from being a mountain isolate, seems to have provided a genetic highway. Nevertheless, there is an international border dividing the population and this has many consequences for the socialization, education, and culture of individuals. Catalan has long been the language of the local people of this valley, and since removal of Franco's restraints, Catalan is again the official language on the Spanish side. However, on the French side, French is now both the official and the common language. In the schools, the French national curriculum is adhered to. In French Cerdanya, the Catalan language was described by a local resident as the language of the grandparents. While many individuals can speak something of the three languages, Catalan, French, and Castilian Spanish, there is a change of common language at the border. Language is an indication of other cultural differences and these exist: many have some bearing on biology. The hours for meals and for sleeping are different on either side of the border; the health-care systems are different; attitudes to pollutants and smoking appear to be different. There are some differences in the structure, methods, and produce of the agriculture. Because of a history of different attitudes to development by the respective central governments, there are today differences in occupations and commerce. In fact, the list of all relevant differences would be long, and an ideal research programme within the human sciences would require a much fuller ethnography of life-style differences, using the field methods of social anthropology, but applied to understanding the aetiology of biological variables.

Study of food intake frequency

In this chapter, the evidence for cultural difference is taken from the study of food habits, which through nutrition affects biology. A 7-day food intake frequency study will be discussed.

Subjects, data, and methods

Two samples of the French and Spanish Cerdan populations were contacted through the schools in the 'town' of Puigcerdá in Spain and the adjacent 'village' of Bourg Madame in France. As would be expected, the schools had wider catchment areas than the two towns, and rural people from distant farms were equally involved in the study. Teenagers in the schools were addressed and a simple questionnaire about their food preferences administered to all between the ages of 11 and 15 (Macbeth *et al.* 1990). A total of 665 children took part, 345 from Spanish schools and 319 from French schools. Significant differences were found between the two national samples of teenagers in their stated preferences (Macbeth and Green in press). The children were also asked to take home four 7-day food-intake frequency questionnaires, one for the teenager, one for the mother, one for the father, and the fourth for a grandparent or elderly neighbour of either sex. Other family and household members were omitted. These questionnaires had columns for times of day and a list of all categories of food items. All that was required was a mark to be made for every food item consumed at any time during the same consecutive days in March 1991. Even so it was for the respondent a tedious task. The methods of studying food intake data for humans have been much discussed (e.g. Cameron and van Staveren 1988) and the problems generally lie in choosing between what is acceptable to the respondents and what is viable for nutritional studies. However, in this study, the main objective was not to obtain measured nutritional quantities but sufficient information on intake frequency to indicate cultural differences that could potentially affect biology. In order to study and compare a large number of people within restricted time and finance, the method used here omits quantities and concentrates on frequencies. While it cannot be claimed that this provided a completely accurate study of nutrition, it provided useful data in a search for cultural differences in food intake.

Foodstuffs were divided into 11 categories that would generally be comprehensible today to non-nutritionists: *Breads; carbohydrates; meats; fish; other proteins; extras* (being nuts, crips, etc.); *vegetables; fruits; sweets and desserts; drinks; other.* Under these headings food items were listed by name. Two versions were available, one in French, one in Castilian Spanish, and everyone was provided with a translation in Catalan. Some 3000 of these food intake frequency questionnaires were distributed, colour-coded for 'teenager', 'mother', 'father', and 'grandparent/elderly person'. The study was based on the same 7 days in March for all respondents. The weeks on either side of Easter were avoided.

The food intake frequency results have allowed many different forms of analysis, but only a summary of results will be given in this overview sufficient to show many significant international differences. For each food item listed frequencies were recorded. Discussed here is analysis of the differences between the populations by three methods. First, means give an indication of difference, but are insufficient for statistical analysis of the significance of those differences. So, Mann–Whitney comparison of rank orders was used as well as a simple χ^2 analysis of the numbers of those who did and those who did not eat any given item.

Results

Of the 3000 questionnaire forms distributed, 1000 were never returned. Of those received many were rejected if they were deemed to be in any way incomplete. However, 648 were valid, 333 from France and 315 from Spain. In this chapter information is not broken down by family role of respondent, but is summarized in Tables 13.3–13.5, where column 1 gives the food items under subheadings, column 2 gives the country that recorded the item more frequently and column 3 indicates the significance of the difference by Mann–Whitney test. Greater statistical detail will be published elsewhere. Many significant differences are found between the two sample populations. Differences that were significant were frequently significant by both methods of analysis (Mann–Whitney test of rank order and χ^2 of proportions who ate).

It was found that some food items were eaten by virtually all people and some, for example bread, were eaten by all, several times. However, there are many more foods in the list which have been eaten only by some individuals and by them only once or twice during a week. It is not surprising to find that food which is not frequently consumed may be eaten more than once in the same week, as once the food item (e.g. game) is in the house it may extend beyond one meal. So, for some foods such as bread, the figure for an average weekly intake frequency for each population has some meaning but for others the zero consumption by some or many individuals gives little meaning to an arithmetic mean.

Meats, fish, eggs, and cheese (Table 13.3) Because the concept of the European meal tends to centre around the foods commonly described in our culture as 'proteins' (Douglas 1975), this discussion will start with frequency of meat, fish, egg, and cheese dishes.

Table 13.3. Meats, fish, eggs and cheese: comparison of food intake frequencies

Food item	Higher frequency in:	Significance of difference (Mann–Whitney)
Meat		
Beef	France	***
Hamburger	Spain	***
Lamb	Spain	***
Pork	–	NS
Ham/bacon	France	*
Sausages	France	***
Salami, etc.	Spain	***
Pâté	France	***
Other charcuterie	–	NS
Game	France	*
Chicken	Spain	***
Turkey and other poultry	France	***
Other meats	–	NS
Total red meat	Spain	***
Total pig meat	–	NS
Total charcuterie	–	NS
Total poultry	Spain	**
Total meat	–	NS
Fish		
White fish	Spain	***
Oily fish	Spain	***
Shellfish	–	NS
Other fish	–	NS
Total fish	Spain	***
Eggs		
Egg dishes, etc.	Spain	***
Dairy products (except liquid milk)		
Cooked cheese	France	***
Raw cheese	–	NS
Yoghurt	France	***
Other dairy produce	France	***
Total dairy	France	***
Total 'proteins'	France	***

Total red meat = beef + hamburgers + lamb
Total pig meat = pork + ham/bacon + sausages + salami, etc.
Total charcuterie = ham/bacon + sausages + salami, etc. + pâté + other charcuterie
Total poultry = chicken + turkey and other poultry
Total meat = total red meat + total charcuterie + total poultry + pork + game
Total fish = white fish + oily fish + shellfish + other fish
Total dairy = cooked and raw cheese + yoghurt + other
Total 'proteins' = all of the above
* $P < 0.05$; ** $P < 0.01$; *** $P < 0.001$.

Table 13.4.   Staples and vegetables: comparison of food intake frequencies

Food item	Higher frequency in:	Significance of difference (Mann–Whitney)
Staples		
White bread	Spain	*
Wholemeal bread	France	**
Total bread	–	NS
Croissants	–	NS
Crackers, etc.	–	NS
Other breads	–	NS
Rice	–	NS
Pasta	–	NS
Breakfast cereal	France	***
Other carbohydrate	France	***
Sweet corn (maize)	France	***
Potatoes	–	NS
Total carbohydrates	–	NS
Vegetables		
Lettuce	–	NS
Greens	Spain	**
Peas	France	**
Green beans	France	***
Dry beans	Spain	**
Lentils	–	NS
Carrots	France	***
Other root vegetables	France	***
Tomatoes	–	NS
Onions	France	*
Leeks	France	***
Garlic	France	**
Olives	–	NS
Other vegetables	France	***

* $P < 0.05$; ** $P < 0.01$; *** $P < 0.001$

There is no significant difference in total frequency of meat consumption, and very few individuals on either side of the border ate no meat all week. Significant national differences are found for beef, hamburgers, lamb, ham/bacon, sausages, salami, pâté, game, chicken, and turkey. All these, except pâté, game, and turkey, were eaten at least once by over 30 per cent of the combined population, and beef by 80 per cent of the French population. The frequency of beef consumption in French Cerdanya was significantly more than in Spanish Cerdanya, but was higher than lamb on both sides. Lamb was consumed

Table 13.5. Fruit and sweets: comparison of food intake frequencies

Food item	Higher frequency in:	Significance of difference (Mann–Whitney)
Fruit		
Fresh fruit	Spain	***
Tinned fruit	–	NS
Frozen fruit	France	*
Dried fruit	–	NS
Other fruit	France	***
Sweets		
Ice cream	France	***
Custard	–	NS
Cake	France	***
Sweet biscuits	France	**
Chocolate	France	***
Other sweet things	–	NS
Sugar	–	NS

* $P < 0.05$; ** $P < 0.01$; *** $P < 0.001$.

more frequently in Spanish Cerdanya. In this study there was no way to check the content of what respondents had called hamburgers, but red meat, predominantly beef is expected. The Spanish recorded eating hamburgers more frequently. The higher rank order on the Spanish side for the subtotal, 'red meat' is highly significant. Doctors on both sides of the frontier had anticipated that a high frequency of pork intake would be recorded, but while it was higher than lamb in France it was lower than beef on both sides; there was no significant difference between samples. However, whereas more French had ham or bacon at least once and up to four times in the week, the Spanish sample had more people who had eaten ham or bacon even more frequently, including some who must have had it once or even twice a day. Salami was eaten more frequently in Spain, but sausages and pâté were much more common in France. When all the meats made from pig are included under the subtotal, 'pig meat', means on both sides of the border exceed those for the subtotal, 'red meat', but there is no significant difference between the populations. A similar situation exists for poultry. When poultry is a composite subtotal including chicken, turkey, and other birds, the difference between the two samples is much less than the comparisons for separate food items.

Regrouping the meats into 'bovine', 'ovine', 'porcine', 'poultry' and 'other' allows comparison with national differences in consumption as listed in Vanbelle *et al.*'s (1990) list of *per capita* consumption in 1988 by nation state within the European Community. France is shown as consuming 25 kg of bovine meat and 4 kg ovine, while Spain is shown as consuming 8 kg bovine and 5 kg ovine, but more poultry. The consumption of bovine meat, including hamburgers, was higher in the Spanish Cerdanya in 1991 than in all Spain in 1988. In summary, while this study has shown no difference in total meat intake frequency, the comparison of meats is interesting in relation to other data on European consumption and health concerns about types of fatty acids.

The greater consumption of the subtotal, 'total fish' by those on the Spanish side is highly significant and reflects a national tradition of fish eating found right across Spain, even in remote inland areas. Vanbelle *et al.* (1990) also draw attention to the high fish consumption in Spain and its low consumption in France in 1988, since when, however, it has been increasing. The higher Spanish levels are shown for white and oily fish, but not for shellfish or other fish. That 30 per cent of each sample recorded marks against 'other fish' shows the inadequacy of the other three categories. Classificatory problems cause an additional difficulty in cross-cultural research, especially where questionnaires are used.

An overall higher Spanish recording of the consumption of eggs was less expected than that for fish, but may be due to the common Spanish tortilla supper. However, recorded data on 'egg dishes' are difficult to use for any analysis of food intake and it is assumed that eggs were eaten in many more ways than recorded, as they are used in so many French and Spanish recipes.

Dairy products (other than liquid milk) fall under several headings in Table 13.3. When totalled there is a clear indication of the more frequent French consumption of dairy products, which was the only difference anticipated by local informants. When reviewed separately, only the item 'raw cheese' shows no significant difference. From observation, it is likely that had the types of cheese been disaggregated there would have been differences. Publication of the fat contents was less standardized on labels of dairy products in Spanish food shops, than on the French side, but were generally lower. This would add further complication to any attempt at nutritional analysis, but higher intake of dairy fat by the French seems indicated.

Staples and vegetables (Table 13.4)   Just as the word 'protein' was justified because of common usage, popular concepts were borne in mind in the distribution of 'carbohydrates' and 'vegetables' throughout the questionnaire. The questionnaire starts with the breads, goes on to rice, pasta, and breakfast cereals; potatoes and sweet corn, after considerable local discussion, were included among the vegetables. The items do seem to have been clearly understood. However, in presenting results a different order is pursued and all the above are included as 'staples' and precede 'vegetables' (Table 13.4).

At least 90 per cent of each population ate white bread at some time, and most ate it frequently; a slightly higher Spanish mean for white bread is balanced by the significantly greater number of French who had eaten wholemeal bread. There could, here, be an important distinction between the *pan integral*, eaten perhaps days old, on the Spanish side and the *pain integral*, generally eaten fresh within the day, on the French side. Such interpretations of vocabulary may complicate this kind of research, but the difference acts to emphasize the relevance of cultural diversity. There was no significant difference for total bread, nor any significant difference for rice or pasta; however, the Anglo-American culture of breakfast cereals has been adopted to a greater extent on the French side, as has sweet corn (maize). The potato, which is an important staple in northern Europe, including northern departments of France, is also frequently quoted as typical here, as it is central to a local traditional dish.

To distinguish the pulses from other vegetables is nutritionally important, but green beans, the pods of a pulse, are popularly considered as gastronomically similar to green peas. Clearly, for a study in the mountains in March, the green beans and peas must have been preserved in some way. Tinned green beans and peas are commonly served at meals throughout France and the French product is exported widely. So, while the frozen vegetables are equally available on either side of the border, the greater French consumption of green beans and peas is probably due to this preference. Although questions on vegetable preservation were not regularly completed by respondents, more French recorded tinned vegetables. On the other hand the Spanish consumption of dry beans was significantly more frequent and it was a surprise that consumption of lentils showed no difference. Dry beans and lentils are common in Catalan dishes and less typical of other regions of France.

There was no significant difference for lettuce, but there was for 'greens'. The words that translate as 'greens' are used in French, Catalan, and Castilian Spanish and if they are taken to mean the same thing (green-leaved vegetables of the cabbage and spinach genera) there was a significant difference in their consumption. Tomatoes may have been underrecorded on the Spanish side as they are used in so many ways. For example where northern Europeans might put butter on bread, the Catalan Spanish throughout the year would rub the inside of a tomato on to the bread before adding ham, salami, or olive oil and garlic. Respondents may have had difficulty deciding when they should record it as a food item eaten, for no significant difference is shown and frequencies are surprisingly low for both samples.

French informants said that one of the big differences between the diets of coastal Mediterranean and Pyrenean areas in southern France is the greater consumption in the mountains of root vegetables, which in this study are shown to have been eaten significantly more frequently by the French. Of the bulb vegetables, onions, leeks, and garlic were also recorded more often by the French. There was no difference in frequency of consumption of olives, and only about a quarter of each population marked down olives at all that week.

Fruit and sweets (Table 13.5)   In this section, the differences are noticeable. More fresh fruit was consumed on the Spanish side, but because of space on the questionnaire categorization of fruit had to be reduced to fresh or the type of preservation. For several sweet items, ice cream, cake, biscuits, and chocolate the frequency of consumption recorded by the French was significantly higher, but there is no way to quantify the amount of sugar intake. These data show choices, from which one would assume more glucose consumption by the French, but observation suggests that the Spanish are more likely to take more teaspoonfuls of sugar with their frequent consumption of strong black coffee. To gain more information more detailed and measured data on food intake are needed.

Discussion of food intake study

The more frequent French choice of dairy fats, sweets, pâté and their lower frequency of intake of fish, chicken, dry beans, and fresh fruit will be noted by those aware of the literature on diet and cardiovascular risks, which is increasingly available for the general public. However, the Spanish had more hamburgers, lamb and, so, total 'red meat'. More detailed discussion of the possible nutritional implications, as well as further analysis, for example by family role of the respondent, are currently in progress.

The prime purpose of this chapter is to give an overview of whether national differences do or do not exist between these two adjacent population samples. They clearly do. What is more, although measured in a very different way, the results are comparable with national differences for the whole of France and Spain for 1988 for the foods listed by Vanbelle *et al.* (1990). This means that even in Cerdanya where personal interviews had suggested there would be Catalan, or even 'Cerdan', similarity and very little local difference in food habits, national influences are shown to be an important cause of the diversity between the two populations.

Discussion

Potential research appropriate to the 1970s optimism for integrative human sciences is therefore developing in the Cerdanya. This valley has a physical unity surrounded by mountains and a common ethnicity claimed by some. Yet the valley has been divided by the Franco-Spanish border since 1659, a frontier which has regularly been crossed even in the times when it was heavily guarded, and the parish registers record many marriages to prove it. While it is past migrations that affect the miscegenation of the present population, cross-frontier marriages and doubtless other mating this century have continued at a high enough rate to make genetic distinction between the two parts of the Cerdanya today unlikely to be statistically significant (Macbeth *et al.* in preparation).

Yet today, because of the border, the languages, schooling, newspapers, and preferred TV stations are different. While on the French side these are typical of much of France, on the Spanish side they show the influences both of Spanish nationality and of the Spanish state of Catalonia. Despite the easy access for local residents to shops on both sides, interviews in 1991–93 revealed that most food shopping was still national. Inspection of recipe books used in kitchens visited were national, rather than local, most published in distant cities, which would be commonly used by people across each of the countries. However much abbreviated in this chapter, these small food studies reflect differences in life-style between two groups of people in adjacent towns on either side of the international border in the valley of the Cerdanya. The differences shown in the food intake frequency data are generally in line with other sources of information on food consumption differences between France and Spain, and these national differences are sufficient to suggest variation in factors affecting biological variables.

This means that nationality may be causing biological diversity between two populations whose natural ecology in one Pyrenean valley does not seem to be different. The statistical information has shown a pattern not revealed orally to the researcher by those inhabitants who claim common local ethnicity and emphasized Cerdan unity. The differences in food preferences expressed by teenagers living few kilometres apart give a little insight into development of this diversity (Macbeth and Green in press).

Conclusions

Although this chapter relates to one mountain valley, its concern with the biological effects of nationality and ethnicity around a boundary that divides two nation states is topical in the Europe of today. Interest in this particular section of that boundary arises because it is easily crossed, but divides a valley that has physical unity surrounded by mountains and, some would say, ethnic unity within Catalonia. The social affiliation of nationality has had considerable influence on marriage patterns, but cross-frontier marriages have been continuing, even though decreasing rather than increasing. Over this century, gene flow is presumed to have been sufficient to make heterogeneity between the gene pools of French and Spanish Cerdanya most unlikely. Nevertheless, national differences in many life-style variables have been observed and have been exemplified in this chapter by a study of food intake. This situation of probable lack of genetic heterogeneity, but every indication of diversity in non-genetic factors may provide an excellent arena for future research on multifactorial characteristics, which is planned.

National differences, through culture, are considered here to be the independent variables liable to cause variation in biological characteristics and not vice versa. It is a sobering thought that the machinations of distant politicians, without local knowledge deciding a boundary almost three and a half centuries ago, have thereby affected the distribution of biological diversity within the valley perhaps more than can be attributed to any local ecological differences.

Acknowledgements

Thanks go to the people of the Cerdanya who recorded their diet for 7 days, to the doctors and teachers through whom contact was made, in particular Jacques Vergé and Enric Subirats, and above all to Alex Green, without whose careful assistance the data would not have been analysed. The support of the Economic and Social Research Council is acknowledged (award number R:-000-232816). Finally, I should like to express enduring gratitude to Geoff Harrison, who tried to teach a social scientist some biology and so inspired this approach to bio-social anthropology.

References

Boyce, A. J., Küchemann, C. F., and Harrison, G. A. (1968). The reconstruction of historical movement patterns. In *Record linkage in medicine.* (ed. D. M. Acheson) Livingstone, Edinburgh.

Cameron, M. E. and van Staveren, W. A. (1988). *Manual on methodology for food consumption studies.* Oxford University Press.

Douglas, M. (1975). Deciphering a meal. In *Implicit meanings.* (ed. M. Douglas) Routledge and Kegan Paul, London.

Harrison, G. A. (1975). Biological aspects of life's quality in modern environments. *Urban Ecology*, 3, 292–299.

Harrison, G. A. and Boyce, A. J. (1972). *The structure of human populations.* Oxford University Press.

Küchemann, C. F., Boyce, A. J., and Harrison, G. A. (1967). The demographic and genetic structure of a group of Oxfordshire villages. *Human Biology*, 39, 251–75.

Macbeth, H. M. (1985). *Biological variation in human migrants.* D. Phil. thesis, University of Oxford.

Macbeth, H. M. (1992). Comida, culture y biologia: comparaciones en un valle catalán. In *Antropologia de la alimentación: ensayos sobre la dieta mediterránea.* I. (ed. Gonzáles Turmo and P. Romero de Solís pp. 107–32, Fundación Machado, Andalucía.,

Macbeth, H. M., Green, A. M., and Castro A. (1990). Gender differences in adolescent views about food: a study of teenage food preferences in a Pyrenean valley. *Social Biology and Human Affairs*, 55, 79–92.

Macbeth, H. M., Green, A. M. (in preparation). In *Food preferences and taste: continuity and change.* (ed. H. M. Macbeth).

Macbeth, H. M., Bertranpetit, J., Salvat, M., and Vigo, M. (in preparation).

Sahlins, P (1989). *Boundaries — the making of France and Spain in the Pyrenees.* University of California Press, Berkeley.

Salvat, M., Vigo, M. Bertranpetit, J., and Macbeth, H. (1992). Proyecto de estudio de la estructura matrimonial de la población de la Cerdaña. *Actas VII Congreso Español de Antropologia Biológica, Granada.*

Vanbelle, M., de Visscher, G., Focant, M., and Teller, E. (1990). *L'évolution des habitudes alimentaires dans la C. E. E.: diversité et convergence.* La semaine internationale de l'alimentation, de la nutrition et de l'agro-industrie, Le Corum, Montpelier.

Vigo, M., Salvat, M. Bertranpetit J., and Macbeth, H. (1992). Estacionalidad del matrimonio en la Cerdaña francesa. *Actas VII Congreso Español de Antropologia Biológica, Granada.*

14

Inside the gurrnganngara: social processes and demographic genetics in north-east Arnhem Land, Australia

N. G. WHITE

Introduction

The Yolngu today number approximately 3200 and occupy an area of about 26 000 square kilometres, bounded by coastline to the north and east and river systems to the south and west (Fig. 14.1). These people, referred to variously as Murngin, Wulamba, and Malag, as well as Yolngu, are the subject of a substantial social anthropological literature, much of it relating to their complex social organization and religion, including art and ritual (see for example Warner 1937; Thomson 1949; Berndt 1951, 1952; Williams 1986; Morphy 1991). Their language, differentiated into a number of exogamous dialects — some so different as to be almost mutually unintelligible — differs in both structure and vocabulary from the languages surrounding it. As a whole, the Yolngu are also genetically distinct from neighbouring language units, that is, tribes. This chapter will deal primarily with the extent and causes of genetic variation within the Yolngu population.

It is known that fishermen from Sulawesi came annually in considerable numbers to the northern coasts of Australia perhaps from as early as the sixteenth century (Berndt and Berndt 1954; Macknight 1972). The influence wielded by these visitors is evident in the art, myth, and ceremony, as well as in the technology and material culture of the region. European contact was spasmodic and temporary in the early nineteenth century and probably did not greatly disrupt the Aboriginal way of life, especially in eastern Arnhem Land. During the first half of this century, however, a number of mission stations were established along the Arnhem Land coast causing Aborigines to leave their own lands to settle into new social and physical environments. With the establishment of an Australian military base near Yirrkala on the Gove peninsula during World War II, and in particular, the commencement of bauxite mining in the region in the late 1960s, changes in the lifestyle of Aborigines have been dramatic, especially in and around the mining township of Nhulunbuy. Changes have been largely confined to the material culture, lifestyles, and diet. The key

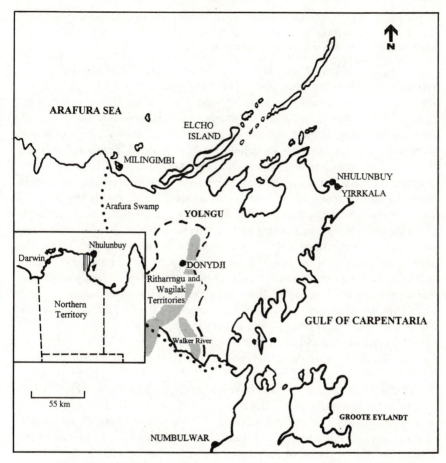

Figure 14.1 Yolngu country in north-eastern Arnhem Land. Territories of the Ritharrngu and Wagilak-speaking people are shown in relation to the 'stone country' of the Mitchell and Bath Ranges (stippled).

elements of social organization, kinship, and religion, remain basically unaltered from that recorded by the earliest anthropologists, which is consistent with the view held by the Yolngu themselves that theirs is an unchanging spiritual world (White *et al.* 1982). Such an attitude was expressed powerfully in a speech made by Yilarama, a Donydji man, at a public meeting held in eastern Arnhem Land on 11 January 1983. This was in response to requests from mining companies to survey Yolngu lands:

We don't know how to change the ruum (tribal traditions and customs; the 'Law'). It's like cement, or a big rock. You can hit it with your fist, or a shovel, or whatever — it won't break. That's how our law is. It is a very old one; our ancestors set it down.

We are not going to change our law the way you white people keep changing yours. Every year you question us about our land. We will not give in to you. You argue strongly for mining, but you will not destroy us.

Yolngu are organized into named land-owning patrilineal descent groups (clans) and territorially based dialect units referred to by the Yolngu as *matha* (in some dialects, literally tongue, or speech). Clan territoriality is based on the 'ownership' of sites of religious significance to clan members: these 'sacred' sites are said to be imbued with the spiritual 'essence' of mythological beings from whom all clan members are believed to be descended. The sacred sites and associated religious paraphernalia such as the sacred painted designs (*minytji*), songs, and rituals, and hence the clans themselves, are linked to religious sites in the territories of a number of other clans by the tracks used by the mythical ancestors during the Creation era (the 'Dreaming'). Both clans and dialect units (with the exception of the Djinang and Djinba) are exogamous — clan members and speakers of the same dialect are forbidden from marrying each other. The land-*using* groups, called bands by anthropologists, are composed of one or more family groups representing a number of clans and while usually resident in the territory of the husband(s), have foraging rights through descent and marriage over the territories of a number of other clans. Bands vary in size according to the season and habitat — the less reliable and/or more scattered the food resources, the smaller and more fluid the groups.

Donydji outstation (or homeland centre), where my biological anthropological field research has been based since 1974, is located near the western slopes of the Mitchell Ranges in inland Yolngu territory (Fig. 14.1). The local group resident at Donydji outstation has fluctuated in size seasonally, and year to year, numbering between 20 and 60 individuals mainly from clans of the Yolngu dialect units called Ritharrngu and Wagilak. Donydji is situated within the territory of the Birdingal clan of Ritharrngu (an area of about 1200 square kilometres), although the people living there have access to both Ritharrngu and Wagilak clan territories which together encompass some 5000 square kilometres. Prior to 1968, families now resident in the Donydji area were relatively nomadic, living as hunters and gatherers largely dependent on traditional food resources. These people were among the few remaining Aboriginal people living in, and off, the bush, despite the fact that they had substantial contact with Europeans occupying mission stations in the region (White 1985).

Geoffrey Ainsworth Harrison is held in high regard by the Aboriginal people living at Donydji: he visited with me in August 1983. Geoff's name came up in conversation during a recent research trip.

Ah, Djepri Arritjin', said my friend Gunaminy, a prominent elder of the Ritharrngu-speaking Yolngu people. 'Yo. Dhumurru ngay bunggawa: liliwaninangay biinguru gapumurnukngara — barrkunguru. Marnggidhanamirringay; djaalthirri marnggithirringay. Galangmirri ngay!' This translates loosely as:

Ah, Geoffrey Harrison. Yes. He is the big boss, the leader, who came from the far distant saltwater place. He is both knowledgeable and a person who wishes to learn. He is clever.

A coastal Yolngu man on being asked to identify neighbouring groups, will usually reply in terms that reflect his own ecological orientation. For example, people living inland will often be referred to using the prefix *gupa* — (nape of the neck) or *diltji* — (back), that is, from his perspective of looking towards the sea, these are people living in the bush behind him, or at the tops of rivers away from the coast. Conversely, inland people will refer to those living on the coast as *durdi* — (base of the spine) or *luku* — (foot), both implying 'bottom country' or 'down-river'. More specifically, they may say *gapu murnuk mala*, saltwater folk. In turn, there are terms used among inlanders to distinguish land-owning groups and/or patrilines within them. For example, there are Marralarrmirri (literally, hair [top] stone flakes with) or Gurrkalarrmirri (penis stone flake with) Wagilak (mythical women who carried stone spear heads) — referring to those Yolngu speaking the Wagilak dialect who own land on the top of the hills containing prized quartzite flakes. There are the Birdingal (a flower of an aquatic *Nymphoides* sp.) Ritharrngu (a tall blade grass, growing near creeks and rivers) — a freshwater clan of Ritharrngu-speaking Yolngu. Even songs that belong to the land-owning groups (clans) are referred to as *matharla' murru* ([passing] by the beach) or *diltjimurru* ([passing] through the bush). There is, however, an interdependence in the religious domain at least, between coast and inland, saltwater and freshwater, which is acknowledged in songs 'owned' by each of the clans. These song cycles celebrate the travels of ancestral beings with whom clan members have a totemic relationship:

Dhirripala [Birrk Birrk] luyun bawuda
Ngulalang Luthunpuy lapa budapurru
Dhunupawuy
Gapuda yindi gunmawili
Mayrikbirrk budapurru
Mayrikbirrk budapurru Ngulalangba
djinbananawuy

From island to shore
the Plover waded,
reaching the mainland at the rivermouth
where the bay is wide
Plover crossed over.
Plover crossed where
the water swirled — as saltwater met fresh

This is a verse of a Wagilak song which follows the mythological ancestral plover on its Dreaming track (that is, on its travels during the Creation Time) as it journeys inland from the coast to the higher, stony country in which is located the legendary stone quarry of Ngilipitji (Jones and White 1988). The song thus links ceremonially, the coastal clans of the Djapu-speaking Yolngu and the Wagilak clans of the interior. It emphasizes both the interrelatedness and the contrast between 'saltwater' and 'freshwater' people (from McKenzie *et al.* 1983).

It is this emphasis on ecological orientation that is at the heart of interpreting population genetic diversity in (at least) the eastern Arnhem Land region of Aboriginal Australia. The methods of human biology and anthropological genetics allow us to *describe* human biological variation, but to understand the *processes* which underlie this variation requires a biological anthropological approach; an approach evident in Geoffrey Harrison's own research and teaching — and which he encouraged in the field studies among the Yolngu upon which I report here. Biological anthropology examines the complex and intimate interactions that exist between the biology of people and their *cultural*, as well as natural, environments. Such investigations rest heavily on fieldwork using the method of participant observation.

The gurrnganngara

A *gurrnganngara* is a place, generally a bough shelter, where Yolngu men gather, often for weeks on end, for secret-sacred rituals. The name derives from the word for dark or shade, and carries here the connotations of 'inside' and secret — away from the public gaze. Here rest the *djuuk*; the *mardayin* — the secret-sacred. Women are prohibited from entering the gurrnganngara and some foods become *dhuyu* (taboo) to the participants. It is a shady sanctuary for the manufacture or preparation of ritual objects — objects that are *mardayindhanha* (made sacred) and which are believed to be imbued with the spiritual essence of ancestral beings. This is the place where the dead are painted and prepared for the departure of their souls, and where male initiates receive religious instruction and are taught the *ruum* (tribal traditions and customs; the 'Law'). Here, too, the *mali* gather (shadows, usually in the sense of spirit images). It is, then, a place of shade and 'shades'.

Inside the gurrnganngara, men sing, to the accompaniment of the *yirdaki* ('didgeridoo' or 'drone pipe'), parts of the great song cycles which belong to their clan. They discuss matters secular as well as sacred. There is also humour. It is a place where the researcher can learn about such things as Yolngu cosmologies and seek information on social relationships of clans and individuals. Notebooks begin to fill with (ideal) marriage arrangements among clans and lineages and with genealogies of clan and band members. The married men receive food sent by their wives — the rest of us rely for our sustenance on kinship and customary sharing, or, more accurately, customary *taking*.

Genetic diversity among Aboriginal tribes — an overview

A good deal of research has demonstrated substantial diversity for allele-frequency traits (mainly blood markers) among the Aboriginal peoples of Australia (for example Simmons 1976; Balakrishnan *et al.* 1975; Birdsell 1993). Variation across the continent is also evident in both anthropometric and anthroposcopic characters (for example Abbie 1957; Macho and Freedman 1987; Birdsell 1993) including those of the skeleton (Pietrusewsky 1984). While a number of these researchers have considered this diversity in terms of Aboriginal origins or microevolution in a range of physical environments, relatively little attention has been given to the influence of culture on gene flow and population differentiation.

Our own work on the heterogeneity of dermatoglyphic traits among tribes (language units) has been reported elsewhere (for example White 1979*a*). This research was based on a survey of 3260 Aboriginal people of full descent from 36 tribes living in the Northern Territory of Australia. Most were from the Arnhem Land region, the sample representing nearly one third of the people living there. In addition to fingerprints, a number of other biological data were collected, including phenylthiocarbamide (PTC) taste ability, red–green colour blindness, hairy pinnae, ear lobe form, and skin-reflectance measurements (which showed that Arnhem Land Aborigines were significantly darker than those people living in the arid centre of Australia (Parsons and White 1976)).

I present here an overview of the results of the analyses of the total ridge count (TRC) data only, since a principal aim of the initial survey was to evaluate the usefulness of this character in assessing genetic diversity at the inter- and intratribal levels and in estimating population genetic affinities. A more detailed account of the intertribal survey of fingerprint traits can be found in White (1979*a*). Total ridge count, of all metrical traits, best satisfies an additive polygenic model for its determination and is least influenced by the environment, that is, the narrow heritability of TRC across all populations studied is the highest of any quantitative character. It was argued (White 1979*a*), that for population genetic studies this trait would be influenced less by genetic drift, sporadic gene flow, and founder events than would Mendelian gene markers. Furthermore, selection is considered unlikely to have been important in fingerprint pattern size differentiation among populations. Therefore, we might expect total ridge counts to provide insights into population genetic diversity that would complement the description of population structure and affinities provided by allelle-frequency traits. In addition, they serve as a useful model for the interpretation of skeletal metrics in assessing biological affinities in space and time.

The tribes surveyed come from two markedly different ecological zones: central Australian tribes from the southern part of the Northern Territory and the remainder from the Arnhem Land region in the Top End of the Territory. The former traditionally occupied large territories in arid to semi-desert areas with correspondingly low population densities — the Pintubi, for example, numbered fewer than one person/200 km^2, and, like many Aboriginal groups living in arid Australia, suffered considerable mortality from drought (Kimber 1990). I have suggested elsewhere (White 1989, p. 173) that in such circumstances 'there is a need for greater mobility of hunter–gatherer bands, with the establishment of long-distance social links through marriage and religious affiliation being advantageous. In times of resource crises this would enable the band to obtain food from groups occupying different resource zones. That is, social mechanisms effectively extend the subsistence range of Aboriginal bands. This argument receives strong support from Tonkinson (1988) who noted for the Mardujarra of the Western Desert that "kinship, ritual, marriage alliances, shared ideology and a host of other cultural elements stress broader linkages which allow for the retention of access rights in the territories of other groups" (p. 161). He goes on to say that any attempts at closure of territorial boundaries would run strongly counter to survival chances in the long term. "In the desert hegemony has to do battle with the social realities of small groups scattered in low density across vast spaces" (p. 162). In less favourable areas we would expect to find, therefore, a high level of boundary permeability between local groups and between tribes, leading to the establishment of chains of dialects and genetic clines. Both are features of Western Desert populations'. The Top End of the Northern Territory is, by contrast, a region characterized by a monsoonal and markedly seasonal climate with greater habitat diversity and a wider range, as well as predictability, of food resources, particularly along the northern coast.

Table 14.1 summarizes the results of an analysis of variance based on TRC for the Northern Territory tribes grouped in a variety of ways according to features of their cultural and physical environments. This shows that language units (tribes) are highly differentiated in their mean ridge counts, coastal groups particularly so, and is consistent with their generally high endogamy rates. Approximately an eighth of the continent, in a band from the south west corner of the Gulf of Carpentaria through Arnhem Land to the Kimberley region in the northern part of Western Australia, is the most linguistically diverse area in Australia: this is matched by its genetic diversity. Overall, the breeding population corresponds closely with language, language boundaries acting as strong barriers to gene flow. Exceptions are found among central coastal Arnhem Land languages where high intertribal marriage rates occur. In this area marriages are common between speakers of languages which are themselves highly differentiated. The close correspondence between the population genetic unit and language may reflect different genetic origins of the speakers of the different languages. Alternatively, and I believe the more likely explanation, genetic differentiation and linguistic differentiation have proceeded in tandem. Conditions conducive to the one may also be conducive to the other; furthermore, the process of differentiation may follow a positive feedback loop, that is, as a language differentiates it is likely to impose increasing restrictions on gene flow (White and Parsons 1973).

Table 14.1   Summary of an analysis of variance (ANOVA with unequal sample sizes) based on total ridge count. Units which show statistically significant among-unit (compared with within-unit) differences are shown in bold type (based on White 1979*b*).

Northern Territory tribes, using language affiliation — 'tribe' — as the basis for within-unit comparisons.

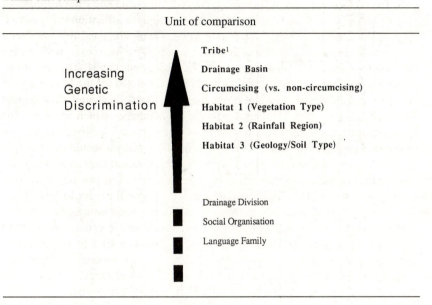

	Unit of comparison
	Tribe[1]
Increasing Genetic Discrimination	**Drainage Basin**
	Circumcising (vs. non-circumcising)
	Habitat 1 (Vegetation Type)
	Habitat 2 (Rainfall Region)
	Habitat 3 (Geology/Soil Type)
	Drainage Division
	Social Organisation
	Language Family

[1] Among coastal tribes >> among inland tribes.

The analysis of total ridge counts points to a strong relationship between genetic diversity and the natural environment of indigenous Australians. Marriage patterns appear to be strongly associated with habitat. These patterns are in turn governed by demographic factors such as population density and tribal size, both of which are also influenced by the physical environment. In Arnhem Land, for instance, coastal territories provide a particularly favourable food economy for hunters and foragers with considerable resource diversity in space and stability through time. These coastal tribes tend to be smaller, with higher population densities, larger bands, and shorter marriage distances than for those tribes living inland, particularly in the arid interior. This relationship between habitat, marriage patterns, and genetic diversity is shown in Fig. 14.2. Particularly striking is the high degree of genetic differentiation among groups of tribes occupying different drainage basins. This may result from the concentration of people around creeks and river systems and away from watersheds (White 1976). Gene flow would be expected to occur more frequently between groups along drainage systems than between people occupying different systems separated by watersheds. That rivers and creeks were preferred corridors of movement for Aboriginal bands is reflected in economic exchange networks and

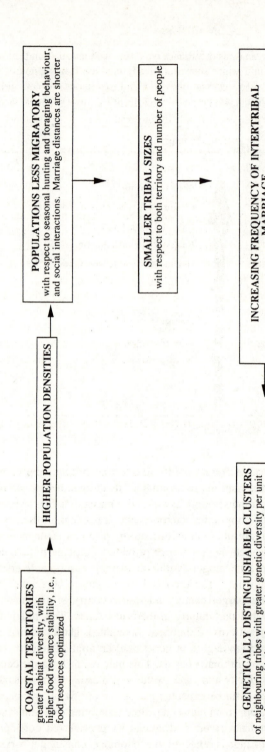

Figure 14.2 An interpretation of the relationship between tribal environments, endogamy rates, and genetic diversity in the Arnhem Land region. This scheme applies equally to the comparison between populations in Arnhem Land and Central Australia (modified from White 1978).

in the 'Dreaming tracks' — paths said to have been followed by mythological beings during the Creation Time. Peterson (1976), working independently from a social anthropological perspective, described drainage basin-based 'cultural area' populations. He, too, argued that by restricting communication, natural boundaries such as watersheds will result in 'cultural areas' that will tend to be endogamous.

While features of the natural environment such as topography, habitat quality, and climate (between which of course there is interdependence) appear to be particularly important in explaining the degree and pattern of genetic heterogeneity among Aboriginal populations, the cultural environment also plays a role. (It is possible, indeed probable, that social and cultural boundaries might themselves reflect natural barriers to communication.) For instance, in addition to the close relationship between language and the deme discussed above, there is the example of male circumcision which, in those tribes that practise it, symbolizes manhood. It is the first stage of male age grading and represents the removal of a boy from the domain of his mother and sisters (this is generally between the ages of eight and twelve years). Entry into the men's domain is, of course, a prerequisite for marriage. It might be expected, therefore, that the cultural boundary represented by the practice or non-practice of male circumcision greatly restricted gene flow across it (White 1976). This was confirmed by the fingerprint ridge count data (Table 14.1).

Social processes, demography, and the genetic differentiation of the Yolngu

Having noted earlier that relatively little attention has been given to the influences of culture on regional genetic variation, there have been even fewer investigations of its role in determining population structure, that is, in genetic differentiation at the local group level *within* a tribe. To this end, research into the extent of genetic diversity and its possible causes within the Yolngu was initiated in 1971. Biological data were collected from 812 Yolngu which, at the time, represented nearly 35 per cent of the Yolngu who were then resident in north-east Arnhem Land.

After completing the biological survey it was necessary to map the land-owning units (clans) and dialects in north-east Arnhem Land to provide a basis for the analysis and interpretation of the data. A detailed distribution of clans and dialect units is in White (1979*b*). It is summarized in Fig. 14.3 which shows the distribution of linguistically related groups of dialects (following Schebeck 1970), and in Fig. 14.4, which shows the patterns of marriage among some of the clans and dialects to be discussed below.

Using the map of dialects as a template, the considerable within-Yolngu diversity in TRC is shown in Fig. 14.5. Indeed, employing Sjøvold's (1973) dis-

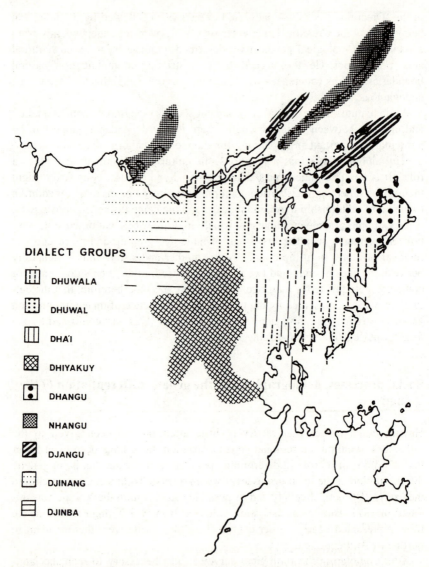

Figure 14.3   The location of dialect groups (classification following Schebeck (1970)) within the Yolngu dialect cluster (from White (1979b)).

tance statistic with four characters believed to be under strong genetic control, nearly 70 per cent of the differentiation observed among Northern Territory tribes was found among territorial units within the Yolngu culture-bloc (Table 14.2). More recently, we have analysed blood-markers in tissue collected as part of our investigations into the medical genetics and immunological status of the

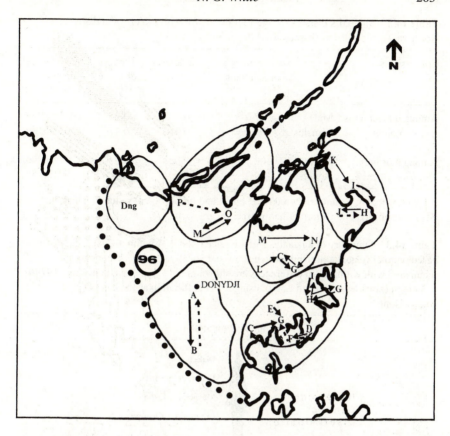

Dng	Djinang	I	Galpu	*Percentage of Marriages involving women from the groups*
A	Ritharrngu	J	Rirratjingu	*shown*
B	Wagilak	K	Warramiri	
C	Dalwangu	L	Marrangu	⟶ 20-39
D	Marrakulu	M	Djambarrpuyngu	
E	Manggalili	N	Wangurri	⟶ 40-70
F	Madarrpa	O	Gupapuyngu	
G	Djapu	P	Leyagalawumirri	- - ▸ >70
H	Gumatj			

Figure 14.4 Approximate boundaries of Yolngu marriage clusters discernible from the dialect and clan affiliations of parents (and spouses where married) of 812 participants in the biological survey. Arrows indicate some major movements of wives among dialect units within these clusters. (The number circled indicates the endogamy rate for the entire Yolngu cultural complex.) Note that 62 per cent of marriages occurred within the Djinang (Dng) dialect. (Based on White 1978, 1979*b*.)

Yolngu (Flannery and White 1993). Genetic distances using Gm haplotypes and Km, ABO, and Hp allele frequencies also indicated a substantial degree of intra-Yolngu genetic diversity (Pagnon 1993). (Fifty-four per cent of among-tribe variation using Roger's (1972) distances existed among Yolngu marriage

Table 14.2 Sjøvold's distances using four traits* for within-Yolngu and among-Northern-Territory tribes (based on White 1979*b*).

Comparison		No. of pair-wise comparisons	Smallest distance	Largest distance	Mean distance ± SD
Among dialect units within-Yolngu	Males	77	0.004	0.230	0.053±0.050
	Females	107	0.010	0.470	0.103±0.100
Among Northern Territory tribes	Males	108	0.003	0.240	0.077±0.066
	Females	109	0.004	0.900	0.157±0.152

* Two fingerprint parameters, total ridge count and proportion of radial loop patterns, PTC taste ability, and pattern of hair on the fingers.

Table 14.3 Summary of an analysis of variance (ANOVA with unequal sample sizes) based on total ridge count. Units which show statistically significant among-unit (compared with within-unit) differences are shown in bold type (based on White 1979*b*).

Yolngu (north-east Arnhem Land), using dialect affiliation as the basis of within-unit comparisons.

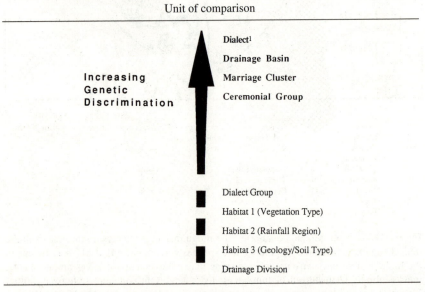

Unit of comparison

Increasing Genetic Discrimination

Dialect[1]

Drainage Basin

Marriage Cluster

Ceremonial Group

Dialect Group

Habitat 1 (Vegetation Type)

Habitat 2 (Rainfall Region)

Habitat 3 (Geology/Soil Type)

Drainage Division

[1] Among coastal dialects >> among inland dialects.

clusters (see below and Fig. 14.4).) Further, analyses of metric and non-metric data from a small sample of crania collected during the 1930s (with the permission of the Yolngu) demonstrated considerable regional variation within north-east Arnhem Land (Bennett 1985).

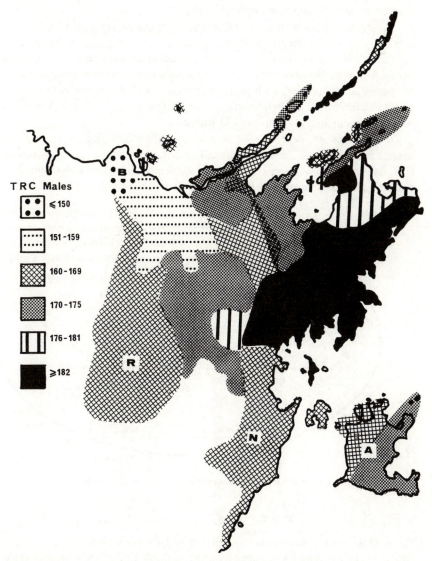

Figure 14.5 Distribution of mean total ridge count, TRC (males only), for Yolngu dialect units and for some neighbouring tribes (B — Burarra; R — Rembarrnga; N — Nunggubuyu; A — Andilyaugwa).

An analysis of variance of TRC for the Yolngu, based on their dialect affiliation, is shown in Table 14.3. As was the case for Northern Territory tribes, the greatest genetic discrimination was among speech communities, here dialects. Again, the greatest diversity occurred among coastal dialects units which occupy more favourable habitats with higher population densities, larger band sizes, and smaller foraging ranges than Yolngu occupying inland territories. There was also a high level of discrimination among drainage basin groupings of Yolngu, presumably for the same reasons as given earlier with regard to the intertribal study. (Here, however, we are dealing with clans and dialects within a tribe rather than between-tribe relationships.) For the Yolngu, crude environmental parameters such as 'rainfall region' and 'vegetation type' are not useful discriminators of population structure as would be expected for this comparatively small area of Aboriginal Australia.

Yolngu share an ideal view of marriage relationships and the passage of women among groups. These are seen as following specific cycles among sets of clans according to a system of bestowal (Morphy 1978): it is 'his mother's mother's brother's patriline that a man looks to for the promise of a wife, a man

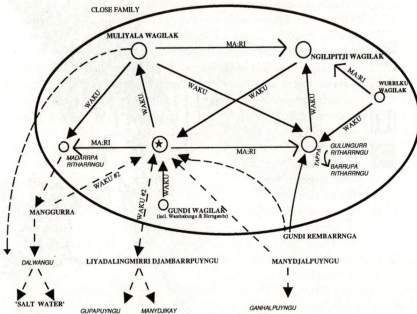

Figure 14.6 An idealized scheme for the relationships between clans grouped as 'close family' from the perspective of some senior men of the Birdingal clan of the Ritharrngu dialect unit (represented by a star). Clans, like individuals, are referred to by kin terms (see text: ma: ri — mother's mother's brother (also MM); Waku — a man's sister's child (also a woman's own child); yappa — sister). For example, Ngilipitji Wagilak call Birdingal Ritharrngu, Waku, with the reciprocal being Nga: rndi (mother). The different fonts used for the clan names represent the two moieties, *Yirritja* (e.g. Ritharrngu) and **Dhuwa** (e.g. Wagilak). The solid arrows indicate the expected movement of women through marriage. This figure is based on a sand drawing by a middle-aged Birdingal Ritharrngu man (T.G.B), in 1978.

has little say in who his daughters should marry, but a considerable say in who his daughters' daughters and sisters' daughters should marry' (p. 213). Such a scheme for the Ritharrngu and Wagilak clans centred on Donydji is shown in Fig. 14.6. (This was copied from a sand drawing made by a middle-aged Ritharrngu man of the Birdingal clan.) The degree to which the ideal scheme accords with the actual pattern of marriage relationships, and the extent to which it is reflected in the genetic structure of the Yolngu, was investigated in this study.

Dialect and clan affiliations of the parents of the participants (and spouses of those who were married) in the biological survey were used to construct a matrix of marriages for the Yolngu. Marriages among dialects and clans were clearly non-random and, on the basis of at least 70 per cent intramarriage, five marriage clusters were discernible (Fig. 14.4). As might be expected, most marriages were between contiguous clan neighbours (Table 14.4). (Fifty-two per cent of marriages occurred within a 20 km radius from the centre of the husbands' clan territories. This compares with 93 per cent within a 8 km radius for the neighbouring coastal Gidjingarli-speaking Anbarra people (White *et al.* 1990).) The predominant direction from which coastal clans obtained wives followed the coastline, just as inland clans tended to marry inland. This may reflect habitat preference; that is, wives come from territories with similar kinds of food resources, which presumably would be advantageous not only because the woman, as the main food provider, would be familiar with the types of resources available, she would also be more likely to know when and where they could be obtained, than would women coming from markedly different habitats. Alternatively, or in addition, the marriage pattern may reflect routes of communication — for instance, coastal Yolngu are known to have travelled considerable distances by canoe to visit kin (Warner 1958; Chaseling 1957).

In the course of discussions on marriage relationships with some senior Yolngu men, reference was made by them to groupings of clans called *mitji*, or 'companies'. These named 'mobs' of people were said to function as 'war' and/or ceremonial units (White 1976). There was substantial overlap between mitji and the recognizable marriage clusters, which is consistent with the obligations, responsibilities, and expectations that exist among wife-bestowing, wife-releasing, and wife-receiving clans.

The analysis of the TRC data (Table 14.3) indicate that there is substantial correspondence between what Yolngu advisers say *should* be the pattern of marriage relationships among their people and the genetically distinguishable subpopulations, that is, the ideal and actual systems of marriage relationships among clans are in broad agreement. For such genetic differentiation to have occurred the marriage clusters must have had considerable stability through time.

Table 14.4   Some Yolngu demographic parameters (based on White 1979*b* and White
et al. 1990).

Population densities (km^2/person)	3–9 (coast), 11–16 (inland)
Marriages between contiguous clans (%)	84
Sex ratio (males:100 females) < 4 yrs age Overall	 Variation by region 108–133 95*; 89.5
Percentage of total population of both marriageable and reproductive age viz: women 15–41 yrs men 25–50 yrs	 37 (coast)–32 (inland)
Polygyny	

Average number of wives/married man
  (max. no. of wives)
	3.5 (coast)–2.3 (inland)
	   (20) (7)

Percentage of all married men who are polygynous	56; 51*
Percentage of married men ≥30 yrs of age who are polygynous	57*
Percentage of men ≥30 yrs of age who have no wives	13*

Completed family sizes
  Females
  Males
	
	3.1±2.1 (coast)–2.4±2.3 (inland)
	4.9–8.1±6.1

Crow's index of potential selection (*I*)	2.08 [$I_m = 0.87$; $I_f = 0.65$]

*(Keen (1982) for 156 Yolngu men from the Milingimbi area, Fig. 14.1.)

Some demographic features of genetic importance

On my first field trip among the Yolngu in 1971, I was keen to establish the biological relationships among the people with whom I was working and from
whom fingerprints and other biological data were being collected. The common
response to my questions (through an interpreter, since at the time I knew little
of the local language), was generally 'we are one family'. This appeared to be
confirmed during my initial interviews, with the majority of younger individuals
surveyed referring to each other as sibs. What a remarkably large family, I
mused. Was this typical of completed Yolngu family sizes? It wasn't until four
of the women and two of the men were acknowledged as mother and father,

respectively, that I became aware of the complexity of kinship and the difficulties it poses for human geneticists.

The social and natural worlds of the Yolngu are divided into two named exogamous divisions termed moieties by anthropologists. The people, their clans and their dialects, fall into one or other of these divisions which they name *Dhuwa* and *Yirritja*. Most plants and animals, and a number of celestial bodies, are also classified as *Dhuwa* and *Yirritja*. Yolngu society and social behaviour is to a very large extent regulated by kinship. Kinship is an egocentric system of social relationships expressed in a biological idiom which 'provides a kind of blue print for almost all interpersonal behavior among the Aborigines' (Tonkinson 1978, p. 43). It is the articulating force for all social interaction (Berndt and Berndt 1977). Aboriginal kinship systems are classificatory in that kinship terms used between people who are biologically related are also applied to unrelated people. The 'web of kinship thus extends far beyond consanguineal and local group limits to include the most distant of kin and former strangers' (Tonkinson 1978, p. 43). Furthermore, siblings of the same sex are classified as equivalent. For example, my father's brothers are classified together with my father and are all called *bapa* in the Yolngu dialects; my mother and mother's sisters are all *nga:rndi*, and father's brothers' children are my brothers (*wa:wa* — older brother, *gutha* — younger brother) and sisters (*yappa*). The relationship between kinship reciprocals ranges from one of mutual avoidance as in the case of a man and his mother-in-law, to open and emotionally close relationships such as between a man and his mother's mother's brother. The intensity of the relationship, and its associated responsibilities, depends on the degree of closeness, that is, whether they are actual kin or distant and biologically unrelated classificatory kin. The Yolngu kinship system incorporates five generations and seven male lines of descent: kin terms are modified by gender and, in the case of brothers, by age. (For a detailed account of the Yolngu kinship system and the rules regulating the various kinship reciprocals, see Warner (1937).) Clans as well as individuals have these terms applied to them (Fig. 14.6). (See also Morphy (1978) and Williams (1986).) Since about the 1930s — for the Yirrkala area at least — social categories in addition to moieties have been used by the Yolngu. These are called *malk*, or 'skin', by the Aboriginal people, and subsections by anthropologists. Subsections divide each moiety into four named categories and are organized according to generation: a man's child belongs to a different subsection from his own (although it is of the same moiety) and depends on which of the two permissible subsections the mother belongs to. The subsection system simplifies the kinship system and thereby accommodates strangers (both Aboriginal and non-Aboriginal) more readily, as well as providing wider access to potential wives.

It is the kinship system which regulates marriage — indeed, it rests upon the 'ideal' marriage rule of a man with his matrilateral first cousin (mother's brother's daughter) according to Warner (1937) and Berndt (1955), or second cousin (mother's mother's brother's daughter's daughter) in the view of Shapiro (1968), Maddock (1970), Morphy (1978), and others. (Genealogies from Donydji contribute little to this debate since approximately equal numbers of actual or classificatory first and second cousin marriages occur.) From my experience there are regional differences — or differences of opinion — regarding marriages between biological cousins. At Yirrkala, for example, some senior men declared that actual cousins should be avoided as spouses, whereas at Donydji, classificatory and real cousins seemed to be equally acceptable.

As with the scheme for marriage relationships among clans, it is important to distinguish between what people declare to be the rule of marriage and what actually takes place. In Yolngu society there are 'correct' marriages that follow the ideal marriage rule and 'wrong' marriages. The incidence of unions between two people who are not related as 'spouse' is unknown, largely because of what, in Aboriginal English, is termed 'straightening-out business', that is the process of legitimizing unions. In such cases the social category and kinship of children of such unions — and of the husband and/or wife themselves on occasions — can, over time, be altered to correspond to the norm, or ideal. From discussions with older male informants at Yirrkala and Donydji, there is little doubt that 'wrong' marriages have always occurred and are not simply a post-Mission development: indeed, they may have been more frequent in the past, when force and violence were more common methods of 'resolving' marriage choice. (An examination of genealogies collected in the 1930s by D. Thomson indicated that a particularly powerful man had, among his twenty wives, some who would be regarded as unequivocally 'wrong' by the Yolngu.) C. H. Berndt (1970) wrote '...the combination of economic considerations, and physical force and threat,...militated against conformity with the ideal of cross-cousin marriage' (p. 41). 'The right and authority to give and to withhold...could traditionally be overridden by the "power to take"...[today] the checks and sanctions that limit or block the power to take are not only more multifaceted...but also much more effective (p. 49).' W. L. Warner was the first anthropologist to work with the Yolngu. He noted that of 72 male homicides which he recorded, '10 killings were due to members of a clan stealing a woman, or obtaining a woman who belonged to another clan by illegal means' (Warner 1930, p. 458).

Some of the genealogies collected from the residents of Donydji (shown in Fig. 14.7) illustrate additional features of Yolngu marriages which have implications for microevolution. It is important for human geneticists to understand some of the difficulties encountered in constructing genealogies of tradition-orientated Aboriginal people such as the Yolngu. I have already referred to the 'straightening out' of 'wrong' marriages to suit the ideal of matrilateral cross-cousin marriage: there is also a strong tendency to employ this ideal model for older generations where details of biological kinship have faded from the memory of those who hold such knowledge — these are generally the older women. There is, too, the problem of distinguishing biological from classi-

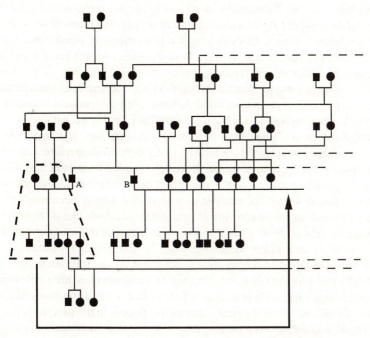

Figure 14.7 This segment of the set of genealogies compiled for members of the Donydji band of Yolngu illustrates some aspects of Yolngu marriages of importance to geneticists. It can be seen that marriages involve actual as well as classificatory matrilateral first and second cousins in polygynous unions. Also shown is the sororate (cowives are related to each other as sisters), and levirate, where a man (**B**) acquires wives and children of a deceased brother, **A** (this is indicated by the arrow).

ficatory kin, and of establishing paternity. This is particularly difficult where there is polygyny and where adoptions are common as a result of window remarriage including the levirate (the wives of a dead man are taken by his surviving brother(s)). These, together with the sororate (actual sisters as cowives in a polygynous union), are all features of the genealogies presented here. In an attempt to obviate these problems for the purpose of estimating the average level of inbreeding in the local group at Donydji, marriage relationships were cross-checked with individuals from all lineages represented, and unions in generations earlier than that of grandparents were excluded, as were those in the youngest generation, since in recent years, road and air travel has substantially increased the marriage range to include spouses from distant communities and tribes — marriages said by some older Yolngu to be 'wrong'. The **average level of inbreeding** so estimated was 0.017, which is similar to that in some Central and South American Indian populations (De Oliveira and Salzano 1969). The highest individual **coefficient of inbreeding** was 0.07 from data over five generations (White 1976). These values do not take into account the biological relatedness of individuals in the earliest generation represented in the genealogies. The avoidance of close inbreeding which is a feature of the Yolngu kinship system, ensuring that women move across patrilines over generations, has probably been important in maintaining genetic variability.

Table 14.4 summarizes some additional Yolngu demographic parameters of interest to population geneticists. (This is based on information collected during the present study as well as on Keen (1982), Government records, and genealogies collected by D. Thomson in the 1930s which are held by the Museum of Victoria.) I have mentioned elsewhere that **population densities** are much higher for coastal people than for those living inland. For the Yolngu, this ranges from about one person to 3 km^2 in some coastal territories to one person to 16 km^2 inland. While the number of Yolngu is likely to have increased following the arrival of Europeans in north-east Arnhem Land, the contrast between coastal and inland population densities can be detected in the earliest reports from this area (Lindsay 1884).

The **sex ratio** at birth (the secondary sex ratio) for populations worldwide is about 106 males to 100 females. The higher than expected sex ratio found in Yolngu children may have arisen from census errors, or be the result of chance events which are likely in small groups of people such as this Australian Aboriginal population, and hence, one cannot safely attribute variations in demographic parameters such as the sex ratio to the effects of any single factor (White *et al.* 1990). If, as I believe, the high sex ratios among infants are due to factors other than chance demographic events, possible reasons for the excess of boys over girls would include the following: a cultural manipulation of the sex ratio through female infanticide which has been reported for Aborigines (Sharp 1940), although opinions vary as to whether this was widespread (Cowlishaw 1978); it may reflect the epidemiology of hepatitis B infection in the Yolngu (Flannery and White 1993); or it may be related to paternal age, maternal age, and birth order, all of which have been claimed to influence the human secondary sex ratio (Ruder 1985). (Married men are often considerably older than their wife/wives. Keen (1982) noted that 9 per cent of Yolngu marriages with husbands older than the wife (88 per cent of total marriages) involved an age difference of at least 30 years. This is a principal reason for widow remarriage and adoptions through the levirate being comparatively common among tradition-orientated Yolngu.) The Yolngu sex ratios may, then, reflect differences in completed family size for females and in polygyny rates, as well as differences in the reproductive span for females in the various Yolngu subgroups.

Estimates for **completed family size** for women varied among the groups surveyed (Table 14.4), with the highest apparent net fertility found in coastal Yolngu groups. As with the secondary sex ratio, there are cultural and/or biological explanations for these apparent differences. My own investigations suggest that abortificants and infanticide were used by Yolngu in the past, although whether or not this was frequent will never be known. Constraints on birth spacing would have been greater for women living in harsher environments. Shorter birth intervals and larger family sizes for women living in richer environments may be associated with better nutrition (especially energy intake and protein consumption) and reduced energy expenditure. As has been reported for the Third World (Rosetta 1992), women living in less productive inland areas might, on the other hand, be expected to experience a greater impairment of menstrual function including more frequent episodes of secondary amenorrhoea, particularly with the more marked seasonal variation in energy expenditure in the food quest, greater seasonal differences in the quantity and quality of the diet, and possibly longer periods of breast feeding (White 1985): certainly there is evidence of seasonal and regional differences in the amount of subcutaneous fat in Yolngu women (Jones and White 1994). Furthermore, in the larger coastal bands there are likely to be more female kin available to assist in the care of pregnant women, mothers, and children. Differences in polygyny rates may also, at least partly, account for the variation in completed family sizes for women among the Yolngu groups (White *et al.* 1990), since there is evidence from other societies that women in polygynous unions have fewer children on average than those in monogamous marriages (Shaikh *et al.* 1987).

Table 14.4 shows that as a result of polygynous marriages there were far greater differences among men in their reproductive success than among women, illustrated by the higher average completed family sizes and correspondingly higher variances among Yolngu men. There is some indication of a higher level of polygyny for men in coastal clans than for inlanders, possibly because of a larger number of potential spouses in these higher density coastal areas (together with a greater ability for men to protect their interests in women), as well as a comparative lack of fraternal generosity among Yolngu in ceding rights to women (Keen 1982; White *et al.* 1990). Polygyny, together with the relatively late age at which a man obtains his first wife, means that many men of reproductive age are without wives (but not necessarily without children!), consequently, while some men make little or no contribution to the gene pool there are others who will make large, and often dramatic contributions. An example was Wonggu, a prominent and powerful member of the Djapu dialect unit with territory in the Blue Mud Bay region on the east coast. His genealogy was recorded by Thomson in the 1930s (held in the Donald Thomson collection in the Museum of Victoria): it showed that he had at least 50 children from his twenty or so wives (a photograph of Wonggu with part of his family is shown in Thomson (1949); see also Chaseling (1957)). There is little doubt that random genetic drift has contributed to the genetic divergence of the marriage cluster (subpopulation) of which the Djapu clans are members. In addition, male fertility differentials will offer a greater opportunity for selection than for females. From a genetic standpoint, discussion of the fertility data is complicated by the fact that it is older men, many of whose reproductive career is nearly completed, who have multiple wives. In addition, many wives (and often the first) are older widows whose reproductive lives are finished.

Breeding population sizes as a proportion of individuals capable of reproducing, were close to 40 per cent, although the figure for the total number of individuals of marriageable age was 5–10 per cent less. (Diez and Salzano (1978) noted that the relationship between the breeding and total population sizes for tribal groups seems to be fairly constant (38–46 per cent) and independent of their ecology. Australian Aboriginal data, on the other hand, do suggest an association with the physical environment (White *et al.* 1990).)

Crow (1958) developed an **index of potential selection**, I (known variously as the index of total selection, index of opportunity for selection, and selection intensity index), in which components of natural selection due to fertility and mortality differences can be estimated using demographic data. It is a measure of the rate of evolution of a population assuming that all differences in fitness are completely genetically determined (Cavalli-Sforza and Bodmer 1971). The greater the value of I, the more opportunity there is for selection to operate. This index has been calculated for various South American tribes which were predominantly hunters and foragers with values between 0.9 (Salzano 1972) and 4.24 (Neel and Weiss 1975), the component due to fertility differences (I_f) being approximately the same as that for differential mortality (I_m), unlike the situation in developed industrialized societies where the larger proportion of the opportunity for selection is due to fertility differences. For the Yolngu, the index of potential selection was 2.08 with the component due to differential fertility being approximately 58 per cent of the total (compared with 46–75 per cent for South American tribes (Salzano 1972; Diez and Salzano 1978)).

A demographic genetic parameter of fundamental importance to the genetic structure of populations is the **effective population size**, (N_e). A loss of genetic variation results from small effective population sizes as a result of drift, although 'rules' (Franklin 1980) that claim to link the minimum size of N_e needed for the long-term maintenance of additive genetic variation have recently been challenged on both theoretical and empirical grounds (Templeton 1994). The precise estimation of N_e is complex. It is particularly difficult in human populations, and especially so for the Yolngu where there have been fluctuations in population numbers; strong restrictions on mate selection with marriages both prescribed and proscribed by social category and kinship; skewed sex ratios; marked differences among men and between men and women in reproductive performance; and where there are loose ecologically based subpopulations (among which there are likely to be demographic differences). In addition, despite a high level of endogamy (96 per cent) recorded for the Yolngu as a whole, there are none the less occasional (and increasing) marriages with surrounding tribes: these tend to involve Yolngu men receiving wives from outside groups rather than women leaving Yolngu clans.

There is no single formula for estimating N_e which incorporates all of the demographic variables and constraints outlined above. Nevertheless, if we apply the formula $N_e = 4MF/(M + F)$ (Kimura and Crow 1963) which is commonly applied to human populations, the effective population size for the Yolngu as a whole, is in the order of 550. This is based on the age and sex structure of the Yolngu population — estimated at 2600 — from census and survey data compiled between 1971–1974 (White 1979*b*). It assumes a tertiary sex ratio of 90 per cent; includes males aged between 20 and 61 years (but because of late marriages for Yolngu men, only half of the 20–31 years age group was used) and females between the ages of 15 and 41 years, and an average of two wives per married man. (With no assumption of polygyny, $N_e = 820$.) Now, clearly, there are subpopulations of Yolngu, and hence the actual effective population sizes would be expected to be considerably less than this gross upper limit, a situation which, according to the migration matrix model of Bodmer and Cavalli-Sforza (1968), might be expected to lead to gene frequency variation, and divergence, among these groups even though there is a 'quite large' exchange between them. This prediction is supported by the genetic evidence.

It is readily apparent from the above comments that Australian Aboriginal population structure varied greatly throughout the continent, a point often overlooked in genetic research (White 1989). For instance, Morton and Keats (1976), in their study of kinship in the western Pacific including Australia, demonstrated for a sample of Australian Aborigines comparable values of local kinship to those found in New Guinea and Micronesia. However, this Aboriginal sample showed a much slower decline of kinship with distance compared with populations in New Guinea, but had a value similar to that found in Oceania. They concluded that 'evidently geographic and social obstacles to long distance migration were much less serious in Australia than in New Guinea, as the tradition of long treks and "walkabouts" suggests' (Morton and Keats 1976, p. 381). The genetic information upon which this analysis is based appears to have been derived largely, if not entirely, from central Australian and Western Desert populations.

Unlike the picture which has emerged for South American Indian tribes, there appears not to have been the constant reshuffling of populations through the fission and fusion of subgroups. However, this model of population structure (Salzano 1972), which has groups of biologically related individuals splitting off to establish new breeding units, may have been important during the colonization of Australia. In a more limited way, it may also have been applicable to the occupation of territories left vacant by the extinction of local descent groups, particularly following European settlement. Overall though, the fission–fusion model does not appear to characterize Australian hunter–gatherer populations. Rather, population structure would seem to differ in form according to the environment in which the population lives. In areas of diverse and stable food resources, such as the Arnhem Land coast, the structure is most easily identified with Wright's (1943) 'island model'. For tribes occupying less favourable territories, especially in arid central Australia, the situation approaches a stepping-stone model (Kimura 1953) or one of isolation by distance.

It is relevant and appropriate, I think, to conclude with a quote from Harrison and Boyce (1972). 'It would seem to us that much more attention needs to be given to behavioural variation, in considering population genetic structure and that imprecise models which take it into account are more practically useful than sophisticated ones that do not' (p. 144). The study of human behaviour adds a fascinating dimension to research into human biological diversity. However, for those whose interest is in elegant theoretical models to describe populations, its complexity can be a constant source of frustration. Yolngu society is nothing if not complex but, being more inclined (or intellectually restricted) to description than to theory. I remain fascinated by these people and their natural and cultural worlds.

References

Abbie, A. A. (1957). Metrical characters of a Central Australian tribe. *Oceania*, **27**, 220–43.

Balakrishnan, V., Sanghvi, L. D., and Kirk, R. L. (1975). *Genetic diversity among Australian Aborigines*. Australian Institute of Aboriginal Studies, Canberra.

Bennett, C. (1985). *Genetic differentiation in the Yolngu of northeast Arnhem Land: a study through time*. BSc(Hons) thesis, Department of Genetics and Human Variation, La Trobe University (unpublished).

Berndt, C. H. (1970). Prolegomena to a study of genealogies in North-eastern Arnhem Land. In *Australian Aboriginal anthropology: modern studies in the social anthropology of the Australian Aborigines*, (ed. R. M. Berndt), pp. 29–50. University of Western Australia Press, Nedlands.

Berndt, R. M. (1951). *Kunapipi*. Cheshire, Melbourne.

Berndt, R. M. (1952). *Djanggawul*. Routledge and Kegan Paul, London.

Berndt, R. M. (1955). 'Murngin' (Wulamba) social organization. *American Anthropologist*, **57**, 84–106.

Berndt, R. M. and Berndt, C. H. (1954). *Arnhem Land, its history and its people*. Cheshire, Melbourne.

Berndt, R. M. and Berndt, C. H. (1977). *The world of the first Australians*. Ure Smith, Sydney.

Birdsell, J. B. (1993). *Microevolutionary patterns in Aboriginal Australia: a gradient analysis of clines*. Oxford University Press.

Bodmer, W. F. and Cavalli-Sforza, L. L. (1968). A migration matrix model for the study of random genetic drift. *Genetics*, **59**, 565–92.

Cavalli-Sforza, L. L. and Bodmer, W. F. (1971). *The genetics of human populations*. W. H. Freeman and Co., San Francisco.

Chaseling, W. S. (1957). *Yulengor: nomads of Arnhem Land*. The Epworth Press, London.

Cowlishaw, G. (1978). Infanticide in Aboriginal Australia. *Oceania*, **40**, 262–83.

Crow, J. F. (1958). Some possibilities for measuring selection intensities in man. *Human Biology*, **30**, 1–13.

De Oliveira, A. E. and Salzano, F. M. (1969). Genetic implications of the demography of Brazilian Juruna indians. *Social Biology*, **16**, 209–15.

Diez, A. A. P. and Salzano, F. M. (1978). Evolutionary implications of the ethnography and demography of Ayoreo Indians. *Journal of Human Evolution*, **7**, 253–68.

Flannery, G. and White, N. (1993). Immunological parameters in northeast Arnhem Land Aborigines: consequences of changing settlement patterns and lifestyles. In *Urban ecology and health in the third world*, (ed. L. M. Schell, M. T. Smith, and A. Bilsborough), pp. 202–20. Society for the Study of Human Biology Symposium 32, Cambridge University Press.

Franklin, I. R. (1980). Evolutionary change in small populations. In *Conservation biology*, (ed. M. E. Soule and B. A. Wilcox), pp. 135–48. Sinauer Associates, Sunderland Massachusetts.

Harrison, G. A., and Boyce, A. J. (1972). *The structure of human populations*. Clarendon Press, Oxford.

Jones, R. and White, N. G. (1988). Point blank: stone tool manufacture at Ngilipitji Quarry, Arnhem Land 1981. In *Archaeology with ethnography: an Australian perspective*, (ed. B. Meehan and R. Jones), pp. 51–87. Department of Prehistory, Australian National University, Canberra.

Jones, C. O. H., and White, N. G. (1994). Adiposity in Aboriginal people from Arnhem Land, Australia: variation in degree and distribution associated v.ith age, sex and lifestyle. *Annals of Human Biology*, **21**, 207–27.

Keen, I. (1982). How some Murngin men marry ten wives: the martial implications of matrilateral cross-cousin structures. *Man* (NS), **17**, 620–42.

Kimber, R.G. (1990). Hunter gatherer demography: the recent past in Central Australia. In *Hunter-gatherer demography: past and present*, (ed. B. Meehan and N. White), pp. 160–70. University of Sydney.

Kimura, M. (1953). 'Stepping stone' model of population. *Annual Report of the National Institute of Genetics, Japan*, **3**, 62–3.

Kimura, M. and Crow, J. F. (1963). The measurement of effective population numbers. *Evolution*, **17**, 279–88.

Lindsay, D. (1884). Mr D. Lindsay's explorations through Arnheim's Land. *Australian Parliamentary Papers* 1883/1884, No. 239. Parliament of South Australia, Adelaide.

Macho, G. and Freedman, L. (1987). *Occasional papers in human biology 4: a re-analysis of the Andrew A. Abbie morphometric data on Australian Aborigines*. Australian Institute of Aboriginal Studies, Canberra.

McKenzie, K., White, N. G. and Jones, R. (1983). *The spear in the stone: a study guide*. Australian Institute of Aboriginal Studies, Canberra.

Macknight, C. C. (1972). Macassans and Aborigines. *Oceania*, **42**, 283–321.

Maddock, K. (1970). Rethinking the Murngin problem: a review article. *Oceania*, **41**, 77–89.

Morphy, H. (1978). Rights in paintings and rights in women: a consideration of some of the basic problems posed by the asymmetry of the 'Murngin System'. *Mankind*, **11**, 208–19.

Morphy, H. (1991). *Ancestral connections: art and an Aboriginal system of knowledge*. The University of Chicago Press.

Morton, N. E. and Keats, B. (1976). Human microdifferentiation in the Western Pacific. In *The origin of the Australians*, (ed. R. L. Kirk and A. G. Thorne), pp. 379–99. Australian Institute of Aboriginal Studies, Humanities Press, New Jersey.

Neel, J. V. and Weiss, K. (1975). The genetic structure of a tribal population, the Yanomama Indians XII. Biodemographic studies. *American Journal of Physical Anthropology*, **42**, 25–52.

Pagnon, J. C. (1993) *Protein and DNA polymorphisms among the Yolngu from north east Arnhem Land: relationship with geography, socio-cultural and linguistic factors*. BSc(Hons) thesis, Department of Genetics and Human Variaton, La Trobe University (unpublished).

Parsons, P. A. and White, N. G. (1976). Variability of anthropometric traits in Australian Aborigines and adjacent populations: its bearing on the biological origin of the Australians. In *The biological origin of the Australians*, (ed. R. L. Kirk and A. G. Thorne), pp. 227–43. Australian Institute of Aboriginal Studies, Humanities Press, New Jersey.

Peterson, N. (1976). *Tribes and boundaries in Australia*. Australian Institute of Aboriginal Studies, Humanities Press, New Jersey.

Pietrusewsky, M. (1984). Metric and non-metric cranial variation in Australian Aboriginal populations compared with populations from the Pacific and Asia. *Occasional papers in human biology 3*. Australian Institute of Aboriginal Studies, Canberra.

Roger, J. S. (1972). Measures of genetic similarity and genetic distance. In *Studies in genetics VII*, University of Texas Publication 7213, (ed. M. R. Wheeler), pp. 145–53. University of Texas.

Rosetta, L. (1992). Aetiological approach of female reproductive physiology in lactational amenorrhoea. *Journal of Biosocial Science*, **24** (3), 301–15.

Ruder, A. (1985). Parental-age and birth order effect on the human secondary sex–ratio. *American Journal of Human Genetics*, **37**, 362–72.

Salzano, F. M. (1972). Genetic aspects of the demography of American Indians and Eskimos. In *The structure of human populations*, (ed. G. A. Harrison and A. J. Boyce), pp. 234–51. Clarendon Press, Oxford.

Schebeck, B. (1970). *A revised linguistic survey of Australia*, (ed. W. J. Oates and L. F. Oates), pp. 225–6. Australian Institute of Aboriginal Studies, Canberra.

Shaikh, K., Asiz, K. M. A., and Chowdhuru, A. I. (1987). Differentials of fertility between polygynous and monogamous marriages in rural Bangladesh. *Journal of Biosocial Science*, **19**, 49–56.

Sharp, L. (1940). An Australian Aboriginal population. *Human Biology*, **12**, 481–504.

Shapiro, W. (1968). The exchange of sisters' daughters' daughters in northeast Arnhem land. *Man*, **4**, 629–40.

Sjøvold, T. (1973). The occurrence of minor non-metrical variants in the skeleton and their quantitative treatment for population comparisons. *Homo*, **24**, 204–33.

Simmons, R. T. (1976). The biological origin of Australian Aboriginals: an examination of blood group genes and gene frequencies for possible evidence in populations from Australia to Eurasia. In *The origin of the Australians*, (ed. R. L. Kirk and A. G. Thorne), pp. 307–28. Australian Institute of Aboriginal Studies, Humanities Press, New Jersey.

Templeton, A. R. (1994). Biodiversity at the molecular genetic level: experiences from disparate macroorganisms. *Philosophical Transactions of the Royal Society of London B*, **345**, 59–64.

Thomson, D. F. (1949). *Economic structure and the ceremonial exchange in Arnhem Land*. Macmillan. Melbourne.

Tonkinson, R. (1978). *The Mardudjara Aborigines: living the dream in Australia's desert*. Holt, Rinehart and Winston, New York.

Tonkinson, R. (1988). 'Ideology and domination' in Aboriginal Australia: a western desert test case. In *Hunters and gatherers 2. Property, power and ideology* (ed. T. Ingold, D. Riches, and J. Woodburn), pp. 150–64. Berg, Oxford.

Warner, W. L. (1930). Murngin warfare. *Oceania*, **1**, 457–94.

Warner, W. L. (1937). *A black civilization: a social study of an Australian tribe*. Harper and Row, New York.

Warner, W. L. (1958). *A black civilization: a social study of an Australian tribe*. Revised Edition. Harper and Row, New York.

White, N. G. (1976). A preliminary account of the correspondence among genetic, linguistic, social and topographic divisions in Arnhem Land, Australia, *Mankind*, **10**, 240–7.

White, N. G. (1978). A human ecology research project in the Arnhem Land region: an outline. *Australian Institute of Aboriginal Studies Newsletter*, **9**, 39–52.

White, N. G. (1979*a*). The use of digital dermatoglyphics in assessing population relationships in Aboriginal Australia. *Birth Defects: Article Series*, **15(6)**, 437–54.

White, N. G. (1979*b*). *Tribes, genes and habitats*. PhD Thesis, Department of Genetics and Human Variation, La Trobe University.

White, N. G. (1985). Sex differences in Australian Aboriginal subsistence: possible implications for the biology of hunter-gatherers. In *Human sexual dimorphism,* (Ed. J. Ghesquiere, R. D. Martin, and F. Newcombe), pp. 323–361. Taylor and Francis, London.

White, N. G. (1989). Cultural influences on the biology of Aboriginal people: examples from Arnhem Land. In *The growing scope of human biology: proceedings of the Australasian Society for Human Biology No. 2,* (ed. L. H. Schmitt, L. Freedman, and N. W. Bruce), pp. 171–8. Australasian Society for Human Biology, Centre for Human Biology, University of Western Australia, Western Australia.

White, N. G. and Parsons, P. A. (1973). Genetic and socio-cultural differentiation in the Aborigines of Arnhem Land, Australia. *American Journal of Physical Anthropology*, **38**, 5–14.

White, N. G., Scarlett, N. H. and Reid, J. (1982). Bush medicines: the pharmacopeia of the Yolngu of Arnhem Land. In *Body land and spirit: health and healing in Aboriginal Australia,* (ed. J. Reid), pp. 154–91. University of Queensland Press, St Lucia.

White, N., Meehan, B., Hiatt, L. and Jones, R. (1990). Demography of contemporary hunter–gatherers: lessons from Arnhem Land. In *Hunter–gatherer demography: past and present,* (ed. B. Meehan and N. G. White), pp. 171–85. Oceania Monograph 39, University of Sydney.

Williams, N. M. (1986). *The Yolngu and their land*. Australian Institute of Aboriginal Studies, Canberra.

Wright, S. (1943). Isolation by distance. *Genetics*, **28**, 114–38.

Index